D1554418

The publisher and the University of California Press Foundation gratefully acknowledge the generous support of the Peter Booth Wiley Endowment Fund in History.

Suburban Empire

AMERICAN CROSSROADS

*Edited by Earl Lewis, George Lipsitz, George Sánchez, Dana Takagi,
Laura Briggs, and Nikhil Pal Singh*

Suburban Empire

COLD WAR MILITARIZATION IN THE US PACIFIC

Lauren Hirshberg

UNIVERSITY OF CALIFORNIA PRESS

University of California Press
Oakland, California

© 2022 by Lauren Hirshberg

Library of Congress Cataloging-in-Publication Data

Names: Hirshberg, Lauren, 1978– author.
Title: Suburban empire : Cold War militarization in the U.S. Pacific /
　　Lauren Hirshberg.
Other titles: American crossroads.
Description: Oakland, California : University of California Press,
　　[2022] | Series: American crossroads | Includes bibliographical
　　references and index.
Identifiers: LCCN 2021037002 (print) | LCCN 2021037003 (ebook) |
　　ISBN 9780520289154 (cloth) | ISBN 9780520289161 (paperback) |
　　ISBN 9780520963856 (epub)
Subjects: LCSH: Imperialism—Social aspects—Marshall Islands—
　　Kwajalein Atoll. | Kwajalein Atoll (Marshall Islands)—History—
　　20th century.
Classification: LCC DU710 .H57 2022 (print) | LCC DU710 (ebook) |
　　DDC 996.8/3—dc23
LC record available at https://lccn.loc.gov/2021037002
LC ebook record available at https://lccn.loc.gov/2021037003

Manufactured in the United States of America

31　30　29　28　27　26　25　24　23　22
10　9　8　7　6　5　4　3　2　1

Dedicated to my parents, Joan and Fred Hirshberg, with love.

We are never as steeped in history as when we pretend not to be, but if we stop pretending we may gain in understanding what we lose in false innocence.

—Michel-Rolph Trouillot, *Silencing the Past* (1995, xxiii)

Contents

Illustrations

FIGURES

MAPS

A Note on Language

Throughout this book I have used the language prominently appearing in primary and secondary sources aimed at English-language readers to trace this history. For example, rather than use "Majel," the Marshallese word for Marshall Islands, or "Ri-Kuwajleen," the Marshallese word for the original Marshallese inhabitants, or the "Kwajalein people" I have used the "Marshall Islands," "Marshallese," and/or "Kwajalein landowners" to reflect the language that most commonly appeared in primary and secondary source documents by US and Marshallese voices as well as in oral history interviews with both populations. As a book that resides at the intersection between US and Marshallese histories, written by an English-language speaker for an English-language readership, I have deferred to this language used by both US and Marshallese historic subjects, while aware of the many deficiencies that accompany those linguistic limitations. In cases where I do incorporate Marshallese translations, I have deferred to the cultural expertise and linguistic skills of Marshallese sources, as well as anthropologists, historians, and cultural studies scholars of the Pacific, as cited in those sections.[1]

There are also a few instances throughout the book in which my referencing of individuals shifts between "Micronesians" and "Marshallese."

These shifts are not intended to suggest a conflation of the two descriptive categories. While Marshallese have been historically categorized as belonging to the regional identification as Micronesians, not all who identify as Micronesians are Marshallese. Nor should either of these two categories be presumed to address the variety of ways that individuals self-identify in this region of the Pacific. Specific island and atoll identifications have also come into play, as have historic rejections of the category "Micronesian" (likewise for "Polynesian" and "Melanesian") as an artificial colonial imposition upon vast geographic, and historically and culturally diverse, regions. The sections in my book that shift in that categorical language reflect how Trust Territory government and military documents described these populations at different times (also indicated in endnotes). When referencing these documents I have kept my language mirroring these shifts as they appeared in the historic evidence. While this may cause some ambiguity, that ambiguity reflects that which is found in the archives and potentially suggests how various US civilian and military colonial administrators may have perceived this category of "Micronesians" as a seemingly homogenous population. My inclusion of this language is not intended to reify that colonial categorization but rather to write in a way that reflects, while analyzing, those historic primary sources.

In analysis where I refer to the population living on Ebeye and working on Kwajalein during the army missile-installation era, I primarily use "Marshallese," or "Ebeye residents." This is because the majority of the population on Ebeye and working on Kwajalein during this period comprised Marshallese individuals. However, it should be noted that Ebeye has historically housed a smaller but growing population of individuals from other parts of Micronesia as well as the Philippines. In addition, many of these individuals have also worked on Kwajalein.

In reference to the missile installation at Kwajalein Atoll, I have tended to use interchangeably broad terms like "missile base" or "missile installation" to avoid confusion, as the installation has birthed various official titles over time. These have included the Kwajalein Missile Range, USAKA (United States Army at Kwajalein Atoll), and most recently the Ronald Reagan Ballistic Missile Defense Test Site (also called the Reagan Test Site or the Reagan Test Site and Space Range). These official titles are only interspersed throughout the book when they reflect primary source language; otherwise they are largely absent.

Finally, I have tried to minimize, as much as possible, the uses of "American" or "Americans" to describe citizens from the United States who have resided on and/or worked at Kwajalein. This is intended to avoid perpetuating a US-centric vision of population identification that obscures the broader region of the Americas.[2] That said, I *do* use "American" throughout the book when referring to cultural patterns, norms, and tropes (including "the American dream" and "American exceptionalism," among others). I also use "American" when this term reflects the language used in primary sources or in oral history interviews as articulated in quotes and/or paraphrases.

Introduction

HOME ON THE RANGE: US EMPIRE AND INNOCENCE
IN THE COLD WAR PACIFIC

"SO WE CAN'T GO WITH RIBELLES?"

Darlene Keju was born in 1951 on Ebeye Island in Kwajalein Atoll, in the Marshall Islands. Darlene was born seven years after the US military had attacked its Japanese enemy on Kwajalein, leveling it, the largest island within the atoll, during the most destructive bombing campaign of the Pacific War. She came into the world five years after the US Navy had begun testing nuclear weapons in the Northern Marshall Islands, a campaign that spanned twelve years. Radioactive fallout plagued Darlene within a few years of her birth, alongside hundreds of other Marshallese. Decades later Darlene developed breast cancer that would spread to her bones and lungs and tragically take her life at the age of forty-five.

Darlene was born during the height of the Cold War. Her life began amid the McCarthy witch hunts in the United States; one year after Paul Nitze of the State Department penned National Security Council Policy Paper 68. NSC 68 called for a tripling of US defense spending to fight global communism and became a blueprint for the massive increase in US military spending that informed the rise of the military-industrial complex in the decades that followed. Darlene's life, like so many other

1

Marshallese lives, was significantly impacted by all of these events shaping the Cold War, just as the generation before them had been shaped by the battles of the Pacific War unfolding in their islands.

While historians have often turned their attention to the Pacific to examine the battle histories of World War II, this book centers the region as a lens into the Cold War and argues that the Marshall Islands are central to understanding that broader global history. *Suburban Empire* argues that global change has both shaped and been shaped by Pacific histories and specifically the consequential events taking place in the Marshall Islands and on Kwajalein Atoll following World War II. With a focus on the Cold War era, this book traces how Darlene's homelands were transformed as they became identified by the US Navy as ideal staging grounds for US development of weapons of mass destruction, a historic and ongoing campaign that has buttressed the rise of the postwar US security state. I examine the US quest for security during the Cold War and the enormous costs paid by Marshallese colonial subjects, whose homelands were taken over to embark on that mission.

One feature of the postwar US security state was its perpetually illusive character, a state of security never fully achievable globally or locally, but something always on the horizon and thus necessitating endless investment in resources.[1] This book is centrally concerned with the costs of this continual quest for security for those coming under the realm of an expanding base empire—the relational *insecurities* produced by this security project—and the historic and ongoing US attempts to erase those costs. As US military and civilian contractors professionally and materially profited from their national security mission, Marshallese paid the ultimate price through their lives, health, lands, and sovereignty. But as this book also traces, as military and civilian personnel attempted to disavow those costs by normalizing the expansion of US bases globally while shrouding the devastating impacts of that mission in a veil of innocence, Marshallese refused to accept the erasure of their lived experiences. Instead, many challenged the colonial conditions framing their lives. Darlene Keju was among those who early on in life pulled back this veil and probed the strange phenomenon that was US military control over her homelands.

As a toddler on Ebeye, Darlene was remembered as curious, always posing questions, foreshadowing a path toward activism as an adult. Her caregiver, Neijon, who lost her mother as US and Japanese soldiers battled in her homelands, recalled the toddler Darlene "always asking questions."[2] She recounted a memory of Darlene watching Marshallese workers returning on a ship to Ebeye from Kwajalein Island, where they had been laboring in support of the US Navy. Observing the three-mile commute that bridged Kwajalein and Ebeye across the atoll, Darlene asked Neijon: 'Why do we [Marshallese] have to wear badges to go to Kwajalein?' 'Ebeye it's part of Kwajalein, isn't it? Why can only a few people go to Kwajalein?'" Neijon recalled: "So I'd answer that it's because it is a ribelle [American] place. 'So we can't go with ribelles?' [Darlene asked.] 'I couldn't answer that.'"[3]

At such a young age, what Darlene already intuited as she watched Marshallese people denied the opportunity to live on their own lands was the remarkable nature of the structure of segregation and surveillance imposed by the US military on Kwajalein Atoll. To Darlene, this seemed curious and required explanation. At the time, US military personnel were living on Kwajalein Island, using it primarily as a support base for nuclear testing in the Northern Marshall Islands and as a fueling station for military activities in the Korean War. In 1951, the year Darlene was born, the navy had displaced all Marshallese workers from Kwajalein to Ebeye, workers who had been living alongside US military residents helping rebuild the island following the war. After 1951, while the military continued to rely on the labor of both US and Marshallese workers to operate its ongoing mission, Kwajalein would exclusively house US workers and their family members. Ebeye became home to the military's commuting Marshallese workforce and their dependents, as well as a growing number of Marshallese displaced within the atoll to make way for expansive US weapons testing. By the mid-1950s, Darlene moved with her parents to Wotje (a Marshallese atoll east of Kwajalein), where her family lived for several years during the peak of the nuclear-testing campaign. By the time Darlene returned to Ebeye in the 1960s to attend a Protestant mission school—her body carrying the invisible but damaging impacts of irradiation—the military had transitioned Kwajalein's activities from supporting the testing of nuclear weapons to the vehicles for their delivery: intercontinental ballistic missiles (ICBMs).

To support this transition from nuclear to ICBM testing during the 1960s, the US Army displaced more Marshallese from home islands throughout the atoll (clearing space for a missile impact zone), while transforming Kwajalein Island into a home for US workers. As a recruitment and retention strategy to lure its most elite workforce, the army created a home away from home for these engineers, scientists, and their families, investing in domestic and consumer luxuries on Kwajalein to support a comfortable suburban family lifestyle. The military mapped a mythical landscape of small-town Americana onto Kwajalein, replete with ballparks, a golf course, the local Surfway and island Macy's, and palm-tree-lined row housing. The island became a space exclusively housing these US families to which Marshallese service workers would commute daily from Ebeye to cook, clean, landscape, and provide childcare and other services. As Kwajalein was restaged as a tropical-style Mayberry in the Central Pacific, Ebeye became the most densely populated space in Oceania, a racialized and impoverished home to those who had been displaced and those in Kwajalein's segregated service sector. This dynamic that emerged during the 1960s was decried by Marshallese activists and political leaders, and by the 1970s and 1980s US and Pacific investigative journalists called it "American apartheid in the Pacific." This segregated labor and residency structure, built to support US missile testing at Kwajalein, persists today.

Darlene Keju's intuition as a toddler that this structure of segregation enacted costs for Marshallese likewise hinted at an awareness of relational gains enjoyed by those foreigners living an exclusionary existence in her islands. The enormous costs Marshallese have continued to pay for seven decades of uninterrupted US weapons testing in their homelands has directly informed those benefits, from the individual research careers of engineers and scientists, to the wealth gained by an array of logistics contractors, to thousands of US salaries earned by workers living subsidized lives on Marshallese lands. But the ultimate prize came through the ascendance of the United States to the position of global military hegemon. This expansion of US military power, buttressed by colonial control over the lands of Marshallese and so many others in the postwar era coming under the US base imperium, calls for an update to President Dwight D. Eisenhower's 1961 warning about the dangers of a rising "military-industrial complex." This book argues that when we center the history of the Marshall Islands and Kwajalein Atoll, the truth of that historic, cautionary speech resides more accurately within the realm of a military-industrial *colonial* complex.

Suburban Empire chronicles how the postwar history of Kwajalein Atoll in the era of US colonial control offers a window into the manifestations of Cold War US expansion as what historian Patricia Nelson Limerick has called an "empire of innocence."[4] While Limerick's analysis focused on disavowal of westward imperial expansion across the North American continent, here I explore how the myth of US innocence in the imperial Pacific was normalized through the physical landscape of small-town suburbia at Kwajalein and the global diplomatic framework of the United Nations. On a global scale, I examine the ways UN sanction of US colonialism in Micronesia through the 1947 Trust Territory of the Pacific Islands Agreement (hereafter the Trusteeship Agreement) enabled one of the most destructive imperial projects to be framed as a "special trust." At the local level, this book focuses on how US military and civilian settlers migrating to support weapons testing on Kwajalein produced and reproduced the cultural façade of small-town suburbia restaged onto this Marshallese homeland.

In the era when US families began migrating to Kwajalein, James Baldwin was reflecting on the violence and destruction of slavery and its legacies alongside the nation's enduring denial of that history. In 1963 he wrote: "One can be, indeed one must strive to become, tough and philosophical concerning destruction and death, for this is what most of mankind has been best at since we have heard of man. . . . But it is not permissible that the authors of devastation should also be innocent. *It is the innocence which constitutes the crime*."[5] On Kwajalein, the innocence of Cold War suburban family life mapped onto some of the most destructive and deadly weapons testing in global history, tests that irreversibly imprinted devastation onto Marshallese lands, bodies, and lives. As Marshallese strategically used the United Nations as a platform to challenge the global structure sanctioning US imperial expansion into their homelands, many also creatively engaged this suburban landscape of innocence erected atop their home islands. In doing so, they unsettled this façade of innocence and its erasure of US colonial destruction in their lands while reclaiming Kwajalein as *their* home. These protests culminated most impactfully in a 1982 movement that Marshallese activists called Operation Homecoming.

This mass sail-in built upon years of challenges to many features of US imperialism, including the structure of segregation at Kwajalein. Some Marshallese protesting against these manifestations of empire on Kwajalein linked their demands to the broader Nuclear Free and Independent Pacific movement rippling across Oceania during the 1970s and 1980s. In doing so they took their place within this vast coalitional movement that reshaped not only Pacific history but the broader postwar history of global decolonization.

This book chronicles this complex history with a focus on how US imperialism took shape locally in the Marshall Islands in the specific moment of the Cold War. This is a story that centers place—tracing the historic transformations of Kwajalein and Ebeye—as these island changes offer a lens on the broader story of how Marshallese navigated the impacts of US military imperialism in their homelands following World War II. US disavowal of empire alongside its vast and destructive expansion is not a new phenomenon, as scholars of US empire and American exceptionalism have revealed. This book turns to the particular Cold War iterations of that imperial formation in the Marshall Islands—a history of *suburban empire*—and how Marshallese navigated its terrain in their homelands.

MARSHALLESE GEOGRAPHY, GEOLOGY, AND GENEALOGY: KWAJALEIN AND EBEYE IN A "SEA OF ISLANDS"

As Darlene Keju watched Marshallese workers commute across the lagoon from Kwajalein in 1951, pondering the segregation structure separating these two islands, she did so while standing on Ebeye's coral's sediment, which rests atop a massive sunken volcano, the geology that created the atoll. Kwajalein Atoll is the largest of the twenty-nine atolls and five islands that make up the Republic of the Marshall Islands (RMI). The atoll resides just above the surface of the perimeter of a collapsed volcano. Ninety-three islets form this single atoll, which follows the coral crest piercing the water. While a deep ocean resides along the outside of the atoll, a shallow lagoon—between approximately 197 and 262 feet deep—forms the interior. From the oceanside, the depth of the atoll rises more than 1.3 miles above the sea floor. Spanning more than 1,000 square

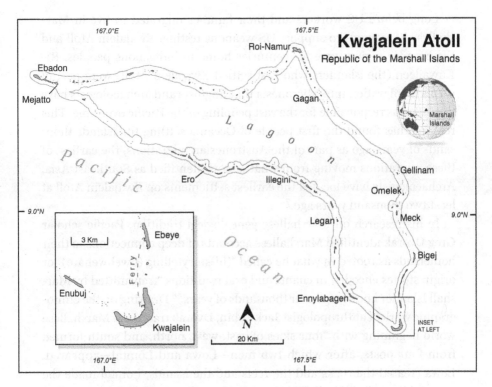

Map 1. Kwajalein Atoll, Republic of the Marshall Islands. Map by Philip B. White.

miles—nearly 81 miles tip to tip—Kwajalein is one of the largest atolls in the world. While the watery distance is expansive, the coral islets comprise little more than 6 miles of land mass altogether as each islet pokes just above the water's surface. Kwajalein islet comprises about 900 acres of land and sits at the southernmost tip of the atoll, approximately 3 miles across the lagoon from the roughly 80 acres that make up Ebeye islet. Kwajalein Atoll resides within the western (Ralik) chain of the RMI, which has a population of about seventy-three thousand. This republic stretches about 772,000 square miles across the Central Pacific and resides approximately 2,300–2,500 miles southwest of Hawai'i. It is some 4,200 miles from Vandenberg Airforce Base in Santa Barbara County, California, the site from which the military has been launching ICBMs at Kwajalein for nearly six decades.[6]

Long before US workers and their families migrated to live in Marshallese homelands to support US weapons testing, Kwajalein Atoll and the broader region were for centuries home to indigenous peoples. Ri-Kuwajleen (the islanders who first settled Kwajalein Atoll) were part of waves of migration into Micronesia that linguists and archaeologists have identified as responsible for the vast peopling of the Pacific over time. This research has found the first people of Oceania settling the islands thousands of years ago as part of the Austronesian migrations, the earliest of these migrations moving from what is now identified as Southeast Asia. Archaeologists have located the earliest settlements on Kwajalein Atoll at least two thousand years ago.[7]

In his research on Marshallese genealogical tradition, Pacific scholar Greg Dvorak identified Marshallese accounts of deep connections to their homelands as rooted in what he called "(hi)storytelling (bwebwenato)" or origin stories encoded in chants and oral traditions "transmitted by Marshall Islander knowledge over thousands of years."[8] Drawing on the ethnographic work of anthropologist Jack Tobin, Dvorak traced the Marshallese world beginning with "four skies of east, west, north, and south formed from four posts, after which two men—Ḷowa and Ḷōṃtal—appeared. Ḷowa created the rocks and the reefs and the islands, Ḷōṃtal made the sea, making it flow in all directions and bringing the first fish, as well as the sky and the birds that flew through it."[9] The origins story also identifies the coming of humans, the beginnings of Marshallese culture and the spiritual world, the organization of communities of men and women into different clans, and their movements to different parts of the islands.[10]

This geography, geology, and genealogy of the Marshallese homelands is part of a vast network of Pacific Islands connected through what Tongan scholar Epeli Hauʻofa identified as a "sea of islands" in a paradigm-shifting essay in 1994. In "Our Sea of Islands," Hauʻofa introduced this framing of the region with the aim to challenge academic imperialism that had historically framed Pacific Islands as isolated and disconnected from the rest of the world.[11] Hauʻofa critiqued what he saw as belittling frameworks that had narrated Oceania as "tiny islands in a far sea," arguing instead for a vision of the Pacific—a geographic feature covering one-third of the earth's surface—as a space of enlargement, where waterways between islands can be understood as oceanic highways of intersecting communities.[12]

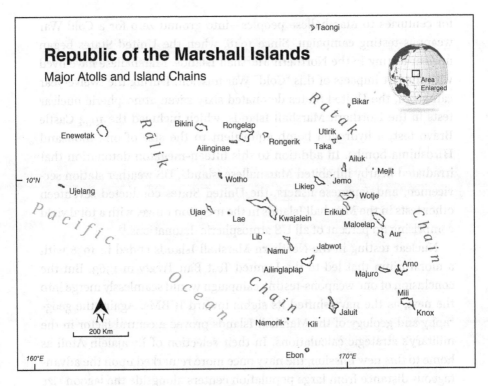

Map 2. The Republic of the Marshall Islands. Map by Philip B. White.

The rich historical, cultural, human, and environmental geography of Oceania celebrated by Hauʻofa was seen through a very different lens when encountered by the US military during the 1940s. Hovering over the Marshall Islands in the wake of global war, the US Navy's gaze would instead see a site of military strategy. Naval commanders saw a geography ideally situated to enable them to test the most destructive weapons in the world. They saw a small population that could be easily displaced. They saw a region located far enough from larger population centers in the United States to make testing these deadly weapons a safe endeavor, at least for US residents.[13] As the region quickly came under formal US control through the UN-sanctioned Trusteeship Agreement in 1947, which would entitle the United States to use the region for global security, these military leaders further saw an opportunity to turn these islands—home for centuries to Marshallese peoples—into ground zero for a Cold War weapons-testing campaign. Since 1946, when the United States began nuclear testing in the Northern Marshall Islands, Marshallese have lived with the hot impacts of this "Cold" War mission. During the twelve-year campaign, the United States detonated sixty-seven atmospheric nuclear tests in the Northern Marshall Islands, which included the 1954 Castle Bravo test, a hydrogen bomb equivalent to the size of one thousand Hiroshima bombs. In addition to this fifteen-megaton detonation that irradiated nearby inhabited Marshallese islands, US weather station servicemen, and Japanese fishers, the United States conducted seventeen other tests in the Marshall Islands in the megaton range, with a total yield comprising 80 percent of all US atmospheric detonations.[14]

Nuclear testing in the Northern Marshall Islands ended in 1958 with a moratorium that led to the Limited Test Ban Treaty in 1963. But the conclusion of one weapons-testing campaign would seamlessly merge into the next, as the navy shifted its sights toward ICBMs. Again, the geography and geology of the Marshall Islands proved a central factor in the military's strategic calculations. In their selection of Kwajalein Atoll as home to this new mission, the navy once more remarked upon the advantageous distance from large population centers alongside the lagoon size and depth, which enabled easier retrieval of missile materials. From the 1960s onward, as missiles were launched toward Kwajalein's lagoon from California's Vandenberg Air Force Base, the atoll became central to Cold War weapons buildup. As Marshallese have borne the enormous costs of this military mission through their increasing insecurity, the atoll has historically and continually buttressed the US security state.

UP AGAINST THE NATIONAL SECURITY
STATE AND CIVILIAN DEFENSE

During the 1970s, Ebeye reached a population of about eight thousand and was identified as the most densely populated space in the Pacific. With nearly twice that many residents in recent years, the challenges of poverty and infrastructural capacity amid extreme density persist.[15] By 2010, with approximately twelve hundred US residents living on Kwajalein's nine-hundred-acre setting, Ebeye's eighty acres housed more than eleven thousand people.[16] That was the year I first traveled to the RMI and visited both islands. In May 2010 I found myself taking a ferry from Kwajalein to Ebeye, embarking on the three-mile commute Darlene Keju had watched Marshallese workers take nearly six decades earlier. Illustrating the persistence of the military's segregation structure between these two islands, I turned to my US friend Rachel, who spoke Marshallese and would act as my translator for interviews on Ebeye, to ask how our Ebeye host, Deo Keju (Darlene's brother), would be able to find us when we disembarked from the ferry. We had never met Deo before, and neither he nor we had cell phones. Rachel and I looked around the ferry and laughed at the ridiculous nature of my question. We were the only White people on a boat transporting hundreds of Marshallese workers home. Upon arriving at Ebeye, we learned that with such a small number of White Americans visiting the island, most Marshallese on the ferry likely assumed we were missionaries or volunteer teachers. Rachel and I stayed on Ebeye, moving through a landscape I had only known through archival research in Honolulu.

During our trip, we walked the streets Darlene had as a child and visited her family's store. I thought about a letter her father, Jinna Keju, had written in 1979 protesting US colonial practices of neglect of the island's infrastructure, neglect that had brought deadly consequences for his family and so many other Marshallese families on the island. Ebeye's hospital was one of many facilities marked by inadequate funding and planning during the US colonial era, where frequent power outages and a lack of sufficient medical supplies and staffing spurred otherwise avoidable health emergencies and deaths. In 1979, Keju wrote to Juan Alcedo, of the Committee on Civil Rights in San Francisco, noting that he understood Alcedo's department had jurisdiction over the Trust Territory. Keju decried US neglect of Ebeye, describing the island's hospital, which served a population of eight thousand and had the highest disease rate in the entire Trust Territory. This was a hospital that constantly ran out of the most basic items, such as bandages and aspirin. "Every year many children die of influenza and diarrhea epidemics that sweep the island because they cannot get adequate treatment at the Ebeye Hospital," Keju explained.[17] "And the Kwajalein hospital is not open to Marshallese on a general basis."[18] Describing his tragic connection to hospital exclusion policies, Keju told the story of his deceased daughter, Darlene's sister. He wrote, "My 29-year-old daughter died five months ago shortly after giving birth because of problems at the Ebeye hospital and the lack of coordination to handle emergencies between the Ebeye and Kwajalein hospitals."[19]

Walking Ebeye's streets nearly forty years later, I passed the Ebeye cemetery, a space I knew housed the graves of many Marshallese children and adults who had died in public health epidemics during this era of US colonial control, a period in which the United Nations had obligated the United States to support and protect the region's inhabitants: their lands, health, and well-being. But this UN sanction also empowered the United States to use Marshallese islands for national security. These graves, many of which represented the deadly conditions of poverty fueling health epidemics, stood as tragic testimony to which of these two mandates had been taken seriously by US colonial representatives in the region. Citing what had become a dual evasion of responsibility for Ebeye by the two arms of US empire in the region (military and civilian), Jinna Keju wrote in 1979 about Marshallese being caught between Trust Territory bureaucracy and the army, where nothing got done. "It can hardly be said that the U.S. is 'protecting the health of the inhabitants' here—as the U.N. says it must—when one looks at the poor condition of the Ebeye hospital and the long list of epidemics that have claimed the lives of hundreds over the years."[20] Keju's letter, echoing the voices of Marshallese activists who came before him and fueling those who would come after, pointed to the contradictions foundational to the Trusteeship Agreement. He discussed segregation between Ebeye and Kwajalein: "It is ironic that we are only 3 miles from 'Uncle Sam' at Kwajalein, with first rate schools, excellent sports and recreational facilities and a decent hospital. But for all practical purposes we might as well be 1,000 miles away, because we have very limited use, if any, of these facilities."[21] By 2010, Ebeye was still home to Kwajalein's segregated commuting workforce, their dependents, and many others who had migrated there in search of work. This was an island that still housed Marshallese and their descendants who had been displaced within the atoll to make way for missile testing, alongside many nuclear refugees and their descendants.

My journey to Kwajalein began on another island continuously impacted by a history of US imperial expansion into the Pacific: Oʻahu. In the home of generations of Kanaka Maoli, who had survived the illegal overthrow of their kingdom in 1893 and its annexation in 1898, I resided in a space increasingly encroached upon by the military.[22] By the time I was digging through archival materials in 2008, the US military controlled 22.4 percent of the land on Oʻahu.[23] But they did not do so without resistance and protest from native peoples and their allies. A historic and ongoing sovereignty movement that challenged the history and legacy of colonialism across the Hawaiian islands began in the 1970s, sparked in part by protests against US weapons testing on Kahoʻolawe island and live fire training in Oʻahu's Makua Valley. As land control has expanded to support space research and the expansive construction of telescopes on Mauna Kea (just as Kwajalein's activities have encompassed research in space technologies), anti-colonial protests have centered attention around reclamation of this sacred space, a movement unfolding daily.

While exploring the history of US colonialism in the Pacific, informed by my studies in Pacific and metropolitan histories, my research took a turn toward Kwajalein after I stumbled across military and civilian contractor welcome manuals from the 1960s that introduced Kwajalein as a replica of small-town suburbia. Aimed at recruiting engineers and scientists to relocate their families to the Central Pacific to support missile research, these manuals showcased Kwajalein's domesticity using imagery reminiscent of US vice president Richard Nixon's and Soviet premier Nikita Khrushchev's famous 1959 "kitchen debates." Sifting through the pictures of modern kitchens and cozy living rooms that filled these manuals, I imagined these US workers and their families moving to this seemingly small-town suburban USA in the middle of the Pacific. I wondered how effective such physical and cultural markers of Cold War suburbia were at convincing those migrating from the United States that they were "at home" in the Marshall Islands, that this was in fact an *American* home. Prior to my second research trip to Kwajalein, I had a revealing exchange with one of the US residents on the island that suggested an answer.

After securing sponsorship to stay on base for the research trip, I arranged several interviews via email with US civilians on Kwajalein.[24] Two weeks prior to my departure, I received an email from one explaining he had Googled me and found that my dissertation title included the word "imperialism" to define US history in the region. He categorized my word choice as "quite provocative."[25] After reading one of my conference paper abstracts, he said I had referred to a "US 'Colonial' period at Kwajalein" and thus surmised "a negatively focused conclusion to [my] work appears to be established," and said he would no longer be speaking with me.[26]

I was reminded of how quickly word spreads in both small-town and island communities after I received emails from several other civilians living on Kwajalein reneging on earlier commitments to speak with me. My Kwajalein sponsor also wrote, panicked about my research intentions. After I had reiterated to her my motivation to thicken analysis of the island's history, particularly given the dearth of US civilian voices in the archives, she decided to continue her sponsorship. During that visit, I learned what a brave move this had been given the degree to which concerns about my visit had rippled through the island, placing my sponsor under intense scrutiny. For me, this experience revealed the extent of the military's success in having transformed Kwajalein into an "American home," a mythical space whose narrative boundaries were taken up by civilian residents and vehemently guarded.

This experience aligned with subsequent encounters in Hawai'i with former Kwajalein residents who proved equally defensive about the island's story. Many civilians who have raised families on the island and made lifelong friendships felt, and continue to feel, deeply connected to Kwajalein. This connection has spawned a nostalgia culture comprising annual reunions, paraphernalia, memoirs, and social networking sites of commemoration. Much of this nostalgia builds upon an understanding, interpretation, and narrative of Kwajalein as an "American home," as residing outside any history of US colonialism and detached from related histories involving Marshallese families and their homes.

One concern this book takes up is how such compartmentalizations have been enabled in part by the historic and continuous distances maintained between American life on Kwajalein and Marshallese life on Ebeye through the military's structure of segregation. This local iteration of a historic disavowal of US empire had its global counterpart in the structure of UN sanction of US expansion, labeling it a "special relationship" through the Trusteeship Agreement. Both structures and narratives armed US civilian workers and family members—individuals like those antagonistic to my visit—with other ways to frame their residency and employment on the island. This disavowal of an imperial past and explanations to situate an exclusive residency on Kwajalein and the material and lifestyle benefits that accompanied that residency have persisted for more than six decades. This framing, embraced by many US residents on Kwajalein from the 1960s through today, has marked their relationship to the island as unrelated to US imperialism broadly or to Kwajalein and Ebeye's history of segregation specifically.

Tracing the reproduction and protection of a mythical portrait of Kwajalein as a US home, *Suburban Empire* reveals how Cold War exceptionalism initially produced under military policies became appropriated by Kwajalein's civilian community over time. Kwajalein's civilian residents did not create the conditions of colonial power they entered into when arriving on the island. But many took up their privileged positions with ease and helped to reproduce that power over time. Because, thankfully, several of those residents and Marshallese living on Ebeye did allow interviews for this project, I have been able to highlight the complexity of these dynamics. And while many seemed to happily embrace their status within this segregated colonial structure, others challenged discriminatory policies toward Marshallese through creative means and distinctive positions of influence on Kwajalein.

Histories of US empire are deeply continuous, geographically broad, *and* historically and locally specific. The context situating US imperial expansion into Micronesia following World War II is no different. Thus, while this book traces Kwajalein's Cold War transformation within broader and deeper histories of US base expansion and imperialism throughout the Pacific alongside connections and continuities with postwar suburban structures of segregation in the United States, it is centered in local Marshallese history shaping how this military imperial project would unfold over time. Likewise, this book peels back the layers on what US expansion looked like during an era of global decolonization and Cold War competition. What were the global and local manifestations of this imperial expansion amid its simultaneous disavowal? How did Marshallese workers, activists, and politicians creatively navigate, accommodate, and challenge that distinctive political, social, and cultural terrain? To answer these questions, I also trace local Marshallese activism as it connects upward and outward to a broader Pacific history of coalition building to challenge the use of Oceania as a "nuclear playground" by imperial powers during the 1970s and 1980s.[27]

THE RISE OF A US MILITARY-INDUSTRIAL *COLONIAL* COMPLEX IN THE MARSHALL ISLANDS

US militarism in the Marshall Islands was not the first experience Marshallese had with colonial control over their homelands. Colonial contact is a relatively recent phenomenon in the region, which as noted earlier was enriched by thousands of years of human history prior to first contact with the Spaniards in 1529. Unlike the Chamorros of Guam and the Northern Marianas, earliest encounters with the Spanish Empire in the Marshall Islands had minimal impact. The naming of the Marshall Islands followed a subsequent encounter in the late 1700s, when British captain John Marshall, commanding a fleet of convict ships from London to Sydney, passed through the region in 1788. This passage marked the "discovery" of the atolls that came to be known on European maps thereafter as the "Marshall Islands."[28] Nearly a century later, US Protestant missionaries arrived in 1857, radically influencing Marshallese customs and promoting European ones in their place. Within a couple decades Germany would create the first colonial outpost and introduce a wage economy in the region, establishing a copra trade. According to anthropologist Holly M. Barker, many Marshallese identified the German period as a significant shift away from "communal self-sufficiency and family to individual income."[29] This first treaty signing in 1878 accompanied Germany's influence on fixing clan relationships by demanding an end to inter-atoll warfare between clans for control over land.[30]

Following World War I and a League of Nations mandate, colonial control transitioned from Germany to Japan. The Japanese instituted a settler approach to the region; what Pacific studies scholar Greg Dvorak calls a "Japanization" of Micronesia.[31] The Japanese colonial era saw a focus on developing education, the economy, and new infrastructure to house thousands of Japanese and Korean settlers who migrated to work in the region in support of Japanese economic endeavors. With the coming of World War II, what had been an era of civilian settler expansion transitioned to a period of militarization as civilian settlers were joined by Japanese military forces who began fortifying the islands in preparation for war.

With victory declared over Japan, colonial control shifted to the United States, which retained control over the region under UN sanction with the 1947 Trusteeship Agreement. This agreement became a key reason the United States selected and carried out the testing of weapons of mass destruction in the Marshallese homelands: retention of internationally sanctioned control over the region. President Harry S. Truman's signing of the Trusteeship Agreement in 1947, which siloed off Micronesia to deter a perceived threat of communist penetration into the region, would come four months after he introduced to Congress his doctrine of Cold War containment. The timing of these two major policies signaled a shift in US international politics, economics, and military expansion foundational to the origins of the Cold War. The Truman Doctrine informed US nation-building activities aimed at erecting an impermeable shield around nonaligned countries against Soviet incursion, ultimately justifying destructive wars in Korea and Vietnam. Within this broader policy of containment, the language of the Trusteeship Agreement positioned the Central Pacific as a region of strategic control: in need of US protection and necessary to facilitating military expansion. As illustrated in the accompanying map, the island regions falling within the Trust Territory of the Pacific Islands covered most of Micronesia and included Yap, Pohnpei, Chuuk, Kosrae, Palau, and the Northern Marianas.[32]

As noted earlier, such expansion contributed to transforming US society toward one that President Eisenhower cautioned by 1961 had become vulnerable to the influence of a military-industrial complex. To understand my claim that centering the Marshall Islands during the Cold War unearths a story more accurately reflecting a military-industrial *colonial* complex, we must first consider the deeper, historic intersections of US empire and militarism. US colonial control in the Marshall Islands intersected not only with precolonial indigenous history in the region and more recent contexts of German and Japanese rule, but also with earlier histories of US imperial expansion into the Pacific and the particularities of US base development over time. As anthropologist David Vine traced in

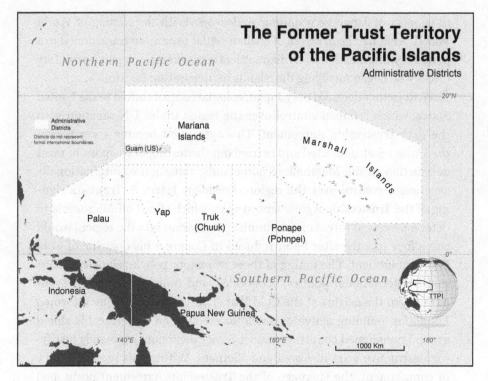

The Former Trust Territory of the Pacific Islands

Administrative Districts

Northern Pacific Ocean

20°N

Administrative
Districts

Districts do not represent
formal international boundaries.

Guam (US)

Mariana
Islands

Marshall

Islands

Palau   Yap   Truk
(Chuuk)

Ponape
(Pohnpei)

0°

Southern Pacific Ocean

Indonesia

TTPI

Papua New Guinea

140°E   160°E   180°

1000 Km

Map 3. The Former Trust Territory of the Pacific Islands. Map by Philip B. White.

his book on these base histories, from its foundations as a self-proclaimed independent nation, US imperial expansion across the North American continent saw the development of a vast network of military fortifications and fortresses to enable that expansion. As Vine pointed out, "while scholars generally identify Guantánamo Bay as the first U.S. military base abroad, they strangely overlook bases created shortly after independence. Hundreds of frontier forts helped enable westward expansion of the United States, and they were built on land that was very much *abroad* at the time."[33] This development began with the first fortification of Fort Harmar, built in 1785 in the Northwest Territory, and was followed by the construction of 60 major forts and 138 army posts over the next seven decades as US settlers moved West of the Mississippi to occupy the homelands of Indian nations.[34] These military establishments rapidly grew during the Mexican American War of 1846–1848 and by the late nineteenth century accompanied the largest acquisition of colonial territory outside the continental landscape following the Spanish American War of 1898.[35] After 1898, US-annexed territories of Hawai'i, Eastern portions of Samoa (renamed American Samoa), Guam, the Philippines, Puerto Rico, and Cuba (identified as a "protectorate" at the time) became increasingly militarized.[36] By the end of World War II, US base expansion spiked, with average construction reaching 112 bases per month.[37] While base expansion retracted in the postwar era, the United States has perpetually maintained "'a permanent institution of bases in peacetime.'"[38] Today, while no foreign base exists on US soil, the United States operates around eight hundred bases in more than seventy countries. Vine explains: "Although few U.S. citizens realize it, we probably have more bases in other people's lands than any other people, nation, or empire in world history."[39]

This base history constitutes one piece of a broader context of US imperialism situating the history of US occupation of Kwajalein Atoll during and following World War II. Under the confines of the Trusteeship Agreement—UN-sanctioned colonialism—Kwajalein became one island colony buttressing what Bruce Cumings has called an "archipelago of empire."[40] In addition to an increase in US economic and political influence during the Cold War, this base network enabled the government to quickly deploy the military anywhere around the world, underwriting the rise in US global hegemony through the threat of force.[41]

Kwajalein's history under US control marked the ascendance of this unprecedented level of US military power during the Cold War, a level of power that provoked President Eisenhower's cautionary statement in his 1961 farewell speech. Warning Americans of the potential consequences that would emerge from the disproportionate influence of a military-industrial complex on their society, Eisenhower was centrally concerned about the impact on US domestic life. He failed to identify the consequences already endured by colonial subjects around the world, whose homes had become the testing grounds for this military-industrial growth. Marshallese became aware of such impacts first through the US nuclear-testing campaign and at its conclusion through Kwajalein's transformation into a missile-testing range. As noted previously, centering Marshallese histories during the Cold War forces us to expand Eisenhower's warning to acknowledge the true costs of a military-industrial *colonial* complex. These stories allow us to better understand how as Eisenhower's speech made visible the costs of the military-industrial complex to Americans, it simultaneously made invisible the costs to colonial subjects like the Marshallese, whose homelands proved essential to buttressing this military-industrial partnership.[42] This complex Eisenhower warned of was in reality a global and transnational phenomenon, not simply a function of the domestic structures within the United States. Nor does the historic example of weapons testing in the Marshall Islands simply illustrate this complex transported to a colonial setting. Rather, I argue that scholars need to attend to the historic *imbrication* of that structure with colonial control.

Nuclear- and missile-testing programs have been foundational to the rise of this military-industrial colonial complex, and this book reveals the various modes of colonial control that enabled this most destructive testing to occur. As we will see, the United States built a vast array of technological capacities through its ability to occupy Marshallese islands, assisted by the geopolitical frame of UN sanction working to disguise that colonial control as something outside the realm of empire. While mythologized instead as a "special trust," a status much more amenable to the geopolitical pressures of a decolonizing world, the colonial dimensions of US governance in the region proved deeply consequential for Marshallese. Thus, while US citizens living downwind from the fallout of Cold War nuclear tests conducted across Nevada and other Southwest locations retained the political right to vote and hold their representatives accountable for the harms they suffered, Marshallese shared no such privileges. As colonial subjects of US empire, Marshallese could not vote out of office those making destructive decisions about their homelands and their bodies; they had no ability to speak back to the state. This was a *colonial* complex that reshaped the social, economic, and environmental worlds of Marshallese with legacies that endure today.

Within the long trajectory of US base expansion over time, Kwajalein came to be one of the most valuable jewels in the crown of this military-industrial colonial complex. In addition to acting as the support base for the twelve-year nuclear-testing campaign that enabled the United States to flex its military muscle to the world during the Cold War, Kwajalein became the site where nearly every ICBM in the US arsenal was tested.[43]

Its unique location, the massive military infrastructure investment, and ongoing US control over the region through the UN Trusteeship Agreement made the base "invaluable to the Department of Defense over time."[44] By the 1980s, President Ronald Reagan would locate the research for his Strategic Defense Initiative, also known as "Star Wars," at Kwajalein, upping the political ante of the installation. This mission was tied to Reagan's shifting geopolitical strategy, which aimed to massively ramp up defense spending, hoping to outspend the Soviet Union and hasten the Cold War's conclusion.

Just as the military-industrial complex within the domestic realm of US society sent exorbitant material benefits of government investment toward private contractors, US paychecks tied to colonial control over Kwajalein also proved substantial. According to the US Army, by 1994 the Kwajalein missile-testing complex had reached a value of $4 billion as a key strategic resource in ballistic missile testing, anti-ballistic missile (ABM) testing, and space and intelligence-gathering functions.[45] This book considers how base profits rippled beyond the salaries and savings of those engineers and scientists living subsidized lives on the island. While those residing on the base included thousands of US workers over time who moved through the rotating door of contract labor, research activities on the island also enriched the pockets of military, engineering, and logistical contractors beyond the atoll. Just as nuclear testing in the Northern Marshall Islands buttressed the salaries and research profiles of countless scientists at the Brookhaven National Laboratory in New York, the Argonne National Laboratory in Chicago, and those employed by the Atomic Energy Commission whose careers advanced through studying the effects of radiation on Marshallese lands and bodies, research at Kwajalein likewise saw an expansion of profits upward and outward. Those lucky enough to win early contracts to transform this Marshallese island into an elaborate landscape dotted with missile facilities alongside small-town suburban infrastructure embarked on a lucrative endeavor. An example is the Honolulu Engineering District of the US Army Corps of Engineers, which captured an early construction contract in 1962 with a substantial portion of the first-phase missile facilities totaling over $55 million.[46] Private contractor Pacific Martin Zachary also won a $15 million contract during this period to construct support facilities on Kwajalein that included fresh- and saltwater systems, bachelor quarters, and a school for the children of incoming scientists and engineers.[47] By 1986, the local Macy's catering to US consumer desires boasted profits of $4 million per year.[48]

The ultimate prize to the United States came not through the enriched pockets and careers of US workers directly connected to missile research at Kwajalein but rather through the role Kwajalein played in greasing the wheels of US ascendance to becoming the sole military hegemon by the Cold War's end. Kwajalein has been key to the iteration of US imperial expansion in the postwar era that has been historically rooted in unrivaled military power and capacity. As Anthropologist Holly Barker has argued, while the Marshallese paid the majority of the price: "The United States achieved global superpower status as a result of its weapons testing in the Marshall Islands" and that status "came at the cost of the health of the Marshallese people and their environment."[49]

In *Base Nation*, David Vine framed Eisenhower's cautionary words alongside base expenditures, noting that "every base built overseas signifies a theft from American society. Reallocating the $75 billion to $100 billion in total annual expenditures on overseas bases would allow the country to roughly double federal education spending."[50] The cost of a modern base in 2015 was equivalent to the yearly cost of a college scholarship for 63,000 students, or health care for 260,000 low-income children or 64,000 veterans, he added.[51] This book asks what the relational costs have been for colonized populations whose homes have buttressed this base empire. When we historically trace the profits of Raytheon, Lockheed Martin, MIT's Lincoln Laboratories, and others, how can we place those profits in conversation with the costs to those indigenous to the regions where this military research and development has flourished? What have been the costs in land loss and ecological contamination, in public health and mortality, in sovereignty and self-determination?

"EMPIRE OF INNOCENCE": KWAJALEIN'S "MAYBERRY" OF THE PACIFIC

Just as Kwajalein's transformation into a space of military control is situated within the vast history of US imperial expansion over time, the disavowal of this imperial process during the Cold War aligns with deeper patterns in American exceptionalism. A dynamic of imperial destruction alongside its erasure has been foundational to the emergence of US empire and the maintenance of this exceptionalist narrative for hundreds of years. Scholars of US empire and settler colonialism have mined the depths of this national mythology, excavating and analyzing its cultural manifestations. Historian Philip J. Deloria traced the cultural history of a US settler society that has "played Indian" for hundreds of years from the Boston Tea Party through 1970s New Wave hippies and the naming and donning of sports mascots today. In doing so, he demonstrated how the contradictions of the American exceptionalist narratives framing settler identity are never far below the surface. This identity has never been fixed in place but rather infused by a vision of nationhood that is always "becoming," one that never resolved the tension of a heavy reliance "upon a British or an Indian foil."[52] He argued: "The plotting out of and explaining of the United States have for a long time meant celebrating the nation's growing power and its occasionally wise, often tragic, sometimes well-intentioned deployment of that power on the continent and around the world. The celebration of national character, on the other hand, has frequently involved the *erasure* of such exercises of power."[53] These deep disavowals and erasures have been central to the particularities of a US base imperium over time and took on distinct inflections during the Cold War. This iteration of Cold War American exceptionalism—this *imperial formation*—conditioned through the UN Trusteeship Agreement, had much cultural precedent to draw upon.[54] During the Cold War, with the United States a major voice shaping UN policy, this new global body played a key role in sanctioning US imperial expansion into Micronesia for military buildup through the identification of such expansion as a "special trust." The Trusteeship Agreement provided a narrative of US benevolence conjoined with an urgent imperative to marry US national security to the fate of global peace. This moment of US imperial expansion alongside erasure of the nature of such expansion reflected shifting Cold War geopolitics. An era of anti-colonial protest and decolonization found the United States and the Soviet Union as two rising imperial powers up against a tide of global decolonization and on the search for allies, and thus committed to avoiding accusations of imperialism. Vine has shown how within this changing geopolitical context the United States began to "exert its power through increasingly subtle and discreet means."[55] In addition to using market influence and international agreements, the United States harvested the fruits of its investments in base buildup to nudge any nations veering off course back in line with economic and political conditions most favorable to the United States.[56]

Nearly four decades of a destructive US weapons-testing campaign unfolded in the Marshall Islands during a period marked on the one hand by Cold War military expansion and on the other by global anti-colonial movements delegitimizing imperial expansion. This conjunction required the expansion of US imperial power in the Marshall Islands to unfold simultaneously with its disavowal. US military personnel and civilian contractors laid claim to their new home in the Marshall Islands through wartime and postwar narratives of sacrifice and national security, while Cold War containment imperatives married the idea of global peace to the expansion of US military power. Just as the UN Trusteeship Agreement offered a global framing of imperial innocence, a postwar spatio-cultural export enabled erasure of the most destructive features of a growing base imperium to likewise take root on a local level. The mapping of a growing number of US bases in the wartime and postwar era with the features of suburban American life infused these spaces tied to the expansion of increasingly destructive US military power with the everyday innocence of Cold War suburban family life.

In recent decades, base studies scholars have begun probing the sacrosanct narrative of national security shrouding the histories of US bases to reveal their historic impacts on local populations. Historians, anthropologists, and scholars of architecture have specifically traced physical and cultural transformations of islands reaching beyond the Pacific into the Caribbean and the Indian Ocean, examining base histories in Diego Garcia, Guantánamo, Vieques, and Okinawa, among other sites.[57] The impacts of this expanding US base imperium have included patterns of displacement, the emergence of exploitative sex economies, and the export and imposition of US racial segregation practices.[58] Kwajalein's history shares many resonances with other base stories, including the imposition of a structure of segregation to organize labor and leisure that scholars Wesley Iwao Uenten and Jana K. Lipman have likewise traced, respectively, in the histories of Okinawa and Guantánamo Bay.[59]

Base expansion in the postwar era emerged alongside new spatial configurations easing discipline over US domestic life—both shifts aimed to contain nuclear families. On Kwajalein, army commanders were not only charged with overseeing the missile-testing mission, but also acted as mayors of a predominantly civilian community. The army erected a tropical-style Mayberry landscape to support family life on Kwajalein, a setting aimed to protect families from threats of nuclear annihilation, resident bachelor laborers, and potential boundary transgressions of a racialized commuting colonial service sector. Compared with other US bases, policing such transgressions of the latter colonized workforce was enabled through the spatial confinement of Kwajalein and Ebeye. Their separation by three miles of reef created a natural barrier, ensuring that segregating these two essential labor forces and enacting surveillance over Marshallese movement on Kwajalein could be easily achieved.

While a distinctive capacity for domestic containment through island-style suburban segregation marks Kwajalein's history as exceptional, the pattern of suburbanization on US bases around the world is not. In his 2007 comparative work, *America Town: Building the Outposts of Empire*, geographer Mark L. Gillem examined this historic trend of suburbanization at US bases in Japan, Okinawa, South Korea, Italy, and Germany. Gillem revealed how, as on Kwajalein, in other outposts of US empire suburban planning mapped bases as familiar spaces for US soldiers and their families residing in foreign lands.[60] Golf courses, baseball fields, and franchise stores dotted Kwajalein's landscape, just as they have these other bases. The suburban transformation of Kwajalein thus resides within a broader pattern in which a vast expansion of US bases globally has come to be seen (or unseen) as a given, unremarkable. These base settings have harnessed signature features of postwar American suburbia, shrouding the expanse of a US base imperium in a veil of innocence. As historian Matthew D. Lassiter found in comparative analysis of US suburban histories, postwar suburbia harnessed a set of bipartisan political values that included "taxpayer and consumer rights, children's educational privileges, family residential security, and *middle-class historical innocence*."[61] Within these broader patterns of postwar suburbia, Lassiter argued: "The dominant ethos of American suburbia has always idealized the present and celebrated the future at the expense of any critical reflection on the past."[62] Accompanying the export of a US suburban landscape to this Marshallese island in the Central Pacific was the simultaneous erasure of any critical reflection on the impacts of a US settler presence in the region.

Kwajalein was one of the most striking manifestations of American exceptionalism in which suburbanization produced US domesticity in a foreign landscape. On Kwajalein, narratives of American domesticity relied on the dehumanization of Marshallese and the positioning of their presence in the region as both foreign and existing to serve Americans. That a landscape of innocence without history was easily embraced by US civilians living on Kwajalein over time has been suggested by Pacific scholar and former Kwajalein resident Greg Dvorak. In his book *Coral and Concrete: Remembering Kwajalein Atoll between Japan, America, and the Marshall Islands*, Dvorak observed that on Kwajalein, "Civilians . . . took little or no responsibility for the injustices the United States had carried out upon the people of the Marshall Islands, from the horrific nuclear tests of the 1940s and 1950s to the numerous displacements that ensued due to irradiation in the Northern atolls and the ongoing missile-testing project in Kwajalein Atoll. Through our very existence in Kwajalein, we were all directly imbricated in the history of the contemporary Marshall Islands, and yet we disowned the past and lived as if this were all just the military's fault."[63] While disavowal of empire may have been one by-product of Kwajalein's suburbanization, this erasure was not the motivating factor for the island's physical and cultural transformation. The military constructed a suburban landscape on Kwajalein as a recruitment tool with the aim to attract and retain a highly prized labor force of largely White engineers and scientists who were already living in postwar suburbia. Kwajalein's built environment was modeled after the New Jersey suburbs to emulate the environment from which a significant cohort of elite workers from Bell Laboratories migrated.[64]

US scientists and engineers from Bell and other contractors began migrating to Kwajalein during the early 1960s to analyze data on missiles launches and interceptions. The installation was staffed by a majority civilian workforce over time; engineers, scientists, and a host of other civilian personnel worked in construction, shipping, and maintenance alongside the commuting Marshallese service sector. During its early years as a missile base, the island transferred from naval to army control and became a government owned contractor operated (GOCO) facility. Former longtime resident Eugene C. Sims, who worked as chief engineer for logistics contractor Global Associates on Kwajalein during the mid-1960s, recalled this transition as fitting into a broader trend aimed to "free up combat military personnel from the day to day operation of military facilities."[65] On Kwajalein this meant civilian contractors and their families often outnumbered military personnel on the island ten to one during the missile-testing era; the base was typically overseen by an army colonel with a two-year tour of duty. [66] As the population fluctuated over time, civilian residency peaked during the 1960s and 1970s, when the island housed between four and five thousand workers and their families.[67] This peak coincided with the height of construction work, which erected missile facilities as well as Kwajalein's residential and recreational amenities. These numbers have declined to a low of around twelve hundred today.[68] In any given year during the six decades of missile testing, Marshallese laborers have accounted for about one-quarter of Kwajalein's workforce.[69]

During the missile era, suburbanization became not only a way for the army to attract its most elite workforce but also a mechanism for organizing space and imposing a disciplinary order on its hybrid workforce. Mirroring suburban construction that architectural scholar Marc Gillem has detailed as informing the US base imperium in recent years, Kwajalein's built environment reflected a "strict hierarchy of architectural forms . . . standardized building styles represent[ing] order and control."[70] While this setting was planned with an eye toward military containment and control on Kwajalein, the island's boundaries proved perpetually porous. Complete dominion over residential social relations could never be fully achieved because bachelors, not just families, resided on the island. These men were situated by the military as potential predators threatening the security and purity of Kwajalein's wholesome nuclear families. Army surveillance policed gender and sexual norms on the island as the military was forced to contend with the reality of bachelors living in close proximity to seemingly vulnerable women and children. Residential and recreational spaces were monitored to keep presumably predatory single men at a distance from families. Military surveillance on Kwajalein proved incredibly effective in policing these boundaries, as army rules disciplining movement could be explained as security measures. Individuals who deviated from such rules and regulations could be, and in many cases were, banned from the island.

It was largely this bachelor population on Kwajalein that helped distinguish the island's suburban landscape from its racially homogenous continental counterparts.[71] Kwajalein's suburbia was not marked by exclusive White residency. But among its US residents, a racially divided setting was informed by class distinctions that found the majority White scientists and engineers arriving with accompanied status and living in family housing. Those coming with unaccompanied status (in jobs like construction, shipping, and dock work) comprised the largest percentage of US workers of color, who lived in a separate area in bachelor dormitories.[72] While the entanglements of class and race influenced housing segregation on the island, Kwajalein's nine-hundred-acre size meant a greater amount of social integration in spaces like dining facilities and recreational activities than was typical in Cold War continental suburbia. In contrast to Dr. Martin Luther King Jr.'s 1960 lament that "one of the most segregated hours . . . in Christian America was 11 a.m. on Sunday," Kwajalein's houses of worship were integrated.[73]

Stark racial segregation infusing the island's suburban landscape came instead through the structure of colonialism keeping Marshallese excluded from residency and from frequenting Kwajalein's consumer and recreational spaces.[74] Military surveillance disciplining Marshallese compliance worked to criminalize Kwajalein's brown colonial service sector. While surveillance over the mobility of residential populations on Kwajalein proved a perpetual challenge for the military, the island's natural boundaries enabled a level of regulation and surveillance between Kwajalein and Ebeye—a more complete form of segregation never fully achieved in continental suburbia. Kwajalein's suburbia perfected what other US suburban spaces could only aspire to in the realm of domestic containment from urban settings.

Further distinguishing suburban life on Kwajalein, the island's small and contained spatiality, where cars were banned and residents traveled via bicycle, contrasted the frontier-style movement of White flight and automobile culture characterizing a sense of mobility and anonymity in its US counterparts.[75] Unlike continental sprawl, Kwajalein's suburbia was profoundly rooted in place. The island has not been a space of expansive

White flight; it was not a landscape marked by redlining or discriminatory FHA loans, so much of which has been the focus of US metropolitan
scholarship.[76] Rather, Kwajalein's suburban landscape was built within a
context of military imperialism that involved displacing resident Marshallese and retaining the island for a US military and civilian population.

While many features of this local context mark the suburban setting on Kwajalein in distinctive ways, the island's physical and cultural
transformation shared linkages with continental histories of suburban/
urban development. Kwajalein was historically marked as a militarized
site of American domesticity, while Ebeye was positioned as an urban and
impoverished site housing foreign labor. Similar to spaces historically narrated as urban in the United States, Ebeye was perceived as a home to
workers, not families: a space foreign to the domesticity of Kwajalein's US
suburbia. As urban historians have shown, during the Cold War the urban
constituted a space of racialized threat from which suburbia provided a
protective family refuge.[77]

If Kwajalein's history sheds light on distinctions in the broader context of postwar suburban segregation, expanding this analysis into the
realm of empire, this story also brings into sharp relief the convergence
between military and spatial forms of domestic containment emerging
during the Cold War. Kwajalein's history coincides with the rise of a US
security state that included continental and overseas imperial implications tied to the expansion of US weapons development activities. Suburbanization served as an effective technology for ordering residency and
labor in a space perceived as perpetually insecure. While the story of suburban containment in the Central Pacific is unique, the island's security
structure shares commonalities with the increasing surveillance appara-
tus characterizing US suburbia in the postwar period. Historian Elaine
Tyler May commented on such intersections between the domestic and
global security state, noting the increasingly "fortress" style of living and
"bunker mentality" characterizing the United States in the wake of the
Cold War.[78] Domestic containment at the turn of the twenty-first century
has been marked by the increasing militarization of the police alongside
the tragic symbol of neighborhood watch coordinators armed with lethal
weaponry and "stand your ground" laws. In this era, as terror in the suburbs has transitioned from Cold War "duck and cover" drills in schools

to "active shooter" lockdown protocol, questions about the relationship between the security state and the suburbs seem particularly prescient. Thus, Kwajalein's history under US colonial control illuminates not only the way suburbia's markers historically moved thousands of miles into the Central Pacific to map this militarized site of US empire with the familiar features of "home," but also how the growing security state and its various surveillance structures have increasingly infused US suburban landscapes during and beyond the Cold War.

CENTERING THE PACIFIC IN THE STORY OF POSTWAR GLOBAL DECOLONIZATION

A site illuminating global and domestic elements of US Cold War containment policy in a region signaling the launch of the nuclear arms race, Kwajalein's history also sheds light on the role of the Pacific in postwar global decolonization. Kwajalein's and Ebeye's relational historic development reveals how within the structure of postwar suburbanization in the context of US empire, the military's segregation of these two essential labor forces initially buttressed but then ultimately helped destabilize US power in the region. As the extreme disparities between life on Kwajalein and life on Ebeye emerged to deadly consequence over time, Ebeye became the site from which the most impactful protests against US militarism and colonial control erupted. This movement followed decades of Marshallese challenges to US colonialism in their homelands through petitions and letters, media interviews, and Senate testimony. Ultimately, when these tactics failed to achieve change, Marshallese landowners, workers, and families began sailing in to reclaim their islands in the late 1970s and early 1980s. The sail-ins exploded within the context of Marshallese negotiations for sovereignty and mass Pacific protests against militarism and empire, signaled by a Nuclear Free and Independent Pacific movement.

Marshallese challenged US colonialism on Kwajalein within the broader context of tensions undergirding an era of global decolonization and Cold War imperial expansion. US colonialism in the Marshall Islands built upon earlier precedent set by continental and overseas imperial histories but was also inflected by the changing context of Cold War competition. These shifts centered on the conflict between a US military strategy built on imperial expansion and a simultaneous public relations campaign aimed at positioning the nation as the promoter of freedom and democracy to the decolonizing world. Like other sites of US imperial expansion following World War II, Kwajalein's story showcases US efforts to wage this propaganda front of the Cold War—a battle for hearts and minds to align decolonizing nations with the nation's political, economic, and military agendas—alongside the contradictions of empire. Disavowal of empire on Kwajalein existed alongside lateral examples of Cold War US imperial interventions around the world. Scholars of American culture and empire have illuminated how the United States projected an image of liberty and equality overseas during the Cold War while struggling to erase historic and continuous contradictions to this narrative evident in domestic and foreign policy.[79] Histories of anti-colonial struggles in Latin America, Southeast Asia, and Africa exposed the contradictions between US Cold War propaganda on global democracy in light of US practices of undermining such values when democratic elections threatened US interests.[80]

The story of Marshallese anti-colonial movements reveals the Pacific to be no exception to a broader global pattern of resistance to imperialism following World War II, while this local movement at Kwajalein also illustrates the extension of these struggles into the final years of the Cold War. Just as the global context of Cold War competition informed and influenced the civil rights movement, as traced by scholars like Mary L. Dudziak, the model of nonviolent direct action also rippled beyond the shores of the United States and found its way into the strategies of Marshallese activists during the 1980s.[81] The largest protest, 1982's Operation Homecoming, incorporated this model of nonviolent direct action into mass sail-ins and reclamation of homelands throughout Kwajalein Atoll.

The rise of the US military-industrial colonial complex during an era marked by increasing support for global decolonization made the importance of disavowing the imperial nature of expansion into Micronesia key to Cold War politics.[82] Early on in the Cold War, the United Nations offered language framing such expansion as a necessary good to ensure both US national security and global peace, legitimating US entitlement to the region. This sanction positioned the United States as a global defender, marrying the language of US national security to global security. In doing so, the Trusteeship Agreement supported a historic level of technological research and development that informed the production of an increasingly destructive range of nuclear and missile weaponry. Kwajalein resided at the center of this history as a site emblematic of US power becoming normalized as a national security imperative rather than an imperial endeavor. The following chapters reveal how, as the United Nations increasingly absorbed newly sovereign nations across the decolonizing world in the postwar period—and began authoring declarations on the rights of colonized peoples—this institution of global governance became a complicated site for both legitimating and challenging the continuity of US imperialism in Micronesia.

THE SPACIALITIES, TEMPORALITIES, AND CULTURES OF US EMPIRE

Suburban Empire traces local and global histories informing the transformations of place and the human geography of this atoll from the end of World War II through the Cold War's conclusion. Centering spatial history, this book considers how people create their own "place-worlds" by drawing on what anthropologist Keith H. Basso calls doing human history through placemaking. To ask "what happened here?" on Kwajalein is not only to trace a story of the islands' physical transformations, but to reveal the human history of that place.[83] Basso has suggested: "What people make of their places is closely connected to what they make of themselves as members of society and inhabitants of the earth.... If place-making is a way of constructing the past, a venerable means of *doing* human history, it is also a way of constructing social traditions and, in the process, personal and social identities. We are, in a sense, the place-worlds we imagine."[84] Similarly, political geographers have noted that we are also *spatial* beings, products of spatial arrangements that proceed us, and collective creators of our spatiality.[85] If this book seeks to uncover how attention to placemaking on Kwajalein reveals a connection to social history, it likewise is steeped in a Marxist tradition that we make our own history, but not under conditions of our choosing. In what follows readers will discover how Marshallese used their agency to survive, accommodate, protest, and find some benefit among the range of changes taking place in their homelands under US colonial rule. Their actions were conditioned by the decisions of agents of US empire whose use of their lands would contribute to US ascendance as *the* military hegemon by the Cold War's conclusion.

While scholarship highlighting the intersection of US and Pacific history in the twentieth century has tended to center Oceania as a vital space for understanding World War II—often as a lens on US or Japanese experiences and rarely with a focus on the histories of Pacific Islanders—this book argues that the Pacific has been equally central to understanding the global Cold War. As the support base for nuclear testing in the Northern Marshall Islands, Kwajalein facilitated the US military's capacity to flex its weaponry muscles before the Soviet Union and the world. The centrality of the Marshall Islands to the development of weapons of mass destruction following World War II helped reshape the global order. The specific role Kwajalein has played in supporting nuclear testing and the historic and continuous ICBM testing has been essential to buttressing the emergence of the United States as the dominant military empire and thus crucial in transforming the postwar global landscape.

Despite this significant role in shaping the postwar international arena, the Marshall Islands have remained largely ignored in studies of postwar global history.[86] Such omissions in scholarship exemplify the historic erasures Epeli Hau'ofa (noted earlier) so poignantly challenged as a form of academic imperialism that historically framed the Pacific Islands as tiny and isolated from the rest of the world, rather than as a space of oceanic connection and enlargement.[87] This book builds on Hau'ofa's and others' reimaginings of scale and historic interconnectivity to show how global change has both informed and been informed by Pacific histories and specifically the consequential events taking place in the Marshall Islands following World War II. As a US military base, a segregated suburban landscape, and a site of anti-colonial protest, Kwajalein's postwar history reorients the global historic compass and clock, reminding us that the Pacific is far from peripheral to this period of world history; rather, it is at the epicenter of some of the most significant changes marking the postwar global order.

By positioning the Marshall Islands and Pacific history at the center of postwar US and global history, *Suburban Empire* not only challenges presumptions about geography, scale, and historic connection; it also forces us to rethink how these categories inform periodization. The history of US weapons testing in the Marshall Islands illuminates how broadly accepted moments marking global historic change, like 1945 and 1989, take on different meanings when informed by the voices of those whose homelands became pivotal to the *unending* state of US wartime preparation. Centering Marshallese lived experiences helps us further question what was "Cold" about this war and consider the hot consequences that misnomer obscures. As legal scholar Mary L. Dudziak has shown US history to be marked by a near perpetual state of war, with "not many years of peacetime" during the twentieth century, it is not surprising that those subjects coming under US dominion during this era found their lives structured by "this enduring condition."[88] The shifts from wartime battle, to postwar nuclear devastation, to ongoing missile testing has made the past seven decades of Marshallese history intimately and tragically familiar with the meanings of US "wartime." Kwajalein's missile-testing practices have continued unabated from the demise of one global enemy through the identification of new targets in an age of war on terror.[89]

Finally, this book also aims to contribute to the broad range of scholarship analyzing the histories of US empire as *cultural* histories. In the following chapters I argue that the impacts of US empire in the Marshall Islands have been manifested through the realm of the material *and* the cultural. One poignant example appeared in a 1946 issue of the *Atomic Blast*. This military-produced local newspaper, aimed at residential personnel on Kwajalein supporting nuclear testing in the Northern Marshall Islands, showcased stories anticipating and celebrating the first atomic detonation at Bikini Atoll. Alongside coverage anticipating the ensuing destruction at Bikini Atoll appeared other news tidbits on the opening of Kwajalein's first miniature golf course and an "Atomic Beauty Queen Pageant" on the island. Such stories geared to inform and entertain US military personnel engaged in real-time acts of colonial destruction and devastation in the Marshallese homelands became a signal feature of US Cold War imperialism in the region. This imperial formation was rooted in the innocence of everyday, small-town, suburban life. This cultural history and its "crime of innocence," emerging at the intersection of the physical and narrative mapping of Kwajalein following World War II as an "American home," persist today. This book closely examines how the everyday innocence of suburban family life has mapped the history of colonialism in the Marshall Islands in ways that connect Kwajalein to the broader normalization of a global US base imperium.

As a toddler on Ebeye, Darlene Keju intuited the importance of marking a phenomenon that over time became unremarkable to so many Americans. She sensed something unnatural as she looked across Kwajalein's lagoon and asked why Marshallese needed passes to visit Marshallese lands, why they were segregated in their homes. In doing so, she probed the *remarkable* character of this base imperium, an act she would continue through decades of activism and advocacy for her people as an adult. Taking inspiration from Keju, this book strives to continue this marking, to further unsettle the ease with which the vast majority of Americans have historically and continually "unseen" the workings of US empire, as well as its impacts on peoples around the world who have come under its sphere. It may be unsurprising that this history was unknown to most US citizens living thousands of miles away from Kwajalein, many of whom have never heard of Micronesia, let alone the Marshall Islands. Out of sight and out of mind, as anthropologist David Vine revealed in his study of this seemingly invisible base empire.[90] But a striking phenomenon unearthed in my research is how effectively the physical and cultural transformation of Kwajalein's landscape has made invisible the destructive and exploitative nature of military imperialism in real time to a large number of US workers living and working on the island.[91] This invisibility at the local level emerged with Americans and Marshallese living in close proximity and yet seemingly worlds apart, a dynamic framed by the military structure of segregation.

RESEARCH METHODS, CONSTRAINTS, AND CHAPTER OVERVIEWS

The raw materials of this book have come from a range of archival sources as well as dozens of oral history interviews. While the vast majority of archival sources were written in English or included translations, many oral histories I conducted on Ebeye required a translator. More than any other group participating in Kwajalein and Ebeye's historic transformations, Marshallese workers and particularly the voices of Marshallese women remained absent from the archives. Thus, a significant component of my translated interviews focused on these women who had worked on Kwajalein over the years, many as domestics.[92]

A significant number of oral history interviews were geared toward gaining a better sense of how this history played out on the ground among Marshallese and US civilians working on Kwajalein. Some interviews retain the requested anonymity as a measure of protection for previous or current research, past or present employment, and/or residency on Kwajalein. Of thirty-three oral history interviewees, only two chose to remain anonymous, noted as such throughout.[93] Luckily, the archives proved rife with the voices of military and Trust Territory officials, which helped detail those governing this deployment of US empire from the top down, and their perceptions of Kwajalein and Ebeye over time. These sources included a diverse array of correspondence, reports, directives, and speeches, alongside interviews captured in several documentary films about Kwajalein's history and military publications like *Stars and Stripes* and *Soldiers*.

While this book has been cobbled together through access to a rich range of sources and voices, my research contains limitations that accompany a lack of residency in the region and linguistic skills, which I navigated through research visits and use of an interpreter.[94] While my research on Kwajalein brings to light details of Marshallese and Micronesian histories more broadly, this project is not a cultural study of the Marshall Islands or Micronesia. I specify this because, in contrast, I *do* see this project as making broader claims about US culture and specifically the cultural forms of empire during the Cold War taking place in the Marshall Islands. My academic training, paired with my cultural and linguistic knowledge, has placed me on firmer ground to bring that lens to this analysis. In addition to linguistic and cultural limitations, my subjectivity, which includes settler, racial, and class privilege, poses further constraints. I write from having grown up with such privileges in both the continental United States and during three years of residency in Hawai'i that enabled me to conduct the majority of my research. While I lacked the opportunity to live on Kwajalein or Ebeye, researching this project from Hawai'i offered a chance to consider both historic distinctions and spaces of overlap in the histories and legacies of US military imperialism.

Residing at the intersection of US base studies, cultural histories of US empire, and urban and suburban historiography, *Suburban Empire* situates Pacific history as central to some of the most significant global changes in the post–World War II era. The book examines global and local scales of these historic transformations through six chapters. Chapter 1 locates the start of US military control over Kwajalein through a World War II battle and the postwar transformation of that history within the emergence of US Cold War containment policy. The chapter largely hovers between the 1940s and 1950s to examine how the Trusteeship Agreement framed US expansion into Micronesia through a narrative of security and benevolence: a "special relationship" aimed at bolstering US defense, global peace, and regional development. I explore how within the dual pressures of perceived Cold War security threats and the changing tides of global decolonization, the Trusteeship Agreement posed contradictory directives, obliging the United States to support Micronesians toward self-determination (including land protection) while sanctioning military use of Micronesian lands for defense. The chapter reveals how priority was given to the latter directive, as most tragically exemplified by the US nuclear-testing campaign in the Northern Marshall Islands, a catalyst in the global nuclear arms race and a campaign for which Kwajalein served as a support base.

Moving between global and local manifestations of US empire in Micronesia, chapter 2 spans the 1950s, 1960s, and 1970s, honing in on land control in Kwajalein Atoll through analysis of colonial leasing histories. The chapter further explores military displacements of Marshallese throughout Kwajalein Atoll to enable ICBM testing and begins to look at the disparate history of investment in and planning of each island's built environments. While chapter 2 focuses on Ebeye—the island housing those Marshallese displaced by the military and the missile base's segregated service sector—chapter 3 relationally explores these dynamics unfolding on Kwajalein during the same period. Situating Kwajalein as a site of Cold War domestic containment, chapter 3 traces military planning, investments, and policies aimed at recruiting and retaining an elite US workforce and their families. The erection and protection of a wholesome family setting on Kwajalein entailed segregation and surveillance over the commuting Marshallese workforce as well as the policing of sexual and gender norms among US residents on the island. The chapter explores how Army policies on Kwajalein, aligning with continental patterns of suburban segregation, criminalized any unregulated movement by a racialized service sector and a residential bachelor workforce.

Building from the relational historic transformations of Ebeye and Kwajalein, chapter 4 offers a cultural analysis of how successful the military was in convincing US workers and their family members that they were indeed "at home" in Marshallese lands. This chapter explores how the particularities of Cold War American exceptionalism, historic patterns of erasure begun by US military and Trust Territory colonial officials in the region, were readily taken up by Kwajalein's civilian residents over time. Chapter 4 places US civilian experiences of Kwajalein during the 1960s, 1970s, and 1980s in conversation with more recent reflections on the island's meanings through a focus on a culture of nostalgia emerging among former residents.

While chapter 4 centers US mythmaking practices that have attempted to situate Kwajalein as an "American home," chapter 5 explores various ways Marshallese have challenged such narratives over time. This chapter stays in the 1970s and 1980s to chronicle Marshallese testimonies before the US Senate in 1976 and the 1982 landowner protest against the conditions of US colonial control. During the historic sail-in, Operation Homecoming, one thousand Marshallese men, women, and children reclaimed their home islands throughout Kwajalein Atoll. I examine how the Senate hearings and the protest constituted two events in which Marshallese most impactfully called attention to the costs of the US security mission in their homelands. Within four years of Operation Homecoming the United States signed the Compact of Free Association with the newly established RMI. Chapter 6 examines the impact of Marshallese protests on the trajectory of decolonization during the 1980s and what this "postcolonial" moment has looked like on the ground for Marshallese amid the continuation of US missile testing on Kwajalein through today.

1 From Wartime Victory to Cold War Containment in the Pacific

BUILDING THE POSTWAR US SECURITY STATE
ON MARSHALLESE INSECURITY

In terms of world society, Micronesia is inconsequential.

—Lt. John Useem, US Naval Reserves, 1946

Don't Americans realize that every life is precious?

—Rongelapese woman, speaking in the 1985 documentary
Half Life: A Parable for the Nuclear Age

THE UNENDING WAR IN THE PACIFIC

John Heine was barely nine years old when war came to his home island of Jabwot in the Marshall Islands. For Heine the war first came through sound. He recalled sitting outside his parent's house under a coconut tree when he heard gunfire overhead, followed by "American planes all over the place dropping bombs everywhere."[1] He recalled that "about 100 Marshallese died in that bombing."[2] Heine survived the war, hiding on various islands after the Japanese military separated him from his family. In the nightmare that had come to his island home Heine witnessed the Japanese beheading his father, who they believed was a potential spy for the United States. Following the war, Heine became a scout for the United States and in time made his way to Kwajalein Island to work for the US Navy.[3]

Heine arrived at Kwajalein after the United States had invaded and captured the island in late January 1944. This campaign on Kwajalein

39

involved more than forty-one thousand US troops.[4] Following the costly battle at Tarawa, where the United States had faced formidable Japanese defenses and suffered significant casualties, the strategy for Operation Flintlock at Kwajalein became one of complete destruction. During the weeklong invasion, the United States dropped thirty-six thousand shells, making Kwajalein the most concentrated bombing site of the entire Pacific War.[5] When victory was declared on February 5, Kwajalein's landscape was left scarred by ordnance dropped at levels "roughly equivalent to the destructive power of a 20-kilton atomic bomb."[6] Only one tree remained standing. The island appeared to one American soldier as if it had been "picked up to 20,000 feet and then dropped."[7]

Characterized by naval historian Samuel Eliot Morison as "one of the most complicated amphibious campaigns in history," the invasion of Kwajalein would be recounted and commemorated by Americans for decades in ways that celebrated American courage and sacrifice while erasing any Marshallese experiences of the battle in their homelands.[8] In addition to excluding memories like those of John Heine, these recollections abstracted the island from its local geography and history, contributing to a broader perception of a war fought in a Pacific theater that lacked any Pacific Islander history or ongoing presence.

Heine recalled in later years the uncertainty and fear that gripped him in the wake of the war, a legacy of postwar insecurity shared by many other Marshallese and Pacific Islander survivors of wartime destruction and devastation. Heine noted that while he could not speak for the entire Marshall Islands population, many his age remained "by-products of the Pacific war," a conflict, he emphasized, "we were not a part of."[9] He continued, "We had no business in it; but we were drawn into it. As a result it is not easy for any of us in the islands to predict our futures."[10]

The ongoing insecurity described by Heine persisted long after the war's conclusion. While the US military came to the Marshall Islands in the 1940s to defeat Japanese forces, declarations of victory would not signal US departure from the region. The US military has instead remained in the Marshall Islands from the 1940s through today. This ongoing military presence that brought devastation to land and life would continue to create the conditions of an unpredictable future for Marshallese. A wartime dynamic in which US security came at the expense of Marshallese insecurity would become an enduring condition. As the navy used Marshallese lands to remain in a perpetual state of wartime preparedness, the distinction between having one's home at the center of a hot versus a "cold" war seemingly became negligible. This "unending war" saw the US military move from testing nuclear bombs to ICBMs as wartime targets shifted seamlessly from a Japanese to a communist enemy over time.

This chapter examines World War II and early Cold War contexts that contributed to positioning the Marshall Islands as a space of entitlement for the emerging US security state. Beginning in the 1940s, cultural and political histories articulated through US war stories and postwar political agreements collectively worked to frame US control over Micronesia as essential to national and global security. The chapter begins by considering how US war stories positioned the Pacific, and Kwajalein specifically, as sites of American sacrifice and self-defense. Over time, these narratives began to frame the region as an object of US possession and entitlement. With signing of the Trusteeship Agreement in 1947, US political leaders drew upon a context of US wartime sacrifice to further position Micronesia—and importantly, indefinite US control of this region—as essential to postwar security. The Trusteeship Agreement framed US imperial expansion into Micronesia as both strategic and benevolent, through dual mandates of regional control for US security and support for Micronesian self-determination. No event more clearly illustrated US disregard for the latter obligation, exemplifying the destructive, colonial nature of US control in the region, than the nuclear-testing campaign. As this chapter turns to that campaign, which lasted from 1946 to 1958, it examines how the impacts of destruction, displacement, and irradiation reveal the contradictions in the American postwar premise that US national security was equivalent to global security. Such claims must be weighed against the ongoing insecurity of those living with the legacies of historic and ongoing US weapons testing in their homelands.

The political tensions of this US imperial project unfolded in an era of global decolonization. The chapter concludes by tracing how, during the 1950s and 1960s, US political leaders, military and civilian administrators, and UN representatives disavowed the destructive impact of US expansion into Micronesia during the Cold War and drew upon colonizing tropes of native incapacity for self-governance to justify indefinite US control.

This deeply rooted American cultural perception of indigenous peoples as unfit to self-govern helped situate control over the region as a project of benevolent tutelage in helping a "backward" and "savage" people move slowly toward civilization. For US military and Trust Territory officials, civilizational ideology helped soften a contradictory stance of supporting self-determination alongside a commitment to imperial control. By the 1960s, Marshallese political leaders would zero in on these contradictions as they challenged such tropes by using the United Nations as a platform to decry US colonialism and destruction in their homelands. In doing so they added their voices to the growing tide of global anti-colonial protest.

FROM BATTLES TO BASES:
REMEMBERING WAR IN THE PACIFIC

The relative paucity of published accounts like that of John Heine reflects a historic erasure of the costs of the Pacific War for those whose home-lands comprised its "stage." Examining some of the earliest and ongoing iterations of the Kwajalein battle story, this section unearths a pattern of US storytelling that unfolded over more than five decades to frame Kwaja-lein as a place where history began with US sacrifice and moved inevitably toward permanent US possession. A trajectory in which "battles become bases," which anthropologist Catherine Lutz has traced across the global US base imperium over time, appeared so fated in Kwajalein battle com-memorations that to question this path would be equivalent to question-ing the broader sacrosanct narrative of US national security.[11]

Most US histories of the Pacific War have largely obscured the voices of Micronesians, narrating the war instead as a battle between two enemies taking place on a "theater" devoid of any local history. The incapacity to perceive these islands as homes for generations of Pacific Islanders came through in some of the earliest political and military categorizations of such homes as "stepping stones" in a broader campaign across the region. Few US historians have taken the time to recover the voices of Microne-sians in recounting the war. It is only in the past two decades that stories like John Heine's have begun to fill the pages of a limited number of col-lections on Micronesian experiences of World War II, researched by a small cohort of historians, anthropologists, and Pacific studies scholars. In one of these volumes, Marshallese survivor Ato Lankio described his experience of losing his home island of Kwajalein during the war. Lankio recalled how when Kwajalein became a major Japanese base in late 1939, the Japanese forced many Kwajalein people to relocate to Namu Island. He recounted, "This was a decision that brought a great deal of sadness, and it was also fairly difficult in terms of the life that we Marshallese led and our own customs. This is because Kwajalein was a location that was extremely important to us . . . there was no negotiation about it, and no one discussed it with us."[12] For countless other Marshallese like Heine and Lankio, World War II proved a life-altering experience, colored by suffering, loss, displacement, and chaos. Memories captured in anthropology collections reveal the trauma of wartime bombardments, violence, and family separations, alongside experiences of survival and resilience and the complexity of postwar relationships and connections between Americans and Pacific Islanders in the war's aftermath. Within these recollections, stories also captured the anguish experienced by many Marshallese and other Micronesians whose lives had become intertwined in social and familial ways with prewar Japanese and Korean settlers after the United States repatriated those settlers following the war. Kwajalein landowner and wartime survivor Handel Dribo reflected on the shock that accompanied the immediate postwar transition from Japanese to US power.[13] In an interview for a 1991 documentary film, Dribo explained that he and thirty-two other Marshallese survived the Kwajalein battle by hiding in a bunker he had built on the island.[14] He said Marshallese on Kwajalein had total confidence in the Japanese capacity to win. Dribo's awareness of the power differential only became clear after seeing the damage wrought by US bombings. He recalled seeing fire all over the island and nothing left standing, not a single coconut or breadfruit tree; "there was not even a single house; everything was burnt."[15] He concluded, "That's how bad it was and that's how powerful the Americans were."[16]

Dribo's account, alongside those of other Marshallese collected decades after the war, detailed both the trauma of witnessing such destruction on Kwajalein and the anxiety of not knowing what would come next under US control. While these recollections reveal how the war indelibly shaped the lives of countless individuals whose homes were chosen by foreigners as sites for battle, Pacific Islander stories remain peripheral, when even present at all, in US accounts and commemorations of the war. Absent any acknowledgment of Marshallese or Micronesian atolls and islands as homes to people with their own histories, American commemorations of the Pacific War have worked to obscure the nature of ongoing US colonial control in the region long after the war concluded. Pacific studies scholars Vicente M. Diaz and Keith L. Camacho have traced this pattern of US celebrations of wartime sacrifice and liberation on Guam and the Northern Marianas, respectively.[17] Likewise, Pacific studies scholar Greg Dvorak analyzed this trope as it appeared in photographs taken on Kwajalein during and following Operation Flintlock.[18] In these images, the "liberation story" visually worked to erase not only Marshallese memories of loss and sacrifice, but also those of Japanese, Okinawans, and Koreans.[19]

Abstracted from any Marshallese context, the Kwajalein battle story was presented as unfolding in a theater in which Pacific Islands became "stepping stones" in a campaign across the ocean. Both Presidents Franklin D. Roosevelt and Harry S. Truman voiced some of the earliest iterations of this narrative in presidential speeches in 1945.[20] While each reinforced an image of the Pacific as an unpeopled theater upon which the US drama of wartime victory unfolded from the executive platform, the ground-level story of soldiers' accounts mirrored this erasure of Marshallese from narratives of the Kwajalein battle.[21] The 1948 and 1966 special issues of the Kwajalein *Hour Glass*, the daily publication serving Kwajalein's US military residential population, featured play-by-play narratives of Operation Flintlock and delineated Japanese and American casualties. Neither issue included any mention of Marshallese present at, or lost in, the battle.[22] In the 1966 issue, author E. H. Bryan Jr. echoed the earlier presidential discourse framing Kwajalein's role as "a stepping stone in the island hopping advance across the Pacific."[23]

In a postwar context of increasing US security interests in Micronesia, the tropes framing the Kwajalein battle story expanded from the theme of abstraction from any local history toward a narrative of inevitable US possession. Tracing a natural progression of Kwajalein from wartime prize to indefinite missile installation, this trope was reproduced over time alongside the history of increasing US investments on Kwajalein for national security. One of the key civilian contractors supporting missile testing on Kwajalein, Bell Laboratories, contributed to this narration with pro-lific documentation of the Kwajalein battle story in its civilian contractor manuals. In 1974, Bell published a thirty-year-anniversary commemo-rative booklet claiming to showcase the first "extensive" history of the invasion.[24] The introduction traced American experiences on the island during wartime, with long-term residency on the missile base thereafter and the seemingly inevitable connection between the two. Among those showcased was Bob Flynn, who had served as an anti-aircraft gunner on the island when he was seventeen years old and was working on Kwajalein again at the time of the booklet's publication. Flynn recounted that after invading Kwajalein in 1944, he was certain he remembered seeing, "what we now know as the 'lone palm' standing alone along the ocean shore. Everything else was rubble. . . . It looked like a burnt out forest. I never dreamed that I'd come back here someday." He added, "Now I play golf all the time by that same tree."[25] In Flynn's account, the survival of the lone tree marked the trajectory from US conquest to US possession and ulti-mately to the transformation of Kwajalein into not only a missile base but also an American home signified by familiar recreation.[26]

The Bell commemorative booklet illustrated how US reproductions of the Kwajalein battle story over time not only positioned the island as a space of US entitlement but also laid the narrative foundations for the restaging of the island as a key Cold War missile installation and suburban American home. The booklet concluded with a reflection on the Kwajalein battle as the narrative moved from wartime victory to colonial conquest. The editor wrote that on February 5, the last day of fighting, "the Stars and Stripes were up on Kwaj." The passage continued: "30 years later, Kwaj and such places as Guadalcanal, Tarawa, Saipan, Guam, Peleliu, and Iwo Jima are remembered as bitterly contested bits of land where half a world war was won."[27] Highlighting the theme of American sacrifice made not only for wartime victory but for postwar control, the editor suggested that many US soldiers who fought at Kwajalein would likely rather forget the island, given the pain and suffering they had endured.[28] Forgetting would certainly be easier, the editor noted. "But perhaps we owe it to ourselves, to *our* island, and to those who fought here to remember the price that was paid for *our* little piece of the Pacific."[29] These discursive moves from wartime sacrifice to triumphal victory to ongoing possession linked to an updated iteration of this inevitable path toward US entitlement through details of Kwajalein's contemporaneous suburban landscape. The final pages of the booklet offered a glimpse of what life looked like on Kwajalein in 1981, including a description of the missile base's numerous amenities, which made the island comparable to any "typical small town in the U.S."[30] The booklet highlighted the top-rated school system and grocery and retail stores, alongside a variety of other conveniences.[31]

The persistence of this framing over five decades came through in a November 2000 article for *Soldiers* magazine, the official magazine of the US Army. Here, author Jim Tennant returned to tropes begun in the 1940s: the stepping stone geography, notable mention of American and Japanese casualties, and the ongoing absence of Marshallese.[32] Not only did this article exclude mention of Marshallese presence, it made no reference to Kwajalein's location within the Marshall Islands. In fact, the only point at which any reference to the Marshall Islands appeared was in a photograph caption describing a US soldier surveying the battle damage. The caption identified the soldier as wearing on his back a "Marshallese-woven bag."[33]

Appearing fifty-six years after the Kwajalein battle, Tennant's article continued to abstract the island from any reference to its geographic location, its indigenous people, or their history. He instead traced the history of the island from wartime battle through its inevitable transformation into a US missile range. Tennant described this fated trajectory through island features that Americans living and working on Kwajalein could have recognized, noting: "A few battle markers and worn-down bunkers are about the only physical reminders that, before it was a world-class missile range with the global mission and all the comforts of small-town America, Kwajalein was a World War II Japanese base with a strategic mission. . . . Today, the island little resembles its war days. . . . Trees have grown where the terrain once appeared as a moonscape from the battle damage. And entire complexes of buildings and huge sensors have been built."[34]

Echoing decades of US storytelling on Kwajalein, Tennant bookended the mythology of the island as one whose history began with the Pacific War and concluded with its ongoing status as a US missile installation. Cementing the erasure of Marshallese in *his*tory, Tennant concluded: "The victory at Kwajalein Atoll could hardly have been more complete. It marked the first time U.S. troops had taken prewar Japanese territory, and it established another key American base in the Central Pacific."[35] Tennant's article reiterated the trope that positioned Kwajalein as inevitably moving from capture to conquest, from postwar possession to indefinite control. As his article mirrored earlier narrative patterns infusing American telling and retelling of the Kwajalein battle, the timing of his piece also signaled a significant transformation in US imperial history since World War II. By 2000, on the eve of the war on terror, Tennant was marking Kwajalein's status as a key base in the Central Pacific and doing so within a broader context of an expansive US base imperium that would reach one thousand bases within the decade.[36]

THE UN TRUSTEESHIP AGREEMENT: MARRYING US NATIONAL SECURITY TO GLOBAL SECURITY

As the production and reproduction of the Kwajalein battle story helped pave the way for US imperial expansion into Micronesia to be framed through the guise of wartime abstraction and postwar entitlement, the Trusteeship Agreement likewise contributed to a broader global narrative legitimating indefinite US control. The Trusteeship Agreement built upon the tropes of American wartime sacrifice and victory that buttressed a framework of postwar US entitlement in the region. But it also expanded the frame to encompass a logic of "strategic denial" during the Cold War. Promising that never again would another enemy threaten the United States from Micronesia, US leaders strategically navigated participation in the Trusteeship Agreement in ways that ensured the United States would retain permanent military control over the region. Taken together, the Kwajalein battle story and the Trusteeship Agreement collectively worked to justify the ongoing US presence on Kwajalein, framing the nation's postwar administrative role in Micronesia more broadly as something outside the realm of empire.

On July 18, 1947, three years after the Kwajalein battle, President Truman ratified the Trusteeship Agreement, siloing off Micronesia from the rest of the Pacific while taking control of Japan's former colonies in the region. Through the Trusteeship Agreement, the newly designated

Trust Territory of the Pacific Islands became one trust within a trustee-ship system set up through the UN Charter. This larger system placed eleven former colonies and territories of the Axis powers under new post-war administration.[37] Out of these eleven territories, the United Nations categorized the Trust Territory of the Pacific Islands as the only "strategic trust." This distinction placed the territory under UN Security Council supervision rather than the UN Trusteeship Council. That positioning gave the United States significant control over the islands through its veto power in the Security Council on any matters the nation identified as threatening national security or international peace.[38] Such power authorized the United States to close off any or all parts of the Trust Ter-ritory to UN inspection or supervision for security reasons as the United States deemed necessary. For the Marshall Islands this provision meant the United States could conduct its nuclear-testing campaign and subse-quent missile-testing mission without outside interference. This "strategic trust" status ensured the region would play a central role in buttressing the postwar US security state.

The UN trusteeship system shared similarities with the post–World War I League of Nations in straddling a contradictory vision for sup-porting self-determination while creating a mandate system for the gov-ernance of territories of former imperial powers.[39] President Woodrow Wilson did not anticipate the employment of his rhetorical commitment to self-determination by an array of colonized populations who embraced this discourse to further their ongoing struggles for independence. The creation of the UN system's support for self-determination took place in the context of several anti-colonial struggles erupting in the wake of the economic and military collapse of former imperial powers alongside the emergence of a new Cold War competition. The latter created incentives for the United States and the Soviet Union to gain alignment with the decolonizing world, pressuring the two imperial powers to at least give the appearance of support for global decolonization.

The US postwar policy of strategic denial meant retaining indefinite control over Micronesia to prevent any other nation from using the region to attack the United States.[40] This strategy risked situating the United States on the wrong side of history in an era of anti-colonial struggle. A Cold War communist threat was used to justify a narrative that married

US national security to global peace and positioned Micronesia as central to this military strategy. A wave of global decolonization required that as the United States expanded its reach into Micronesia, it simultaneously disavowed the imperial nature of that expansion. That disavowal took many forms and would bring to the surface conflict and contestation among the various constituencies of US expansion in the postwar era. These high-level discussions included debates over what the postwar status of Micronesia should be, with the US Department of Defense expressing a preference to annex the region. As anthropologist Robert C. Kiste found: "More sensitive to international opinion of the time, the U.S. Department of State realised that the era of colonial expansion was over, and the acquisition of new possessions was no longer respectable. Reflecting the American myth, the Secretary of War [Henry L. Stimson] argued that acquiring Micronesia would not be an act of colonialism. Rather, the islands were necessary for the defence of the free world, and 'To serve such a purpose they must belong to the United States with absolute power to rule and fortify them. They are not colonies; they are outposts.'"[41] Stimson's clear effort to gain permanent control of the region while disavowing the colonial nature of that project hinted at the global pressures framing this moment of postwar military expansion. The UN sanctioning of US imperial expansion through a special trusteeship agreement put the United States in a position to prove that its postwar role in the world would be dominant but not imperial.

Tensions emerged as the contradictions of the agreement's security directive, which placed the United States in the role of global military hegemon, butted up against the development directive that obligated the United States to support Micronesian self-determination. US representatives participating in the structuring of the Trusteeship Agreement did so with one eye on long-term control in the region and the other keenly observing the postwar climate of anti-colonial struggles. The Trusteeship Agreement's article 5 committed the United States to ensure the territory played its part in maintaining global peace, which included establishing military bases in the region.[42] This part of the agreement charged the United States with carrying out these obligations for international security as well as local defense and the maintenance of law and order in the Trust Territory.[43] Contrasting with the directives of article 5, article 6 delineated an array of US obligations aimed at ensuring the region's inhabitants would achieve self-determination. These measures included support for political education, health care, economic sustainability, protection against discrimination, and protection against land loss.[44] The original language of article 6 included a directive to the administering authority to support the region's inhabitants toward "self-government."

Signaling the Cold War tensions bubbling up during the UN negotiations for the Trusteeship Agreement, the Soviet representative to the United Nations proposed this additional text: "or independence as may be appropriate to the particular circumstances of the trust territory and its peoples and the freely expressed wishes of the people concerned."[45] US ambassador Warren Austin initially rejected the inclusion of the word "independence" but eventually offered a "'qualified acceptance" of both the language and the principle.[46] To explain his initial hesitancy, Austin said: "The United States feels that it must record its opposition not to the principle of independence, to which no people could be more consecrated than the people of the United States, but to the thought that it could possibly be achieved within any foreseeable future in this case."[47]

The unspoken preeminence of article 5 over article 6, in conjunction with this ambiguous timeline for potential Micronesian independence, helped marry the postwar US national security strategy to a narrative of global defense through an open-ended directive that marked the Trust Territory as a space central to ensuring both. This was a mission with no endpoint. There was no benchmark for measuring how the United States or the United Nations would determine that international peace and security had indeed been successfully achieved. Nor was there any identifiable rubric for gauging the exact point at which Micronesians could be trusted to chart their own political path. The absence of any definitive timeline for either of these events informed the ongoing nature of US military control over the region. This convenient ambiguity likewise positioned Micronesia and particularly the Marshall Islands to become a permanent feature of the expansive postwar US security state.

As former US ambassador to the United Nations Donald F. McHenry wrote, the Trusteeship Agreement proved to be riddled with contradictions from the get-go, given the dual mandates to use the territory to ensure international security *and* to promote development toward self-government in the region.[48] One way to address such contradictions was to draw upon tropes emerging from the Kwajalein battle story: entitlement to postwar possession rooted in wartime sacrifice. According to this logic, the United States was entitled to retain indefinite control over the region to ensure that a site where US soldiers had spilled blood was never used to attack the nation again. This came through in Ambassador Austin's advocacy for US control at the Security Council meeting for negotiating the Trusteeship Agreement: "Tens of thousands of American lives, vast expenditures of treasure, and years of bitter fighting were necessary to drive the Japanese aggressors back from these islands. These islands constitute an integrated strategic physical complex *vital* to the security of the United States. The American people are firmly resolved that this area shall never again be used as a springboard for aggression against the United States or any other member of the United Nations."[49] Austin's statement tied a narrative of US sacrifice to ongoing postwar security and rounded both out by connecting US defense to that of the international community. Such a formula worked to justify not just temporary governance in the region, but indefinite control. McHenry highlighted how these arguments connected American sacrifice to a rationale for permanent control through strategic denial in his 1975 book *Micronesia: Trust Betrayed*, in which he explained that following World War II, two arguments dominated military thinking: "the United States should retain possession of the Pacific Islands" and "the United States should remain the most resilient and formidable military power in the world."[50] Both could be ensured through a strategy of "denial": the prevention of any other power from controlling the region again.[51] This project of strategic denial had no foreseeable conclusion.

That a vision for permanent US control over Micronesia existed even prior to and informed the Trusteeship Agreement negotiations was suggested by early planning for postwar governance in the region. This goal of retaining permanent control was articulated in the 1946 curriculum at the Stanford University School of Naval Administration. The school trained naval officers in short-term governance methods for the immediate postwar period. The school's pedagogy included the writing of anthropologist Lt. John Useem of the US Naval Reserves, whose Social Reconstruction in Micronesia curriculum articulated an ideal of indefinite control in

Micronesia. He wrote: "Political orientation would define the relationship of the natives to Americans; this encompasses the basic programs the United States will pursue in its *permanent* territorial governing of the area, the degree of native self-government which will be permissible, and the status of various local ethnic groups."[52] To ensure permanent control, Useem recommended the United States provide natives with sociological guidance. This included "the accommodation of native institutions to American patterns, the rehabilitation of dependent groups, and the guidance of the whole acculturation process."[53]

Stanford's postwar educational materials instructed naval officials on how to build a long-term, permanent US presence in Micronesia. The curriculum included a section titled "Comparative Colonial Administration," whose papers covered British, Australian, Japanese, and Dutch approaches to colonial rule.[54] US colonial history was covered in one paper on US Indian service, but this part of the curriculum was categorized as within international law and organization.[55] The separation of US settler colonial policies from comparative colonial studies further exemplified the strength of US exceptionalist narratives even within a context of instruction on how to become a better colonial administrator. This curriculum hinted at what would become an ongoing challenge in governing the Trust Territory of the Pacific Islands: how to effectively govern as a colonial power while disavowing the colonial nature of that governance.

Useem's instructional materials highlighted the postwar tensions that necessitated the United States appearing within the eyes of a global audience as powerful but not imperial, as a nation participating in a postwar family of nations. In this story, the United States was the most dominant but not oppressive power. Useem's teachings articulated what would be an enduring conundrum for those US representatives charged with administering the Trust Territory in the coming decades: a collective recognition that *how* the United States governed the Trust Territory would likewise signal to the world what kind of power it would be in the postwar period. During this era, there was ongoing global concern about how the United States would negotiate its disproportionate level of influence in the burgeoning global structure of the United Nations. Useem foreshadowed this dynamic, demarcating what was at stake with US governance in Micronesia. He pointed to the risks of the US administration failing from within due to debates on civil or military control or from without because of incompetence and conflict with UN-sponsored trusteeship principals. "In terms of world society, Micronesia is inconsequential," he remarked.[56] However, the way the United States governed in the Pacific would indicate to peoples around the world how the nation "live[d] up to our commitments in the nascent world organization."[57]

Echoing the World War II battle stories positioning Micronesia as a space without people or history, Useem's paper again reinforced a framing of the region as solely existing to serve the strategic interests of the United States. Useem articulated this dehumanizing perception of Micronesia in the same year the navy began testing nuclear weapons in the Marshall Islands. The devastation wrought through land destruction, displacement, and radiation-related diseases accompanying this nuclear campaign most tragically exemplified which mandates of the Trusteeship Agreement were prioritized and which were ignored.

DOMESTICATING EMPIRE: BOMBS, BASEBALL, AND BEAUTY QUEENS IN "A PLACE WHERE HARDLY ANYONE LIVES"

No event more vividly illustrated the US wartime and postwar perception of Micronesians homelands as "inconsequential" than the nuclear-testing campaign, spanning 1946 to 1958. The history of nuclear testing in the Marshall Islands and the use of Kwajalein to support this mission showcased the range of approaches taken by the military to cast one of the most devastating acts of colonial destruction during the Cold War through a frame of innocence. This included the use of religion to explain Marshallese exile from their homelands. It also involved the production of a setting of US suburban innocence on one Marshallese homeland, Kwajalein, as it became the naval support base from which other Marshallese homelands were destroyed with atomic bombs. Collectively these acts worked to obscure the enormous costs paid by Marshallese in land, lives, and health in the US Cold War pursuit of national security. This perpetual US quest for security was marked by a fundamental contradiction: by the nuclear campaign's conclusion, the United States had created a nuclear arsenal capable of destroying all life on the planet.

Within a year of dropping the first two atomic bombs on Hiroshima and Nagasaki, the navy had identified the Northern Marshall Islands as a prime location for testing. The distance from large population centers and small size, which allowed the navy to easily displace the indigenous inhabitants, were among reasons cited for the region's selection.[58] The navy framed the removal of the 167 Bikinians from their homeland through use of religious discourse, drawing upon the deep roots of US missionary influence in the region that had begun in the 1850s. Filmed footage depicted Commodore Ben H. Wyatt explaining to Bikinian leader King Juda that nuclear testing was "for the benefit of all mankind and to end all world wars," and Juda agreeing to lead his people away from their island in a seeming act of mutual consent.[59] But Bikinian Alab Lore Kessubuki recalled that in reality, his people left out of fear. "We didn't feel we had any other choice but to obey the United States," he said.[60]

After the navy had displaced the Bikinians, the Northern Marshall Islands came to constitute the space where the United States most overtly flexed its nuclear muscles before the Soviet Union and the world. Over twelve years, the United States detonated sixty-seven nuclear tests with a total yield that comprised 80 percent of all US atmospheric detonations.[61] The first tests, in July 1946, constituted a mass spectacle of US military might strategically timed to overlap with the celebration of US independence. Operation Crossroads consisted of the Able and Baker tests. The navy welcomed forty-two thousand onlookers, including military, scientific, and technical personnel and observers, to bear witness to the first US atomic detonation outside Japan and the Trinity test site in New Mexico.[62] The decision to make Operation Crossroads a global spectacle—one that guaranteed international awareness of the destructive military capacity of the United States, and particularly the Soviet Union—signaled the atomic gunshot starting the Cold War arms race.

In a pattern that would persist from the nuclear through the missile-testing eras, this first detonation at Operation Crossroads involved making one Marshallese homeland permanently uninhabitable while turning another into an accommodating home for US personnel. This practice of spatial production amid destruction involved mapping features of

KWAJALEIN
TEED-OFF
COUNTRY CLUB

REMINDS ME OF HOME - IT'S SO DIFFERENT.

Figure 1. "Kwajalein Teed-Off
Country Club," cartoon in *Atomic
Blast*, June 22, 1946 (US Army).

small-town American life onto the Marshallese homeland Kwajalein, as
it was used as a support base for nuclear testing. This came through poignantly in the first edition of the *Atomic Blast*, a newspaper published
for US military personnel residing on Kwajalein and Enewetak who were
working to support the nuclear campaign.[63] In the June 15, 1946, issue,
released two weeks before the Able detonation, headlines expressed excite-
ment about the coming test, highlighting press plans to provide a "'ring-
side'" seat for the world at the detonation.[64] The same edition also ran
stories on the "Guinea Pig" major league baseball competition on Kwajalein but lamented the limitations on this representing true "major league
ball." The article explained that in lieu of the real deal "softball [had]
replaced the national game, at least until the boys get back to the states."[65]
The same edition of the *Atomic Blast* also included a story on the opening
of "Teed-Off" on Kwajalein, "the only 18-hole miniature golf course in the
Pacific area." This fun spot had a "compactly constructed layout" and was
also known as the 'Teed Off Country Club.'" The story advertised that "200
putters and sufficient golf balls" were available for anyone who wanted to
take a crack at the prize money offered for high scores.[66]

Signaling the success of this advertising, the following week's issue
of the *Atomic Blast* carried the headline "Hundreds Attend Golf Course

Opening" over a story celebrating the throngs of officers who took part in this special event. The article traced the golf course opening and was accompanied by an illustration of the new country club feature. The illustration's caption, "Reminds Me of Home—It's So Different," was an early iteration of the ways the military had begun to mark Kwajalein as an American home through the construction of these signs of everyday Americana on the island.[67] It also suggested the ways military personnel may have begun to respond to the export of American life to the Central Pacific with an ambiguous embrace.

Within a week of the newspaper's celebration of the miniature golf course opening, the publication featured more headlines in anticipation of "A-Day" alongside a new story signaling the opening of a special competition.[68] This article, "Atomic Queen," noted: "In the belief that men working on this important scientific test have several other things on their minds, the editors of the 'Blast' today announce the opening of a contest to select the most beautiful girl-friend or wife of the men stationed here. The girl selected by the board of competent judges will be appropriately named 'The Atom Queen'"; the winner was announced shortly after the June 30, Able detonation.[69]

The bomb used in the Able test was named *Gilda*, for Rita Hayworth's character in the film *Gilda*, to signal the "bombshell" nature of this unprecedented destruction. Pacific scholar Teresia K. Teaiwa has shown how this sexualization of atomic testing was apparent early on in French designer Louis Reard's naming of the "bikini" swimsuit after the atomic testing at Bikini.[70] As Teaiwa argued, this naming worked to erase the violence, destruction, and devastation of the tests, with the bathing suit manifesting "both a celebration and a forgetting of the nuclear power that strategically marginalizes and erases the living history of Pacific Islanders."[71] The stories appearing in the *Atomic Blast* further show this work of erasure in real time enacted locally on Kwajalein as the tests were taking place. Those supporting the campaign were involved in mapping the features of Cold War American home life—replete with all of the gendered and recreational aspects of that physical and cultural landscape—onto Kwajalein while they were engaged in the destruction of Marshallese home life. This was the production of American innocence on Kwajalein through landscape, the domestication of US imperial destruction.

As US soldiers were making a home for themselves on Kwajalein, the Bikinians were displaced to a new home on Rongerik Island to make way for Operation Crossroads.[72] Within five months, the Kwajalein Island commander penned his monthly report acknowledging the Bikinians had already expressed a desire to return home.[73] He commented on their willingness to cooperate and stay as long at the navy needed and framed their longing to return to Bikini as undoubtedly "motivated by that age-old desire to return "home.'" In doing so, he characterized the Bikinian's plight as a form of relatable nostalgia, generically familiar, rather than a trauma of colonial displacement and atomic destruction.[74]

Despite Bikinians having expressed concern about food shortages on Rongerik two months into their stay, it was not until July 1947, more than a year later, that a medical officer inspected conditions on Rongerik and reported the Bikinians were "visibly suffering from malnutrition."[75] Anthropologist Leonard Mason confirmed the islanders were near starvation.[76] While the Trusteeship Agreement mandated the United States "safeguard the life, liberty, and general well-being of the Trust Territory," the Bikinians spent two years struggling to survive on Rongerik until the navy finally evacuated them.[77] On March 14, 1948, the 171 nuclear refugees were transported to Kwajalein, where they lived in a segregated tent camp for the next seven months.

As US military personnel "teed off" at the Kwajalein's country club miniature golf course, Bikinians lived an isolating existence on the island. Kilon Bauno recalled: "We lived a strange life on Kwajalein. From day to day we were frightened by all the airplanes that continuously landed very close to our homes. We were also frustrated by the small amount of space in which we were permitted to move around. . . . We were afraid of this alien environment and almost from the day we got there we began thinking about other places to live."[78] The Bikinian struggles on Rongerik and Kwajalein—their well-being and survival a mere afterthought to military officials—became a routine feature of US empire in the decades to follow. As the US military turned Marshallese islands into target practice and Kwajalein into a quaint and comfortable American home, Marshallese fought to survive the deadly and destructive impacts of the US security mission. The military invested billions of dollars in developing weapons of mass destruction in the Marshall Islands over the next six decades. Yet

Figure 2. Bikinians gathered next to their housing at Kwajalein Camp, 1948. Photo by Leonard Mason. Permission to reproduce granted by Pacific Collection, Hamilton Library, University of Hawai'i-Mānoa.

any investment to support those whose displacement enabled US military power to grow on an unparalleled scale was scant and only given begrudgingly following Marshallese protests.

Documenting this pattern of neglect early on, the Marshall Islands governor sent a civilian administration report to the chief of naval operations detailing the Bikinians' plight. Issued one month into the Bikinians' stay on Kwajalein, the report blamed Bikinian struggles on "an accumulation of errors incident to the original move from Bikini."[79] He attributed this to a superficial assessment of the challenges and argued that the first month of their stay on Kwajalein should be dedicated to "establishing a sense of security and self-respect after their unfortunate experiences with displacement and under-nourishment."[80]

While euphemistically framing the navy's failure to respond to early warnings of Bikinian starvation as "unfortunate," the Marshall Islands governor's attention to Bikinian trauma proved noteworthy among official

Figure 3. Road between two rows of housing for Bikinians at Kwajalein Camp, 1948. Photo by Leonard Mason. Permission to reproduce granted by Pacific Collection, Hamilton Library, University of Hawai'i-Mānoa.

reports. Some US sources documenting Bikinian arrival at Kwajalein even framed the event as celebratory, erasing the destructive conditions prompting their refugee status. The *Marshall Post Inquirer*, a bilingual (English and Marshallese) weekly publication distributed throughout the Marshall Islands, ran a series of articles narrating the Bikinians' journey to Kwajalein.[81] Within this mix, one *Inquirer* story spun the act of colonial destruction and displacement into a yarn about the mundane, the everyday, and even the humorous recognition of cultural commonalities. The author wrote: "A touch of human nature was displayed by one of the Marshallese families just departure [*sic*] from Rongerik. It seems that a Marshallese husband and wife are capable of family disputes also."[82] The story described how one man leaving Rongerik refused to travel on the same ship with his wife. Despite efforts to convince him otherwise, he chose to arrive on a later date rather than accompany her.[83] This carefree tone, finding humor in a presumed domestic quarrel, overlapped with another article that lightened the traumatic experience of exile through the trope of celebration. This came through in an *Inquirer* story describing the welcome reception for Bikinians on Kwajalein as a party at the labor camp that included gifts, dances, and songs. The article explained, "By the Marshallese from Bikini a very good time was had by all."[84]

The tone of these articles again signaled early iterations of a pattern that increased over time, in which US documentation, celebration, and commemoration of life on Kwajalein worked to sanitize the devastation inflicted by historic and ongoing weapons testing in the region. Here the stories included the euphemistic framing of nuclear refugee arrivals, but they built upon the earlier articles documenting Americana through softball competition, miniature golf openings, and beauty pageants, all layering tropes of innocence atop the historic unfolding of imperial destruction. A focus on the humdrum of everyday life in the islands (for Americans *and* Marshallese) would continue to infuse storytelling on Kwajalein for decades. These US mythologies collectively and cumulatively erased Marshallese experiences of trauma caused by the US weapons-testing campaigns. For Bikinians, trauma not only preceded their arrival at Kwajalein but also followed their departure to a new home on Kili Island in November 1948. The poorly planned resettlement again revealed the military's disregard for the UN Trusteeship obligations to protect the region's inhabitants from harm. Because Kili lacked a lagoon, anchorage for dropping supplies and fishing proved nearly impossible. The island thus became yet another space where Bikinians struggled to survive as they faced food shortages throughout the 1960s.[85]

Six years after the Bikinians had left Kwajalein, another group of Marshallese came to the island as nuclear refugees. Unlike the Bikinian seven-month residency, these Marshallese stayed just three months, leaving after medical examinations and temporary treatment. Their arrival was also prompted by an emergency evacuation. But this one came after, not before, detonation. For these nuclear refugees, the journey was marked not only by the trauma of displacement but also by the detrimental health impacts of irradiation.[86]

On March 1, 1954, under the code name Castle Bravo, the navy detonated a fifteen-megaton hydrogen bomb at Bikini Atoll. This bomb was so destructive that its radioactive impact contaminated islands within a 275-mile periphery. The navy initially anticipated that the bomb, detonated one year after the Soviet Union tested its hydrogen bomb, would be 250 times more powerful than the bomb dropped on Hiroshima. It turned out to be 1,000 times more powerful.[87] As the blast lifted hundreds of millions of tons of sand, soil, and coral upward into the atmosphere, wind moved radioactive fallout east, covering Marshallese living in the atolls of Rongelap and Utirik, a boat of Japanese fishermen, and US servicemen surveying the weather on Rongerik Atoll.[88]

Not only did the military fail to immediately evacuate the irradiated populations, it also neglected to give the Marshallese living on nearby islands any warning about the test. What ensued was the irradiation of more than 240 Marshallese living in nearby islands, where radioactive fallout contaminated their bodies and their lands. With no instruction to remain inside their homes, many Marshallese consumed contaminated food and water. The exposure to lethal doses of radiation would plague Marshallese and their progeny for multiple generations, continuing through today.

Three days after the blast, the navy evacuated to Kwajalein Marshallese from the contaminated islands of Rongelap, Rongerik, and Utirik. One survivor arriving from Rongelap, Entry Enos, recalled the experience: "When we arrived on Kwajalein, we started getting burns all over our bodies and people were feeling dizzy and weak.... After two days something appeared under my fingernails and then my fingernails came off and my fingers bled."[89] At the time of the Marshallese evacuation, the US Atomic Energy Commission (AEC) issued a press statement to the US public about this "routine atomic test."[90] The statement noted, "U.S. servicemen and people from Rongelap, Ailinginae and Utirik were taken to Kwajalein 'as a precautionary measure.'"[91] The statement continued, "These individuals were unexpectedly exposed to some radioactivity. There were no burns. All were reported well.'"[92] This press statement followed documented evidence of Rongelapese vomiting and suffering from nausea, diarrhea, and itching skin and eyes.[93]

In recent years scholars have begun exploring this history of irradiation, tracking the impacts of Marshallese displacement, death, and intergenerational disease and interrogating the navy's failure to evacuate Marshallese prior to the detonation.[94] The historic devastation wrought by the

Bravo Shot on Marshallese likewise afforded once in a lifetime research opportunities for US scientists from Brookhaven National Laboratory, who would spend decades studying the impacts of radiation on the Rongelapese population.[95] As scientists arrived at their homeland, Rongelapese voiced complaints and suspicions about being treated as experimental subjects rather than receiving adequate medical care for their ailments.[96] Nelson Anjain was among the many Marshallese whose bodies provided the data buttressing this research. He recalled Americans telling him and other islanders that their home was safe after the blast but observing that US doctors conducted all exams from boats offshore. He suspected they would not stay on the island with the Marshallese because they knew it was dangerous and posed the question: "I wonder if they would have done the same thing if this place was in America."[97]

Within a year of the Bravo detonation, the US *did* destroy and irradiate a place in America; a fake suburban replica erected to prepare Americans for the doomsday scenario in which nuclear family life would become "nuclearized family life."[98] As Marshallese survivors like Anjain grappled with the very real horrors of irradiation, the Federal Civil Defense Administration was busily planning this hypothetical catastrophe, which constituted the "largest civil defense spectacle staged at the Nevada Test Site."[99] As anthropologist Joseph Masco detailed, "On May 5, 1955, 100 million Americans watched on television a 'typical' suburban community blown to bits by an atomic bomb."[100] In one test within a larger series of tests called Operation Teapot, which carried a price tag of $19.4 million, more than two hundred companies participated to study the potential impact on all elements of nuclear family life: suburban homes, clothing fabrics, and frozen and canned foods exposed to nuclear radiation.[101] Such attention to detail included examining the burns left on the clothing of mannequin families, who were shown on a national tour following the detonation. "J.C. Penney's Department store, which provided the garments, displayed these postnuclear families in its stores around the county with a sign declaring 'this could be you!'"[102]

This parade of burned mannequin clothing in 1955 occurred the year after Brookhaven scientists examined the real burns scarring the necks, torsos, and arms of Marshallese survivors of nuclear irradiation after their evacuation to Kwajalein. The ongoing effects of irradiation remain

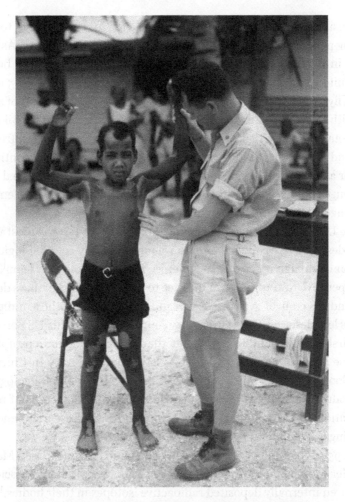

Figure 4. "Dr. Conrad Examines Native Boy on Kwajalein."
Project 22-Operation Castle (Bikini/Enewetak) Test Activities.
Courtesy of the National Archives and Records Administration.

with Marshallese today; the region has become home to the highest rate of thyroid cancer in the world and has seen new forms of cancer, birth deformities, and miscarriages among the impacts. The United States has never legitimized allegations of intent, but in 1983 the nation did enter into a formal agreement with the Marshall Islands that recognized US responsibility to compensate Marshallese "for loss or damage to property or persons" as a result of the nuclear-testing program.[103] As delineated in Section 177 of the 1983 Compact of Free Association between the United States and the RMI, Rongelapese were awarded $2.5 million annually over fifteen years.[104] This compensation would be part of a package with slightly greater and slightly lesser amounts allotted for Bikinians, Enewetakese and Utirikese that was contested and challenged from day one and over more than three decades. Today, Marshallese continue to sue for an amount that adequately addresses the intergenerational health challenges and loss of life and land, and for truthful acknowledgement of the range of atolls and islands impacted.[105]

The US decision to use Marshallese homelands to test the most world's most destructive weaponry to date was informed by colonial logics. The nuclear campaign resided at the intersection of US Cold War fears fueling an imperative to stay ahead in the race to create weapons of mass destruction and US control over the region and a perception of those indigenous to it as less deserving of security. Few sources captured this US perception of Marshallese insignificance better than the documentation of a Marshallese visit to the AEC's Argonne National Laboratory in Chicago. A close look at footage taken of this visit reveals the colonial ideology used to devalue Marshallese lives and obscure the costs to victims of nuclear irradiation as US scientists promote the enormous research benefits of studying this population.

In 1957, four Rongelapese, two Utirikese, and one unexposed Marshall Islander were taken to Argonne National Laboratory, where US scientists measured internally deposited radioactive isotopes in their bodies.[106] The visit was filmed and guided by an unseen narrator taking the viewer on a virtual tour of the Argonne facilities and introducing the viewer to those being researched.[107] As the camera lens hovers on the smiling faces of seven Marshallese men, the narrator identifies the men as "fishing people; savages by our standards."[108] Honing in on one Marshallese man identified as "John," the narrator reminds the viewer that "John, as we said, is a savage; but a happy, amenable savage."[109] He acknowledges that John reads and is a pretty good mayor, but that John's "grandfather ran almost naked on his coral atoll."[110] The film then follows John on his journey into the radiation detector room, an act framed as a new "ritual" for John and the other Marshallese "savages." Once the "ritual" is completed by all, the narrator explains the men would now return to their homes "in the Marshall Islands, in the middle of the Pacific Ocean, *where hardly anybody lives.*"[111]

Reassuring viewers that the use of Marshallese homelands for nuclear tests was justified by the obvious insignificance of the region, the narrator's final words also foreshadowed a self-fulfilling prophecy. Given the US decision to risk irradiating Marshallese homelands, the atolls would indeed become places incapable of sustaining life, places where hardly anyone *could* live over time. John "the mayor" would remain in the spotlight years after the Argonne film as his son, Likoj Anjain, who was exposed to the Bravo shot's radiation at the age of one, became the first documented leukemia victim of the hydrogen bomb. Likoj Anjain died from acute myelogenous leukemia in 1972, just shy of his thirtieth birthday.[112]

"Don't Americans realize that every life is precious?"[113] This question was asked by a Rongelapese woman as she stared piercingly into the camera in Dennis O'Rourke's 1985 documentary film *Half Life: A Parable for the Nuclear Age.* The profound challenge posed by this question was one Marshallese continually put forth to the United States and to the world as they protested their colonial status under the UN Trusteeship Agreement for nearly four decades. US responses to these challenges highlighted the tensions undergirding a US sense of entitlement to the region for security purposes as it butted up against a postwar context necessitating a disavowal of empire. The next section examines US attempts to reconcile these tensions in an era of global anti-colonial protest erupting amid these destructive US weapons-testing campaigns.

AGAINST THE TIDE: IMPERIAL EXPANSION
IN AN ERA OF GLOBAL DECOLONIZATION

The devastation wrought by nuclear testing in the Marshall Islands during the first decade of the Trusteeship Agreement that obligated the United States to protect the lives and lands of the region's inhabitants showcased the contradictions embedded in the directives of US security and development support in the region. The navy justified testing these weapons of mass destruction in the Marshall Islands through a logic that global security and peace depended upon US national security. But this narrative neglected to consider Marshallese as part of that global family. What would security look like for Marshallese in these years?

As has been shown, the mission to buttress US security came at the cost of increasing insecurity for Marshallese. It also accompanied US efforts to erase those costs as military and civilian colonial administrators faced the postwar conundrum of how to maintain a colonial regime through an anti-colonial stance. We have seen how efforts to mark the US presence in the region through a veil of innocence included the beginnings of Kwajalein's early transformation into an accommodating small-town suburban home for US personnel. This spatial and cultural production alongside nuclear destruction accompanied the use of deep colonial tropes to mark the costs of such destruction as seemingly insignificant because of who was bearing them. US rationale justifying nuclear testing echoed the writing of Lt. Useem's 1946 perception of "Micronesia [as] inconsequential."[114] But Useem's paper also encouraged US leaders not to forget that a global audience would be watching how they governed this region. He believed this approach would signal the role that the United States would play in the United Nations, and more broadly on the global stage. We conclude this chapter by examining how those administering the Trust Territory government attempted to oversee an anti-colonial, colonial regime. This confounding project aimed to buttress the US security state while downplaying the relational costs in Marshallese insecurity. As we will see, Marshallese ensured that US efforts to erase their lived experiences under this destructive colonial regime would fail over time.

Given the devastating consequences of nuclear testing, the first decade of the Trust Territory administration gave Marshallese ample reason to doubt how much the United States could be trusted to protect their lands and lives. In the spotlight of a global audience watching as Cold War objectives and global decolonization pressures collided, US representatives were tasked with reassuring Micronesians and the world of their commitment to support self-determination at the same time they were destroying Marshallese homelands. US Navy rear admiral Leon. S. Fiske offered one early approach to this challenge. In 1950, the year before the Trust Territory transitioned from postwar temporary naval governance to civilian administration under the Department of the Interior, Fiske gave a speech to UN representatives from his position as deputy high commissioner of the territory.[115] In addition to reminding UN representatives of American sacrifice in the region—the price paid for territorial control in men, money, and combat years—Fiske drew upon another story, deeply rooted in US settler colonial ideology to explain indefinite control over Micronesia. In this story, US governance was not of an imperial exploitative nature, but rather one of benevolent tutelage, an effort aimed at guiding a backward people, "savages" like "John the Mayor." To justify this framing, Fiske relied on the myth of native incapacity for self-governance.

While not parsing words on the preeminence of security concerns informing US control in the region, Fiske made room to address the other piece of the Trust Agreement mandate: supporting the region's inhabitants toward self-determination. He did so by lauding American efforts to teach a "backward" people the ways of modernity. Fiske expressed faith that the indigenous inhabitants of Micronesia could learn to emulate American ways but it was unclear how long that instruction might take: *when* exactly the natives would be capable of going it alone. While stressing the indeterminate nature of timing such tutelage, Fiske was happy to report on the accomplishments already evident to date. Such achievements "reflect the practical idealism which is the American way of life.... Our Western conception of democratic self-government has been some 2000 years evolving.... It is gratifying to realize that these people of primitive and feudal culture are making slow but real progress towards the attainment of self-sufficiency and self-government visualized for them by the United Nations."[116]

A recurrent theme of native reliance on American tutelage was used to justify why the United States should not leave the region in "the foreseeable future." It became a self-fulfilling prophecy for the Trust Territory over time. By the 1960s, US policies in Micronesia were characterized by economic neglect and an overarching agenda to create dependency across the region to ensure the United States could always maintain strategic control. From the first years of naval governance through the transition to a civilian colonial administration, Americans living and working across the region rationalized Micronesian dependency as an incapacity to self-govern by drawing on deeply rooted perceptions of native peoples as primitive and irrational. Historian David Hanlon analyzed these caricatured stereotypes in his 1998 *Remaking Micronesia: Discourse over Development in a Pacific Territory, 1944–1982*. "The perceived backwardness of the people of the islands added further justification to the need for military government . . . the Navy characterized social traditions and indigenous forms of political government as primitive, feudalistic."[117] While this US imperial approach to legitimizing control in the Pacific by depicting indigenous peoples as incapable of self-governance certainly preceded the Trust Territory era, as scholarship on Hawai'i and the Philippines among others has revealed in recent years, these paternalistic, racist, colonial logics took on new valence during the Cold War.[118] As Cold War scholars have traced, these logics traveled widely across a global Cold War landscape as US politicians applied them to justify imperial policies aimed at ensuring decolonizing nations transitioned to independence in ways that aligned with US interests.[119]

As postwar waves of decolonization rippled across the world, Trust Territory officials came under increasing pressure to prove that a structure smacking of colonialism was something else. In the propaganda battlefront of the Cold War, as two imperial powers vied for the allegiance of decolonizing nations, the status of the Trust Territory became a site of confrontation. In June 1953, the Soviet delegate to the United Nations, Mr. Zonov, gave a speech to the Trusteeship Council criticizing US administration of the Trust Territory, referencing the Trusteeship Agreement directives obliging the United States to create social, political, and economic conditions to support the region's inhabitants toward self-government or independence.[120] Zonov noted that "all power in the Territory is in the hands of the United States officials," explaining no indigenous inhabitants held any major administrative positions.[121] Trust Territory high commissioner Frank Midkiff rebutted Zonov by emphasizing the dangers of prematurely returning political control to Micronesians. Midkiff highlighted US efforts to train Micronesians for administrative positions prior to promoting them, lauding the merits of gradual transformation.[122] Spoken before the United Nations just three months after Joseph Stalin's death, Midkiff's words were haunted by not-so-subtle allusions to a landscape of purges and gulags. He described a hasty approach as involving the kinds of "violent or cataclysmic" change often reserved for contexts of "unduly oppressive and restrictive conditions," which he claimed did not apply in Micronesia.[123]

Excerpts from Zonov's speech and Midkiff's rebuttal appeared in the *Micronesian Monthly,* a newsletter pitched to employees of the Trust Territory government, suggesting Trust Territory administrators took seriously how US governance over the region was being globally framed and publicized. The contrasting portraits of US administration in Micronesia foreshadowed a dynamic that would continue to see Trust Territory representatives put in a position to defend ongoing governance within a context of global decolonization. As the Cold War progressed, the United States came under increasing pressure to demonstrate how Trust Territory policies were motivated by support for Micronesians rather than imperial strategic interests. This was a public relations mission that became difficult to balance alongside growing US military interests in the region.

The importance of maintaining the mythology of a nation rooted in resistance to empire rather than one simultaneously founded upon settler expansion came through in Midkiff's assertions about Trust Territory administration. He concluded the *Monthly* piece with a telling observation on one major challenge for implementing effective change in the Trust Territory: how to govern the territory without any formal colonial infrastructure. Maintaining the myth of American exceptionalism, Midkiff signaled this conundrum by expressing concern about the administrative structure staffed by primarily temporary employees, which lacked stable, long-term careers for Trust Territory personnel. He explained that this structure existed to achieve one Trusteeship Agreement objective: to prepare Micronesians to replace a substantial percentage of US employees. He then said, "We do not have within our federal system of employment a *colonial* service. Broadly speaking, we have only the Civil Service and the Foreign Service systems. Neither of these is entirely suited to the Trust Territory employment situation."[124]

Perhaps unintentionally, Midkiff exposed the central contradiction of the Trusteeship Agreement and the broader public relations challenge facing the United States in an era of anti-colonial protest: How does one govern a colonial territory while convincing oneself and the world it is not? Midkiff may have identified something akin to British colonial service in India as more fitting to the challenges he faced in administering the Trust Territory. But presiding over a historic and ongoing pattern of extending colonial rule while simultaneously disavowing that process posed logistical obstacles. As anthropologist Robert C. Kiste has written in regard to US power in the Pacific following World War II: "The American inability to see itself as a colonial power had significant consequences. The United States never saw a need to create a colonial service, train administrators to work abroad, or develop an explicit colonial policy. From the American point of view decolonisation was the business of others and the United States did not anticipate the need to prepare for the process."[125]

US Trust Territory government officials justified long-term control over Micronesia through an argument of entitlement based on wartime sacrifice, postwar security needs, and Micronesian incapacity for self-governance. These intersecting logics informed the mission of those overseeing postwar US expansion into Micronesia while also leaving these ambassadors of empire in a bind by the 1960s as tensions increased over the ongoing colonial nature of US control during an era of global decolonization. In a rapidly shifting international landscape, the United States was moving counter to the tide of world perceptions on the legitimacy of colonial rule. This global shift eventually restructured the United Nations in a way that made it a complicated forum for both legitimating and critiquing US colonial power through the conditions and contradictions of the Trusteeship Agreement.

By the early 1960s, the tensions between US colonial control over Micronesia and the need to disavow this control extended beyond those administering the islands. A growing array of Micronesian and American critics began publicly probing the conflict between the US military defense mission and the Trusteeship Agreement's directive to support Micronesians toward self-determination. A significant impetus spurring such criticism was the overall state of the Trust Territory. A 1961 UN Trust Territory visiting mission revealed that US neglect of article 6 of the agreement allowed the region's infrastructure to deteriorate to such devastating effect as to give rise to the descriptor "rust territory."[126] Critiques of US administration in Micronesia began appearing in mainstream US magazines during the 1960s, including the *New Yorker* and the *Saturday Evening Post.*[127] In the same period, the United Nations began authoring resolutions on decolonization that increasingly put pressure on the United States to justify continued and indefinite administration of the Territory, especially given how devastating the first decade of US administration had been for Micronesians. Also by this time, the majority of the original eleven territories under the trusteeship system had become independent or integrated into a neighboring territory. This pattern found the US acting counter to a clear trend in postwar political transitions.

The pressures to acknowledge a global climate of anti-colonial protest while simultaneously defending US control over Micronesia emerged in a classified report commissioned by the Kennedy administration to assess conditions in the region. Following the 1961 UN visiting mission, President John F. Kennedy called for this investigative report to help strategize solutions to problems identified by the mission.[128] In May 1963, a survey headed by Harvard economics professor and later assistant secretary of state for economic affairs Anthony M. Solomon visited the Trust Territory to report on economic, social, and political developments. With UN pressure mounting in support of decolonization, Solomon's group was charged with offering recommendations that would lead to programs and policies to quicken the rate of development in the region. The group aimed to discover whether or not the region's inhabitants could make an "informed and free choice as to their future, in accordance with U.S. responsibilities under the Trusteeship Agreement."[129] While the Solomon group's findings were initially marked unclassified, the entire contents became quickly classified at the insistence of the Department of the State. According to former US ambassador Donald F. McHenry, state officials wanted to suppress criticism contained in the report that could be used against the United States at the United Nations. More important, he added, they wanted to cover up secret political objectives referred to throughout the report.[130]

The Solomon group found that after two decades of US administration, the region's infrastructure was worse than when the United States first took power. The report characterized the Trust Territory economy as largely stagnant and identified minimal progress in social development. Solomon's group found the majority of Micronesians illiterate and struggling to survive through agriculture and fishing. The report noted that given this reality, the United States was coming under increasing criticism from the press, the United Nations, and Micronesians themselves. The report stated:

> Despite a lack of serious concern for the area until quite recently, Micronesia is said to be essential to the US for security reasons. We cannot give the area

up, yet time is running out for the US in the sense that we will soon be the only nation left administering a trust territory. The time could come, and shortly, when the pressures in the UN for a settlement of the status of Micronesia could become more than embarrassing. In recognition of the problem, the President, on April 18, 1962, approved NSAM No. 145, which set forth as US policy the movement of Micronesia into a permanent relationship with the US . . . the memorandum called for accelerated development of the area to bring its political, economic, and social standards into line with an *eventual permanent association*.[131]

The Solomon group's suggestions for solidifying US permanence included preparing a favorable plebiscite for 1968.[132] The plan was to convince Micronesians, through long-overdue investments, to vote for a permanent relationship with the United States. The Solomon group attempted to raise awareness in the White House that continued control of the Trust Territory implicated the United States as "moving counter to the anti-colonial movement."[133] To combat this perception, the group recommended the White House include independence as an option in the plebiscite because if the United States implemented the recommended programs, Micronesians would show "little desire" to vote for it.[134] According to the report, the United States needed to at least give the appearance of acting in good faith with the trusteeship mandate of supporting Micronesian self-determination.

Having contextualized the two contradictory directives guiding US policy in the region, the Solomon Report addressed the tensions of colonial control amid its simultaneous disavowal. It posed a solution to this foundational conflict: the United States should increase Micronesian dependency so Micronesians themselves would "freely choose" US permanence. This solution addressed the period's decolonizing political pressure while simultaneously supporting the continued Cold War military mission.

The report's recommendations, presented to President Kennedy in October 1963, were never implemented because Kennedy's assassination followed within a month. After Kennedy's death, the group charged with implementing the recommendations disappeared along with any substantive focus on Micronesia. While numerous efforts followed to reestablish an interagency body on Micronesia issues, Vietnam quickly became the White House's focus.[135] Despite the dissipation of any *official* strategy from Washington to achieve Solomon's recommendations, the essence of the group's suggestions—ensuring permanent association by promoting economic dependency—took shape across the region over time.

US investments in the Marshall Islands became centered on the Kwajalein missile range, with the base playing a central role in shaping the Marshallese path toward decolonization. The Solomon Report remained classified until 1971, when a student at the University of Hawai'i's Micronesian collective discovered and exposed it. Publication of the report's introduction in the school newsletter merely confirmed the suspicions of Marshallese political leaders and activists, who had been challenging the consequences of this approach to territorial control for years.[136] Throughout the 1960s, Marshallese leaders had been decrying the colonial nature of US power in the region, trying to hold the nation to its UN mandate to support Micronesians toward self-determination. As the United Nations absorbed an increasing number of newly sovereign nations across the decolonizing world, Marshallese petitioned this global body to intervene on behalf of their ongoing colonial situation. The United Nations occasionally sent visiting missions to the territories during the 1960s to oversee US administration. But the primary power of UN oversight resided in making recommendations on conditions in the Trust Territory and suggesting areas for improvement. The UN role was limited to supervision, not governance: "to encourage and recommend, not to make laws and carry them out."[137]

While unable to pass laws for the Trust Territory given the veto power of the United States, the United Nations did offer a forum in which Marshallese could express grievances. In that respect, the United Nations became a stage for Marshallese leaders to voice their right to self-determination within the broader theater of the Cold War and the wave of global anticolonial protest. One of the early challenges to US control over the region came through a 1968 Marshallese resolution sent to the United Nations from the Marshallese legislature, the Nitijela.[138] Coauthor and chief Amata Kabua prefaced the 1968 resolution with a letter asking the United Nations to reconsider the Trust Territory's legal and political status. He asserted that the resolution constituted "one of the first attempts by the peoples of Micronesia to cry out to the world for help in righting the unjust neocolonial situation under which we now exist."[139]

The resolution cited Trusteeship Agreement language obligating the United States to foster development of political institutions to promote self-government and to support economic advancement and self-sufficiency. The Nitijela argued that the United States had attempted to transplant into the region a system of government closely resembling itself, one irrelevant to Micronesia's political conditions.[140] It charged the United States with refusing to discuss possibilities of independence or alliance with countries other than itself in considering political alternatives for the Trust Territory. Three years prior to any public knowledge of the Solomon Report, the local implications of the report's recommendations were globally broadcast as the Nitijela noted how apparently the United States took for granted continued association whether or not this reflected Micronesian desires.[141] The Nitijela explained how the United States "for over twenty years deferred any program of political education for the inhabitants . . . [leading to] the number of Micronesians in policy-making positions remain[ing] distressingly small.[142] Finally, the resolution characterized US policies in the region as "positively destructive of the respect for human rights and for fundamental freedoms which the United States under Article 75c of the United Nations Charter is required to promote."[143] The Nitijela concluded by petitioning the Security Council to review the entire basis for continued US presence in the region. It advised the council to revise or abolish the Trusteeship Agreement in order to promote Micronesian well-being.

The Nitijela resolution represented a direct challenge to US imperialism in Micronesia by employing Trusteeship Agreement language as a frame through which to hold the United States accountable to its documented UN commitments. In doing so, the Nitijela picked apart nearly every agreement directive and uncovered US failures to meet its obligations in each case. Further unsettling US efforts to disavow the colonial nature of its control over Micronesia, a Marshallese editorial appeared in the *Marshall Islands Journal* a few weeks after the Nitijela's resolution went to the United Nations. The privately owned journal carried the tagline "Marshall's Free Press" and provided a rare media outlet in the region voicing challenges to the US administration.[144] The editorial encouraged Marshallese and all Micronesians to embrace the Nitijela's resolution and demand justice, equality, and dignity for themselves. It warned: "If the people's demands are ignored . . . they will find themselves much as America's Indians found themselves. For they will have lost their land and their culture. They will be doomed to an endless second-class existence."[145] The editorial continued to describe the more than two decades of trusteeship efforts to cover up the "ill-disguised colonialism taking place in Micronesia."[146]

Such critiques of US colonialism not only attested to the ongoing failures of the Trust Territory administration to uphold the mythology of American exceptionalism in the Marshall Islands, they also signaled what became a pattern in which Marshallese linked their protests to comparative colonial histories and struggles. As this chapter has revealed, while Trust Territory officials strained to reconcile the contradictions of overseeing an anti-colonial, colonial regime, Marshallese found no such obstacles to situating their colonial reality alongside that of other colonized subjects.

Following receipt of resolution no. 71, the United Nations publicly criticized US colonialism in the region while confirming its impotence to hold the United States accountable to any of its stated obligations. Within a year of the Nitijela protest, a UN subcommittee published a report entitled "Military Activities and Arrangements by Colonial Powers in Territories under Their Administration, Which Might Be Competing in the Implementation of the Declaration on the Granting of Independence to Colonial Countries and Its Peoples." As suggested by the title, the report addressed the contradictory tension between the US defense mission in the Trust Territory and the stated goal of supporting the regions' inhabitants toward independence. The report offered an interpretation of the Trusteeship Agreement that contrasted with US practices in the region. In its recommendations, the subcommittee elevated the importance of supporting the region's inhabitants over military defense. It also questioned the equation of US base buildup with global peace: "It is obvious that the military personnel, equipment, naval and air force facilities, and bases maintained by the colonial Powers go far beyond the defense requirements of these small territories and that they are directed against third parties in the global military strategy of the colonial Powers and their allies . . . in addition to creating a threat to international peace and security [such activities] . . . affect adversely the economic, social and political advancement of the Territories and have resulted in alienation of the land and natural resources of colonial peoples."[147] The committee recommended the colonial powers discontinue alienating lands of Trust Territory peoples for construction of bases and return the lands to their rightful owners.[148] The tone of the report reflected a potential response to the Nitijela resolution but also to increasing global attention to what many around the world viewed as a destructive US colonial campaign in Southeast Asia.

The 1969 UN subcommittee report counterposed the US mission to promote national security and international peace with the mission to support Trust Territory inhabitants toward decolonization. The report argued that military buildup in indigenous peoples' homelands indeed harmed those inhabitants. Given that UN power remained limited to commissioning reports and offering recommendations, its arguments had little to no influence on the United States. The report's only influence may have been in contributing to the US decision to withdraw from the UN General Assembly's Special Committee on the Situation with Regard to the Implementation of the Declaration on the Granting of Independence to Colonial Countries and Peoples. Two years after the subcommittee report was issued, the United States stopped participating on this committee with no explanation.[149]

PALM TREE PLACEMAKING: FROM THE NUCLEAR CAMPAIGN TO THE MISSILE-TESTING ERA

By the late 1960s, Marshallese condemnation of US colonial control in their homelands covered the broad range of US attacks on Marshallese humanity. The Nitijela resolution denounced the destruction and devastation wrought by US weapons testing, the authors decrying the use of Bikini and Enewetak for the nuclear campaign. The resolution stated: "The Marshallese people do not believe that such explosions are consistent with the maintenance of international peace and security."[150] The resolution also condemned Marshallese living conditions under the military's missile-testing program on Kwajalein. The Nitijela criticized US Army policies on Kwajalein that created "the most rigid form of segregation [existing] . . . in which Micronesians are not permitted to live on the same islands as the Americans, to shop in . . . the stores, or even take home with them anything of value which Americans might freely give them."[151]

This inclusion in the resolution reflected growing concerns about the army's segregation policies on Kwajalein, policies that accompanied the construction and maintenance of a small-town suburban home for American workers on the island. Within a year of the nuclear-testing campaign's conclusion, the United States had designated Kwajalein Atoll as the location for testing the vehicles upon which to deliver nuclear warheads: ICBMs. Weaving these two weapons-testing campaigns together were palm trees, literally rooting seeds of displacement and destruction from one campaign to the next.

In 1946, as the navy began preparing Bikinians for their journey away from home, it removed twenty-five hundred palm trees from Bikini to replant on Kwajalein, "for the purpose of improving the appearance of the island."[152] This project to beautify Kwajalein foreshadowed how the missile-testing era that began at the nuclear campaign's conclusion would be marked by thoughtful planning and substantial investment in the island's transformation. Removed to enable the destruction of a Marshallese home on Bikini, the replanted palms helped landscape Kwajalein's built environment during the 1960s, the erection of a new home for American scientists, engineers, and their nuclear families.

The framing of US entitlement in the region that began during World War II moved through the Cold War, reinforcing the notion that Marshallese homelands existed to support US interests. As nuclear tests were replaced with ICBM tests, Americans again found themselves golfing and playing baseball on this Marshallese homeland. At the same time, Marshallese again found themselves struggling to survive under conditions of US colonial governance marked by economic neglect and disregard. The creation of a small-town suburban setting to house Americans on Kwajalein was a project that built upon further displacements of Marshallese in Kwajalein Atoll to nearby Ebeye Island. Ebeye's transformation into a space to house those displaced and the military's growing service sector unfolded in line with Kwajalein's transformation as linked histories of colonial land and labor control.

2 New Homes for New Workers

COLONIALISM, CONTRACT, AND CONSTRUCTION

> The history of the Marshall Islands during the three dec-
> ades of American rule has been the saddest history we can
> remember. History will show that it was we Marshallese
> who had the "trust" while America had the "territory."
>
> —Ataji Balos, 1976

THE METROPOLE AND THE METROPOLITAN
IN THE MARSHALL ISLANDS

In 1966, Marshallese landowner Handel Dribo wrote to Trust Territory
high commissioner Maurice W. Goding expressing his concerns about the
US eminent domain policy on his island of Ebeye. Dribo detailed how the
Trust Territory attorney general had recently visited Ebeye and communicated to Dribo that his six acres would be taken for construction purposes.[1]
He explained that he had already given much of his land for public use for
the Ebeye hospital, a church, a school, and hospital employee housing.
Dribo requested that the Trust Territory government allow him to retain
his last acres of land to rent out so he could support the 130 people dependent on him. Dribo wrote that he was proud to share land with the US
government "for constructing means to hold the world peace."[2] But he "did
not understand that [he] could be caught in this 'Eminent Domain' law."[3]
He asked: "Just what will my people do now? We have no education—we
have no power."[4]

Ten years later, Dribo reflected on his sense of powerlessness in testimony he gave before the US Senate Subcommittee on Territorial and

Insular Affairs. Dribo explained how he had lost his land after signing a Trust Territory lease. He stated: "The reason I gave my signature was out of some fear. There was a word that was used which is more fearful than a sword in my hearing. . . . If I refused to sign, they could claim it by *eminent domain*. This was their weapon."[5]

Dribo's letter and subsequent testimony offer a glimpse into one local manifestation of US colonial land control over the broad region that came to be called the Trust Territory of the Pacific Islands. While chapter 1 explored how US imperialism in Micronesia expanded amid the backdrop of shifting Cold War geopolitics and was framed by UN sanction, this chapter delves into the local iterations of US military colonialism at Kwajalein Atoll. The process of transforming Kwajalein into a suburban refuge for the military's residential workforce centered on controlling land and labor in the region. Land control came through displacements of resident Marshallese and other Micronesians living within the atoll and coercing unjust leasing agreements with Marshallese landowners for those newly vacant lands. It also entailed the use of eminent domain, as Dribo decried, in attempts to build and maintain infrastructure for those displaced by the military, its segregated service sector, and their dependents.

Dribo's story of land loss links with a broader history of military displacements throughout Kwajalein Atoll and a history of coercive leasing to gain long-term control over the islands from which Marshallese residents and workers were displaced. But it also illustrates how the export of investments, policies, and cultural norms to produce an American suburban home on Kwajalein was paralleled by the construction of a segregated urban home on Ebeye. This metropolitan dynamic required policies like eminent domain, a tool used across urban landscapes during the 1950s and 1960s to enable the acquisition of private property spanning Los Angeles to San Diego, Denver to New York. In these and other cities, the homes of urban communities of color were identified as "blighted" to justify residential displacements that cleared the way for the construction of freeways, public parks, or in the case of Los Angeles, Dodger Stadium.[6] What unfolded on Ebeye during the 1960s was also framed through what might be considered "blight," but unlike in the US continental landscape, where many urban communities of color experienced blight as a result of federal redlining policies and structural segregation, impoverished landscapes on

Kwajalein and Ebeye emerged as a direct result of US colonial policies. Here we see the replication of one feature of metropolitan segregation, but within the context of the imperial metropole.

While chapter 1 analyzed the relationship between US security interests and increasing Marshallese insecurity centering the impacts of weapons testing, this chapter considers another realm of insecurity tied to US colonial development on Ebeye. This local history reveals a new set of deadly costs borne by Marshallese in the name of US weapons testing. These included land loss and displacements to and within Ebeye and the resultant public health challenges to survive on the island's increasingly dense and impoverished infrastructure amid the spread of preventable disease and death. Just as US colonial administrators had done during the nuclear campaign, in the missile-testing era they also disavowed the devastating impacts of their policies. The new insecurities accompanying residency on Ebeye emerged because of US policies of displacement, segregation, labor recruitment, and economic neglect. But the manner of disavowal shifted in this story. For the military, Ebeye's struggles would be relegated to the realm of the Trust Territory government, now tasked with developing a home for the military's segregated service sector and those it displaced for weapons testing. Trust Territory administrators would in turn point the finger of blame for Ebeye's increasing impoverishment back at the military. Marshallese rejected these deflections of accountability and took to the global stage to decry US neglect of its UN trusteeship obligations to support and protect the region's inhabitants.

This chapter explores the colonial tensions undergirding the military's dependence on land and labor to carry out weapons testing on Kwajalein, alongside its distancing from the repercussions of such dependencies. I begin by examining colonial policies that transformed Kwajalein Atoll into a key Cold War site for US weapons testing by focusing on the contraction of Marshallese lands through leasing. Discussion of the construction of new homes for those displaced and those who became the military's segregated service sector all living on Ebeye follows. Each of these steps constituted an essential and contested process in laying the foundations for long-term military control over Kwajalein Atoll, ongoing control that shaped the contours of Marshallese decolonization decades later.

The first of three chapters to consider the history of land and labor control and the construction of new landscapes to support US weapons testing, this chapter begins to examine how Marshallese navigated this changing colonial terrain. As the military began erecting and containing a segregated suburban missile base on Kwajalein Island to house incoming US workers and their families (the subject of chapter 3), it had also been working with Trust Territory government representatives to contract for lands throughout the atoll through coercive leases. The construction of new homes for those the army displaced for missile testing and for its segregated service sector accompanied the leasing of Marshallese lands, as did a pattern of mythmaking that erased this history as it was unfolding. Begun by army narratives and taken up and reproduced by US civilians living on Kwajalein, this mythology framing Kwajalein as an American home (the subject of chapter 4) continues today. Marshallese leaders like Handel Dribo most dramatically challenged these myths and policies through ongoing protest against US colonial control over their lands.

THE (EMINENT) DOMAIN OF EMPIRE, PART I: LAND CONTROL ON KWAJALEIN

Dribo's letter of protest was haunted by deeper histories of US settler colonial expansion. As he described misunderstanding the "weapon" of eminent domain used to obtain control over his lands, the resonances of indigenous land dispossession on the North American continent through colonial treaty-making histories bled into this moment of US imperialism in the Pacific during the Cold War.[7] But at Kwajalein Atoll, this colonial land grab also intersected with twentieth-century municipal policies such as eminent domain, which targeted and displaced racialized communities across US metropolitan landscapes. To adequately examine the collective impact of these policies, I turn first to US leasing history on Kwajalein and Ebeye.

US Trust Territory and military officials charged with negotiating land leases in the Marshall Islands did so informed in part by a US settler history of land acquisition aimed at privatization and intergenerational wealth accumulation. This settler context was foundational to a broader history of imperial expansion aimed at dispossessing indigenous peoples from their lands within and outside the continent and the ongoing disavowal of that history. As discussed in this book's introduction, control of Marshallese lands through US leasing practices also contributed to intergenerational wealth accumulation for thousands of US workers over time. But the process looked different from settler colonial expansion across the continent. Colonialism in the Marshall Islands was based on strategic military interests, not a settler project in which property could be permanently owned and passed from one generation of Americans to the next. Land control for long-term use had to abide by the Trusteeship Agreement's mandate to protect the region's inhabitants from permanent land loss. Thus, land acquisition had to be temporary, even if temporary meant a ninety-nine-year lease. This structure was guided by overtly stated *strategic* rather than economic concerns. The US security strategy in Micronesia during the Cold War involved using indigenous lands to build up military capacity and for strategic denial, meaning no other military power could have a presence in the region. Unlike continental settler colonialism, US wealth accumulation from settlement on Kwajalein did not come through landownership. Instead it came through salaries and wages earned living a subsidized lifestyle on Marshallese lands, a privilege that allowed temporary US settlers to save and invest their earnings in property elsewhere. This distinct mode of colonial extraction resides within a realm that historian Naoko Shibusawa has identified as "military settler colonialism."[8]

Just as the nuclear-testing campaign revealed, disputes over land control at Kwajalein Atoll were another example of how the Trusteeship Agreement directive obliging the United States to protect Micronesians from land loss came into conflict with military desires to control these lands for weapons testing. Marshallese attempted to reveal these contradictions and negotiate within a context of vastly unequal power relations. Marshallese landowners negotiated leases against the backdrop of prior colonial administrations and with a broker bringing its own settler colonial context to the negotiating table. Having traced some of the deeper and broader contexts of US settler colonial and imperial expansion in the introduction, in this chapter I provide context on Marshallese land traditions. This context reveals how Marshallese and Americans negotiated these contracts from their own distinct cultural and historic relationships to land use and ownership.

US approaches to land negotiations in the Marshall Islands were informed by deeper histories of colonial land control merging with new postwar strategic opportunities. In contrast, Marshallese would arrive at the negotiating table informed by a different historic relationship to their land. This was a cultural context that had not historically involved privatization. While leasing negotiations would take place between various US administrators and Marshallese "landowners," it is important to qualify what this title meant in a Marshallese context. As Pacific scholar Greg Dvorak has written, "Where whole clans and multiple individuals have links to the same land, the idea had typically been more one of custodianship, being able to use the land and reap its benefits on behalf of one's lineage. In many ways, it is not that one owns the land, but rather that one is *owned by* that land, that one belongs to it and passed it on to the next generation appropriately."[9] As a matrilineal society, land usage rights were traditionally passed down generation to generation to other family members through the eldest woman in that family. When this woman passed away, land rights moved to her brothers and sisters in order of their age, starting with the eldest. When all siblings died, the land rights passed to the next generation, starting with the children of the oldest woman of the previous generation.[10] Marshallese lineage or clan lines, called *bwij*, provided land use rights for lineage members, who traditionally lived on and exploited the resources of their small land parcel, called a *weto*, the most typical type of inherited land. Each *weto* comprised a section of land extending from lagoon to ocean, allowing for all resources within this range—including dry land and resources extending into the reef—to be utilized. According to anthropologist Holly M. Barker, claims to *wetos* depended on each individual knowing the boundaries and history of those parcels, with the "power to recognize and validate land claims rest[ing] in the hands of customary authorities," while also acknowledging that "no single person own[ed] the land."[11]

Marshallese society revolved around a three-tier approach of reciprocal land use rights. The *irooj* (chiefs who maintained authority over clans and the land), *alab* (land managers), and *ri-jerbal* (workers) comprised the three major divisions. Historically, *irooj* remained responsible for taking care of the people, and in turn the people provided food and labor for their chiefs. The *alab* oversaw day-to-day land maintenance and reported back to the chiefs while ensuring everyone was provided for. This symbiotic yet hierarchical structure, in which workers cultivated the land and the chiefs and managers provided workers access to the land for survival, constituted the foundations of Marshallese land organization and relational society: the Marshallese political economy.[12]

While the US colonial period introduced new and consequential changes to land use and land rights, Marshallese land organization had begun adapting to the presence of colonial administrators as early as the 1870s and 1880s under the first colonial era of German rule. But as detailed in the introduction, the traditional land structure remained largely undisturbed during both the German colonial and Japanese settler colonial eras, only shifting with Japanese fortification during the mid-1930s. While Micronesian landholder titles remained protected by the Japanese civilian colonial administration, these protections diminished during Japanese militarization.[13] The US Navy found few records concerning landownership in the Marshall Islands at the end of the war, as the Japanese had removed all of value, and Marshallese kept no written records. Thus, at the conclusion of the war the navy took land Japanese administrators had purchased or seized in the late 1930s or early 1940s, with the view that Japanese "public land" was 'alien property," to be controlled by the United States as the "successor sovereign."[14]

Within this context of successive colonial histories informing land use in the Marshall Islands, US military commanders, Trust Territory administrators, and Marshallese landowners faced the challenge of negotiating leases between parties of vastly unequal power. Marshallese landowners had little to no leverage to deny the occupation of their lands, a critical feature of the contractual production of these islands as "leased" spaces. What did it mean for Marshallese landowners to negotiate these leases with parties who had significantly greater power and authority to enforce or rescind these contracts? Such "negotiations" enabled colonial land control to be masked under the pretense of mutually agreed upon contracts, thus satisfying the trusteeship directive obliging the US to protect Micronesians against land loss.[15]

Marshallese landowners received no compensation for their lands in the immediate postwar era. It was not until a decade later, after landowners had continually voiced concerns before the UN Trusteeship Council, that the secretary of the interior and the secretary of the navy signed an agreement that created the conditions within which Marshallese could begin negotiating compensation for land use. The 1955 agreement positioned the Trust Territory government as the middleman in negotiations between the US military and Micronesian landowners, referring to the former as US "using agencies."[16] In cases where landowners were unwilling to lease their land, the Trust Territory government was given the authority to acquire that land through eminent domain and offer fair compensation.[17] This three-party negotiation structure implemented in 1955—between military officials, Trust Territory representatives, and Marshallese landowners—made the efforts of landowners struggling to prevent the United States from taking their lands additionally challenging. Landowners found themselves dependent upon one arm of US empire (the Trust Territory government) to negotiate their land protection against the other arm (the military), whose interests and resources carried far more weight and influence than the former's.

Infused with colonial hierarchy, tension, and suspicion, this tripartite system of land negotiations moved forward in the late 1950s as the United States for the first time acknowledged the need to compensate Marshallese landowners for occupancy of Kwajalein Island. Negotiations would last several years, spanning the transition of Kwajalein from a naval base supporting the Korean War and the nuclear-testing campaign through its transition into a missile range in 1960. Soviet success in launching Sputnik and testing its first ICBM in 1957 hastened the US decision to establish a missile base at Kwajalein.[18] After a few years of stalemated negotiations during the late 1950s, the United States offered Marshallese landowners $500 per acre for "indefinite use" rights to their land.[19] Presuming Marshallese naiveté in dealing with a cash economy, US representatives placed $300,000 in single dollar bills on a table in front of 192 landowners.[20] Kwajalein Irooj (chief) Amata Kabua led the other landowners out of the room, refusing the offer. Lacking faith in the United States as a fair negotiator, Kabua petitioned the UN Trusteeship Council in 1959 to intervene on behalf of the landowners, constituting an early effort to call upon the United Nations to enforce its stated principles. Kabua addressed the council, explaining why Marshallese would not sign an indefinite use agreement.[21] He argued that Marshallese landowners would "always believe that in principle a piece of land occupied on an indefinite use rights basis is no different from one that has been bought or annexed."[22] He added, "The Kwajalein people consider the offer unfair and unjust and shall to the end seek the justice to which they are entitled under the Human Bill of Rights."[23]

Kabua's testimony warned of how the use of Marshallese lands for a mission aimed at ensuring greater security for American families thousands of miles away would create new forms of insecurity for Marshallese locally at Kwajalein Atoll. He did so by explaining to the Trusteeship Council the contrast in valuing land versus money in Marshallese society, emphasizing how the former brought far greater security for Marshallese than the latter. Kabua noted that a family could cultivate an acre of land and yield enough crops to care for their daily basic needs and those of all family members. A landless person could barely support himself, let alone his entire family, with the meager US compensation offer. This was particularly important given that US occupancy necessitated the importation of nearly all food.[24] Foreshadowing the challenges soon to face many landless Marshallese displaced to Ebeye, Kabua cautioned that if the US forced Marshallese to lease their land for such little compensation, "a new class of paupers will be created overnight."[25]

Confirming Kabua's suspicion of working with bad faith negotiators unconcerned with Marshallese well-being, Trust Territory high commissioner D. H. Nucker issued an executive order a few months after Kabua's petition condemning all "private property for public use."[26] This order defined the land affected as any area the high commissioner determined was needed for public use.[27] The order accompanied naval plans to transform Kwajalein into a missile installation and further damaged US efforts to garner trust among Marshallese landowners. As the importance of the missile-testing program to the United States became more evident, Marshallese continued to petition the Trusteeship Council for support in getting just compensation for their lands and to address the dire living conditions emerging on Ebeye. The Trusteeship Council encouraged the United States to negotiate a settlement, but only did so after the first successful missile interception launch on Kwajalein. The interception heightened the military's sense of urgency to resolve all remaining Marshallese land claims to enable long-term, uninterrupted control over the island. In 1964, paramount chief (Iroojlaplap) Lejolan Kabua signed a lease for Kwajalein with the Trust Territory government and the US military. The agreement allowed the military to lease Kwajalein for $1,000 per acre for ninety-nine years. While double the initial US offer, the compensation still amounted to less than $10 per acre, per year, to each landowner, making the lease little more than a "gesture," according to Pacific historian David Hanlon.[28]

The 1964 lease agreement proved critical in setting the terms by which Kwajalein Island would be brought into an expanding US base imperium. Trust Territory administrators characterized the 1964 lease as a triumph after years spent negotiating on behalf of the military and Marshallese landowners. Few, if any, Marshallese landowners drew the same conclusion. Reactions among many landowners and political leaders exemplified their continued struggle to remove the façade of a mutually agreed upon contract between equal parties that masked a context of colonial coercion and intimidation.

While the lease negotiation constituted an act of coercion, it also created a platform from which Marshallese would continue to challenge US colonialism before the United Nations and the world. In 1968, Kabua appeared again before the UN Trusteeship Council, this time representing the Marshall Islands Nitijela (legislature), with a resolution regarding US land acquisition of Kwajalein. As detailed in chapter 1, this resolution called attention to the "neo-colonial situation" Marshallese existed under and requested that the United Nations reconsider the legal and political status of the Trust Territory. It also detailed the process by which the United States had acquired Kwajalein, noting that landowners were "forced to surrender" approximately 750 acres of land for about $10 per acre per year in "an area where land is scarce and therefore precious beyond the comprehension of outsiders."[29]

The Kwajalein lease was contested not only by the Nitijela, but also by Trust Territory representatives who felt caught in the precarious position of balancing obligations to protect Micronesian land rights while helping seize those lands for military use. Within a year of the Nitijela resolution, High Commissioner Edward Johnston expressed such concerns in a letter to Secretary of the Interior Walter J. Hickel. Illuminating how the contradictions of colonialism impacted his capacity to do his job, Johnston criticized the land acquisition process and its impact on weakening Micronesian trust. He requested that the entire approach to military leasing authorized by the 1955 agreement be reviewed and reconsidered.[30] Johnston wrote about the challenge to inspire confidence among Micronesians and incorporate them into a Trust Territory government that supported them on the one hand while negotiating their land dispossession on the other.[31] Such opposition, voiced by those charged with administering the Trust Territory region, revealed the porous nature of an American exceptionalist narrative framed through a Trusteeship Agreement that disavowed US colonialism in the region. Johnston's critiques highlighted the challenges facing Trust Territory administrators tasked with carrying out such contradictory policies on the ground. His concerns echoed the conundrum, analyzed in chapter 1, faced by these officials hired to administer an "anti-colonial," colonial regime.

The 1964 lease agreement held firm until 1979, when additional compensation was made to landowners, only after they staged sail-in protests to reoccupy their lands. As discussed in chapters 5 and 6, Kwajalein landowners would continue these protests through the 1980s, in efforts to assert greater influence on ongoing leasing negotiations as Marshallese navigated a path toward decolonization.

THE (EMINENT) DOMAIN OF EMPIRE, PART II:
LAND CONTROL ON EBEYE

By the time the army secured the 1964 lease for land control on Kwajalein, the island had been an exclusive home to its US workers and their dependents for thirteen years. In 1951, the navy displaced to Ebeye all "Micronesian workers" who had been living on Kwajalein following World War II to support US military activities.[32] At that point, the naval administration determined that US military personnel and native laborers should live on separate islands. This switch to keep Kwajalein a space of exclusive US residency meant that over time the heavily resourced military could focus on investments and planning for quality of life facilities aimed at creating the most accommodating setting for its US workforce. The task of supporting its Marshallese workers living on Ebeye would fall to the underfunded Trust Territory government. The military's colonial policies of displacement and exclusion, which informed Kwajalein's leasing history, also determined how land control on Ebeye relationally emerged over time. Leasing on Ebeye proved a complicated mix of land control in a home that housed displaced and segregated workers alongside a growing number of Marshallese displaced to make way for missile testing, all of whom contributed to unsustainable population growth on the island. This rising density marked life on Ebeye with new forms of insecurity as the island became an essential site buttressing the US quest for national security.

As Kwajalein landowners struggled throughout the 1950s and 1960s to obtain adequate compensation for use of their land, Ebeye landowners found themselves crowded out of their homes as an increasing number of Marshallese arrived on their island through military displacements and in search of jobs on Kwajalein. Whereas Kwajalein had become increasingly populated as it was fortified by the Central Command for the Japanese Imperial Navy during the 1930s and 1940s, Ebeye housed fewer than twenty people on the island in the prewar era. Prior to 1946, the island was primarily a home for the wives of Marshallese chiefs. According to historian David Hanlon, land on Ebeye was divided into ten *wetos*, with ownership rights "shared among a paramount chief or *iroij*, 4 lineage chiefs called *alab*, and approximately seven hundred lineage members, many of whom lived elsewhere in the greater Kwajalein Atoll."[33] The US Navy disregarded this land tenure structure in 1951, when it displaced to the island all Micronesian workers living on Kwajalein.

By displacing its Micronesian workforce to Ebeye in 1951 and disregarding Ebeye's land tenure structure, the navy created challenges for Marshallese landowners and their families living on Ebeye with nowhere else to go. Like colonial practices governing land use on Kwajalein Island, when the navy first displaced the Micronesian labor camp of more than 559 workers and their dependents from Kwajalein to Ebeye, it did so in the absence of any formal lease agreement or compensation for land use. Following the labor camp displacement, Ebeye landowners faced greater restriction on access to their lands, which were used to support an increasing number of Marshallese migrating to Ebeye in hopes of finding work on Kwajalein. A 1954 monthly activities report produced by Trust Territory administration captured landowners' concern about their island being transformed to support military activities on Kwajalein, noting that they felt they should "be allowed to utilize their own land to suit their needs."[34] District land titles officer W. C. White reported: "Ebeye landowners viewed the new laborers residing on Ebeye as 'outsiders' and had requested an evacuation of the whole operation."[35]

Trust Territory reports identified the deadly challenges emerging for Ebeye landowners and residents, tied directly to displacements and alienation from their lands: the ongoing cost of Marshallese insecurity underwriting the US security mission. White's report foreshadowed the tensions that would increase over time as Ebeye landowners struggled to accommodate the needs of US military operations, which sowed the seeds for unsustainable population growth, poverty, and public health crises on the island. The same year of White's report, Marshall Islands district anthropologist Jack Tobin published a report signaling the dire conditions already facing those on Ebeye just three years into the labor camp removal. He warned that density and poverty would become greatly exacerbated in the decades to come.[36] Concerned about the risks to Marshallese health and well-being on Ebeye, Tobin recommended the US return Marshallese islands that had been alienated by Japanese and/or American forces during the war to their former landowners, many of whom lived on Ebeye.[37]

In the 1960s, Ebeye landowners signed leases for their lands, but just as Kwajalein landowners had found, this process was laden with intimidation and coercion. For Ebeye landowners, leases were directly linked to language included in the 1964 Kwajalein lease obligating the army to "improve the economic and social conditions for Marshallese people, particularly at Ebeye."[38] As Ebeye's inadequate infrastructure deteriorated during the early 1960s, Trust Territory administrators had identified the army as responsible for Ebeye's unsustainable population growth due to continued displacements and labor recruitment for Kwajalein. Citing the 1964 lease obligations, the Trust Territory government insisted the Department of Defense fund a renovation and development project on Ebeye.[39]

The army's resultant investment plan for Ebeye created an approach layered with colonial land control policies in the region and displacement tactics that echoed those used against "blighted" communities in racially segregated, urban landscapes in the United States. The $7 million development project introduced the first land leases on Ebeye in 1966, and in doing so further marginalized Ebeye landowners.[40] This was because the army refused to fund any support structures on Marshallese-controlled land. To appease the Department of Defense, the Trust Territory government acquired control of all land on Ebeye through long-term leases exacted under the threat of eminent domain.[41] The Department of Defense demanded the Trust Territory government demolish all existing structures on the newly leased land without compensating landowners for destruction of their buildings. Ebeye landowners were thus forced to abandon their lands and pay rent for using any new structures built on their land after implementation of the new leasing arrangement. Historian David Hanlon noted that this project offered an "ironic twist to an already perverse, badly distorted situation."[42] The military's development project roused disdain among all major landowners on Ebeye, all but one of whom agreed to lease their lands "rather than face confiscation through eminent domain."[43] The twenty-five-year lease arrangement compensated Ebeye landowners with just $8 per month per acre of land, a payment far too low to support individual and family subsistence.

Just as colonial leasing of Kwajalein evoked outcries, Ebeye landowners protested these unjust practices. Kwajalein landowner Amata Kabua advocated on behalf of Ebeye landowners from his position in the Marshall Islands Congress (MIC) on April 4, 1966. He requested the Congress of Micronesia (COM) investigate US leasing practices on Ebeye, noting that he regretted "very much that the Administration has resorted to condemning private land at Ebeye and Kwajalein Atoll by the process of eminent domain," adding that he considered this "a punishment for the landowners who frankly informed the Administration that they could not live on $8.00 per month" per acre of their land.[44] Warning that the precedent being set on Ebeye could ripple out to the rest of Micronesia, impacting the home islands of those comprising the COM leadership, Kabua added: "If a piece of land on Ebeye could be conveniently seized from its owner by legal means, same will hold true for thousand other pieces of land elsewhere in the Trust Territory."[45]

Two weeks after Kabua wrote his letter, Ebeye landowner Handel Dribo sent his letter (noted at the start of this chapter) to High Commissioner

Goding. The letter was also published in the *Marshall Islands Journal*. Reiterating Dribo's and Kabua's warnings of long-term repercussions, Hermios Kibin published a letter in 1968 in the local publication *Ebeye Voice*, condemning the foreign nature of eminent domain policies in the Marshall Islands. Kibin wrote to the editor, lamenting: "Our islands in a sense belong to the Americans but we are alien to them. They can do anything they want under the present eminent domain law. . . . How long the Demon-Law will exist is a question of time."[46] Kibin also addressed the impact of the law on landowners' children. He explained: "The younger generation who have land rights on Ebeye, Kwajalein and other islands involved live in constant fear of what will happen in the future. . . . How much land will be fed to this greedy law in order to satisfy its need and what do we get for our precious land in return?"[47] Marshallese challenges to US leasing practices during the 1960s continued throughout the 1970s and 1980s and informed a series of sail-in protests that garnered greater compensation for landowners of Kwajalein and the mid-corridor islands.[48] Ebeye landowners remained constrained by the eminent domain policies and the ongoing transformation of the island into a support site for the army's missile-testing mission on Kwajalein.

The use of eminent domain on Ebeye to address failing infrastructure reflected similar patterns facing urban communities of color in the continental United States identified as "blighted" during the 1950s and 1960s. Where histories of redlining and segregation in metropolitan areas across the United States had created conditions of blight, which were then used to justify eminent domain to displace those communities, on Ebeye a comparable process unfolded as a result of colonial policies.[49] The military's displacement and segregation policies and labor recruitment strategies to support operations on Kwajalein accompanied its disavowal of any responsibility to address the resulting density and poverty emerging on Ebeye. Instead, eminent domain was used to try to address a crisis created under these colonial conditions, further alienating Marshallese landowners from their lands. The remainder of this chapter explores how these historic and ongoing colonial displacement and disinvestment policies informed the creation of a new home for the military's segregated workforce on Ebeye. In doing so, I move from analyzing the contraction of Marshallese homelands through colonial leasing histories to looking at the built environment erected atop them.

DISPLACEMENTS AND DENIAL:
NAVIGATING COLONIAL DEPENDENCIES

Ebeye emerged as a setting marked by rising insecurity alongside the island's increasingly central role in supporting the US security mission on Kwajalein and the military's disavowal of that dependency. The military's efforts to obscure an interdependency between Kwajalein and Ebeye to carry out its mission was eased by the 1951 labor camp displacement and ongoing segregation thereafter. This structure of segregation enabled a shift in responsibility for planning infrastructure on Ebeye, which ultimately aimed to benefit the military, onto the Trust Territory government. The Trusteeship Agreement had created contradictory directives that gave the military the freedom to use Micronesian islands for base development while making the Trust Territory government responsible for supporting development across Micronesia in nonmilitary spaces. This separation of responsibility offered in some ways a clever solution to the incompatibility of Trusteeship Agreement directives. That separation, combined with the military policies of displacement and segregation, empowered the army to take on one responsibility, the Trust Territory government the other. As the military met the objective of missile testing over time, it created new barriers for the Trust Territory government in meeting its mandate of sustainable development on Ebeye.

The conflicts between these two arms of U.S. empire—the military and the Trust Territory government—hinged in part on debates over Ebeye's status as a nonmilitary space. While not housing missile-testing equipment like Kwajalein, Ebeye nonetheless was essential to military operations on Kwajalein by the early 1960s. But the military never fully acknowledged this reality. The lack of military investments in Ebeye over time, even as Marshallese faced deadly conditions, reflected this disavowal. From the end of World War II, when the navy recruited Micronesians to help clean up the island, through the next six decades of military activity on Kwajalein, Marshallese workers consistently comprised a significant portion of the military's labor. During the missile-testing era they constituted at least a quarter of the workforce, waxing and waning alongside the numbers of US personnel on the island. Military activities on Kwajalein historically and continuously depended on labor housed on Ebeye and the use of the island as a repository for those displaced by the military. Since the 1960s, the Marshallese service sector has remained an uninterrupted and crucial support to military and civilian life on Kwajalein. Reflecting on this long history of US dependence on Marshallese labor in 2010, Kwajalein senator Tony de Brum said he "would like to see Kwajalein try to test its missiles without them."[50] A discussion that same year with a civilian on Kwajalein who wished to remain anonymous further illuminated this dynamic. She described how following 9/11, the military banned Marshallese laborers from coming to Kwajalein for "security" reasons. Within a day of the ban, the army reversed the policy, given its detrimental impact.[51] Military operations and the lifestyle afforded to Kwajalein residents through Marshallese labor has never existed without Ebeye.

And yet despite a history of interdependence marking Kwajalein and Ebeye's relational development over time, the military has only begrudgingly and on rare occasion acknowledged any responsibility for Ebeye. The army's 1966 development project was the exception, not the rule, and was carried out in a way that exacerbated struggles for Ebeye landowners. As the military expressed little concern for its service workers on Ebeye and invested minimally in their well-being, tension developed between the Trust Territory government and the Department of Defense. Resentment brewed as Trust Territory administrators were charged with footing the bill for worsening conditions on Ebeye over time. These administrators often viewed Ebeye's problems as directly caused by the military on Kwajalein. For the military, ongoing segregation policies between Kwajalein and Ebeye embodied a solution to the conflicting goals of the Trusteeship Agreement. By banning Micronesian residency on Kwajalein, the army could fulfill its mission on the cheap, leaving the Trust Territory government to foot the bill. The resulting infighting between the two further illuminated how this local iteration of American exceptionalism at Kwajalein was buttressed by the global sanction of the United Nations. The UN Trusteeship Agreement enabled a façade of US civilian versus military interests in the region, as if the two did not belong to a shared imperial mission.

Perceived by the military as a space to house labor, not families, Ebeye's landscape emerged over time in stark contrast to the abundant investments and meticulous planning at Kwajalein. While the built environment on Kwajalein aimed to support engineers and scientists, seen as deserving

amenities to support family life, recreation, and consumption (detailed
in chapter 3), Ebeye's transformation reflected minimal attention to even
the most basic necessities for survival. Emblematic of the divergent perceptions of each island and the needs of those living on them was Senator de Brum's recollection of the 1951 labor camp displacement. De Brum
was a child visiting Kwajalein when the navy moved the camp to Ebeye.
When asked if he recalled the navy explaining to Micronesians why they
were being moved, he chuckled, presumably at the naivete of the question.
"They didn't explain. They didn't have to and they didn't try to. . . . As you
know the labor camp site now is a golf course."[52]

While not explaining it directly to the those displaced, the navy did provide a justification in its official documentation of the camp removal. The
rationale exemplified an early iteration of the use of eminent domain: the
colonial creation of blight that was then used to push for removal of
the resulting blighted community. While the previous section examined
how this practice unfolded on Ebeye in 1966, as eminent domain was used
to displace Marshallese, mirroring patterns unfolding across the urban
United States during the same period, the navy had already modeled
this tactic on Kwajalein fifteen years earlier. According to Trust Territory
district anthropologist Jack Tobin, the navy decided to declare eminent
domain on Kwajalein to remove the Micronesian labor camp after its
population had swelled to 559 residents by 1950, creating an eyesore for
the military. Conditions in the camp "presented a squalid, shantytown
appearance, contrasting sharply with the spick and span buildings of the
adjacent military establishment," Tobin wrote.[53]

Captain Cecil B. Gill, commander of Naval Operating Base Kwajalein
and governor of the Marshall Islands, detailed these conditions in his proposal to move the blighted labor camp to Ebeye. According to Gill, the
native labor camp on Kwajalein was "entirely inadequate" and so densely
situated it posed a fire risk.[54] Gill remarked that because the navy had
built living quarters for Micronesian laborers on Kwajalein using salvaged
materials that it neglected to maintain over time, the task of improving this
camp would be more expensive than simply displacing workers to Ebeye.
These inadequate and dangerous living conditions had emerged due to
US investments in housing and infrastructure for its US military personnel alongside neglect for anything comparable for the native workforce.

Gill affirmed that the navy had not considered any meaningful support for its Marshallese workforce on the island, noting that in "long range plans for Kwajalein, no facilities have been inserted into the blueprint for native use."[55] He also cited complications in feeding Micronesian workers at Kwajalein's mess hall, given that food prices were higher than native wages.[56] Rather than pay Micronesian workers enough to afford food on Kwajalein or invest in safe and sustainable housing, the navy opted for the cheaper solution of displacement to Ebeye.

But according to Gill, the decision to remove the camp was rooted less in monetary concerns and more in a desire to protect the culture of native workers. Gill said the most important consideration in the navy's decision centered on removing "Marshallese from intimate contact with service personnel and those modern influences with which the natives are unable to cope."[57] Echoing a common colonial myth of "fatal impact," in which Westerners have history and native peoples have culture, and ongoing encounters between the two would risk devastating a presumed, static culture of the native population, Gill argued for the need to protect Marshallese from this fate.[58] Gill emphasized this primary goal of cultural protection, while noting a secondary consideration of military cost-saving benefits that came through offloading the bulk of native housing expenses onto the Trust Territory government. On December 30, 1949, the Trust Territory high commissioner agreed to cover $25,000 of the estimated housing construction cost of $33,200. This amount, drawn from the Trust Territory treasury, would be replaced from Naval Station Kwajalein funds "if" and when they became available at a later date.[59] This offloading of costs to support the military mission on Kwajalein onto the Trust Territory government constituted the start of what became a long-term policy. Following the labor camp displacement, the military continued to depend on the labor of Marshallese workers to support its security mission while wiping its hands of any material responsibility for those workers living on Ebeye; that task now fell onto the Trust Territory government.

While Gill's focus on cultural protection attempted to cast a veil of innocence over the labor camp removal, disavowing the preeminence of material concerns governing this decision, displaced workers and the Trust Territory administrators charged with supporting this newly segregated labor sector immediately challenged such claims of benevolence.

Questioning Gill's assertion that Marshallese would be better off living under their own economy on Ebeye, Trust Territory chief administrator S. C. Anderson wrote to the high commissioner addressing Marshallese concerns about the move. He explained: "The Marshallese reaction is one of apprehension and uncertainty in respect to their ability to afford to pay rent and subsist themselves on imported foods (as all food must be imported at Ebeye). They are wondering if they will have any take-home pay left after these expenses."[60] Anderson's letter pointed to challenges likely to face Marshallese moving to Ebeye given the lack of thoughtful planning for the move. He noted that the navy had made no provisions to allow private enterprise on Ebeye and asserted that naval and Trust Territory use of eminent domain policies to remove the village obliged them to assist in establishing private business on Ebeye.[61] Sharing the concerns of displaced Marshallese, Anderson's assessment cast doubt on Gill's justification for moving these workers to a place where they could better live under their own customs. He framed Gill's explanation as one that ignored the broader impact of US militarism throughout the atoll, which had rendered economic self-sufficiency untenable.

Foreshadowing the comparisons between quality of life resources on Kwajalein and Ebeye made by Marshallese over time, Anderson's letter also noted that the camp displacement lacked any plan for a Marshallese standard of living. He encouraged the military to limit labor requirements to ensure that Ebeye's population would not exceed more than 370, to avoid overcrowding.[62] Thus, at the moment of the camp's removal to Ebeye, population growth, unsustainable infrastructure, and quality of life issues were identified as serious concerns by Marshallese and Trust Territory representatives. Echoing this early warning about how living conditions could quickly devolve on Ebeye, anthropologist Jack Tobin described the new housing for the labor camp on Ebeye as a "shanty town" in appearance.[63] He identified continuities between the military's minimal investments in native housing on Kwajalein and the Trust Territory administration's inadequate funding and planning for housing on Ebeye.[64]

Anderson and Tobin observed and anticipated a range of Marshallese grievances that would inform protests in the coming decades. It is worth emphasizing that as Marshallese struggled with disease and death under Ebeye's failing infrastructure in the 1960s, 1970s, and 1980s, these

Figure 5. Building on Ebeye, 1954. Photo by Jack Tobin. Permission granted by the Pacific Collection, Hamilton Library, University of Hawaiʻi-Mānoa.

Figure 6. Father and son on Ebeye, 1957. Photo by US Navy.

conditions were anticipated and documented from the moment of the labor camp's removal in 1951. But these early warnings fell on deaf ears. The enormous and avoidable costs paid by Marshallese over time, which included preventable diseases and deaths arising from failed infrastructure on Ebeye, reflected a continuity in the US colonial approach to the region from the nuclear through the missile-testing eras. This was the dehumanizing colonial logic that saw the lands and lives of Marshallese as primarily existing to serve US interests and the region as broadly "inconsequential" otherwise. The familiar expectation that Marshallese would absorb ever-increasing levels of insecurity in the name of US national security persisted.

THE LABOR QUESTION IN THE TRUST TERRITORY

While the military's 1951 labor camp removal and accompanying segregation policies worked to physically distance it from any sense of accountability for its Marshallese workforce, a discourse of native worker dispensability provided a cultural terrain complementing such distancing. The labor question—of how best to make US empire *work* across the broad expanse of Micronesia—arose in the moment of colonial turnover from Japanese to US control following the war.[65] Gill addressed the question locally on Kwajalein when explaining his decision to remove all native workers from the island. As Gill detailed his rationale for the labor camp removal, he probed an issue that would inform military protocol in the region for decades thereafter: the necessity of native labor. Did the military really *need* native workers, he asked? "Obviously no," he answered, but added that this labor was "cheap and useful."[66] Gill's assessment in 1950, of this unnecessary but cost-saving luxury of seemingly disposable workers, reflected and fueled a pattern of military apathy to its service sector on Kwajalein thereafter.

Unlike many other US bases that emerged around the world following World War II, the installation at Kwajalein relied on this "cheap and useful" workforce in the postwar era, never shifting toward a primary reliance on labor from outside of Micronesia to staff its service needs.[67] This contrasted with other base histories, for example the base at Guantánamo, about which historian Jana K. Lipman has traced how during the same period, from 1964 onward, the navy shifted its staffing approach toward contract labor to uncouple the base from its location in Cuba in the wake of the revolution. At this point, the navy began recruiting from other "developing" nations, turning to a heavy reliance on Jamaican guest workers to staff its service needs.[68]

Military labor on Kwajalein, however, has consistently depended on a majority of Marshallese workers to support military activities since the end of World War II. In the early years of this labor policy, critics warned of the potential consequences of relying on and segregating this support sector to Ebeye. Alongside his concerns about housing and public health on the island, district anthropologist Jack Tobin encouraged the military in 1954 to replace Marshallese workers with either military or civilian US personnel in order to stem the growing crisis already facing landowners and displaced workers on Ebeye, problems of density and poverty he predicted would only worsen in time. If the military relied on American workers to staff service needs, Marshallese migrating to Ebeye to work on Kwajalein might return to their home atolls.[69] But the military ignored Tobin's recommendation and instead persistently built on its initial cost-saving model of displacing while depending on this "cheap" labor sector. Its ongoing policy of segregation enabled the military to continue offloading the costs of housing and infrastructure to support this workforce onto the Trust Territory government.

This dynamic that emerged on Kwajalein—of depending on while devaluing Micronesian labor—reflected a broader pattern throughout the Trust Territory and the tensions rippling through colonial efforts at labor control following World War II. As historian David Hanlon has chronicled, in the postwar period military administrators recruited Micronesian laborers to help rebuild the infrastructure that US bombs and wartime combat had destroyed. The military had largely demolished the economy and infrastructure the Japanese had created in the region during their settler colonial rule, a period of unprecedented economic growth in Micronesia. Following the war, the United States repatriated the region's Japanese and Korean laborers, crippling the economy across Micronesia. In the wake of these decisions, US colonial administrators began scapegoating Micronesian labor for the economic challenges facing the region, while relying on those same workers to help rebuild areas devastated by the war.[70] In the Marshall Islands, employing Marshallese laborers meant accommodating their preferences to be close to home and helping them adjust to a new conception of time under a capitalist economy. This challenge, common throughout the region, had influenced the Japanese to depend less on Micronesian labor in their development plans.[71] Economic development had succeeded under Japanese rule because the settler colonial nature of that rule brought thousands of Japanese and Korean laborers to live in the region and help build the economy.

From the earliest years of US colonial governance in the region, labor management proved a central concern to naval and Trust Territory administrators. Both struggled with the task of cooperatively navigating the transformation of societies based largely on sustainable agriculture, fishing, and supplemental copra trade into a wage economy directed at benefiting US interests in the region. A 1951 children's literacy book produced by the High Commissioner's Office in the Trust Territory's Department of Education illustrated (literally and metaphorically) early US efforts to indoctrinate Micronesian children into a normalized system of work. The book was among materials aimed at teaching six-year-old Micronesian children English. *Three Children* shows Micronesians (specifically Chuukese children) as "good" because they "work."[72] The text and images of the book narrate Micronesian boys and girls working to help their parents. Several pages paint a portrait of good, working Micronesian children and adults, culminating in final images locating the children "where they are" in space. In these images, the "good" and "working" children find themselves in a Micronesian village (here a Chuukese village) marked by the US flag.[73] Thus, among many messages communicated in this English literacy book was that good Micronesians work, and they do so in a US-controlled space.

As *Three Children* offered one example of how the civilian arm of US empire creatively spread messages normalizing the value of work across the broader Trust Territory region, military attempts to position Micronesians as valued through work also occurred locally on Kwajalein. One year after *Three Children* was published, a 1952 naval memorandum on employment protocol offered a report enumerating "native labor" rules and regulations on Kwajalein. These included work hours, dress code, and time-off policies, along with an extensive section on native employee physical requirements. In it, the commander noted that "careful examination will be made to determine whether the applicant is suitable for labor. Minor defects are not considered cause for rejection provided they do not greatly interfere with function and provided they will not be aggravated by work."[74] To clarify what would be considered minor or major defects, the commander's report described an exhaustive list of "native body parts" for inspection. These included eyes, ears, teeth, nose and throat, head and face, neck, spine, lungs, heart and blood vessels, abdomen, pelvis, the genito-urinary system, skin, the extremities, and the nervous system. The report paired each body part with information about accompanying conditions that constituted cause for employment rejection. A general list of disqualifying diseases and conditions followed the body part breakdown.[75] This scrutiny further attested to the dehumanization of those indigenous to the region, marking their bodies as functioning solely as cogs helping to turn the wheels of the US military machine.

This colonial project to recruit and control "good" and "healthy" Micronesian bodies also meant balancing the tension between Marshallese workers becoming acclimated enough to participate in a wage economy on Kwajalein but not *too* savvy so that they might undermine US colonial control over that economy. This concern surfaced in a 1952 memorandum focused on Marshallese domestic labor on Kwajalein. Marshallese domestics served Kwajalein's military during the 1940s and 1950s and throughout the island's transition to a missile base in the 1960s. Illustrating the postwar demand for domestic servants alongside an impetus to control wages, Commanding Officer M. E. Arnold of the navy issued a memorandum to military personnel clarifying rules about employment of domestics on Kwajalein. The 1952 memorandum stated that Arnold had become aware of military personnel encountering difficulties in hiring domestic servants. He said some had cited problems due to a lack of standardization in wages and working conditions. Arnold identified apparent "competition" among prospective employers in offering extra wages or inducements to prospective employees as potentially contributing to hiring challenges.[76] To address these concerns, Arnold issued directives on employing domestics that delineated expected wages, with a maximum monthly rate of $31 for a forty-hour workweek.[77] He said employers could offer a raise to those domestics working longer than six months, but no extra gifts in the form of cash should be given as an inducement to accept employment. He qualified that if an employer wanted to give something extra, lunches, leftover food items, and cast-off clothing were suitable options.[78] Arnold concluded his memorandum by asking for cooperation to ensure all Kwajalein residents could enjoy equal opportunity in employing domestic servants. Any continuation of lucrative gift inducements that could lure domestics and create an "artificial increase of the wage scale of Marshallese domestics to an unreasonable level" threatened to undermine this goal.[79]

In this instance, US colonial goals of retaining "good workers" in the Trust Territory, and locally on Kwajalein, butted up against the desire for controlling just *how good* these workers got at capitalism. Arnold's concern was that Marshallese domestics, clearly in high demand on Kwajalein, might exercise agency in leveraging their value for higher wages. This concern for curbing Marshallese capacity to use their labor power for their own benefit continued through the missile-testing era. By the 1970s Marshallese workers would be voicing concerns about wages, hiring, and promotion discrimination on Kwajalein, a topic taken up more closely in chapter 5.

CREATING A HOME FOR WORKERS, NOT FAMILIES, ON EBEYE

As military and Trust Territory administrators worked to discipline Marshallese labor toward serving the emerging missile-testing mission on Kwajalein in the 1960s, they came into increasing conflict with each other over who would be responsible for the collapsing housing and infrastructure on Ebeye erected to support these workers. The military's foundational outlook on native labor as "cheap and useful" continued to inform its approach to investments and planning for Ebeye during this contentious time. While the military persistently depended on its segregated workforce on Ebeye and the island's use as a depository for the increasing number of Marshallese throughout the atoll that it displaced for missile-testing purposes, its willingness to take any responsibility for conditions on Ebeye remained minimal.

The structural continuity of segregation between Kwajalein and Ebeye helped normalize the military's lack of accountability to those it displaced to enable missile testing and the service workers supporting its mission. Trust Territory representatives continuously expressed frustration at the resource-rich military, whose presence on Kwajalein spurred the conditions for Ebeye's crisis while only seldomly, minimally, and begrudgingly contributing any resources toward alleviating that crisis. Ultimately, the contradictory missions of the Trusteeship Agreement led these two arms of the same imperial body to point the finger of responsibility for Ebeye at each other throughout the 1960s and 1970s. All the while, Ebeye's colonized subjects continued to suffer the deadly repercussions of that inaction.[80]

Ebeye's population continued to increase throughout the 1960s and 1970s as a result of displacements, labor migrations, and family growth. Within the first year of the labor camp displacement of 559 to Ebeye in 1951, the island population had swelled to 1,200. By 1966, that number had more than doubled, reaching 4,500.[81] Ebeye's deadly poverty grew as the Trust Territory government failed to maintain housing and infrastructure in line with rapid population growth. As conditions on Ebeye worsened throughout the 1960s, tensions bubbled to the surface between military and Trust Territory government officials as they came together to address their respective responsibilities in the region. At a 1964 conference in Honolulu, Trust Territory officials convened with representatives from the army and the MIC and condemned the military for shirking its responsibilities in the region. One representative noted: "The Department of Defense must recognize its responsibility for properly supporting the Ebeye economy which is so closely tied to Missile Range activities on Kwajalein."[82] Challenging military frugality when it came to addressing Ebeye's dire situation, the representative concluded: "The defense activities have caused the problem. Therefore, the defense activities should solve the problem, with money limitations as a secondary consideration."[83]

Trust Territory representatives hurled criticism at the military within a context of extreme budgetary differences. These disparities found a poorly resourced Trust Territory government trying to address insurmountable infrastructure challenges on Ebeye. As the army and Trust Territory officials squabbled over accountability, Kwajalein's research program "swung into high gear" following the successful Nike Zeus missile interception in May 1963, with "$500 million a year . . . allocated for anti-ballistic missile research."[84] Despite what became a seemingly endless stream of funds flowing toward this cutting-edge defense technology and suburban quality of life facilities on Kwajalein over time, when it came to supporting mere sustainability on Ebeye, the military's wallet remained tightly gripped. By the mid-1960s, as Kwajalein's meandering walkways routed through cozy housing, swimming pools, and ballparks, Ebeye's housing largely comprised small houses "constructed from surplus materials[,]" some with walls made of crating materials and roofs made of sheet metal.[85] With dilapidated buildings evoking the specter of a shantytown residing three miles from Kwajalein's utopian suburban landscape—a dynamic journalists came to label "American Apartheid in the Pacific" by the 1970s—the military was continually called upon to contribute to improving conditions on Ebeye. Intermittently the army agreed to do so, reluctantly and sparingly.

The $7 million development project noted earlier in the chapter was the largest army investment on Ebeye, but it ultimately failed to spur long-term improvements, given an underestimation of population numbers and infrastructure needs. As detailed earlier, this project, spanning 1964 to 1966, fueled grievances related to its requisite eminent domain policy. Closer examination of how the army wanted this funding spent reveals the zero-sum-game mentality informing its support for Marshallese infrastructure. A 1965 meeting with representatives from the Trust Territory government, the Nike X Project, and the Honolulu Engineering Company brought to the fore debates over how army funds should be used.[86] Articulating a logic that Ebeye residents needed to forgo certain housing amenities to pay for others, Lt. Col. Durham suggested eliminating kitchen cabinets in homes, which cost $200 each for 280 units, to save the military approximately $56,000. These savings could then be applied to increasing electrical wiring capacity in the houses.[87] Likewise, the army would fund porches *or* kitchen cabinets for Ebeye homes, but not both.[88]

Such penny pinching when it came to Ebeye improvements, alongside massive investments in Kwajalein, represented a continuous military logic that moved seamlessly from the initial labor camp displacement in 1951 through the 1960s and 1970s. While the army continued to depend on

Marshallese labor to operate its mission on Kwajalein—a dependence that has persisted uninterrupted for six decades—any commitments to support sustainable conditions within which those workers were segregated to live continually reflected those fitting a population viewed as "cheap and useful." By the 1960s, the impact of military frugality when it came to Ebeye had already spurred deadly catastrophes. Diseases spread quickly on Ebeye, an island marked by water shortages, inadequate sewage treatment, and an overburdened and underresourced hospital. By 1963, district anthropologist Tobin's early warning about health risks proved tragically accurate as preventable diseases moved through Ebeye. These included a polio outbreak that left many paralyzed and deadly epidemics of gastroenteritis and influenza.[89]

The inadequacy of the army's development investment in realistically addressing the crisis on Ebeye was identified by Trust Territory officials, who delineated insufficient housing and sanitation and warned of the ongoing spread of preventable diseases as a result. A 1966 coauthored letter from the assistant commissioner of community services and acting assistant commissioner in administration to the Trust Territory high commissioner asserted that the army's plan could "only result in exceedingly substandard housing which will, in effect, exchange the current Pacific slum for a Pacific tenement."[90] In the end, the army's improvement project, which enacted disastrous eminent domain policies across Ebeye, led to the construction of seventy-seven additional residential units and new water and electricity systems and sewage facilities, the latter of which ultimately failed in part due to poor planning. The military planned housing and infrastructure improvements to accommodate a population of twenty-five hundred people, when the actual population by 1966 had reached forty-five hundred.[91]

Over the next twelve years, Ebeye's population grew to eight thousand. US attorney Mary M. Kearney, who had been working to help secure compensation for Kwajalein landowners at the time, offered an image of this density. She described it as comparable to placing the entire population of the United States into the state of Connecticut. In 1978, the US population was about 224 million people. Kearney added that Connecticut's resulting population "would be considerably less than that of Ebeye."[92] A brewing storm of public scrutiny, spurred by hundreds of investigative articles decrying the disparities between Kwajalein and Ebeye penned throughout the 1960s and 1970s, finally forced the military's hand to address the situation on Ebeye. Through an extensive fact-finding report, the army strategically disavowed comparisons made between Kwajalein's abundance and Ebeye's deprivation by framing Ebeye's living conditions in relation to the "outer islands," where Marshallese practiced sustainable agriculture and fishing and lived without running water and electricity. The 1977 report concluded that while Ebeye's schools and medical facilities were hardly up to par with American standards, "Ebeye facilities represent a significance in quality of life compared to the almost non-existent medical facilities and (comparatively) extremely limited school facilities on most other islands."[93] Such comparisons aimed to get the army off the hook for Ebeye while simultaneously, and perhaps unintentionally, highlighting the failure of the civilian arm of US empire—the Trust Territory government—to support greater development across the region.

The army's comparisons of Ebeye with the outer islands enabled a justification for its relative lack of investment when compared with Kwajalein. This approach positioned Ebeye as connected to the rest of Micronesia and Kwajalein as within the realm of the US base network, removing Kwajalein from any Marshallese territoriality or context. This effort to situate Kwajalein within a US national framework and Ebeye within a Micronesian one—to push against comparisons being made between the two islands by Marshallese and other critical onlookers—was in tension with approaches to development within the broader Trust Territory region. While the army was busy recreating an American suburban landscape on Kwajalein to recruit its elite US workforce to the island, Trust Territory administrators had been drawing on policies aimed at addressing other examples of segregated and racialized urban poverty in the United States. In addition to the use of eminent domain, these officials were employing remedies introduced by President Lyndon B. Johnson's War on Poverty. During the mid-1960s, coinciding with the findings of the Solomon Report, Micronesians became eligible for Johnson's Great Society programs. This led to Trust Territory inhabitants receiving federal program benefits, including food subsidies and employment training programs "mostly designed for urban America."[94] As historian David Hanlon noted, "Johnson's program for a Great Society sought to revitalize a declining nation and, in its extension to the Trust Territory of the Pacific Islands, offered Micronesians the status of an American minority group."[95]

Just as urban historians Thomas J. Sugrue, Robert O. Self, and Eric Avila have written on postwar histories of Detroit, Oakland, and Los Angeles, some iterations of suburban and urban relational development made their way to the US imperial Pacific.[96] While the army aimed to situate Kwajalein within an exceptional landscape of suburbia, the relational export and application of urban policies and programs to Ebeye likewise situated the island within a space of relative comparison. This proved an inconvenient consequence of colonial policies in this region and thus was disavowed in the army's understanding of the dynamic between the two islands. By the 1970s, Ebeye illustrated the most extreme case of population density throughout the Trust Territory (and the entire Pacific), and Trust Territory planning and investments were perpetually unable to keep pace with the infrastructural challenges generated by the Kwajalein missile program. The army's effort to position Kwajalein within a comparative framework to the United States, while distancing Ebeye from any US context despite this broader colonial development strategy situating the region through US domestic programs for addressing poverty, signaled another dimension to the tensions of US colonial control over the region.

Military representatives maintained the view that a dynamic of structural segregation and material disparity between the two islands was not historically connected, and that Marshallese should instead frame their lifestyle expectations in line with the rest of Micronesia. This military effort to control not only the labor sector working on Kwajalein but the relative expectations of those workers ultimately failed, as Marshallese increasingly voiced their own ideas about the homes and infrastructure they deserved as workers on Kwajalein and residents on Ebeye throughout the 1970s and 1980s.

Faced with this onslaught of criticism, the army remained consistent in disavowing any responsibility for the *hybrid* workforce it depended on for its mission. The 1977 fact-finding report explained that the "'quality-of-life' facilities on [Kwajalein] are those believed by the Army, and developed over some 12 years of experience, to be those appropriate for maintaining a high standard of performance and effectiveness from a small, concentrated, well-educated, affluent community."[97] Comparing Kwajalein's quality of life facilities with those on other bases, the army emphasized the importance of investing in an atmosphere that inspired and retained productivity from its American workforce. Whereas American workers required incentives for recruitment and to maintain productivity, the army knew Marshallese living on Ebeye would show up to work with or without such luxuries. The mobility of US workers and their families migrating to Kwajalein contrasted with that of Marshallese; the former came of their own free will and could leave anytime. As noted, many Marshallese arrived in Ebeye through displacements, while others came in hopes of finding a job on Kwajalein. Given the Trust Territory government's failure to adequately invest in other economic growth across the region, the army knew its service labor would remain consistent whether or not it invested in Ebeye. The army was the best game in town. This combination of wage labor on Kwajalein and lack of viable economic alternatives meant the army would have a steady supply of service workers regardless of how dire conditions became on Ebeye.

Further justifying military expenditures to support Americans on Kwajalein, the army's fact-finding report stated: "It must be remembered that Congress appropriates RDTE [Research Development Test and Evaluation] funds specifically for the operation and maintenance of the National Range at Kwajalein."[98] Disavowing responsibility for Ebeye, the report continued: "The monies must, by law, be spent for the purpose appropriated, and cannot be used for other purposes such as improvements on Ebeye or care for Marshallese."[99] Such statements erased the essential role of Marshallese labor in ensuring the successful "operation and maintenance" of the missile range and downplayed army reliance on Ebeye to house these workers and those it displaced. Just as in the continental United States, structures of segregation in the Marshall Islands worked in ways that enabled service and white collar labor to be interdependent while at the same time helping to obscure that mutual dependence.

Given the rare and begrudging occasions when the military *did* financially contribute to Ebeye, it is worth considering how such contributions were framed over time. The army historically identified these intermittent investments as charity versus obligation, as gifts rather than entitlements. According to the army, contributions to Ebeye constituted welfare to a needy neighbor rather than UN obligations, compensation for colonial displacements, or concern for the life-threatening conditions facing a significant segment of its workforce. In his 1968 correspondence to Principal Deputy Assistant Secretary of International Security Affairs R. Earle II, Colonel Donald B. Millar listed Kwajalein's annual support services to Ebeye, noting: "We have very close daily association with the Marshallese, which has developed mutual respect and admiration, appreciation of customs and tradition and possibly the best of all, a close bondage of personal friendship."[100] He continued, "Our help and assistance is offered not by direction or out of cold necessity, but through genuine interest, brotherhood and humanity."[101] Millar's summary of the support services provided to Marshallese by Kwajalein included "scheduled ferry boat service (Tarlang), twice daily, six days a week, between Kwajalein and Ebeye."[102] Identifying ferry service as among the army's "help and assistance" for Marshallese was curious because these workers, who comprised the base's *segregated* labor sector, could not perform their duties without transportation to the island. Marshallese workers did not earn enough to afford daily water-taxi fare. Millar's list also included Kwajalein community donations for Marshallese scholarships. Nine years later, the army's fact-finding report echoed Millar's tone of benevolence, applauding the Kwajalein Women's Club members for their volunteerism and annual fundraising for Ebeye. The military recommended the continuation of the club's charitable offerings, which included $30,000 in donations and the sale of inexpensive clothing.[103]

This historic and ongoing emphasis on a "good neighbor" frame reflected what historian Jana K. Lipman has likewise found regarding the naval base GTMO at Guantánamo in Cuba during the 1940s and 1950s. She identified "good neighborliness" as a slogan that was "injected with North American superiority and benevolence into [a] 'neighborly' rhetoric."[104] As in Cuba and the Marshall Islands, this trope of charity and benevolence has also been traced more broadly across the history of base expansion through what anthropologist Catherine Lutz has described as the myth of US bases as gift-giving "wealth generators" rooted in American sacrifice and "altruism."[105] In her collection on the bases of US empire, Lutz revealed the paradox of this myth of "giving" so often located at bases "taken" by the United States during wartime and kept thereafter.[106]

PROTECTING KWAJALEIN'S "FORBIDDEN FRUITS"

This concept of the "good neighbor" may have offered public relations opportunities for the army as it came under increasing scrutiny for the dire conditions on Ebeye, but the proximity suggested by the category of neighbor also posed risks. This perception came through in army justifications for limiting investment in Ebeye over the years. The army saw such investments as threatening its ability to protect Kwajalein from the presumably covetous nature of its proximate neighbor. Given this fear, the army argued in favor of keeping Ebeye in a state of crisis so as not to encourage further migrations, migrations that would bring even more Marshallese closer to Kwajalein. This concern came through in the 1977 fact-finding report, in an army recommendation for how the Trust Territory government should use twelve acres of land the coast guard had recently returned to Ebeye. The Trust Territory government had suggested constructing a new high school, given the lack of educational resources on the island to serve its resident population. The army responded that this would not be prudent due to the likelihood of the school further increasing Ebeye's population. The report stated, "The pressure of large numbers of teen-agers so close to Kwajalein and its resources and attractions *(mostly forbidden fruits)* could cause social problems."[107] By stressing the importance of keeping Ebeye in a state lacking appeal for new migrants, the army ignored the fact that the existing teen population had no public high school on Ebeye to attend. Ebeye's educational infrastructure could not accommodate its population, and the cost of sending kids away to school on other islands was prohibitive for most parents.

The army's recommendation further revealed how it viewed its Marshallese workers on Ebeye in contrast to its American workers on Kwajalein. American workers were members of families whose children deserved privileges like education; Marshallese workers were not. The army advised: "Any radical improvement in facilities or capabilities to improve quality of life must be considered carefully to insure that such improvements do not further increase the desirability of immigrating to Ebeye."[108] The report added, "A deliberate, *go-slow policy* should be followed with attempts to assess the long term social consequences of each considered measure prior to its being put into effect."[109]

The army's recommendations reflected the ongoing predicament facing these two arms of US empire in the region and their contradictory directives under the Trusteeship Agreement. How would the Trust Territory government and the army achieve the right balance between keeping conditions on Ebeye stable enough to support the military mission on Kwajalein while avoiding improving life *too* much and spurring further migrations that could seemingly threaten the tranquility of life on Kwajalein? How would the army protect Kwajalein, an island abundant with "forbidden fruits" blossoming from massive US investments to support US workers and their families? This conundrum struck at the heart of the military need for "cheap and useful" labor but not necessarily the dependents of those workers—or perhaps only when those dependents reached an age or capacity to become "cheap and useful" workers themselves. The army needed Marshallese living in the middle of the atoll to move out of the way to enable missile launches, but they did not need those displaced peoples to demand sustainable living conditions in their new homes on Ebeye.

The army's recommendations reflected anxiety over unsustainable population growth on Ebeye, a migration process military policies had initiated and quickly lost control over. Determined to avoid any challenge to its colonial presence in the region, the army opted to encourage keeping life intolerable enough to dissuade others from migrating to Ebeye. This approach dismissed the struggles facing those already living on Ebeye, many of whom could not return home given the army's designation of their homes as within its missile impact zone. It also reflected an ongoing logic that informed the divergent history of investments and planning on Kwajalein and Ebeye: two islands the military would consistently depend on to carry out its security mission in the region for more than six decades but an interdependency the military perpetually disavowed. Finally, it reflected the continuity of the foundational dehumanizing colonial logic discussed in chapter 1: that these islands were seen as valuable only for their role in supporting US security interests. The army's efforts to protect Kwajalein's "forbidden fruits" and contain such luxuries for the island's most elite US workers and their families informed a set of segregation and surveillance policies that further enshrined Kwajalein within the trappings of postwar US suburbia.

3 Domestic Containment in the Pacific

SEGREGATION AND SURVEILLANCE ON KWAJALEIN

> On Ebeye, which is only a couple of miles away from
> the multi-billion-dollar military complex on Kwajalein,
> Micronesians live among rats. On Kwajalein the
> U.S. warlords live like gods.
>
> —"A True Micronesian," March 19, 1968

> The dominant ethos of American suburbia has always
> idealized the present and celebrated the future at the
> expense of any critical reflection on the past.
>
> —Historian Matthew D. Lassiter

BORDERS OVER BRIDGES: SEGREGATING KWAJALEIN

During the 1960s, the US Army ran service between Kwajalein and Ebeye on the four-hundred-passenger *Tarlang* ferry, transporting hundreds of Marshallese workers daily between this segregated landscape. The *Tarlang* offered one way to reconcile the military's dependence on Marshallese workers—this service sector essential to Kwajalein's successful operation—with the simultaneous desire to keep Kwajalein exclusively for housing its US workforce and their dependents. Ferry service from Ebeye and the security checkpoint on Kwajalein has enabled strict surveillance over movement between Kwajalein and Ebeye for more than five decades, and as noted in chapter 2, has been one mechanism for helping to isolate

Kwajalein's "forbidden fruits" from those residing in the segregated confines of Ebeye.

While ferry service connecting the two island populations has become normalized over time, the military's decision to maintain a hybrid and segregated workforce, enabled through this transportation technology, was never a foregone conclusion. For decades, proposals for a causeway to bridge the three miles of lagoon separating the two islands have been repeatedly put forth by Marshallese leaders. The military has consistently shot down these proposals despite the opportunity for potential cost-saving benefits. The editor of the regional newspaper the *Marshall Islands Journal*, Giff Johnson remarked on the military's decision to avoid this transportation solution, one he argued could have saved them tens of millions of dollars on boats and gas over the decades.[1] He explained: "If you look at the decision over the years to not build a causeway, [this] tells you something about the psychology of the Army. They want; they've *always* wanted to be separate from Ebeye."[2]

The US military's decision to keep the two islands disconnected marked a divergence in colonial policy in the region. Under the Japanese colonial administration, a railroad had been constructed that ran across the reef at low tide between Kwajalein and Ebeye, and a power grid was shared, enabling Marshallese access to electricity and communications technology. Late Marshallese senator Tony de Brum and his friend and former Kwajalein resident Cris Lindborg reflected on their shared efforts to advocate for a bridge and greater integration between the two islands.[3] Lindborg said she believed the army seemed more concerned with protecting resources for Americans than with security, and she lamented how this desire for greater integration was "just our little dream," a prospect the military would never consider.[4]

As Lindborg observed, while the broader security of Kwajalein as a military base historically governed aspects of containment and surveillance policies on the island—as it would on all US bases—these concerns converged during the Cold War with an imperative to secure what Mark Gillem has called emerging "America Towns" across an expanding base empire.[5] The creation and containment of an "America Town" on Kwajalein meant the specificity of military base protocol overlapped with the maintenance of a segregation structure established to protect nuclear family life and consumption. Military policies governing Marshallese access to the island worked to hoard life-sustaining resources like water and food, as well as consumer resources that a typical middle-class family could expect in the continental suburban landscape of Cold War America. Containment policies were also designed to regulate sexual intimacy between Americans and Marshallese, as well as within the American family and bachelor communities residing on the island.

To protect American family life on Kwajalein, the army deployed two sets of segregation policies to monitor the movements of its Marshallese workforce and to manage relations among American workers. *Inter*island segregation—keeping American and Marshallese workers separate—built upon the naval policy to displace Micronesian laborers from Kwajalein to Ebeye Island in 1951, which marked Kwajalein as a space of exclusive US residency thereafter. *Intra*island segregation was achieved by separating resident bachelors from US families living on Kwajalein. The latter policy was linked to the relationship between housing and employment on Kwajalein, which historically paired class status with family privileges. This meant a largely White cohort of scientists and engineers arriving with professional training and higher pay received "accompanied" status and could bring their dependents to live in the island's suburban family housing area. Kwajalein's working-class cohort arrived with unaccompanied status and thus lived in separate bachelor dormitories.[6] At the peak of the island's labor demands during the 1960s and 1970s, this latter cohort included a significant portion of workers of color laboring in construction and other manual labor. Military surveillance thus monitored two primary groups of workers on Kwajalein: the more racially diverse, US working-class residential population, and the segregated, colonized, Marshallese workforce commuting from Ebeye. The military treated both as potential threats to the security of the wholesome nuclear family, suburban lifestyle it promoted to lure its most elite workforce to move to Kwajalein.

Centering on the historic intersections of the postwar military-industrial colonial complex and Cold War suburbanization, this chapter closely examines US policies supporting a mission for Cold War domestic containment on two levels: a broader security quest aimed at protecting the national home thousands of miles away and efforts to secure a replica of that home locally on Kwajalein. In doing so, it further illuminates the portrait of how Kwajalein became restaged as an American home in the Marshall Islands. Building on the first two chapters, this chapter explores how surveillance and segregation worked to enfold Kwajalein within the framework of an American home, reinforcing a colonial sense of entitlement through mapping the veil of suburban innocence onto Marshallese lands.

A HOME FOR NUCLEAR FAMILIES AND NUCLEAR WEAPONS IN THE MARSHALL ISLANDS

During thirteen days in October 1962, as President Kennedy and Soviet premier Khrushchev hurtled toward a nuclear high noon, US engineers on Kwajalein remained closely tuned into the missile crisis informed by their research. Three months earlier, Kwajalein had launched its first successful missile interception. Kwajalein's missile scientists and engineers were the prized workers whose recruitments and retention mobilized the military to transform this Marshallese island into the most inviting suburban family setting possible. The military transformation of this Marshallese island into a segregated suburban missile installation made Kwajalein a key site for two Cold War global and domestic iterations of the US security state: the rise of the military-industrial colonial complex and suburbanization. At Kwajalein, the history of both postwar markers of US suburban empire surfaces across the same nine hundred acres.

The military planned Kwajalein's suburban landscape as a labor recruitment tool. Unlike the Marshallese service sector segregated to Ebeye— workers the military always depended upon but also took for granted as readily available—luring US engineers and scientists to the Central Pacific required a different approach. The military's challenge to entice this elite workforce was commented on in a Bell Laboratories retrospective: "It was 1960. . . . John F. Kennedy began sparring with Richard Nixon for the Presidency. And in Morris County, New Jersey, Bell Labs husbands began coming home to Bell Labs wives with the second biggest proposal of their lives: 'How would you like to go to Kwajalein?'"[7] To convince US scientists, engineers, and their families that relocating to the Marshall Islands would cause little disruption to their familiar suburban lifestyle, the military planned a tropical suburbia on Kwajalein replete with shopping, a K–12 school, churches, movie theaters, swimming pools, ballparks, and palm-tree-lined row housing.[8]

Welcome manuals introducing US workers to Kwajalein showcased an array of residential, recreational, and consumer amenities, reassuring these families they would not have to sacrifice the American dream when leaving their homes in the United States; they could find that dream restaged in the Marshall Islands. Americans on Kwajalein need not worry about grooming setbacks, as they could visit the neighborhood beauty parlor or barber shop. Likewise, they could keep up with the latest fashions by shopping at the island Macy's, and find all their favorite foodstuffs at Surfway. Avid readers could enjoy a new library stocked with over ten thousand books. The welcome guides even detailed how island dining halls and social clubs hosted special theme nights at which personnel could dine on hometown favorites like prime rib.[9]

The annual Kwajalein Karnival illustrated the degree of thoughtful planning and investment that went into exporting small-town American life to the middle of the Pacific to familiarize this Marshallese island for elite families. The Karnival, which began in 1950 to serve military personnel and their dependents and raise money for a US Navy relief fund, included music, track and field and swimming events, "train" rides for children, a dunk tank, and floats.[10] The annual event became a huge attraction during the missile-testing era. It was held around Memorial Day each year and planned for many months in advance. By the 1960s and 1970s it had culminated in a full-scale fairground that included a wide array of games and attractions, ranging from bingo to "dunk the mermaid"; food stalls selling corn dogs, fish and chips, and cotton candy; and even a number of rides like a carousel and a small Ferris wheel.[11] The annual Karnival was also one of the rare occasions when Marshallese were invited onto the island to share the event.

This expansive array of small-town suburban family recreational and consumer amenities converged with the natural beauty of a tropical landscape that left individuals and families with fond memories over the years of biking down palm-tree-lined streets and ambling from their row housing to "Emon beach" for refreshing dips. "Emon" is a Marshallese word meaning "it is good." And it *was* good for these US families on Kwajalein,

Figure 7. Kwajalein Karnival, 1972. Photo by Terrance Elliot, Kentron. Courtesy of Bill Remick.

who were living a subsidized lifestyle in this tropical small-town suburban setting. In a 1980 directive to incoming personnel, Army colonel Peter F. Witteried reflected on the success of decades of military investments to create a home away from home for the nation's premiere scientists and engineers and their dependents. He wrote: "The unique beauty of this isolated atoll is everywhere evident [making] the location ideal for accomplishment of the technological mission also [contributing] to a *storybook* setting for the Kwajalein community."[12]

As a site of Cold War military expansion and suburbanization, Kwajalein's heavily funded landscape marked the base as a key military investment, central to buttressing the postwar US security state. While chapter 2 traced the limited military investments and planning for Marshallese workers on Ebeye, this chapter compares how this contrasted with the funding that went into producing this small-town suburban utopia at

Kwajalein. The seeds for this storybook setting were planted long before scientists and engineers arrived with their families, with early construction for US military personnel occurring in the wake of wartime devastation. As noted in chapter 1, Kwajalein was among the mostly heavily bombed targets in the Pacific during World War II. With the island leveled in 1944, postwar reconstruction involved clearing debris and ordinance to build early infrastructure like hospitals, barracks, and storage and garrison units. By the 1950s, construction expanded to support a surge in base activity on Kwajalein due to the island's position along supply routes to Korea and support for the navy's nuclear testing campaign in the Northern Marshalls. During this period, military construction included family residential units, bachelors' quarters, swimming pools, tennis courts, the air terminal, and movie theaters.[13]

Another construction boom followed the conclusion of the nuclear campaign, when the navy designated Kwajalein the site for testing ICBMs. Over the next four decades, Kwajalein's landscape was transformed into a multi-billion-dollar missile complex alongside an expansive, tropical suburban residential and recreational playground for US workers and their families. By 1964, one military official commented upon the extent of Kwajalein's transformation: "From the scarred battleground of 1944, Kwajalein [became] a clean, modern, attractive, self-contained community closely resembling most small modern American cities."[14]

In these years of transformation, the number of US residential personnel waxed and waned, reaching a peak of about four to five thousand during the late 1960s, coinciding with the peak of construction on the island.[15] During this period, workers poured in from the continental United States and Hawai'i to contribute to the construction and shipping demands of this new island home. These unaccompanied laborers lived and worked on the island in close proximity to the engineers and scientists laboring in missile research and a growing cadre of other skilled laborers employed in positions to support this growing small-town community that included teachers, nurses, and doctors. While scientists and engineers did not constitute the largest number of personnel on the island during these construction peaks in the 1960s, the military's investments and planning reflected the greatest attention directed at the needs of this highly coveted community of elite workers.

Lifestyle incentives on Kwajalein paired with significant financial incentives. In addition to salary bonuses, military subsidies afforded many US workers the opportunity to save a sizeable portion of their income. Because Kwajalein prohibited private vehicles and housing remained subsidized, employees avoided spending money on these typically large investments in contrast to their stateside counterparts. According to a finance column in the Kentron employee newsletter in 1975, employees working for eighteen months or longer on Kwajalein could expect to save nearly 50 percent of their gross earnings. This compared with a US national average at the time of about 8 to 10 percent after taxes. This telephone and communications contractor explained how that calculation even took into account a two- to four-week stateside or overseas vacation among its Kwajalein personnel.[16] Oral history interviews with current and former employees confirmed that these financial incentives historically and continually constituted the primary lure for US workers. A conversation with one longtime Kwajalein resident in May 2010, who wished to remain anonymous, explained that the potential to pay off debt and accumulate substantial savings remains an important motivation. Other former residents commented on how Americans working on Kwajalein over the years seemed able to save enough money through avoiding housing costs on Kwajalein to invest in properties elsewhere.[17]

Today, in addition to multiple swimming pools and movie theaters, ballparks, shopping centers, and the golf course, the island is home to a bowling alley, a youth center, a skate park, and racquetball and tennis courts, among various other quality of life facilities. Paired with a range of financial incentives including rent-free living and tax-free shopping, the military has been able to present an alluring package to help bring thousands of US workers to temporarily settle on Kwajalein for nearly six decades. For many self-identified "Kwajers" the experience of residency on the island was so impressionable, they have longed for their island home upon departure. Many fondly recall its utopian landscape through the consumption of popular memorabilia iconizing this time and place in their lives as "Almost Heaven."

Not only did opportunities for social mobility await the Americans migrating to work locally on Kwajalein; the material benefits of missile research on the island also lined the pockets of contractors living in the

United States. In this respect, one can see how Kwajalein's "almost heavenly" delights profited many US workers during the Cold War. One can imagine how the suburban lifestyle created on Kwajalein also helped to subsidize a comparable lifestyle stateside for executives at private corporations like Lockheed Martin, Raytheon, and Bell Laboratories. Early contracts to support building the island's elaborate landscape of missile facilities alongside small-town suburban infrastructure were lucrative, as were contracts catering to American shoppers on the island.[18]

These Cold War consumer needs were attended to, in part, by the island's Macy's. This Kwajalein fixture, first named during the Korean War, grew during the missile era to stock, by the late 1960s, "imports of Hong Kong furniture, brassware from India, and rare pieces of Jade and Ivory from other faraway places."[19] According to former resident Eugene Sims, who traced the history of the store in his memoir, *Kwajalein Remembered*, the franchise carried a solid inventory of "children's clothing, toys, small furniture appliances, and general cookware by the 1980s," and by 1986 the store handled over forty-two hundred line items across about forty-five departments. He boasted that by this period, "The store grossed some 4 million dollars annually and employed a staff of about 37 people."[20]

From Macy's profits to those of a range of logistical and engineering contractors on Kwajalein, this suburban missile installation erected atop Marshallese land came to constitute one strand within the broader web of the expanding US military-industrial colonial complex during the Cold War. This was a story of imperial suburbia converging with the postwar military industrial complex that featured many of the same prominent figures. The material benefits of Kwajalein's missile research expanded outward from individual salaries and savings for those employed on the island locally—comprising thousands of US workers moving through the rotating door of contract labor on the island over time—to financial benefits reaching military, engineering, and logistical contractors. The island enriched personnel connected to this range of contractors over the decades, including the research and development engineering firms Raytheon, Lockheed Martin, MIT's Lincoln Laboratories, and Bell Laboratories, among others. As nuclear testing in the Northern Marshall Islands buttressed the salaries and research profiles of scientists from Brookhaven National Laboratory in New York through Argonne National Laboratory

Figure 8. Macy's department store on Kwajalein Island, ca. 1969–1975 (US Army). Courtesy of Bill Remick.

in Chicago and others connected to the AEC—forging lucrative partnerships between university and industry research to fuel the military industrial complex—the missile-testing era continued this trajectory. As careers were built from the 1950s on for US scientists studying the effects of radiation on Marshallese lands and bodies, Kwajalein's missile-testing program likewise enriched the pockets of an untold number of those employed by military, government, private, and university institutions in the name of US national security and global peace.

The market for the weaponry researched and developed on Kwajalein grew rapidly through the late Cold War. By 1982 missile research development, production, and deployment saw military sales for missile systems and parts amount to $5.2 billion.[21] With continued military investments in Kwajalein under the Reagan administration, by June 1989, "The United

States had one half billion dollars of real property investment alone in Kwajalein Atoll. Replacement cost of the facilities [by that point, was] estimated to be about $2 billion."[22] As the installation transitioned seamlessly following the Cold War's conclusion toward ongoing missile and space research, the army reported Kwajalein's value reaching $4 billion by 1994.[23]

Kwajalein constituted a key location signaling the expansion of the US military-industrial complex during the Cold War, one that enhances our understanding of the colonial dimensions to Eisenhower's framework. US control over this region, its power to use Marshallese land to produce military technologies, not only enriched the individual pockets and careers of those connected to this research, but also put the United States on a military, political, and economic footing that greased the wheels toward its ascendance as the sole military superpower by the end of the Cold War.

BOMBS IN THE BURBS: SECURITY AND INSECURITY ON KWAJALEIN

The construction of Kwajalein as a suburban nuclear family refuge within eyeshot of a missile launch pad and radar technologies primed and readied for nuclear war marked the landscape with the dualities of Cold War security and insecurity. This convergence echoed spatial and cultural tensions traced by Cold War historians emerging across the postwar continental landscape. Historian Kate Brown has chronicled this contrasting experience of small-town suburban security in Richland, Washington, where plutonium engineers worked to unearth and process materials for nuclear war. They did so within an atomic city fondly recalled for its safe, secure, and segregated landscape: a "model" community where one could leave their door unlocked at night.[24] This sense of suburban security amid profound insecurity, marked by the work these Cold War scientists and engineers were carrying out, also infused Kwajalein's landscape. This duality of Cold War security and insecurity showed up as well in historian Elaine Tyler May's research on the retreat to the refuge of suburban family life as one American response to Cold War insecurities: "To alleviate these fears, Americans turned to the family as a bastion of safety in an insecure world, while experts, leaders and politicians promoted codes of conduct and enacted public policies that would bolster the American home. Like their leaders, most Americans agreed that family stability appeared to be the best bulwark against the dangers of the Cold War."[25] This pattern May found marking continental suburbia also traveled to Kwajalein and in doing so constituted defining features of US suburban empire during the Cold War. On Kwajalein, the humdrum of everyday family recreational and consumer life reinforced the façade of suburban security, diverting attention from the insecurities embedded in the installation's Cold War mission. As ICBMs traveled five thousand miles across the Pacific from California's coast to splash down in Kwajalein's lagoon, a mission perpetually linked to the prospect of mutually assured destruction, Kwajalein's workers and families carried on with softball practice, Cub Scout meetings, and outdoor movie screenings at the Rich. Just as continental suburbia offered a myth of security—a refuge from threats posed by the Soviet Union and nearby urban uprisings challenging racial inequality—Kwajalein's segregated suburban setting offered comparable comforts.

Massive military investments over time dotted Kwajalein's landscape with small-town suburban amenities alongside the most cutting-edge missile technologies. Following Kwajalein's first successful missile interception in July 1962, the Nike Zeus project, the island's technology expanded as the Department of Defense quickly decided the Nike Zeus would serve to inform the construction of a more sophisticated ABM system called Nike X.[26] Accompanying the shift in technology development, the base transitioned from naval to army administration in 1964.[27] Kwajalein's missile facilities thereafter grew to include more advanced radar and satellites capable of tracking and targeting ICBMs launched from within and outside the atmosphere. These facilities layered the island with a fantastical, futuristic landscape, all within eyeshot of small-town suburban structures.

How Kwajalein's aura straddled Cold War utopian/dystopian symbols—the portrait of nuclear family security alongside nuclear apocalyptic insecurity—appeared poignantly in a 1977 article in a regional periodical. In his *American Pacific* story, "New Heights Attained over Kwajalein," journalist Harry Hargett vividly captured this paradox. Hargett detailed a recent "rocket launch" on Kwajalein, describing how as the technicians launched their weapons, their faces turned toward the sky to follow the ascending rockets. He wrote: "From the determined look on the faces of these dedicated young men, America need never fear of being overtaken in the arms race with other nations. 'I hope this project will be a success!' quipped one of the technicians. 'We worked night and day on this. Even our parents helped.'"[28] At this point in the story, Hargett unveiled the background of the *young boys* involved in this "model rocket derby," their Cub Scout affiliations, and their resulting scores. Positioning the boys as America's future hope in the arms race through their emergent rocket skills, Hargett likely intended the article to be read as satire. But the meta nature of his piece could also be read as prescient given the Cold War context and the reality of the boys' lives on Kwajalein. The production and reproduction of weapons development technicians, as imagined through this article, helped normalize and domesticate US military imperial expansion in the postwar era by framing it as a family affair. The story offered a sanitized version of the arms race through the humorous and innocuous frame of a small-town Cub Scouts' competition: the very emblem of innocence and vulnerability infusing U.S. nuclear family life.

The duality of suburban security amid Cold War insecurity also infused the language of military and civilian contractor manuals and on-site tours guiding incoming personnel to Kwajalein. Instructing new residents on how to navigate the hybrid suburban-military setting, manuals described security-fencing-surrounded radar transmitters and special tunnels built for secure movement through the facilities.[29] As historic missile tests unfolded in real time on Kwajalein, personnel were reminded of the centrality of their work to the broader Cold War mission. Two years before the Cuban missile crisis, a tour of the Nike Zeus facilities stated: "Whether or not we have our defense ready in time will depend to a significant extent on the quality and timeliness of the construction, installation and testing done here at Kwajalein."[30] The tour continued, "It is not a one-man job; all people on the island are needed to support in some way the big task of making Zeus do the job that is expected."[31] The tour detailed the Zeus missile capability to intercept incoming missiles traveling at fifteen thousand miles per hour while warning of the all-encompassing threat of attack. This could come from any side of the planet, from offshore submarines, earth satellites, or lunar bases.[32] Theirs was a mission marked by apocalyptic risks: "In this game, time is precious, precision is essential. . . .

[T]he threat seems insurmountable." To counter this threat, "all people on the island are needed."[33]

The increased insecurity experienced by all residing in Kwajalein Atoll who lived within eyeshot of ongoing missile touchdowns created exceptional professional opportunities for Kwajalein's scientists and engineers, an unprecedented degree of intimacy with their work. These US scientists and engineers constituted an elite cohort given the opportunity to participate in missile research in a way that few of their counterparts could in the United States. They had the chance to witness and survive the deployment and interception of missiles in close proximity. As noted in a Bell Laboratories retrospective report commemorating Kwajalein's employees, "by any conceivable standard, the Kwajalein experience was an extraordinary one."[34] The report noted that "in a defense program broadly concerned with what is referred to as the 'unthinkable,' many people worked exclusively with hypothesis and prediction--except at Kwajalein ... [where] the countdowns were real, the engagements were live, and the results—far from being theoretical—were concrete and clear."[35] The opportunities that came with participation in such "concrete" operations likely coincided with unimaginable pressure on those operating the missile facilities, many of whose families resided within a stone's throw of any missile-testing errors.

That US personnel and their families migrating to Kwajalein did so at great risk was apparent in the island's safety instructions. One visitor welcome guide indicated that during certain "technical operations on the island" all individuals, except authorized personnel, must "take cover."[36] Other operations required "lights out."[37] The manuals encouraged those visiting or living on Kwajalein to consult the island's daily newspaper to keep informed of all designated safe areas and rules to be followed during these various operations.[38] Such warnings revealed the porous nature of the façade of security suggested by the island's suburban family refuge. In reality, those choosing to raise families on this key Cold War missile installation were in effect sitting ducks. They settled into an environment only as safe and secure as the accuracy of those operating the missile range on Kwajalein and at Vandenberg Air Force Base in California. The military chose Kwajalein to be the target of missile launches in part because the region was identified as having a small population. This avoided the problem of launching ICBMs over large population centers in the United States.

The transformation of Kwajalein into a key Cold War missile installation to buttress national security thus created a new site of insecurity in the Marshall Islands, as Kwajalein Atoll now became vulnerable to testing errors and a potential target of foreign attack. The atoll's newly insecure status posed threats not only for Americans living on Kwajalein Island and Marshallese commuting to work there, but also for thousands of Marshallese living within the atoll. While Marshallese living three miles away on Ebeye did not receive the same security warnings given to US personnel and families on Kwajalein, some expressed awareness of their vulnerability residing in such close proximity to missile testing. In Adam Jonas Horowitz's 1991 documentary film *Home on the Range*, Ebeye resident Que Keju shared his fear of "knowing that a warhead could destroy a sizeable area, just one of them, and having to think about 12 or 13 all at the same time dropping on Kwajalein Atoll. I mean that's pretty berserk. I mean it's outrageous."[39] Fellow Ebeye resident and cousin Harold Keju echoed Que's concerns. He stated with nervous laughter, "When I see those things, I really scared . . . that's gonna be the end of the world."[40] As discussed in chapter 1, the Kejus' sentiments underscored the experience in the Marshall Islands of an "unending war." Their experiences signaled the psychological impact of having one's homeland selected to be a key location in the ongoing project of US military preparedness. The internalization of this anxiety is one by-product for Marshallese whose lands have been used to buttress the US security state, an impact that endures today.

These colonial transformations in the Pacific that created new risks for Marshallese echoed similar US military acquisitions nearly a century earlier in Hawai'i as Native Hawaiians saw Pearl Lagoon transformed into a site of US military strategic interest during the late nineteenth century. Less than four decades after the illegal overthrow of the Hawaiian kingdom, that lagoon became ground zero for World War II on December 7, 1941, a "date which would live in infamy" for Americans. President Roosevelt's iconic words occluded the meaning of this sacred Hawaiian space under a narrative of a Japanese sneak attack against the United States, further obscuring the settler colonial nature of US control over Hawai'i. This settler presence placed not only US service members residing at Pearl

Harbor at risk for such attacks, but also Native Hawaiians dispossessed of their lands, whose colonial condition now positioned them in proximity to these vulnerable wartime attacks on their homelands.

These specific vulnerabilities accompanying US empire in the Pacific, mapped onto Kwajalein Atoll through weapons testing, unearthed shared risks between Americans and Marshallese alongside significant divergences in the range of insecurities introduced by military policies and practices in the region. While Kwajalein housed cutting-edge military technology alongside an array of family, recreational, and consumer amenities, as chapter 2 detailed, Ebeye's landscape was marked by a scarcity of life-sustaining resources. The distance mapping the security of daily life between the two islands was powerfully illustrated in comparative technological feats and failures marking each. One remarkable achievement applauded on Kwajalein was described in the 1964 Nike X Project pamphlet: "The ZAR and the Battery areas have separate power plants, which together could provide enough power for a town of 22,000 people."[41]

We've already seen that while Ebeye and Kwajalein shared a power grid under the Japanese Empire, with the transition to US empire, power plants constructed on Kwajalein remained isolated from Ebeye.[42] Thus, while Kwajalein's engineering feats reached the capacity to power a town of twenty-two thousand residents, Marshallese living three miles away on Ebeye faced the insecurities of frequent power outages impacting such life-sustaining resources as hospital infrastructure and refrigeration of fresh foods, all of which have historically shaped daily life, with a level of precarity that continues today.

This power to have power, and the insecurities that accompany a lack of such power, was apparent in President Eisenhower's cautionary on the military-industrial complex in 1961. As anthropologist David Vine noted, eight years before Eisenhower's famous warning in his farewell speech, he offered a comparative analysis with domestic spending and argued: "Every gun that is made, every warship launched, every rocket fired, signifies in the final sense a theft from those who hunger and are not fed . . . the cost of one heavy bomber is this: A modern brick school in more than 30 cities. It is *two electric power plants, each serving a town of 60,000 population.*"[43] Eisenhower warned of the military-industrial complex and how military spending took from American domestic life to fuel this machine.

But in the context of Kwajalein and Ebeye, this comparison not only calls into question the relative costs of global security sought through military buildup and the impacts on domestic infrastructure; it also brings into view the costs of denying life-sustaining investments for colonized populations whose lands and labor enabled the military buildup. It expands our lens to see a military-industrial colonial complex.

These differential investments on Kwajalein and Ebeye informed the varying degrees of security felt by US and Marshallese residents. Kwajalein's landscape straddled a dual atmosphere of suburban security and Cold War insecurity, a small-town refuge within eyeshot of missile radar, satellites, and missile launch pads. Both US residents on Kwajalein and Marshallese on Ebeye had front-row seats to ICBMs arriving from California to penetrate Kwajalein's lagoon. Such intermittent "light shows" reminded all watching of the vulnerability of each island positioned in the line of fire. But Ebeye's landscape also included additional life-threatening risks posed by unprecedented density and overstressed infrastructure that emerged under US colonial administration. As Kwajalein's landscape featured ballparks, swimming pools, and movie theaters, Ebeye was mapped by dilapidated buildings and crumbling infrastructure. In addition to sharing with US residents on Kwajalein the threat of mutually assured destruction, Marshallese on Ebeye faced daily insecurities posed not only by frequent power outages, but also by water shortages and inadequate sewage treatment that spawned deadly epidemic outbreaks.

These disparities in colonial investments and disinvestment were disavowed under the broader frame of the US security imperative, which obscured the historic and perpetual costs of increasing insecurity borne by Marshallese to further that end. That enormous price paid by Marshallese for the US Cold War mission was marked and challenged in a 1968 letter to the UN Trusteeship Council. The anonymous author, presumably Marshallese given letter details, signed as "A TRUE MICRONESIAN" and protested the use of Kwajalein to test missiles. The author explained that the United States had signed the Trusteeship Agreement twenty-one years earlier, committing to help the people, but had done little to date. The letter stated: "Billions of dollars have been spent in the Trust Territory for military purposes, yet a few million dollars have been spent by the United States toward the fulfillment of the agreement."[44] The author continued,

"On Ebeye, which is only a couple of miles away from the multi-billion-dollar military complex on Kwajalein, Micronesians live among rats. On Kwajalein the U.S. warlords live like gods."[45]

Further pointing to the insecurities created by the US military mission in the region, this "True Micronesian" called into question the Trusteeship Agreement's support of the idea that US security meant global security. The author demanded that the United Nations urge the United States to use "at least some of that billions of dollars that is being used for military armament to improve my islands, before it all goes for military equipment which someday might wipe out you and me and the rest of mankind from this earth."[46] As this author highlighted, not only was the US quest for security illusive—a goal aimed at the capacity to destroy humankind threatened everyone, including Americans—but the immediate price of pursuing that goal was being paid by Marshallese. The "True Micronesian's" letter revealed how military efforts to culturally construct and contain an American home on Kwajalein as something outside a context of empire were always tenuous, perpetually in need of defense. As far as the army was concerned, so were the physical boundaries separating Kwajalein and Ebeye. As the gulf of abundance and scarcity marked the two islands with security and insecurity, the army created increasingly punitive policies to protect Kwajalein's resources for its US residential population. Over time, this practice of policing the psychic and physical borders of Kwajalein through segregation and surveillance increasingly criminalized the military's commuting, Marshallese service sector.

FROM DOMESTIC CONTAINMENT
TO CONTAINING DOMESTICS

In 1961, Neilat Zackhrias moved with her family from her home island of Ailinglaplap to Ebeye. Over time she began working as a domestic on Kwajalein. After more than four decades of living on Ebeye and intermittently working on Kwajalein, she reflected on the starkest differences she noticed between the two islands. She shared these impressions with me in her home on Ebeye in 2010. According to eighty-six-year old Zackhrias, what most distinguished life on Kwajalein was that it was "very strict."

She explained that access to the island required permission and identification cards. When asked how many times she had been on the island after performing her work, she laughed at the presumably ridiculous nature of the question and replied: "no times." When work finished she went home, "didn't stay."[47] Zackhrias's words echoed other Marshallese women who in interviews had also cited the island's security structure as a defining feature that set Kwajalein apart from other Marshallese islands. Eighty-one-year-old Gertruth Clarence saw life as much more difficult on Kwajalein than on her birth island of Jaluit. She explained that on Jaluit she could do "whatever she wants, she doesn't need things like security clearance to go places."[48] Eighty-three-year-old Kenye Kobar had worked as a domestic and in laundry service on Kwajalein for several years and identified the biggest difference between Kwajalein and Ebeye as the "security clearance . . . [needed] to get onto Kwajalein."[49]

These reflections signal the historic structure of segregation that hardened over time as Kwajalein's and Ebeye's built environments diverged under US colonial control. They echo what historian Jana K. Lipman has traced from domestic workers at GTMO, who likewise observed constricted mobility on the base. As one domestic worker, Maria Boothe, recalled, during the 1950s at GTMO, "You could walk only in certain zones, you couldn't go here, you couldn't go there, and you couldn't buy things in the stores. . . . It was like another country."[50] For Marshallese domestic workers, the physical transformation of Kwajalein into a segregated suburban missile range during the 1960s was accompanied by a disciplinary shift as well. Under the watchful eye of the military, Kwajalein became a setting marked by strict security: a space of Cold War domestic (servant) containment. As the military's segregation policies increasingly excluded its colonial service sector from access to resources on Kwajalein, mirroring the Jim Crow landscape that fueled the civil rights movement in the United States, Marshallese and some American allies challenged what they viewed as racial discrimination on this exported suburban replica.

Comprising Kwajalein's lowest paid employees, commuting Marshallese laborers historically worked in landscaping, facility maintenance, sanitation, food services, and other wage labor. While many Marshallese men worked beautifying the outer edges of Kwajalein's homes through landscaping, Marshallese women supported American family life from the interior as domestic servants.[51] The military's residential exclusions that positioned domestics and other Marshallese workers as commuters were buttressed by strict guidelines regulating daily curfews for this colonized labor force. US scientists and engineers both worked and lived within the island's suburban family setting, while Marshallese arrived daily from Ebeye. If Marshallese did not vacate Kwajalein by a certain time each day, they faced disciplinary consequences. A 1961 Bell Laboratories guide for incoming Kwajalein employees informed American workers about the availability of "Marshallese women" for "domestic help for $1.50 to $1.80 per day, depending upon the size of the family."[52] The manual noted: "They are transported to Kwajalein in the morning and returned to *their* island (Ebeye) at the end of the day."[53] The Bell guide added that maids would be hired on a first-come, first-served basis as there were not enough women to provide a "domestic servant" for every family.[54]

The Transport Company of Texas's welcome guide offered specifics on curfew policies: "Some of the Marshallese women on Ebeye Island come to Kwajalein to help with the house work and care for children."[55] The guide instructed: "These women are brought over from Ebeye by boat and arrive about 7:30 a.m. They are returned to Ebeye at 4:45 p.m."[56] Emphasizing the restriction against Marshallese residing on Kwajalein past work hours, the guide stated: "None are allowed to remain overnight or into the evening."[57] The guide also noted that "maids are also given physical examinations at the hospital before being employed."[58]

These physical examinations signified a common colonial predicament centered on the desire to employ colonial subjects in the most intimate settler spaces while also addressing fears of potential diseases contaminating this realm of intimacy.[59] Combined with the army curfew policies, such regulations collectively signified the precarity of the military's dependency on a labor force it devalued and distrusted but could not operate its missile-testing mission without. The military met this challenge of how to navigate these labor dependencies through increasingly punitive policies aimed to protect American nuclear family life from the perceived risks that could come with intermingling between these workforces. These rules and regulations aimed to monitor and control any unregulated movement on the island. In the 1960s, Kwajalein became a site of increasing surveillance, an island where such movement would be criminalized and punished, a structure that remains in place today.[60]

During the 1960s, segregation and surveillance policies contributed to military efforts to remake Kwajalein into a space of American domesticity, positioning American families as at home in the Marshall Islands and Marshallese as the foreigners. This portrait was buttressed by a built environment signaling that the solution to Cold War insecurities posed by looming threats of mutually assured destruction could be found in the maintenance of order through contained suburban domesticity and postwar consumer access.[61] This postwar culture of mass consumption overlapped with what historian Matthew D. Lassiter identified as a bipartisan politics that included values centered on "taxpayer rights" and "family residential security." [62] The combination buttressed a Cold War political identity of "middle-class historic innocence" that shaped suburban landscapes in the United States and traveled to their colonial replica on Kwajalein.[63] This convergence of postwar suburban politics rooted in nuclear family security and consumerism took on foreign policy implications when showcased before the world by Vice President Nixon in his historic 1959 "kitchen debate" with Soviet premier Khrushchev at the world exposition in Moscow. On Kwajalein, the military drew upon this emerging Cold War propaganda equating American freedom with consumption in welcome manuals sent to incoming civilian personnel. Lined with images of modern kitchens, cozy family living rooms, and stores like Surfway and Macy's that stocked a variety of foodstuffs, clothing, and other items, these manuals aimed to reassure Americans that their decision to relocate to the middle of the Pacific would not mean sacrificing their freedom to consume. As the military reminded US workers and family members that they could enjoy the American dream thousands of miles from home through access to American consumer life, it enacted increasingly restrictive and punitive policies to ensure this access was an exclusive privilege of Kwajalein residents.

The first set of military policies aimed at denying Marshallese access to consumer resources on Kwajalein was issued in January 1968. The army's new rules prohibited "Micronesians" from shopping at the island's stores and freely patronizing other island facilities. In an open letter to American residents in the Kwajalein newspaper, Colonel Frank C. Healy

Figure 9. Kwajalein kitchen, from Kwajalein Test Site, US Army Material Command
Welcome Guide, 1968.

explained that the new policies aimed to prevent unfair competition with
Trust Territory merchants on Ebeye, who could not offer tax-free items
like Kwajalein's stores. He also detailed how Micronesians' shopping on
Kwajalein interfered with Ebeye businesses by reducing sales tax revenue
on the island while also making stock maintenance extremely difficult
on Kwajalein. Healy noted that Kwajalein's store managers struggled to
adapt to "the less predictable desires of some 4,000 Micronesians residing on Ebeye," causing American shoppers to suffer.[64] The competition
Healy spoke of had emerged because US taxpayer subsidies supported the
shipping of fresh produce and higher quality products to Kwajalein to be
sold to Americans at lower prices, a luxury not extended to consumption
on Ebeye.

The army's lengthy list of regulations included rules for Marshallese *and*
Americans. Concerned that Americans might buy goods for Marshallese,

the policy instructed that all purchases by Kwajalein residents had to be for personal use or gifts only given to immediate family members. Gifts purchased for those on other islands had to be valued at $15 or less and could only be given during Christmas. The army prohibited Kwajalein residents from bringing with them when visiting Ebeye any food or alcohol or any other items not approved through an authorized pass. Army rules also limited the hours within which Marshallese workers could eat at Kwajalein's eateries.[65] The late 1960s saw an influx of US workers to Kwajalein, and army policies aimed to ensure no Americans had to wait for meals on account of Marshallese workers.

The army's new policies and surveillance practices further marked Marshallese workers as not only foreigners in their homeland but also criminals. The regulations noted that a system to record items given to Micronesians would be maintained, and all items removed without proper authorization would be confiscated. Any violations would be reported to the "Police Blotter," and those abusing purchasing privileges would undergo investigation. Consequences for violations included the impoundment of goods and fourteen days' suspension of entry authorization, which could jeopardize employment status.[66] Over time the army erected a security checkpoint at the ferry dock for Ebeye where guards could inspect all items leaving Kwajalein daily, a structure that remains in place today.

The military's dehumanizing methods for increasing surveillance over Marshallese workers are apparent in a 1968 photograph in the Trust Territory's *Micronesian Reporter*. The image, appearing in P. F. Kluge's article "Micronesia's Unloved Islands: Ebeye," shows the panopticon figure of a White American guard watching over Marshallese domestics en route to Kwajalein on the *Tarlang* ferry. Revealing the criminalization of Marshallese workers, the caption reads: "The guard is tired. He works the night shift and the morning boat is the end of his day. But for the hundreds of Marshallese who jam the decks of the Tarlang, the day is just beginning. And other guards will scan their comings and goings on Kwajalein."[67] Kluge's photograph illustrates the military's degradation of and lack of respect for its Marshallese workers. The image exemplifies how the army designated this population, without whom Kwajalein could not operate, as criminals needing surveillance.

Figure 10. US guard on *Tarlang* ferry at Kwajalein Atoll, 1968. Photographer unknown.

This image of a criminalized Marshallese service sector commuting daily from Ebeye to Kwajalein on the *Tarlang* under the watchful eye of guards evoked criticism from both Marshallese and Americans over time. In his first novel, *Melal: A Pacific Story*, former Kwajalein resident Robert Barclay centered analysis of Marshallese workers' daily humiliations commuting on the *Tarlang* to Kwajalein under strict surveillance. While historic fiction, *Melal* captured what Kwajalein's curfew policies and security checkpoint inspections may have felt like for Marshallese through Barclay's main character, Rujen Keju, a Marshallese waste worker on Kwajalein. *Melal* begins with Keju on Ebeye boarding the *Tarlang* to reach work on Kwajalein. Rujen is the father of two sons, Jebro and Nuke; the latter's name was not accidental. Nor should it be lost on the reader that

Jebro had six fingers on one hand due to his deceased mother's exposure to nuclear radiation.

Themes of trespassing litter *Melal*'s pages. After Rujen secures a position for his son Jebro as a waste worker on Kwajalein, the reader learns:

> Like his father and all Marshallese who worked there, Jebro would need to catch the *Tarlang* to Kwajalein in the morning and then back again before six in the evening (unless specifically authorized for overtime) or be fined for trespassing--a fine more than twice his daily pay. He would not be allowed in the American stores or restaurants, and he would be searched at a checkpoint before leaving. Not even a Pepsi bought from a machine was allowed on the boat back to Ebeye. Jebro wondered, when he went for his orientation on Wednesday, if a sign outside of one of the American clubs was a joke, a mistake, or a serious warning. It read, in Marshallese but not English: NO MARSHALLESE ALLOWED ON THESE PREMISES. ANYBODY CAUGHT WILL FACE IMPRISONMENT AND WILL BE RUINED.[68]

The 2002 publication date of *Melal* suggests the 1968 policy's enduring impacts for Marshallese and for US civilians observing these practices, particularly as these policies became hardened over time following Marshallese protests on Kwajalein, explored in chapters 5 and 6. Having frequently traversed between Kwajalein and Ebeye, and residing on the island during these protests in the 1980s, Barclay's focus on segregation and surveillance as key themes in the novel constitutes one literary attempt to unveil the island's enduring discriminatory history. Barclay punctuates those themes by using teenage Marshallese Jebro's initial encounters with the structures of exclusion on Kwajalein as he takes in the absurdity of Marshallese positioned as trespassers on Marshallese islands, presuming this might be a mistake or even a joke.

In addition to journalistic responses and Barclay's retrospective literary critique, the army's 1968 regulations garnered an immediate backlash from Marshallese and Americans in various positions, all decrying their discriminatory nature. Following their implementation, the Marshallese Nitijela (legislature) sent its resolution no. 71 to the United Nations. Touched on in chapters 1 and 2, the resolution not only called attention to the "neocolonial situation" within which Marshallese existed, but specifically discussed the conditions of discrimination on Kwajalein. Resolution coauthor Marshallese Iroij (chief) Amata Kabua wrote that on Kwajalein "the most rigid form of segregation [existed] . . . in which Micronesians are not permitted to live on the same islands as the Americans, to shop in . . . the stores, or even take home with them anything of value which Americans might freely give them."[69] Echoing Kabua's plea before the United Nations, Marshallese worker Lomes McKay expressed his frustration in a local publication. In the November 12, 1968, issue of *Ebeye Voice*, McKay decried Marshallese being discriminated against by the army and Trust Territory office on Kwajalein. In a letter to the editor, he described visiting the Trust Territory office on Kwajalein to get permission to shop at Macy's. McKay said he was treated with suspicion, asked to confirm if he was indeed a teacher multiple times.[70] McKay added, "If we need something but our stores here on Ebeye don't have them, we would like to use Macy's. Because of discrimination against Marshallese, we cannot shop there."[71]

Reactions against the new army policies also came from Kwajalein residents. Former Kwajalein teacher Mary. E. Russell sent a letter to the United Nations in October 1970 expressing concern about discrimination on Kwajalein. She wrote that she had worked on the island between 1968 and 1969 and asked the United Nations to answer a series of questions addressing this discrimination, including "why [Americans] must only give items of no commercial value to the Marshallese when we leave and break up our trailer home on Kwajalein?"[72] John D. Beall, of Ventura, California, wrote to his senator, George Murphy, also expressing concern about Kwajalein's policies. In his April 24, 1970, correspondence, Beall described how while working on Kwajalein he had been "disgusted with the American treatment of the natives."[73] He noted, "They cannot buy in the white man's stores on this island and are being robbed on their own islands by a monopoly that sells bread for 80 cents a loaf, $1.05 for a can of spam."[74]

A letter to the editor penned by *Ebeye View* publications adviser Chris Christensen on April 27, 1971, addressed the tensions between US dependence on Marshallese service labor alongside challenges posed by the island's segregation structure. Christensen responded to an article appearing in the same issue that detailed a recent visit by Ebeye's sixth-, seventh-, and eighth- grade girls to Kwajalein to enhance their homemaking skills. The experiential learning included showing these Marshallese youths the variety of home economic resources on Kwajalein, facilities to help the girls learn about health and proper attire.[75] She wrote: "Field trips to the Surfway or the laundry seem to be a curious exercise of the learning process[.] (Come on in natives and see wonderful things we've got—however don't touch. And by all means get out of your head any ideas of shopping here with us.)"[76]

For the US officials charged with administering the civilian realm of the Trust Territory, the army's 1968 regulations were seen as an affront to the US mission in the Pacific. Working as the Trust Territory district administrator representative on Ebeye, Dr. William Vitarelli was outraged by the military's indifference to its Marshallese workers. In the 1968 *Micronesian Reporter* article cited earlier, Vitarelli said he "hoped that the Army would realize its responsibility to the people who sweep its floors and cook its meals. . . . But the responsibility goes as far as paying money. After that, it's get the hell out and don't take anything with you."[77] Territory high commissioner W. R. Norwood also challenged the army to repeal the 1968 regulations. In a letter to Colonel Healy, Norwood explained that Marshallese on Ebeye found the new policies and their tone demeaning, adding that he would, too. He viewed the new restrictions as "offensive to the Trust Territory Administration and as seriously encumbering our ability to deal effectively with the already difficult Ebeye problems which are almost entirely the result of the KTS [Kwajalein Test Site] programs."[78] Echoing the tensions and conflict over funding responsibilities for Ebeye highlighted in chapter 2, the army's segregation policies further illuminated the tensions embedded in the contradictory mandates governing these two arms of US empire in the region.

Alongside army policies controlling purchase and removal of goods on Kwajalein, another new set of rules restricting the freedoms of Marshallese domestics also spurred a backlash. These rules began in December 1967 when the Kwajalein Test Site issued a directive that Marshallese maids could no longer use Kwajalein's laundry facilities to do their own washing.[79] The military defended the policy as necessary because Kwajalein's facilities had come under strain due to an influx of American employees on the island. According to the army, the increased population meant Kwajalein's laundry facilities could no longer support both American and Marshallese workers. The new policy exacted particular hardships on

Marshallese women because Ebeye lacked laundry facilities as well as sufficient water for drinking and handwashing clothes.

Since the 1960s, water shortages on Ebeye have illuminated Marshallese colonial status and substandard living conditions. Water became a key contested resource between Ebeye and Kwajalein, highlighting the vast gulf between sustainable living conditions on each island. While Marshallese labor enabled a domestic suburban refuge on Kwajalein, Ebeye lacked adequate water for drinking and sanitation. The image of Marshallese workers carrying empty jugs daily to work on Kwajalein to fill up with clean water has become emblematic of the extreme disparities informing life for Kwajalein's US personnel and its segregated Marshallese workforce. This Marshallese practice has persisted for decades to enable survival on Ebeye. As Kwajalein's multi-billion-dollar base has retained its utopian suburban landscape today, Marshallese workers continue to end their workday lugging jugs of clean water home to an island that has historically and continuously lacked a sufficient amount of this life-sustaining resource.

The army defended its 1967 laundry policy as necessary due to a strain on facilities and to prevent Marshallese women from carrying bundles off Kwajalein that could hide illegally obtained goods.[80] Such policies further criminalized Marshallese workers on Kwajalein. With a lack of laundry facilities and clean water on Ebeye, the laundry policy evoked an immediate outcry from Marshallese workers. Within a day of its announcement, a collective of twenty Marshallese representatives including workers and political leaders wrote to Colonel Healy emphasizing the importance of Kwajalein's laundry facilities.[81] Asserting their contribution to Kwajalein's defense mission, the authors described the importance of wearing clean, ironed clothing when working alongside Americans. They noted that without access to Kwajalein's facilities, they would be limited to handwashing on Ebeye, where there was not enough water for drinking and washing. The letter concluded, "We feel strongly that this rule will bring great hardship for our people who participate with your important mission."[82] Highlighting the essential role of Marshallese workers in the national security project on Kwajalein, the collective challenged the military's tendency to ignore this dependency, a tendency that allowed the army to distance itself from any responsibility for Ebeye.

A group of Marshallese women also sent a letter to Healy challenging the laundry policy and alluding to potential consequences if it remained in place. Signed only "Marshallese Maids" (suggesting job security concerns), its authors detailed the hardships brought on by the new rules. Describing their twelve-hour workday on Kwajalein as a schedule leaving minimal time to care for their own families on Ebeye, the maids questioned why they could not use laundry facilities in the houses where they worked.[83] Stating that they understood why Kwajalein's growing population meant they could no longer use the public facilities, they added that American families had communicated a willingness to let them use their house machines. They asserted that they would hate to quit their jobs, but conditions had become very difficult and they wanted an explanation for this new policy.[84]

Healy's response to the maids revealed the degree to which army commanders policed both the physical *and* narrative boundaries of Kwajalein as a space of exclusive American domestic and consumer privileges. In addressing the maids' concerns, Healy explained that if American women chose to work, they did not do personal chores while on the clock. He wrote: "This is true on Kwajalein as well as back in the United States. . . . If the Marshallese Maids are striving to meet American standards of living, then they must accept the fact that to earn a day's pay a day's work must be done in return."[85] Mythologizing both American and Marshallese women's options, Healy obscured the imperial history structuring the experiences of American workers on Kwajalein and Marshallese workers on Ebeye.

Further disavowing US empire, Healy concluded his letter emphasizing that army regulations had not intended to be arbitrary or unduly restrictive, but rather aimed to benefit Marshallese and Americans. He stated, "It is hoped that they [the Marshallese] will be encouraged by it to build up private enterprise of their own on Ebeye, and concentrate more fully on improving their situation by hard work and initiative as have these Americans whose ways they are striving to emulate, rather than by taking advantage of the easiest solution to every problem."[86] Positioning Marshallese within the familiar "bootstraps" narrative, Healy further naturalized Kwajalein as an American home, outside the realm of empire. In his portrait, Americans on Kwajalein enjoyed privileges because of hard work, not because they arrived in a colonial territory where their housing, shopping, and even laundry were subsidized. Suggesting that Marshallese on Ebeye could attain the degree of economic stability characterizing the American way of life on Kwajalein ignored the colonial structure under which its Marshallese workforce lived and the essential role of military operations on Kwajalein in determining that lifestyle.

Healy's exceptionalist narrative and the army's broader efforts to obscure the imperial nature of the US presence in the Marshall Islands would continue to be challenged by Marshallese workers, political leaders, and US residents on Kwajalein throughout the 1970s and 1980s. In addition to voicing their concerns, some Americans and Marshallese simply ignored the army regulations. Interviews with several former Marshallese domestics indicated that American families continued to allow them to do laundry in their homes after the implementation of the new rules.[87] These laundry-inspired subversive acts revealed the instability of army control on Kwajalein, fault lines that would continue to grow throughout the 1970s and 1980s.[88]

POLICING INTIMACY BETWEEN AMERICANS AND MARSHALLESE ON KWAJALEIN

In addition to highlighting the potentially demeaning impact of the army's criminalizing policies on Marshallese, Robert Barclay's novel *Melal* explored another tension rippling through the structure of segregation between the two islands: intimacy. Concerns about the potential corruption of nuclear family life on Kwajalein surfaced through fears of proximate sexual transgressions on the island. The military tried to curb such deviances by disciplining social intimacies between Marshallese and Americans and between Kwajalein's resident bachelors and resident families. The former scenario, and how the complex array of relationships operated in reference to Kwajalein's segregation structure, was conveyed in *Melal* through the character of Rujen's cousin, Lazarus.

Barclay's inclusion of Lazarus offers a lens into the challenges complicating intimate relationships between Americans and Marshallese. Readers meet Barclay's Lazarus as Rujen heads to work. En route, Rujen encounters

Lazarus coming from the home of his American girlfriend on Kwajalein. After bragging to Rujen about his sexual exploits, Lazarus launches into a description of all the luxuries he enjoyed while staying in this American girl's place: the big TV, a puffy, comfortable couch, air conditioning, and endless bubble baths. He adds, "and when we get married then I'll be living over here as an American, and you—all my family—can visit anytime you like!"[89] After Lazarus asks Rujen not to say anything until he has "become American," Rujen promises he will not. But he adds: "'I hope you know that because you are the man, that when you marry your American wife she will become a Marshallese, not the other way around.'"[90] To which Lazarus responds, "'You lie!'" Rujen replies: "'I'm joking—of course if you marry an American then you become one, *I think*.'"[91]

This passage highlights how relationships between Marshallese and Americans always existed within the confines of policies governing movement, access, and privileges between Kwajalein and Ebeye. His depiction of neither Lazarus nor Rujen as particularly sure about how it would work with a Marshallese man and an American woman speaks to how army policies pervaded and complicated the most intimate realms of social interactions between these two communities. The fictional exchange between the two obscures the fact that Lazarus's access to residency on Kwajalein would have been linked to the class status of his American girlfriend; if her job came with accompanied status, then marriage would give him this "American" privilege. Barclay's decision to narrate American and Marshallese intimacy through a Marshallese man and an American woman seems curious, since this dynamic proved far less common than American men with Marshallese women and girls. Had Barclay chosen the latter, he may have been able to delve more deeply into some of the more coercive patterns that have historically developed in the Marshall Islands and throughout Micronesia in such relationships. When asked why he decided to go with this less common dynamic for *Melal*, Barclay acknowledged such relationships were indeed exceptional. But he said he based Lazarus's relationship on a couple he knew while living on Kwajalein.[92] He added that American men on Kwajalein seeking Marshallese women on Ebeye was far more common. He said sometimes these men would keep them on Kwajalein in their bachelor's quarters for the weekend, "against the rules of course."[93]

Barclay is pointing here to a deeper historic challenge of regulating intimacy between the two islands, a challenge that brought regulations on access to Kwajalein, not Ebeye. As alluded to in the contrasting border regulations between Kwajalein and Ebeye and highlighted in Barclay's discussion of intimacy between Americans and Marshallese, it was not accidental that while Marshallese were excluded from living on Kwajalein, no such prohibitions existed against Americans living on Ebeye. Just as US colonial policies governing residency on Kwajalein and Ebeye diverged, so too did early policies regulating social visits. Marshallese were prohibited from staying overnight on Kwajalein, but early on Americans could stay overnight on Ebeye after securing permission.[94] Daytime travel to Ebeye required no authorization. In her ethnographic research, Sandra Crismon found that access to Ebeye became stricter during the 1970s as problems with American men (sometimes called "Ebeye Rangers") going to Ebeye to have sex with young Marshallese women spurred regulations on Americans staying overnight on Ebeye.[95] That such regulations may have failed to achieve complete control over such behavior became evident in 1989 correspondence from Ebeye officials describing the problems with drunken Americans on Ebeye, noting that "Kwaj residents 'consider Ebeye their private playground' where 'anything goes.'"[96]

While less abundant than other documents addressing access to and movement within Kwajalein, archival materials revealed how control over Marshallese women and girls was a pressing issue for military and civilian communities on Kwajalein and Ebeye over time. Military rules allowing Americans to stay overnight on Ebeye after gaining permission alluded to a more common pattern of sexual economies historically emerging alongside US bases.[97]

As suggested by both Crismon's ethnographic findings and my archival research, while segregation policies restricted Marshallese access to Kwajalein, Americans and Marshallese managed to establish an array of intimate connections over time that transgressed these boundaries. Such intimacies sparked anxieties that surfaced in meeting minutes from the Kwajalein Atoll Inter-Island Community Relations Committee, suggesting the obstacles the military faced in disciplining multiple labor sectors on Kwajalein and particularly Marshallese female workers serving residential spaces of US bachelors. The committee formed in 1968 as an attempt to bring together representatives from Kwajalein and Ebeye to address tensions between the two islands, particularly centered on the military's policies of exclusion and discrimination against Marshallese workers. As meetings held throughout the 1970s and 1980s continued, concerns surfaced about Marshallese women and underage girls staying overnight in the bachelor quarters. Discussions centered on the issue of "problems" created by Ebeye women who stayed overnight illegally and the risk that weekend work created for Marshallese girls getting into "trouble."[98] Brainstorming how to approach such problems, attendees, including civilian and military representatives from Kwajalein and civilian representatives from Ebeye, proposed an array of potential solutions. They collectively suggested the military keep maids off island after 5:30 p.m., prohibit Marshallese weekend labor, and give bachelor quarter maids a separate area to do their washing and ironing (presumably to minimize intermingling with bachelors). Kwajalein Missile Range security also stated no Ebeye residents would be granted visiting privileges in the bachelor quarters, nor would anyone under eighteen be allowed entry, adding that "a list of female residents charged and found guilty on the B.Q.s [bachelor's quarters] of trespass will be furnished Chief Magistrate Ebeye."[99]

This range of solutions reinforced the double standard that punishment for perceived sexual transgressions was imposed on Marshallese women and girls, not American men. The notion that responsibility for disciplining domestics should take place on Ebeye through traditional chiefly authority, local island security, and parental oversight also surfaced in several discussions. One 1979 meeting highlighted the disciplinary role Iroij (Chief) Lejolan Kabua could play if given the names of Marshallese girls found trespassing in bachelor quarters. During this discussion, committee members also suggested an exchange badge system be implemented to ensure no domestics could remain on Kwajalein overnight without the knowledge of Kwajalein *and* Ebeye security personnel. Reinforcing the idea that deviant sexuality remained an Ebeye issue, Kwajalein community representative Alice Buck stated that "the problem of Ebeye girls in B.Q.s" could be solved by greater involvement by Ebeye parents, who could give the Ebeye magistrate their daughters' names so the magistrate and police could make sure these girls received no passes to get to Kwajalein.[100] Indicating that sexual relations existed beyond the confines of labor, and across a potentially significant age gap, the group also suggested discontinuing the Ebeye girls' softball team practice on Kwajalein.[101]

These meeting minutes illuminated how military attempts to control access and movement between these two islands remained unsuccessful in containing the more intimate aspects of individual lives. They also suggested that solutions would continue on Ebeye with the aim of controlling female workers coming to Kwajalein rather than the bachelors presumably inviting them to stay. Both civilian and military representatives seemed less bothered by the existence of sexual intimacy between American men and Marshallese women or girls, as long as such transgressions remained at a distance from wholesome nuclear family life on Kwajalein.

While concerns expressed at the community relations meetings revealed a pattern of potentially coercive relationships existing between underage Marshallese girls and American men (not uncommon throughout colonial Micronesia), the meetings also hinted at other kinds of relationships emerging between the two islands. One discussion about marriage between Americans on Kwajalein and Marshallese on Ebeye revealed the challenges of navigating such relationships across segregated landscapes.[102] The issue came up in 1978 when Marshallese committee members asked why Kwajalein's residents who moved to Ebeye after marriage could buy materials to build new homes at lower prices than Marshallese on Ebeye paid. The committee suggested that costs for these materials be made equivalent for those living on Kwajalein and Ebeye.[103]

As committed relationships developed between Marshallese and Americans, so too did concerns about the varied privileges and costs associated with where couples cohabitated. With rare exception, couples lived on Ebeye because the US partner hired to work on Kwajalein arrived with unaccompanied status. This meant US bachelors arriving at Kwajalein could not have an American or a Marshallese partner live with them on the island, a class privilege reserved largely for the island's scientist and engineer community. Following the labor camp removal in 1951, partnered Marshallese residency in family housing on Kwajalein would not come through Marshallese employment status for more than four decades. The first Marshallese worker to be promoted to a position carrying accompanied status (and therefore allowed to move his family from Ebeye to Kwajalein) did so in 1995, nearly a decade after formal decolonization.[104]

INTRAISLAND SEGREGATION: KWAJALEIN'S SEPARATE SPHERES FOR US RESIDENTS

If concerns about "deviant" intimacies between US and Marshallese workers informed military efforts to discipline Marshallese women and girls on Ebeye, another set of policies regulating movement among Americans signaled the difficulties involved in creating a wholesome portrait of nuclear family life on Kwajalein. While the displacement of all Micronesian workers from Kwajalein in 1951 afforded an opportunity to prohibit sex between the two labor communities thereafter from the island's emerging suburban family setting, the military had no such luxury with the island's residential bachelor population. Unable to fully contain nuclear families through complete island separation from these bachelors, the army worked to police separate spheres *within* Kwajalein.

The project of restaging small-town suburbia on Kwajalein involved military governance over the island in a way that promised protection for its most elite workers' families. But this portrait of suburban utopia sat in tension with the military's labor dependencies, which found US nuclear families residing on a nine-hundred-acre island where a commuting colonial workforce moved through this space, and an equally "threatening" bachelor workforce resided in close proximity. In addition to keeping a close eye on the commuting Marshallese service sector, this entailed military surveillance over the large cohort of resident bachelors working in construction and other manual labor on the island. In this hybrid labor setting, such surveillance aimed to contain a portrait of nuclear family life on Kwajalein—mapping American domestic orderings of race, gender, class, and sexuality onto this site of global military expansion.

While interisland segregation kept American and Marshallese workers separate, intraisland segregation separated resident US bachelors from US families on Kwajalein. The latter policy linked to the relationship between housing and employment on Kwajalein that historically paired class status with family privileges. This meant the largely White cohort of scientists and engineers arriving with professional training and higher pay received "accompanied" status and could bring their dependents to live in the island's suburban family housing area. Kwajalein's working-class cohort arrived with unaccompanied status and thus lived in segregated bachelor dormitories. As noted in the introduction, at the peak of the island's labor demands during the 1960s and 1970s, this latter cohort included a significant portion of workers of color. Working primarily in construction, docking, and shipping, this bachelor cohort constituted the largest labor force on the island during the 1960s and 1970s, comprising approximately 60 percent of the workers.[105] Labor demand peaked during this period to support the growth of construction on Kwajalein and saw a significant contingent of Japanese American and Native Hawaiian bachelors arriving from Hawai'i. One of Kwajalein's longest residents, Jimmy Matsunaga, said he recalled when the island hit peak employment of "maybe 5,500 residents," at least 2,000 having come from Hawai'i.[106] Matsunaga also came to Kwajalein from Hawai'i in 1966 and worked in shipping services.

While Kwajalein's residential workforce comprised a majority of civilian workers, the racial dynamics in the 1960s and 1970s mapped onto similar patterns on bases in more recent years, traced by architectural scholar Marc Gillem. In his book *America Town*, Gillem revealed how class and race overlapped in the military's hierarchical housing structure: "Officers mostly white and generally well paid, live in one area of an outpost at lower densities. Enlisted soldiers, 23 percent African American, 8 percent Hispanic, and not well paid, live elsewhere at higher densities."[107]

Military surveillance monitored two primary groups of workers on Kwajalein: the more racially diverse, US working-class residential population, and the lower-paid, colonized Marshallese workers commuting from Ebeye. The degree of freedom of mobility on Kwajalein signaled one's position within a social ladder also marked by gender, in addition to colonial subjectivity and employment status. Such hierarchies included divisions between military and civilian status and within civilian labor. During the mid-1960s, the army demarcated areas throughout Kwajalein in which access would be limited to certain groups. Those areas included family housing. Tying national security to such regulations, army correspondence noted that "it is the policy of this command to allow the greatest possible latitude consistent with the security and safety requirements of the island."[108] In addition to areas more obviously connected to security concerns—those that remained fenced with guard posts, had office buildings, and had work centers—the letter identified limited entry into residential housing and recreational sites.[109] It noted that socializing in family housing remained restricted to residents. Nonresidents required invitation by a resident and needed to proceed directly to and from their destination without loitering. Any repairmen or others carrying out business errands could enter the residential area but not unattended quarters unless working in pairs or if the occupant gave specific written permission on the repairman's work order.[110]

Even movement from within family housing to recreational settings came under military surveillance. The army noted those desiring to move between dependents' housing and the beach for reef or shelling could do so via direct route to the destination, returning to family housing without stopping along the way. Access to the island's array of recreational and social areas was also guided by rules marking some spaces open to families or women and others restricted to bachelors. Reflecting a range of hierarchies governing island affairs, some social clubs constricted access based on military or civilian status; others privileged employees of certain contractors over others. While the Crossroads Club (named for the 1946 atomic test Operation Crossroads) remained open to all personnel and dependents, the Yokwe Yuk Club (named for the Marshallese greeting "love to you") was restricted to officers and their dependents.[111] Only male civilian personnel could socialize at the Ocean View Club. The MZC Kwajalein Country Club was private, open only to employees of the construction contractor Martin-Zachry and their guests.[112] Another way the military regulated space in recreational areas was through gendering movie theater seating. The island's oldest outdoor theater, the Richardson, remained open to all, but seating divided attendees by yellow seats for bachelors and white for dependents.[113] The Roxy movie theater, located in the dependents' housing area, exclusively served families.[114]

Swimming pools served as another site for spatially organizing the island around gendered lines. Kwajalein's dependent pool remained open to families and visiting female personnel. The bachelor pool exclusively served men living in barracks or bachelor's quarters or just transiting through Kwajalein.[115] These social club and recreational facility divisions mirrored the ways that housing divided Kwajalein through the separation of families from bachelors. The island contained three types of housing during the early years of the missile range: bachelor officers' quarters, dorm-style military barracks for nonofficer bachelors, and family quarters

Figure 11. Dependents' swimming pool on Kwajalein Island, 1963. Photo by Robert C. Kiste. Permission granted by the Pacific Collection, Hamilton Library, University of Hawai'i-Mānoa.

that served civilian and military families.[116] While no military rules separating bachelors and families included overt language on race, and the military did not officially track or publicly report Kwajalein's resident racial demography, the connections between race and class suggest overlap with how these categories operated in continental suburban segregation.

As already noted, the island's highest-paid workers arriving with accompanied status comprised the largely White cohort of scientists and engineers. The largest non-White residential population on Kwajalein would be found among the bachelors who worked in construction and other manual labor. Thus, military concerns about bachelors potentially preying upon the wives and children of scientists and engineers reflected fears that entangled lines of class, gender, sexuality, *and* race. One of the most profound examples of military efforts to contain the island's nuclear families was a street sign prohibiting bachelors from entering dependents' (family) housing area. Former residents recalled seeing the sign up during

Figure 12. No trespassing in dependents' area sign on Kwajalein Island, ca. 1966–1968. Photographer unknown. Courtesy of Bill Remick.

the 1960s and 1970s, noting that it prohibited bachelors from moving beyond 6th Street, the intersection separating family housing.[117]

Concerns about sexual deviance among US bachelors on Kwajalein during the 1960s and 1970s had deeper roots, echoing earlier fears informing military discipline of gender and sexuality dating back to World War II. Such regulations aimed to contain both women and men on the island, mapping Kwajalein through norms of patriarchy and heteronormativity.[118] During World War II, army rules had sought to control male sexuality on the island, both by protecting men from each other and by securing the small population of women working largely as nurses. Several cases surfaced through wartime court martial orders during winter 1944 and spring 1945 charging naval personnel with crimes of "sodomy" and "scandalous conduct tending to the destruction of good morals."[119] For those found guilty, the charges carried sentences that included twelve months' confinement and dishonorable discharge. As historians Allan Berube and Margot Canaday's research revealed, this local iteration on Kwajalein mirrored broader military policies of dishonorable discharges of those identified as homosexual during World War II, which prevented these soldiers from enjoying the GI benefits that launched a whole generation of US male veterans and their dependents into the middle class in the postwar era.[120]

Likewise during the war, the navy had articulated a commitment to protecting the small number of American nurses on Kwajalein from the potential threat of American bachelors. An August 1945 executive notice informed male officers about nurse's quarters visitation policies, delineating the hours within which male officers could visit the quarters' living room as guests of nurse residents.[121] The navy expected officers calling at nurses' quarters to do so "properly dressed in cotton uniform or similar appropriate uniform for their service force."[122] Hinting at the navy's difficulty in regulating intimate encounters in an island environment, the notice declared: "No officers will be admitted to the Quarters in bathing attire."[123] A second memorandum issued that same month prohibited male members of the armed forces from entering any areas occupied by women, with the qualification that the earlier directive detailing specific visitation times remained the only exception to this policy.[124] The notice warned that any violations would "result in prompt disciplinary action."[125]

As Kwajalein transformed from a wartime naval base to a Cold War missile installation, the population of US women on the island shifted from this small contingent of nurses to a wider range of residents that included wives and mothers, nurses, teachers, secretaries, and a small number of highly trained professionals. With this new wave of arrivals in the 1960s, Cold War–era gender norms informing the continental suburban landscape seem to have been mapped onto Kwajalein. Accessing the experiences of this majority-White female population living and working on Kwajalein over the years is difficult given a dearth of sources on the subject. But insights from oral history interviews and scant archival materials paint a portrait of limited social mobility. One civilian resident noted that Kwajalein has maintained a "Leave It to Beaver" aura of 1950s gender roles through the present.[126]

During the missile era, Kwajalein's gendered landscape appears to have mirrored patriarchal conditions structuring women's lives in the United States. The majority of women arriving on Kwajalein in the 1960s came as wives and mothers. If they worked beyond the unpaid economy of childrearing and homemaking, they often faced employment options similar to those for women in the United States: primarily secretarial, nursing, and teaching positions. An exception to this pattern, and a potential nod to the growing feminist movement in the continental United States, appeared in civilian contractor Kentron's celebration of the International Women's Year. Here, the contractor highlighted female employees in a 1975 company newsletter.[127] Among Kentron's more than thirty-five female employees profiled, Nancy Olson worked as a motion picture processor for the company, while Grace Scheidegger was employed as one the first chief telephone operators on Kwajalein and oversaw seven other employees. While Kentron draftswoman Janine Cox identified her position in the company as interesting, she expressed her disappointment that women still received unequal treatment across the board. She explained: "Doors still remain closed for most women. And pay equality is still below wages of men as regards same occupation/same responsibilities."[128] Cox failed to specify whether she was referring to the working world in general or her experiences working for Kentron on Kwajalein, but she did not cite the latter as an exception to her broader statements.

In addition to laboring within the island's paid and unpaid economies, some women engaged in volunteer activities aimed at addressing challenges facing Marshallese on Kwajalein Atoll and across Micronesia. As noted in chapter 2, this work was often used as public relations material by the military. These women organized various social and charitable groups, with the most prominent being the Yokwe Yuk Women's Club. In 1963 the club opened a shop at the Kwajalein air terminal to sell Micronesian handicrafts. Proceeds from the craft sales went to providing educational scholarships at schools throughout Micronesia. The COM acknowledged the far-reaching impact of the club's work in 1975 through a House resolution of appreciation honoring its contributions.[129]

While some women seem to have taken pride in their charitable work alongside other labor on Kwajalein, oral history interviews also revealed grievances about the challenges women faced over the years. Echoing the malaise of a generation of largely White, middle-class women identifying with Betty Friedan's "problem that has no name," detailed in her iconic *Feminine Mystique* in 1963, several women have pointed to Kwajalein's landscape as one in which women's professional training went unused. They noted that on Kwajalein, women often worked in jobs for which they were overqualified. Because families historically came to the island through a husband's employment in male-dominated fields of science and engineering (and continue to do so today), highly educated and professionally trained women often lacked jobs matching their degrees and skills. One woman concluded Kwajalein was an ideal space for male work and recreation but less fulfilling for women.[130] The continuity of a largely male-oriented professional employment structure in a setting of separate spheres for families and bachelors has mapped the island with resonances of Cold War gender norms in ways that have outlived many of those in the United States.[131] As Sandra Crismon found in her ethnographic research on Kwajalein, gender norms among US residents historically layered Kwajalein with a 1950s American aura, at least for men. One resident explained that even in the 1980s, "I always thought it was about 1956. . . . Women did not work here. Only a few wives worked." Over her long experience, one resident observed that the base's distance from the states tends to be a disadvantage for women and a terrific advantage for men: "This is the perfect place for men . . . because they all get to be five years old, wear their shorts to work, ride their bicycles, and play softball. They don't have to do house upkeep [and don't have to pay for it.] So it's a wonderful place for men. It's very hard on women . . . women are in limbo out here. If you have any kind of career, it's on hold. . . . So, we're non-people."[132]

NUCLEAR FAMILY BREAKDOWNS AND ADVENTURES IN BABYSITTING

Policies on housing and mobility that historically linked class, gender, sexuality, and nuclear family protection continue to spatially arrange Kwajalein. Military efforts to preserve this portrait of wholesome nuclear family life have occasionally led to unexpected consequences. In a setting where class, family status, and housing remain linked to a deeper island history informed by fears about deviant sexuality, family breakdowns can prove exceptionally challenging. Such was the case for one family that arrived on the island with accompanied status several years ago and had to negotiate new living arrangements following a painful divorce.[133] When this middle-class, White couple split, the spouse whose job rank gained him family housing status continued caring for their children in his suburban home. The now ex-wife, who worked in an unaccompanied status position on island and had only received family housing through her husband's job, had to move into bachelor's quarters and became one of a few single American women living in such quarters in recent years. Because bachelor housing continues to exclude any individuals under the age of eighteen, the wife's young children could not visit or stay with their mother in her new accommodations. She had to conduct all visits either at her place of work, at the island's public dining facilities, or in other recreational areas.

While this middle-class White mother presumably would not have been viewed as a predatory bachelor preying on Kwajalein's wives or children nor one feared to be cavorting with underage Marshallese female workers, her predicament exemplifies how military policies rooted in such concerns continued to inform the island's contemporary social and spatial arrangements. While bachelors remained segregated from families, the rules governing their accommodations also attempted to prevent engagement with minors in their dormitory rooms. Both policies suggest a continued fear surrounding Kwajalein's suburban landscape's less traditional and presumably suspicious resident worker: the bachelor.

This mother's story hints at a dysfunctional twist on Kwajalein's historic and ongoing "Leave It to Beaver" setting. One can read her story as actually reinforcing this atmosphere by serving as a cautionary tale to those considering disrupting the sanctity of the nuclear family structure on Kwajalein. As long as families maintained a June and Ward Cleaver appearance, island rules separating workers by class (and race as it has been historically entangled with class) remained in their favor. Those who diverged from this portrait would have to derive their own strategy for navigating the island's hierarchical class and family structure. The continuity of a ban on those under age eighteen from entering bachelor workers' quarters—regulations rooted in historic concerns about intimacy between these bachelors and underage Marshallese domestic servants—reveals how traces of these colonial policies continued through the "postcolonial" era on Kwajalein. For the army, domestic containment as a historic mission to secure American nuclear families remained entangled with policing categories of gender, sexuality, race, colonial subjectivity, and class.

Former resident and retired MIT engineer Lynn A. Jacobson reflected on the significance of military policies aimed at regulating potential sexual and gendered deviance on the island and the way it shaped the lives of US families and bachelors. In his 2013 self-published memoir, *Kwajalein: An Island Like No Other*, Jacobson shared a story that again hinted at the fears infusing army efforts to keep bachelors at a distance from the island's Wallys and Beavers, or in this case its Patty Dukes. Contributing to Kwajalein's growing nostalgia industry, which in part comprised several self-published memoirs, Jacobson's book compiled sixty-two short vignettes pieced together from his memories and those of fellow "kwaj-ites." These stories draw upon recollections from Jacobson's multiple tours on the island spanning 1964 to 1972. Noting many details and dates as approximate, his story "Extra Income," with the subtitle "Babysitting," suggested a scenario in which the army failed to fully isolate its wholesome family setting from the potentially corrupting influence of resident bachelors. The story follows a sixteen-year-old girl on Kwajalein as she arrives at the island bank one afternoon to close out her account. Upon noticing the amount in her account, the bank teller calls her father. He explains that the daughter has come to close her account and emphasizes his concern that she is only sixteen. The father responds: "'Look George, she's been babysitting every night all summer—ever since school let out—getting home really late. She says even though she will only be a junior next year, she wants to get a head start on her college fund. She must have three or even four hundred dollars saved up by now.'"[134] The bank teller explains he will do whatever the father wants, but he thought the father should know her balance has reached over $12,000 (a value of $45,000 in 2014). After a long pause, the father responds: "'Don't do anything and *please* don't mention this to anyone. I'll be there in fifteen minutes.'"[135]

Keeping in mind Jacobson's caveat of memory approximations, the inclusion of this particular vignette in a memoir aimed at showcasing the island's distinctiveness highlights the challenges faced by the military in disciplining its hybrid workforce. The task included preventing this kind of scenario—one in which a sixteen-year-old girl appears to have engaged in sex work with men on the island—from tainting the veneer of Kwajalein's wholesome family setting. Following the story, in a subsection titled "Preliberal Times," Jacobson editorializes on how Kwajalein's leaders felt it was their duty during this period to "safeguard the moral fiber and ethics of their community."[136] He notes that by opting to not employ single women to avoid "potential problems," Kwajalein's site designers exacerbated such problems by placing high school students at greater risk of bachelor attention. Echoing patriarchal norms of male entitlement infusing the island's segregation policies, Jacobson concludes: "Single males, prevented from what Mother Nature had intended them to pursue, will find a way—it's always that way and always will be."[137]

Jacobson's story illuminated the complicated nature of the US military's domestic containment mission on Kwajalein: the recruitment of thousands of workers over time to labor at protecting a national family thousands of miles away, while working to protect the replica of that prized yet vulnerable family model locally. Just as the goal of securing and containing a mythical portrait of wholesome family life would prove illusory for many in continental suburbia, so too would these mythologies ring hallow when mapped onto new landscapes of American domesticity in the Pacific. As Americans worked to restage home in the Marshall Islands, the contradictions embedded in their imperial project to expand the security state always lurked in the porous nature of such domestic containment efforts.

4 "*Mayberry* by the Sea"

AMERICANS FIND HOME IN THE MARSHALL ISLANDS

We're not in the Marshall Islands here, we're on Kwajalein.

—US resident on Kwajalein, 2016

IMAGINING KWAJALEIN AS AN AMERICAN HOME:

On July 28, 2019, the *Boston Globe* published a cartoon entitled "Meet the 'Kwaj' alumni." The multipanel satire noted that "of all the alumni groups found in Boston the most unusual is the cohort of folks who lived on Kwajalein."[1] One panel illustrated the range of amenities lining Kwajalein's landscape today, including the bowling alley, swimming pools, skate park, and golf course. Alongside these small-town suburban accoutrements, the caption added: "About 1,000 technical and support staff, and their families, live in this *Mayberry-Sur-Mer*."[2]

The cartoon appeared in Boston's newspaper as a link to the Massachusetts Institute of Technology (MIT), whose Lincoln Lab in Lexington had been providing radar engineers to Kwajalein for decades.[3] That "*Mayberry* by the sea*" was used to liken Kwajalein to a portrait of small town USA is not surprising. This popular cultural reference to Andy Griffith's America has surfaced in recollections of the island by current and former residents over the years, as has "Leave It to Beaver." These gestures to small-town American innocence of an earlier time captured on television have long saturated expressions of longing for this Marshallese island by many former "Kwajers," who have created an expansive nostalgia industry over the years. This has included self-published memoirs, social networking sites, the production of an array of island memorabilia available for purchase, and annual reunions that have brought together thousands of former Kwajalein residents for decades.

The reference to Mayberry was also not distinctive in situating the installation at Kwajalein with a connection to home within the broader US base imperium. In his expansive study on the US bases dotting the globe, anthropologist David Vine recalled: "At many bases I visited, people often invoked Mayberry, the mythical small town in the Andy Griffith Show, to describe base life. Beyond the comfortable living arrangements and the numerous amenities, they meant the comparison to capture feelings of security, community, and connection on base."[4] American understandings of Kwajalein as this distinctive and secure, tight-knit community have infused a flourishing nostalgia industry, in which former residents often narrate the island by abstracting it from any context of US colonial history in the region. The stories many former residents have told over time about Kwajalein often lack any acknowledgment of historic or ongoing Marshallese struggles to navigate and survive the US military presence in their homelands, a history deeply linked to facilitating their presence on Kwajalein. These erasures continue today. In correspondence with a current Kwajalein resident, the extent to which civilians have readily embraced and reproduced the military's abstraction of Kwajalein from any Marshallese context over time was evident. Wishing to remain anonymous in our interview, the resident reflected on my question about the persistent absence of Marshallese in American ways of remembering their time on the island. He was not surprised by such omissions and said, "Yeah . . . we're not in the Marshall Islands, we're on Kwajalein."[5]

Building on the analysis of colonial displacement and segregation policies and differing investments and planning approaches to developing Kwajalein and Ebeye in chapters 2 and 3, this chapter delves into US cultural framings of Kwajalein. It follows the traces left by Kwajalein's civilian residents to better understand how effective military investments and segregation policies were in creating a landscape in which the most prized workers and their families truly came to see themselves as *at home*. In doing so, I return to my introductory discussion of anthropologist Keith

Basso's concept of a "place-world." Basso identified this as "a setting constructing social traditions and, in the process, personal and social identities"; recalling Basso's claim: "We are, in a sense, the place-worlds we imagine."[6] To examine how Kwajalein as a "place-world" was imagined by those elite workers and their families, for whom the island was physically and culturally transformed, the discussion moves from the previous chapters' analysis of global and local colonial land control and construction to examine the *stories* people tell about this place. These narratives emerging from the island's civilian residents reveal the intersection of their imagining of Kwajalein with their imagining of themselves. In this way, these stories offer a lens for viewing the conjunction of social, cultural, and spatial histories taking root at this site of US empire in the Pacific.

During the nearly six decades of Kwajalein's status as a missile installation, thousands of US workers and their family members have come to call this Marshallese island "home." By examining the stories of those who inherited, embraced, and reproduced a narrative of US belonging on Kwajalein, one can see the cultural imprint of civilians in this placemaking history. Some former residents (largely kids or adolescents on the island at the time) have produced probing literature and scholarship that has critically reflected on these contradictions, while others have remained the fiercest guardians of Kwajalein's American mythology, true defenders of the island's storied past. Their "unseeing" of the structural inequalities constituting suburban segregation on Kwajalein was yet another cultural export to the central Pacific marking this island as a familiar American space.

This chapter begins to excavate stories told about Kwajalein during and beyond the era of US colonial control. It provides an additional means to illuminate how American exceptionalism has been deployed to explain suburban segregation in spaces of overseas empire or within suburban empire. While this chapter focuses on stories produced by Kwajalein's civilian residents and former residents, chapter 5 explores the various ways Marshallese activists and political leaders have disrupted these myths of US entitlement in their islands and reclaimed the narrative of home.

This chapter asks: How successful were the military's built environment and segregation policies in convincing US workers and family members they were "at home" on this Marshallese island? In exploring answers, I center one piece of a larger puzzle filled in by civilians themselves, without whose labor the US military would have no missile base.[7] I argue that the role of cultural production is as central to the process of place-making as are material investment and physical construction. This chapter chronicles how US civilians took up the narratives familiarized in the physical landscape that the military thoughtfully planned for them. But as will be made evident, they also brought their own contributions to culturally constructing Kwajalein as their home; their *Mayberry-Sur-Mer*.

"KWAJERS" AND THEIR "GUESTS": NORMALIZING US PRESENCE AND MARSHALLESE ABSENCE ON KWAJALEIN

In 1988, a civilian contractor welcome guide directed at temporary visitors to Kwajalein proclaimed: "*Our* island is beautiful and a wonderful place to visit or live, we ask that you help us keep it that way through your actions as our guest."[8] I begin this chapter by investigating how Americans came to understand Kwajalein as their home to the extent, as noted here, that they could define others—including Marshallese—as *their guests* in the Marshall Islands. Kwajalein's storied production and reproduction as an American home relied on normalizing American settlement and Marshallese residential exclusion, and doing so by disavowing the military colonial context informing that setup. This erasure of history enabled Americans to make their home in the Marshall Islands and simultaneously imagine Marshallese as guests in their own homelands.

One of the more extensive self-published memoirs contributing to the Kwajalein nostalgia industry exemplifies how Kwajalein's abstraction, begun by military discourse, was readily taken up by civilians over time. The memoir does so by dedicating the book to "All those who have known the 'Kwaj condition.'"[9] In addition to author and former resident Eugene C. Sims's take on this common ailment afflicting former residents as they struggled to adapt to life beyond the island, the "condition" was and is commonly joked about ubiquitously, appearing across social networking sites, at annual reunions, and in other mediums of nostalgia.[10] This "Kwaj condition" might entail adjustments such as wearing shoes and socks again (vs. flip-slops), mobility beyond bicycling, and feeling overwhelmed by the variety at abundant supermarkets and department stores after facing limited fare on Kwajalein.[11] Many Americans suffering from the "Kwaj condition" seemed to experience the island through the lens of a utopian, tropical suburbia, a home where they raised a family or were raised as children. This nostalgia for an island-style American dream erected on a US military base was not unique to Kwajalein. In her social history of Guantánamo, historian Jana K. Lipman also found a similar form of longing among former US base residents. She detailed such nostalgia through the voice of Joyce Hughes Matthews, who recalled being ripped from her "beloved GTMO," alongside more than twenty-four hundred other American women and children evacuated during the Cuban missile crisis.[12] She lamented: "'There is no special place in my heart that can conjure up visions like those of GTMO. . . . I am still waiting for the day that I can return to my home and one more time walk the beaches and stand on the soils that I have come to love.'"[13] Like Matthews's nostalgia for a home from which nearby Cubans remained excluded, countless Americans have historically and continually longed for the home they found in the Marshall Islands, which also residentially banned Marshallese.

For some, this deep sense of connection to the place even infused the olfactory sense. Kwajalein was a smell that evoked a feeling of protective attachment. This came through powerfully in the conclusion of Pacific scholar Greg Dvorak's book about the island. Constituting both a secondary source analysis and primary source reflections on Dvorak's own experiences living on Kwajalein as a child, *Concrete and Coral* included a section entitled "The Fragrance of Home." Here Dvorak recalled a visit he had made to Kwajalein and his encounter with a fellow "Kwaj Kid." Dan, like Dvorak, had spent some of his childhood growing up on the island. When Dvorak met him, Dan was living and working on the island as an adult. Dvorak recalled coming across a group "of single men and women in their thirties, most of whom are strangers to me, and it is as if I have just stepped into small town America."[14] He said Dan realized Dvorak was also a Kwaj Kid, and remarked:

"Bet you love this place, dontcha? I mean that water, the sound of these palm fronds, swishing around up above us. . . . Kwaj is a smell right? . . . It's like this perfume that puts you to bed at night. . . . if you grow up here for a long time, and you really love these islands, you feel connected to it and you know you belong here. . . . I feel like I have to protect this place, not for

America but for the island itself. . . . I guess the smell here is like home. . . .
[I]f you could bottle up this smell somehow and you could tell all those
people out there what it's about, they'd understand Kwaj once and for all.
They'd get that it's not all about missile testing and the army and all that. It's
about feeling connected to this place. . . . You know how it is—as a Kwaj Kid
I gotta be out here, gotta do my part so no one else comes and messes it up.
I love this place and so I wanna take care of it somehow. I feel like *that's* my
real job."[15]

Dan's reflections, as recounted by Dvorak, signaled a protective impulse
over both the place but also how the island was understood. For Dan,
his mission on Kwajalein diverged from the broader military one that
recruited Americans thousands of miles to the Central Pacific to work and
live. This "Kwaj kid's" experience growing up in this tropical small-town
USA transformed his purpose for being there: a reimagining of place and
self together.

To reimagine Kwajalein as an American home meant relationally
reimagining Marshallese as not at home but rather Americans' guests.
This framing drew upon and reproduced historic military explanations
of Marshallese *residential absence* alongside a racialized, commuting
labor presence on the island. The military positioning of Kwajalein as an
American home involved narrating who was foreign and domestic to the
island: who belonged, who was a legitimate presence, and in what capacity that legitimacy was accorded. One might imagine that US workers
and families settling on Kwajalein might simply presume Marshallese
residential absence alongside a commuting labor presence could be easily understood as common military base protocol. The explanations military and civilian contractors gave to civilian employees and families for
the absence of Marshallese suggest that the recruiters were aware of the
constructed character of the space. Welcome guides for incoming workers
offered an explanation for Marshallese displacements from their lands
alongside introductions to Marshallese as an available service sector to
support American family life on Kwajalein. These welcome manuals did
not simply frame the 1951 removal of the Micronesian labor camp from
Kwajalein, but also traced how hundreds of displacements throughout
Kwajalein Atoll to Ebeye over time made Ebeye an island of Marshallese
residency and Kwajalein an island of American residency.

These guides welcoming American employees framed Marshallese displacements using the language of safety and security. Displacement was done to protect Marshallese. Words like "evacuation" and "repatriation" were used to detail colonial displacements. For example, a Bell Laboratories welcome guide explained the 1961 military displacements of more than two hundred Marshallese living in the mid-corridor of Kwajalein Atoll, on Lib Island, to allow for missile testing: "As a precaution, 234 native residents of the island of Lib, were repatriated to a new village on Ebeye. With their evacuation, the 'Zeus Corridor' was officially open for traffic."[16] Bell positioned these military displacements as a story of homecoming rather than one of Lib Islanders being forced to move to an island upon which many had no land rights or connections. Likewise, a narrative of "evacuating" Marshallese to open the area for "traffic" framed the process of uprooting people from their homelands as a logistical step along a path toward clearing space for an inevitable missile-testing freeway.[17] In this respect, movements to and within the atoll became linked through a broader framework of natural and purposeful flows, rather than stories of contested colonial displacements. Americans migrated to their new home on Kwajalein, as Marshallese migrated to their new home on Ebeye. Both movements served the broader cause, a Cold War mission that aimed to keep all protected and secure.

Some US military and civilian contractor narratives acknowledged the importance of land to Marshallese. But in doing so, each story framed land scarcity, loss, and displacement as linked to other factors outside of US control. In one instance, the military tied land scarcity in the region to progress ushered in by US public health support. Welcoming new employees to Kwajalein in 1968, a US Army Material Command guide detailed the social importance of land to the Marshallese. It noted, "Land is considered to be the most valuable asset to the Marshallese who are dependent on it for their day-to-day existence."[18] The manual then lamented that "due to rapid increase in population since the introduction of better sanitation and medical facilities, a shortage of available land will eventually result."[19]

Four years later, a Bell Laboratories guide to the Marshall Islands contextualized for incoming US workers the history of Marshallese land tenure, situating US "administration" as following two other "colonial" regimes in the region.[20] In this story, Marshallese land loss was linked to an innate incapacity for self-governance. The guide explained that under German and Japanese colonial rule, Marshallese chiefly authority became weakened, particularly in control over land. The manual stated that while young Marshallese still strived for the privileges of being a chief, they were "not organized into any cohesive entity. That they ever will be is doubtful in the face of the transparent self-interest which dominates their thinking."[21] Echoing colonial language analyzed in chapter 1 that suggested Micronesian inability to self-govern, the Bell guide offered a narrative of self-defeating self-interest to explain ongoing Marshallese land loss. This framework conveniently obscured any context of US colonial land control in the region for weapons testing.

MARSHALLESE PRESENCE ON KWAJALEIN: "THE COMMUTER RACE"

While residentially absent, Marshallese *were* on Kwajalein daily for work. Americans coming to Kwajalein in the 1960s were introduced to Marshallese through their status as commuting laborers. Indeed, this presence of Marshallese in service labor positions contributed to a sense of American entitlement to exclusively reside on this Marshallese island. The luxury of having a Marshallese domestic servant supporting suburban family life signified a sense of social mobility for many US workers. As noted in chapter 3, US families settling on Kwajalein during the 1960s were introduced to Marshallese workers in military and civilian contractor welcome manuals detailing rules and regulations about curfews for this segregated workforce.

As welcome guides delineated these rules, they also provided specific details on the *racial* characteristics of these laborers. In a section entitled "Basic Micronesian Racial Stock," a 1961 Bell Laboratories welcome guide contextualized Marshallese racial characteristics while accounting for variations in physical appearance among Pacific Islanders. The manual identified "the full-blooded Micronesian islanders . . . [as having] complicated *breed* lines."[22] Suggesting an almost species-like differentiation—a narrative connected to deeper colonial language depicting natives as "savages"—such descriptions, situated alongside regulations on Marshallese labor, positioned these workers as a racially foreign presence on Kwajalein. Marshallese were commuters who entered America each morning and returned to Micronesia at the end of the day. The Bell guide further noted that Micronesian "genetic elements [are] associated in the adjacent south and east Asian countries with 'Mongoloid' and 'Caucasoid' racial types and, to a smaller extent, with 'Negritoid' and 'Australoid' types."[23] The manual continued on to distinguish Marshallese physical features from those of other Micronesians. The guide noted that "while the peoples of the West and Central zones (Palau, Truk and Ponape) tend to have Mongoloid type characters somewhat more emphasized, including medium to round (brachycephalic) heads and rounded faces[,] ... those in the Marshalls to the east appear rather more Caucasoid in type, as are their Polynesian neighbors, with longer narrower heads and faces."[24] The Bell guide concluded by lamenting "scientists still know all too little about the physical characteristics of the Micronesian peoples."[25]

The descriptions offered in this Kwajalein welcome manual highlighted a common colonial desire to categorize and catalog seemingly significant physical variations among populations—a project harkening back to the early to mid-twentieth-century eugenics movement and earlier craniology studies informing social Darwinism. That these narratives appearing in this 1961 civilian contractor guide drew upon previous military analysis was suggested by earlier iterations of these passages on Micronesian racial characteristics appearing in Stanford University's 1948 School of Naval Administration *Handbook on the Trust Territory of the Pacific Islands*. The inclusion of the text from the 1948 handbook suggests that the Kwajalein introductory manuals likely pulled the passages from these publications geared at postwar training for Trust Territory administration.[26] These texts appearing again more than a decade later in Kwajalein's personnel manuals exhibits the staying power of such racialized cataloging of Micronesians. By the 1960s, the descriptions were working to further domesticate Americans living on Kwajalein by distinguishing Americans from who they were not. Americans were not a racially foreign other, but rather the unmarked race, domestic to their new island home.

The history of Pacific Islander racialization and particularly Micronesian racial othering has deep roots in American culture, tied to the emergence of the field of anthropology.[27] Scholars of the Pacific have traced racial othering of Pacific Islanders as foundational to the academic discipline, but also infusing American and European popular culture through painting (e.g., by Paul Gauguin), novels, film, television, periodicals like *National Geographic*, and a robust tourism industry.[28] Contractors writing Kwajalein's manuals who included these passages on "Micronesian racial stock" may have done so anticipating a curiosity, suspicion, or even fear among incoming Americans in regard to their new "brown" neighbors. While it is difficult to identify any one clear motive behind the manuals' inclusion of these texts, one can see how such narratives, through their abstraction and objectification of Marshallese people, helped obscure the history and continuity of Marshallese land dispossession under US colonial rule. This language reinforced the colonial placemaking process on Kwajalein by normalizing a dynamic of belonging and exclusion on the island.

Given that social constructions of race have historically and continuously signified *place* in US landscapes, it is worth meditating on the export of these racializing logics, or as sociologists Michael Omi and Howard Winant labeled them in the 1990s, the racial *formations* to this site of suburban segregation in the US imperial Pacific.[29] Merging the insights of Omi and Winant's discussion of the historic specificity of racial production with attention to placemaking, I ask to what extent these racial logics became altered or involved the creation of new racial formations on Kwajalein. In what ways did perceptions of racial difference between Americans and Marshallese, but also between Americans themselves, emerge in place and time to mark the island as a recognizable *or* exceptional American space?

Marshallese accounts of experiencing racism on Kwajalein have tended to appear more often in interviews for investigative articles, petitions to the United Nations, and US Senate testimony, and rarely in oral history interviews. An exception was my interview with former Ebeye high school principal and Marshallese landowner Julian Riklon, who had been involved in Marshallese protests against the US military in the 1980s. During a May 2010 interview in his home on Ebeye, Riklon shared with me his impressions of how racism worked in relation to Marshallese labor on Kwajalein. Riklon grew up on Ebeye and worked with US missionaries

Figure 13. Julian Riklon on Ebeye
Island, 2010. Photo by author.

on Kwajalein for several years helping translate the Bible into Marshallese and explained that he saw many good Americans on Kwajalein who understood Marshallese needs and seemed willing to help.[30] But he added, with a slightly nervous chuckle, that along with these good people "there are people who don't care, who look down on us, think we are just a bunch of people who. . . . [H]ow should I say, like people who don't like colored people?" He continued, "Some of them would like to get rid of the people who are working there, just . . . fire them from their jobs."[31]

Riklon stood out among Marshallese oral history interviewees in overtly acknowledging racism on Kwajalein. Given historic and cultural distinctions around the topic of racism in the United States and the Marshall Islands, the potential discomfort with discussing the topic during interviews should not be surprising or read as an absence of racialized experiences. Many factors explain these hesitations or limitations that surface during interviews, not the least being the fact that a White American woman was asking the questions. In contrast to the exceptional nature of Riklon's candid response, several Americans who had lived and worked on Kwajalein seemed quite comfortable reflecting on what sorts of racial logics may have informed how Americans understood Marshallese presence and absence on the island.

Commenting on how racism operated on the island in recent years, one American working on Kwajalein, who wished to remain anonymous for job security purposes, identified it as the underlying cause for the island's "schizophrenic" atmosphere.[32] She explained that overt racism seemed culturally unacceptable for Americans in 2010, the year of the interview. But, she added, because "this place is inherently racist," people living on Kwajalein have to rationalize their participation in that system. She said most do so by justifying the island's racially segregated structure as a security issue. She noted, however, that this rationale proves untenable when Americans consider Marshallese exclusions from shopping centers, seemingly secure spaces. This Kwajalein resident characterized the island's atmosphere as a "*hyper*-America . . . more American than America," about which civilians often experienced extreme nostalgia when they moved away. As noted earlier, an expansive nostalgia industry played a role in assuaging the struggle of former "Kwajers" to adjust to life after leaving. This resident explained that for Americans who lived on Kwajalein, this nostalgia was for an "idealized time in the past," typically the 1950s, but a 1950s that never really existed in the first place. She likened the image most to "Leave It to Beaver" and noted that Americans who left tended to most miss the privileged and practical ease of their lives on Kwajalein. She added that for many, this privilege involved the luxury of having Marshallese domestics and servers. In her observation of Kwajalein's social and racial dynamics, the island may have become the realization of small-town suburban life for many Americans who previously only saw that portrait represented in the fantasy of television back at home.

Former resident and novelist Robert Barclay also reflected on Kwajalein's racialized landscape, a topic he made central to his novel *Melal*. Just eight years after publishing *Melal*, which captures American racial condescension on Kwajalein through subtlety and paternalism, Barclay elaborated on his observations of how racism operated on the island. Barclay offered an interesting read on how American perceptions of Marshallese on Kwajalein may have differed from American impressions of other racialized service labor or even colonial counterparts in the US landscape. Linking race, class, and place, Barclay discussed American perceptions of

Marshallese via the lens through which they viewed Ebeye. He explained this perception thus: "You have sort of short dark people who live in poverty, and you just look and say no I don't want to be a part of that."[33] Barclay explained that most Americans seemed to interact with Marshallese in a manner devoid of overt racism. Instead they employed a paternalistic approach. He said many expressed a belief that their American presence helped Marshallese people. Americans frequently asserted that Marshallese should be happy that Americans gave them clothes and other discarded items. Barclay laughed when recalling how Americans seemed to often wonder where the Marshallese would be without them. He recalled that when confronted with such questions, "I'd think, 'well . . . they'd probably be on the island!'"[34]

Alongside a pattern of paternalism characterizing American interactions with Marshallese, a range of meaningful relationships and instances of solidarity existed that exemplified a refusal to fully accept military efforts to bound these communities. In addition to the emergence of romantic relationships, detailed in chapter 3, a variety of close relationships were forged between many Americans and Marshallese over the years. On occasion some civilian residents on Kwajalein even used their positions of privilege to resist military policies that buttressed a hierarchical dynamic separating the two populations. For example, Cris Lindborg gained a reputation over the years for sneaking foods or gifts to Ebeye, skirting military rules. Born in Argentina, Lindborg met her American husband during his medical internship in Panama, and both came to Kwajalein in 1981 when her husband took a job as the island physician. Lindborg talked about her experiences in getting to know the Marshallese people as among the highlights of her time on Kwajalein.[35] She described Kwajalein as a beautiful and safe community, particularly from the perspective of a mother raising young children. But she never understood why Kwajalein and Ebeye remained segregated. In her own acts of subversion, Lindborg sidestepped army regulations as often as she could, but she noted that Kwajalein remained a space of rules, not democracy. She said that under a military structure, you followed the rules or you were out.[36] She nearly met this fate during her tenure when she almost got banned from Kwajalein for trying to bring a turkey off island to share with Marshallese friends in Majuro (the Marshallese capital) for Thanksgiving.

Figure 14. Jimmy Matsunaga on Kwajalein Island, 2010. Photo by author.

Civilian rumors also identified Jimmy Matsunaga alongside Lindborg as among those civilians reputed for skirting army rules to help Marshallese workers on Kwajalein. Matsunaga gained a reputation for using his position as manager of transportation and shipping services on Kwajalein to help promote and increase wages for Marshallese employees at any opportunity he could. During a 2010 interview, Matsunaga confirmed that he came by this reputation honestly. When asked if he believed his managerial practices were distinctive among Kwajalein's employers, he said they seemed more the exception than the rule.[37] Both Lindborg's and Matsunaga's actions suggested potential discomfort with Kwajalein's discriminatory practices toward Marshallese. Their behavior also revealed the creative ways each negotiated their own privileged position on Kwajalein to push beyond military barriers separating the two islands and a cultural landscape normalizing such inequities. It is not clear if or how their own experiences with citizenship or race may have informed such choices (Lindborg being Argentinean, Matsunaga being Japanese American).

When Matsunaga retired after more than forty years of employment on Kwajalein, he was thrown going away parties on Kwajalein by his American friends *and* on Ebeye by his Marshallese friends. This was a dual honor that Matsunaga seemed to take great pride in.

Many Americans and Marshallese managed to develop personal relationships over the years through job connections, friendships, or romantic bonds, all traversing the complicated physical and cultural terrain riddled with colonial, military, class, and racialized hierarchies. A significant cohort of US residents on Kwajalein also seemed to maintain limited understanding of the Marshall Islands broadly, and Marshallese people specifically. A common criticism by those Kwajalein residents who *had* spent a substantial amount of time on Ebeye was the seemingly absurd fact that so many individuals who lived on Kwajalein for years never made the three-mile journey across the lagoon to the only other largely populated island within more than 250 miles. Some even expressed derision toward those they knew who had traveled to Australia or Japan during their tenure on Kwajalein while never traveling to Ebeye. Former resident Cris Lindborg spoke disdainfully about the pride with which some would share these facts, recalling how these Americans boasted about their lack of time on Ebeye during multiyear tours on Kwajalein. She said most Americans viewed Ebeye as dirty and uncomfortable.[38] In an interview, Kwajalein resident Bob Butz acknowledged falling into the cohort of those who had never visited Ebeye. But instead of boasting about that fact, he expressed embarrassment. After explaining that the highlight of his experience living on Kwajalein for more than seventeen years was getting to know his Marshallese staff (he managed the island golf course), Butz admitted with a tinge of shame that he had not been to Ebeye once during that time.[39]

Dvorak also commented upon this phenomenon in *Coral and Concrete*, noting that "few of the Americans on Kwajalein ever ventured to Ebeye, even though we could see the islet on the horizon."[40] His inclusion in his book of a conversation with "Lisa" during a visit suggested Dvorak's irritation with this pattern of Americans on Kwajalein. He recalled: "Lisa passes me a drink and asks: 'What's it like on Ebeye this time of night? I've never been there after dark; hell I've almost never even been there during the day!'"[41]

This consideration of American time on Ebeye is not to suggest Americans should have indulged in colonial entitlement to easy and open access to the island, a luxury Marshallese lacked on Kwajalein. Rather, it is meant to highlight that a consistent message among those Kwajalein residents who *had* spent a considerable amount of time on Ebeye was a shared criticism of those Americans who avoided the island. This pattern hints at a level of discomfort some individuals may have felt residing within Kwajalein's segregated landscape as they distinguished themselves from fellow residents who uncritically accepted and perhaps even celebrated the boundaries separating the two islands.

"THE ALOHA STATE . . . OF MIND"

For the many Americans living on Kwajalein who avoided Ebeye over the years and remained primarily connected to Marshallese people through labor relations, the ways in which Marshallese history or culture infused their understanding of where they resided remained limited. For some, the small-town suburban landscape merged with the tropical setting to layer Kwajalein with what may have felt like a more familiar aura: a mythical pan-Polynesian culture. From the 1960s through today, a visitor transiting through Kwajalein might be just as likely to be welcomed by residents with the Hawaiian greeting "aloha" as with "iokwe" (the Marshallese traditional greeting).[42] During the island's tenure as a missile installation, many US residents embraced this "spirit of aloha" as a key marker of their experience on Kwajalein. Symbols of Hawaiian culture surfaced in island publications during the 1960s and 1970s, marking the lives of teens and their contractor-employed parents. These ranged from "aloha-style" student council events featured in the island's yearbook to Hawaiian warrior illustrations adorning pages of civilian contractor newsletters.[43] I next consider how some Kwajalein residents used this caricatured, touristic vision of Hawaiian culture to translate and familiarize this Marshallese island as an American home.[44] In doing so, I explore how the export of this trope from one site of military settler colonial occupation in the Pacific to another worked to disavow US empire in both. Converging with suburbia's cultural markers of innocence that helped enable US residency on Kwajalein to be understood as outside the realm of empire, this celebration of "aloha" on the island positioned Kwajalein as hospitable, an invitation reinforcing a sense of colonial entitlement to the region.

While the mapping of Kwajalein with images of this touristic cultural trope may have emerged in part to make the island more familiar and thus more accessible to Americans, it also seemed linked to changing demography over the years. While today Kwajalein's residential workforce largely comprises White Americans, in the 1960s and 1970s a substantial portion of the island's blue-collar workforce arrived from Hawai'i. Several civilians shared varying perspectives on how socially integrated the island seemed during that period. Some narrated Kwajalein as a space where people from all walks of life worked and socialized together. Others identified the largely Japanese American and Native Hawaiian workers migrating from Hawai'i as tending to socialize more among themselves and more openly with Marshallese than with the largely White American population.

Having lived on Kwajalein longer than most workers, Jimmy Matsunaga reflected on what this Hawaiian presence meant for him. Matsunaga came to Kwajalein from Hawai'i in 1966 and remained on the island for more than forty years. His lengthy tenure inspired a special feature in Kwajalein's daily newspaper the *Hour Glass* in 2006. In it Matsunaga reminisced about his early days on Kwajalein during the height of Hawaiian cultural influence on the island. He recalled: "'There were a lot of people from Hawai'i. . . . I would say at the highest point there were maybe 5,500 [residents], I would say out of that at least 2,000 were Hawaiian.'"[45] He noted: "'There was a lot of aloha spirit, the feeling of Hawai'i.'"[46] During an interview, Matsunaga elaborated on this "aloha spirit," explaining that given the large number of Kwajalein employees from Hawai'i during those years, the community tended to treat each other like brothers and sisters and often shared luaus and local foods.[47] He said during the 1960s and 1970s everyone mixed and had a feeling of camaraderie.[48]

The presence of such a large number of workers from Hawai'i on this US base in the Marshall Islands points to complex labor circuits traversing the US imperial Pacific during the postwar era. Just as military colonial conditions on Kwajalein would spur Marshallese to protest and try to reclaim their islands by the 1980s, so too had military bombings and training in Hawai'i inspired Hawaiians during the 1970s. The modern

Hawaiian sovereignty movement, which is ongoing today, was in part formed in response to US weapons testing on Kahoʻolawe Island and live-fire training in Makua Valley during the 1970s and 1980s.

These Pacific migrations prompted by US empire have not remained unidirectional over the years. Familiarity with Hawaiʻi has also been informed by Marshallese migrations there. For many Marshallese, Hawaiʻi has become intimately known. It has been an important space of education (a site where many Marshallese political leaders attended school during the 1960s). Hawaiʻi has also become the primary destination for health care for Marshallese, particularly since residency restrictions eased with the Compact of Free Association during the 1980s. For those Marshallese suffering the ongoing impacts of radiation-related illnesses and high rates of diabetes that accompanied changing diets under the US colonial regime, Hawaiʻi became a central site for medical care and resources.[49]

As Marshallese and Native Hawaiians have traversed this revolving door between their home islands in the US imperial Pacific, many Americans living on Kwajalein have also mapped their perceptions of "aloha culture" onto the island through increased access to Hawaiʻi. For thousands of US workers and families, moving to Kwajalein meant frequent contact with Hawaiʻi, as visits home to the continental United States were routed through Honolulu. That lasting imprint of Hawaiʻi on Kwajalein remains evident today. Hawaiʻi has become such a central part of the Kwajalein experience for many Americans over the years that certain sites in Honolulu have been marked by this enduring sense of community. As Jimmy Matsunaga shared, if one wanted to find a recent "Kwajer" either moving to Honolulu or traveling en route back and forth, one could simply show up in the morning at Honolulu's Ala Moana mall food court to find old colleagues and friends socializing.

Alongside labor demographic and logistical factors contributing to a greater connection between Hawaiʻi and Kwajalein, suggesting why performing "aloha culture" became common on Kwajalein over the years, Kwajalein residents have also pointed to other explanations. One resident raised the possibility that Americans on Kwajalein have appropriated and celebrated a touristic version of Hawaiian culture to help make sense of their lives in the Pacific. An interview with this Kwajalein employee, who wished to remain anonymous, revealed that Americans continued to greet each other today with "aloha" more often than "iokwe." She believed Americans on Kwajalein seemed more comfortable embracing their version of Hawaiian culture over Marshallese because they viewed this version of island culture as more accessible and more elegant.

Author and former resident Robert Barclay echoed this observation, noting the difficulty Americans seemed to have embracing Marshallese culture. He saw this as another way that Americans "othered" Marshallese. While growing up on Kwajalein during the 1970s and 1980s, he said he observed Americans unable to grasp Marshallese culture: "The problem is that Marshallese culture is just too foreign from American culture for a lot of Americans to embrace it. So what they instead do is they adopt their touristic view of Polynesian culture and apply that instead, that's why they'll say 'aloha' instead of 'iokwe.'"[50] As Hawaiian scholar Haunani-Kay Trask argued in *From a Native Daughter*, the tourist appropriation of "aloha," the Hawaiian word meaning "love," and "above all a cultural feeling and practice that works among the people and between the people and their land," became another tool of colonialism. "The point, of course, is that everything in Hawai'i can be yours, that is, you the tourists', the non-Natives', the visitors'. The place, the people, the culture, even our identity as a 'Native' people is for sale. Thus the word, 'Aloha' is employed as an aid in the constant hawking of things Hawaiian."[51]

The use of "aloha" by those residing on Kwajalein can also be understood as another cultural iteration of incorporating this Marshallese homeland into the sphere of US empire, further marking the island as a space of American entitlement. In his book *Playing Indian*, historian Philip J. Deloria traced a history of US settlers appropriating Native American culture while acquiring Indian land and using their performance of "Indianness" to lament what they perceived as having disappeared. He noted: "The dispossessing of Indians exists in tension with being aboriginally true. The embracing of Indians exists in equal tension with the freedom to become new."[52] "Playing Hawaiian" on Kwajalein may have worked to similar effect. While seemingly less rooted in a lament for disappeared Marshallese, this settler performance of a readily accessible colonial caricature on Kwajalein may have eased the process of Americans finding themselves anew, making home on Marshallese lands through the invitation of "aloha."

It is also possible to read the embrace of Hawaiian culture on Kwajalein as one way in which the island was brought into the broader frame
of belonging to the United States in a moment of historic political transition. On August 21, 1959, just one year before US civilians began arriving
on Kwajalein to support the Cold War missile-testing mission, Hawai'i
became the fiftieth state.[53] With Hawai'i being the only Pacific island
state, perhaps Americans' perceived familiarity with the islands through
popular culture and this changing political status made it a natural fit
for helping translate Kwajalein into a familiar reference point. By exporting a touristic vision of Hawai'i onto Kwajalein, Americans narrated both
Pacific colonies further into the domestic realm of the United States during the Cold War, disavowing the historic and ongoing imperial nature of
US control over each.

THE MYTH OF THE AMERICAN MELTING
POT ON KWAJALEIN

Another way that mythologies of Hawai'i may have converged to help sig-
nify Kwajalein as an American home is through US perceptions of Kwajalein as an exceptionally racially inclusive landscape. Just as Hawai'i has
historically and continually been celebrated as a seeming racial utopia,
Kwajalein has been lauded for this distinguishing characteristic by former and current residents.[54] While many Americans have acknowledged
racial discrimination directed toward Marshallese on Kwajalein, many
have simultaneously likened American relations on the island to the sorts
of narratives of racial harmony that enshroud these exceptionalist fanta-
sies about Hawai'i. Both island regions have come to constitute progressive spaces within American imaginaries, spaces seen as able to avoid the
kinds of racism mapping the continental United States.

This came through among the nostalgic reflections of former residents
on these aspects of daily life that were seen as distinctive on Kwajalein.
In the *Winston Salem Journal*, Sue Ellen Moss wrote about living on
Kwajalein during the 1960s in an editorial entitled "Culture Shock."[55] She
described returning home to North Carolina in 1963, at age seventeen,
and experiencing the shock of racism in the United States. Having grown

up on Kwajalein, Moss wrote, "On this small island there were civilians, enlisted personnel, contractors and subcontractors who were of all shapes, sizes, colors, religions, beliefs and origins. No one thought anything about those who were 'different' from them. What a cultural shock it was to return to North Carolina where people were judged by the color of their skin, the way they talked, their sexual orientation, and their social status."[56] The editorial was posted on May 29, 2016, to a Kwajalein social network site, a particularly robust one capturing Kwajalein memories and nostalgia. One response to the post came from a former Kwajalein resident (cited anonymously here): "Living on Kwaj was a microcosm of how the world should be. If you were white, you turned brown. If you were brown you were no different than whites. One church for all faiths; one school for all students; one lifestyle enjoyed by all." This online exchange poses a puzzle: How could a site marked by colonial exploitation and such extreme segregation that it was decried as exemplary of US "apartheid" in the Pacific by the 1970s be remembered through celebratory images of interracial harmony and equality for all?[57]

Just as the myth of a racial melting pot on Hawai'i has historically and continually worked to divert attention from historic and ongoing settler colonial land dispossession and racial inequalities structuring life for Native Hawaiians, these tropes of liberal racial inclusion were layered onto Kwajalein's landscape to similar effect. It may not be accidental that these narratives historically emerged together. Like the mythology working to obscure settler colonial structures mapping Hawai'i's landscape through a national framework of racial inclusivity, a similar process on Kwajalein helped cloak a space of extreme *colonial* segregation with a veil of innocence through a tale of *national* racial progress. As I examine the contradictions of these myths as they took root on Kwajalein, I show how they contained gaps large enough for the hauntings of US history's most violent chapters of White supremacy to seep through.

The *Winston-Salem Journal* exchange highlighting Kwajalein's exceptional, racially inclusive atmosphere echoed a pattern of observations from several current and former residents. Many described this distinct feature on Kwajalein by comparing the island to the American South. This comparison may be linked to the fact that a significant number of former Kwajalein employees have lived in the South and thus had that comparison in mind when thinking about Americans' interactions with each other. Echoing Moss's editorial, Robert Barclay categorized the racial environment between Americans on Kwajalein as exceptionally open and inclusive compared to other communities where he had lived in the United States. He recalled the shock of reintegrating back into the Southeast, where he witnessed overt racism for the first time while working in Virginia after growing up on Kwajalein. Barclay said he found the separation between Blacks and Whites at his Virginia jobsite a dynamic he never saw among Americans on Kwajalein. He said he never recalled any problems with racism among the Americans.

Barclay offered an interesting hypothesis about why race may have operated differently among US workers on Kwajalein, an analysis linking racism and classism. He felt that because everyone on Kwajalein was employed in some capacity, no residential population existed that could be racially categorized as lazy. Aside from accompanied versus unaccompanied employment status distinctions that impacted housing opportunities, Barclay said most housing on Kwajalein was assigned through a lottery. Therefore neighborhoods seemed to be racially integrated, although a divide remained between bachelor and family employee housing. As noted in chapter 3, this meant a degree of housing segregation, given that there were more workers of color living in bachelor quarters during the boom years of construction on the island, with the predominance of White knowledge workers living in family housing. Echoing several other civilian interviews, Barclay explained that the small size of the island community meant greater social integration; inevitably everyone ended up on softball teams and bowling leagues together and sat next to each other in church.[58] Most current and former residents interviewed agreed Kwajalein was too small for people to not get along. Several said those who could not handle living within the confines of this small island community tended to leave soon after arriving.

Kwajalein's seemingly exceptional intraisland racial integration in social and recreational life emerged in relation to extreme segregation marking the island's historic and ongoing connection to Ebeye. Some awareness of the differences in how race relations worked *among* Kwajalein residents compared to *between* US residents on Kwajalein and Marshallese residents on Ebeye was suggested in Sandra Crismon's ethnographic research.

One resident shared with her: "If you're a Kwaj resident, the amount of prejudice you're going to see in your life is slim to none. If you are not, if you are an Ebeye resident, the amount of prejudice you're going to see is going to be pretty blatant. It's almost like people have to have prejudice against somebody, and since they can't be prejudiced against other people on island, they pick the Marshallese."[59]

While several former residents have celebrated this absence of racism against Americans on the island—one even boasting Kwajalein was "the only place in the world where someone can move from Huntsville, Alabama, where they have lived their entire life, and the first year they're here, let their daughter go to prom with a black guy" not all agreed with this depiction of racial bliss.[60] Former Kwajalein resident C. J. Johnson was one of two African American kids living on Kwajalein during his high school years (the other being his younger sister). Johnson's father was employed as Kwajalein's commanding officer, and thus his family lived in the predominantly White family housing area of the island, one of the few African American families on island to arrive through military service. Moving to Kwajalein with his family just before September 11, 2001, Johnson recalled his immediate sense of discomfort upon disembarking the plane. He said, "As a black kid you can sense these things right away."[61]

Explaining that he was always welcomed on Ebeye, Johnson said he had a complicated relationship to belonging on Kwajalein. One instance that highlighted this was an experience with the island yearbook *Ekatak*, which means "to study" in Marshallese.[62] In a set of photographs taken grouping high school seniors into various categories (the common yearbook trope marking who was "most likely to succeeded," "funniest," "best dressed," etc.), Johnson was placed in a photograph grouping him with the only other brown kids on the island.[63] These teens comprised a small group of Marshallese students who were attending school on Kwajalein as part of a postcolonial school integration program (discussed in chapter 6). The yearbook editors captioned the image "street kids."[64] Insulted by the racist tone, Johnson went to the editors and demanded they change the section. The editors complied and moved Johnson into a grouping with mixed racial backgrounds. The resulting image showed the students wearing cowboy hats and was now captioned "outsiders."[65] Johnson recalled his exchange with the editors, in which they seemed to understand why he was angry. But he also remembered his peers seeming less congenial and implying he had been overreacting. These divergent experiences among Kwajalein's teenagers potentially helped explain why Johnson said he and his best friend—a blonde-haired, blue-eyed boy—had such different recollections of their time on the island. He said this friend longed for his days on Kwajalein, feeling deep nostalgia for that time in his life, while Johnson did not. Johnson did make a point to note, however, that he never felt the racism on Kwajalein came from a place of intent or cruelty, just ignorance.[66]

As a medium capturing the sentimental commemorations of childhood and adolescence, the *Ekatak* yearbook offers a useful view of suburban social norms illuminating features of community life on Kwajalein. It provides an additional text for examining how the experiences of children and teenagers wove into and buttressed the disavowal of empire in the Marshall Islands and helped frame the portrait of suburban innocence on the island. Unbeknownst to Johnson, the *Ekatak* photography marking his racialized experiences on Kwajalein built upon deeper roots of the yearbook's role in racially mapping the island. The yearbook has historically and repeatedly illuminated limits to the seemingly celebratory portrait of a racial utopia on Kwajalein. A pattern of photographs appearing in *Ekatak* during the 1960s and 1980s offers a reminder of how some of the nation's most violent episodes of racial terrorism bled into this replica of small-town USA erected in the space of the US imperial Pacific.

The earliest set of these images appeared in the 1967 issue of *Ekatak*, in which a photo spread illustrating the island's high school costumed dance (presumably for Halloween, given the timing) showcases images of an attendee dressed in a Ku Klux Klan robe. The photos are framed under what became a common American shorthand for Kwajalein, "the rock," in a feature celebrating a costumed event entitled "The rock rocks with Kwaj hops." This *Ekatak* section includes images of this individual dressed as a Klansman on one side of a photospread next to images celebrating an "aloha style" student council event on the other.[67] The individual wearing the Klan costume appears in several images, roaming around the dance, alongside text reading: "Ghosts and goblins haunted the teen club for a howling good-time in October." [68] One image shows a close-up of the Klansman posing for the camera.[69]

The 1967 *Ekatak* also featured an image of high school students cele-brating "sophomore slave day" on Kwajalein, in which a caption depicting the idea that one student has been sold to another reads: "For this I paid real money??"[70] In this photograph, the presumably enslaved, younger, male student is mocked and degraded by having to don female cloth-ing and jewelry.[71] Slave day became an annual celebration at Kwajalein's high school, one that entailed interclass hazing: older students demean-ing their younger peers. In the 1982 *Ekatak*, the event most overtly drew links to the violence and brutality informing US slavery, layering these symbols onto Kwajalein's small-town suburban replica in the Marshall Islands. In this issue, several images show White high school students (and one brown student) appearing with chains around their arms, legs, and necks.[72] The multi-photo spread centers a group image with a White male student holding a whip while standing next to his peers, who are bound in chains. All, except the one brown student in the image, are sporting toothy grins. Below the group photo are three separate close-up images of individual students presumably being led off the auction block, two by chains around their wrists and one by a chain around her neck.[73] Former resident Robert Barclay (who lived on Kwajalein in the 1970s and 1980s) remembered slave day, saying he also recalled the image of a friend who celebrated the annual event by wearing blackface, an image he shared with me during our correspondence in November 2019.[74]

That an individual went to Kwajalein's high school dance costumed as a Klansman in 1967, or that students celebrated slave day and performed a slave auction in chains, may be less suggestive of island racial dynamics than of the reality that the yearbook's adult supervisory staff chose to publish these photographs, featuring them as prominent spreads across the pages. In extensive archival research, including the daily newspaper and several oral history interviews, I was not able to find any evidence of a noteworthy response on Kwajalein to the Klan costume or the yearbook's publication of these images from the dance. Likewise, no evidence surfaced in my research that indicated any protest or criticism of the 1982 slave day images or the wearing of blackface on the island to commemorate this annual event.

As cultural historian Rhae Lynn Barnes has revealed in her research on amateur blackface minstrelsy, such casual depictions and performances of these violent racial chapters in US history were ubiquitous in US yearbooks during the twentieth century.[75] The images spanning the pages of *Ekatak* during 1960s and the 1980s signaled foundational features of the US racial caste system: the slave auction and domestic terrorism of the KKK. Their appearance in this high school yearbook—a medium symbolizing a space of innocence within the island's suburban landscape—suggests that these features of racial hierarchy and terrorism were an important piece of the cultural layers mapping America's segregated suburbia. Not only did symbols of culture travel from the United States to the Pacific, but the actual materiality of these items physically found a way to this island. One can ask: How did a Ku Klux Klan robe physically materialize on Kwajalein? This was not a form of clothing that had any local historical resonance in the Marshall Islands. Thus, one can only presume that a Klan robe landed on Kwajalein in one of three ways: an individual packed it in their luggage when moving to the island, this person sent for it (through purchase or shipped by a friend or family member), or someone stitched it together while living there.

It matters that the costumes and performances of the KKK, slave auctions, and blackface traveled thousands of miles to the Central Pacific, familiarizing this segregated suburban replica as a distinctly American home. As architectural scholar Marc Gillem has argued, "America's outposts are *simulacrums of suburbia*, copies based on a specific script meant to tie the homeland and its territories."[76] In the *Ekatak* yearbook, the haunting of chains, whips, and the familiar white robe may have also worked to tie this suburban copy back to its homeland, to familiarize Kwajalein through the recognizable American family tree that has always born a "strange fruit."[77] Buttressing Kwajalein's transformation into an American home was the export of American racial logics—those that signaled belonging and exclusion, privilege and entitlement within the US context.

Histories of lynching and slavery are never far from those of segregation in the United States, historically and continuously policing who belongs where and how boundaries and control over mobility are perpetually linked to these violent pasts. The images in *Ekatak*, reveal how a receptacle of youth sentimentality, this literary and visual time capsule containing memories of innocence and carefree suburban family life on Kwajalein, could also cast a shadow over those memories and call into question mythologies of the island as a space of exceptional interracial harmony. It may not be possible to identify any one reason why these symbols showed up on Kwajalein or how they were interpreted by those living on the island. But one can speculate on the work such images may have done in this distinctive setting of colonial suburban segregation by considering the role such racial signifiers have played in ordering US landscapes over time.[78] Perhaps a setting marked by extreme racial segregation separating Kwajalein's American and Marshallese workforces but where segregation between Americans was less stable necessitated such cultural signposts. The *Ekatak* photographs visually haunted the island with reminders of dominant White supremacist structures. In doing so, they suggest how the restaging of an American home in the Pacific may have required at least some visual aids to reinforce the natural pecking order through these most powerful and violently enduring narratives of belonging and exclusion in US history. Central to that history and American identity has always been the way that place is mapped racially and how those contours of apartheid landscapes emerged through violence and terrorism. In this way, Kwajalein's storied landscape was also mapped with racial signifiers easily intelligible to any American settling on this suburban landscape in the US imperial Pacific.

CONTAINING THE NARRATIVE OF HOME: UNSEEING KWAJALEIN AND EBEYE'S SHARED HISTORY

The *Ekatak* images and C. J. Johnson's experiences suggest the difficulty in disconnecting a portrait of life on Kwajalein from any broader racializing contexts. American efforts to maintain a cultural narrative of Kwajalein as separate from Ebeye proved just as tenuous. While this chapter earlier discussed how US workers and family members understood the absence and presence of Marshallese on Kwajalein, I turn now to consider how Kwajalein and Ebeye were relationally seen, or *unseen*. How did Kwajalein's civilian residents understand the dynamics of segregation marking the gulf between the two islands? What sorts of easily accessible, racializing tropes did they draw upon to obscure any connection between their colonially privileged suburban lifestyle on Kwajalein and the life-threatening poverty facing Marshallese segregated on Ebeye?

As this chapter has traced, US workers and families migrating to Kwajalein historically arrived to a space in which Marshallese were residentially excluded. For many of these workers and their dependents, Marshallese were a foreign, racialized "other" who commuted from elsewhere to serve them. Thus, for Americans, Ebeye's status as a home to Marshallese, in contrast to Kwajalein as a home for them, was the norm upon arrival. Perceptions of the *kind* of home Ebeye was and what that implied about the *kinds of people* who lived there were also shaped by a range of frameworks familiar to Americans. While the colonial context might have offered up tropes of "native savagery" (as discussed in chapter 1), metropolitan signifiers of race and urbanity, "culture of poverty" ideologies were just as readily on deck from the mid-1960s onward.[79] As noted earlier, for many individuals living on Kwajalein, the effortlessness through which such familiar tropes might come to mind to justify their segregated suburban lifestyle was likewise informed by having never visited Ebeye during their tenure on the island. Pacific studies scholar Greg Dvorak commented on this phenomenon, describing "the ease with which Americans blame the Marshallese for being incapable of sustaining their society, even with American assistance, and they point to Ebeye as an example of this."[80] He added, "In the end, most of them have to swallow and believe that whole message in order to live here."[81] American scapegoating of Marshallese for Ebeye's impoverished conditions went hand in hand with a willed effort to remain unaware of and incurious about any historic relationship between the two islands. Dvorak explained: "Americans have historically rationaliz[ed] that their gated existence on the base has nothing to do with Ebeye, or by foreclosing Ebeye as an unfortunate but inevitable consequence of failed development. In the imaginary of the suburban lifestyle of Kwajamerica, Ebeye thus serves as a metaphorical 'dump' that helps many Americans to rationalize a colonial lifestyle."[82]

That many of Kwajalein's civilian residents have continued to easily take up and vehemently guard the explanations offered by the military that disavow any responsibility for Kwajalein and Ebeye's colonial, segregated development over time was evident in reactions to a recent documentary film made about the two islands. In an interview, a former Kwajalein employee discussed how Americans on Kwajalein described the short film, *Rocket Island*, produced by ABC Australia in 2009. This employee recalled how many on Kwajalein bristled at the suggestion of American privilege on the island after they watched the film's opening scene, which featured Kwajalein residents enjoying a leisurely al fresco meal at the beach while being served by Marshallese waiters.[83] She said Kwajalein residents argued this beach dinner represented an exceptional event. This longtime resident refuted this suggestion, emphasizing that no Americans served each other food in the dining cafeteria or snack bar on Kwajalein. Only Marshallese and other "brown people" served and cleaned.[84] She also said the beach dining event occurred four times a year. She said Americans complained when this scene quickly shifted from that of a segregated country club setting on Kwajalein's beachfront to images of Ebeye's dilapidated houses, which illuminated the stark contrast between the two islands.[85] The dual imagery alluded to American privilege alongside Marshallese deprivation. This introductory framing, presenting an apartheid-like contrast, was laced with the undertones of racial privilege and racialized oppression that even the casual viewer could not have missed.

That some if not many US workers and family members living in a segregated suburban landscape have worked to unsee any structural relationship between their privilege and a racialized population living in urban poverty is not surprising. If a majority of US residents on Kwajalein were probing deeply into this context to question their surroundings, it would present an exceptional break with patterns of US history and the cultural context from which these workers migrated. In that respect, the history on Kwajalein is unexceptional. Similarly, a defensiveness about being perceived as individually racist, or even the projection of accountability for struggles on Ebeye onto perceived Marshallese cultural pathologies, is also predictable within the broader realm of US cultural history during and following the Cold War. To reflexively reject the notion of settler or racial privilege that might unsettle understandings of individualism and bootstrap-model mythologies that bleed into deeply held notions of meritocracy is to be expected. Such framings have always enabled US citizens who have benefited from histories of colonial and racialized structural inequality to unsee these conditions and uphold some of the most deeply cherished visions of what it means to be an American.

Of course no *individual* civilian arriving at Kwajalein created the colonial conditions of structural inequality framing Kwajalein and Ebeye's relationship. Nor have individual and collective benefits from these conditions necessarily had to do with individual *intent*. Rather, participation in a larger colonial military structure has drawn upon American roots of racist and colonial logics, mapping these spaces in ways that layer onto much deeper and broader goals of empire: control over land and labor. In this case, such control has not been about extraction of resources in the way one might think of traditional extractive colonial models or even intergenerational land inheritance by US settlers across the continent and other colonial spaces.[86] On Kwajalein, colonial control of land and labor has been rooted in strategic military objectives that have buttressed the rise of the military-industrial colonial complex: the ascendance of a US military empire. And in this way, cultural narratives framing life on Kwajalein as fundamentally disconnected from Ebeye have been yet another export further mapping the island with familiar cultural tropes that layer onto deeper histories of American disavowal of empire.

During the Cold War, suburbia's physical and cultural forms mapped a racially segregated landscape—one sociologists Douglas S. Massey and Nancy A. Denton defined as "American Apartheid"—across the continent through a veil of innocence. Those physical structures and cultural forms made their way to this suburban replica in the Marshall Islands.[87] As Dvorak observed, on Kwajalein, "histories are sanitized and landscaped over by peaceful grassy lawns, idyllic beaches," noting that the army labeled this "'beautification.'" He added: "Kwajalein today is strikingly picture-perfect. Amnesia is bliss."[88] The "bliss" Dvorak identified reflects what novelist James Baldwin called "the crime of innocence" in *The Fire Next Time*, discussed in this book's introduction. It is worth recalling here Baldwin's discussion of historic accountability, in which he proclaimed: "I know what the world has done to my brother and how narrowly he has survived it. And I know, which is much worse, and this is the crime of which I accuse my country and my countrymen, and for which neither I nor time nor history will ever forgive them, that they have destroyed and are destroying hundreds of thousands of lives and do not know it and do not *want* to know it."[89]

This chapter has made a case for the central role of culture in understanding the transformation of Kwajalein within the broader history of US empire. I return here to where I began, with my analysis of "imperialist nostalgia," which anthropologist Renato Rosaldo has argued helps facilitate the "capacity to transform the responsible colonial agent into an innocent bystander."[90] Rosaldo explained that this nostalgia "uses a pose of 'innocent yearning' both to capture people's imaginations and to conceal its complicity with often brutal domination."[91] On Kwajalein, such complicity required not simply passive ignorance, but also active engagement: it took *more work* in this landscape of colonial exploitation and extreme segregation to unsee that context. This is one feature that makes Kwajalein exceptional: the degree of effort it seems to take for the countless Americans who have reveled in nostalgic connections to the island as a beloved American home to uphold this mythology in a landscape where the conditions of colonial and racialized subjugation have been and continue to be so stark, so seemingly impossible to unsee. Kwajalein perfects what continental suburbia could not, thus making those contradictions that much more apparent. It makes the "crime of innocence" more ripe for prosecution.

Further exemplifying this *active* work of inscribing Kwajalein's landscape with a veil of innocence, Eugene C. Sims's memoir *Kwajalein Remembered* (discussed earlier) serves as one medium of nostalgia that also gestured to an awareness of the island's contested history. While the bulk of Sim's book detailed various transformations of Kwajalein over time through a trove of folksy stories chronicling events like the construction of the first hair salon in 1953, the history of dogs and cats on Kwajalein, and the trajectory of the island Macy's, a concluding chapter identified a history of Marshallese protest. In this section, Sims honored the army's long tenure of governance on the island (twenty-nine years at the time of publication) and alluded to this historic movement, explaining: "It has not been an easy task and the road has been full of chuckholes. Through it all the Army has weathered the political intrigues, the Greenpeace demonstrations, the Marshallese sail-in of 1983–4, the demands by environmentalists, and a host of ridiculous governmental bureaucratic garbage. . . . To this has been added the abusive and sometimes completely erroneous information put out by all of the media. In this writer's opinion the Army has done a commendable job."[92]

Sims's *inclusion* of "the Marshallese sail-in," even if to laud the army's commendable governance, indicates that his *exclusion* of Marshallese from much of the rest of the book was not unintentional. Rather, the active work to erase or discount Marshallese history seems foundational, *necessary*, to imagining the island as an American home. For Sims and so many other former residents of the island, seeing Kwajalein as an American home over time entailed a historic and persistent *unseeing* of the island as a Marshallese one. In this instance, Sims allowed some room for this history of colonial conflict to briefly seep into the memory, but just enough to be dismissed as among one of many "chuckholes" the army had to overcome. By marking and then discounting the protests, Sims added his voice to those of the many Americans on Kwajalein over time who have disavowed US empire in the region.

This chapter has argued that a focus on the role of civilian residents of Kwajalein and their cultural understandings and reproductions of mythologies about the island has contributed to its being shrouded in a veil of small-town suburban innocence. What began as a military recruitment tool to lure an elite workforce and their families to the island—the construction of a utopian suburban landscape—was easily embraced by civilian residents over time, and by some idealized and longed for following their departure. This constituted a shift from the 1960s challenge to sell Kwajalein to elite scientists, engineers, and their families (described in chapter 3). The change suggests the effectiveness of the army's investments and thoughtful planning over time, which transformed the island into a tropic suburban utopia. This was remarked upon by Test Site director colonel Rod Stuckey in his reflections on Kwajalein's ongoing allure. In 2017, he described the island to journalist Steve Johnson as "'Mayberry in the middle of the ocean,'" and explained that "the hardest thing isn't getting people to live on the islands, but rather to come home after they've lived there."[93]

MOVING KWAJALEIN AND EBEYE INTO THE GLOBAL SPOTLIGHT

While many current and former US civilian residents on Kwajalein struggled to see any connection between their lives on the island and Marshallese lives on Ebeye, such was not the case for a growing number of local,

US, and global media outlets during the 1960s, 1970s, and 1980s. As the optics of segregation drew scrutiny from outside observers, articles decrying the extreme divergences in conditions between Kwajalein and Ebeye spanned the pages of an array of publications, including nationally and globally recognized publications such as the *New Yorker,* New York's *Newsday, The Nation, TIME,* and *National Geographic Magazine,* as well as regional publications such as *Pacific Magazine,* the *Micronesian Reporter,* and *Pacific Islands Monthly.* As military policies mapped the two islands through familiar dynamics being historically contested in the United States and South Africa, these two homes became legible to these observers and ripe for critique. Several journalists lambasted what they identified as "apartheid conditions," publishing exposés with headlines such as "The U.S. Army's Ghetto-Islet in Micronesia," "Ebeye: A Pacific Ghetto?," and "Ebeye: Apartheid, U.S. Style."[94] From the 1960s onward, journalists, activists, and Marshallese political leaders worked to promote the narrative of Kwajalein as relationally connected to the framing of Ebeye, rupturing the cultural portrait created and reinforced by US residents on Kwajalein as one abstracted from this context.

By the 1980s, these articles began covering another event that exploded in response to this history of US colonialism in the Marshall Islands. This event, which Sims identified as simply another "chuckhole" in the army's list of headaches, was the mass sail-in protest of Marshallese landowning families in 1982 to reclaim their homes throughout Kwajalein Atoll.[95] This movement followed years of Marshallese condemnation of the colonial conditions framing their lives, frequently through petitions, speeches, and testimonies before the United Nations and at historic US Senate hearings. After these routes proved ineffective, Marshallese organized and put their bodies on the line through nonviolent direct action. In doing so, they challenged the physical and cultural façade Americans had constructed of Kwajalein as *their* home, one that situated Marshallese as foreigners in their own lands. No event more dramatically unsettled this narrative of American entitlement in the region, while spurring an aggressive military defense of this myth, than the 1982 sail-in protest, aptly called Operation Homecoming.

5 Reclaiming Home

OPERATION HOMECOMING AND THE PATH
TOWARD MARSHALLESE SELF-DETERMINATION

> They think that we were stealing something important
> from them. But it was really *they* were stealing something
> important from *us*.
>
> —Julian Riklon, 2010

> The Kwajalein people say they will shut down the vital test
> range before they will suffer 50 more years of apartheid-
> like conditions in Ebeye. It may well be that the future of
> the US nuclear weapons programme rests in the hands of
> 5,000 Kwajalein landowners on their remote Pacific atoll.
>
> —Giff Johnson, 1982

"SEEING STARS" ON KWAJALEIN

In June 1982, one thousand Marshallese men, women, and children sailed throughout Kwajalein Atoll to reclaim their islands in a movement they called Operation Homecoming. Through this protest, Marshallese individuals upended the mythical frame of Kwajalein as a site of American belonging. In doing so, these landowning families reminded the most powerful military in the world, and a local and global audience watching, that this was *their* home.

Operation Homecoming interrupted US missile testing on Kwajalein for four months, incurring unanticipated expenses for the military. Marshallese protestors strategically timed the sail-in to try to influence the nature of political negotiations toward decolonization. They also took advantage of the military's vulnerability to having missile testing interrupted at a time when Kwajalein had become so central to the broader US arms race, that their mass sail-in could impact some of the most high-profile tests of the Reagan administration. The military responded to the unarmed, nonviolent protest with violence and punitive measures imposed on the entire Ebeye community.

One individual on the receiving end of this brutal response was Julian Riklon, a protest leader who was beaten unconscious by US guards on the first day of Operation Homecoming. Riklon was not the first, nor would he be the last, Marshallese protestor assaulted while challenging the conditions of US military colonialism in their home islands.[1] But Riklon's case was the most publicly documented by the media. On the first day of Operation Homecoming, Riklon arrived at Kwajalein and joined about two hundred other Marshallese protestors, primarily women and children, in a march to the jailhouse to challenge the imprisonment of thirteen of their leaders.[2] Riklon recalled in an interview his effort to use his fluency in both Marshallese and English to help translate for this group standing outside the jailhouse. Instead of welcoming this service, the Kwajalein police chief ordered Riklon's arrest, and police dragged him to the jailhouse, where they beat him unconscious. Recounting the scene, Riklon chuckled, noting that's when he "saw stars."[3] When he came to, Riklon remembered lying on the ground and hearing the cries of Marshallese women and children outside who were throwing rocks at the jailhouse to hasten his release. Riklon said the police soon complied, setting him free to calm the commotion. When asked why he thought the police responded to him with such violence, Riklon said: "Oh, I don't really know. They think that we were stealing something important from them. But it was really *they* were stealing something important from us."[4]

Operation Homecoming temporarily ruptured the façade of American belonging on Marshallese lands that the military and civilians living on Kwajalein had been erecting since the 1960s. While not the first instance of Marshallese challenges to policies or narratives marking their homelands as solely existing to serve US strategic interests (as traced in previous chapters), Operation Homecoming and the events leading up to this historic protest signaled a turning point. The protest erupted in the wake of consequential US Senate hearings held on Ebeye in 1976 that captured Marshallese concerns about their future political status, the historic and ongoing health and infrastructure crisis on Ebeye, and the structure of segregation on Kwajalein. The hearings and Operation Homecoming both constituted pivotal chapters in a longer trajectory toward Marshallese decolonization.

As landowners reclaimed the narrative of Kwajalein as a Marshallese home, they also signaled their role in the broader process of Marshall Islands decolonization, as control over Kwajalein and awareness of the island's value to the United States became the primary node on which Marshallese sovereignty would hinge. In the era of global decolonization that spanned the 1970s and 1980s, the US Army struggled to retain unmolested control over its colonial investment in Kwajalein. Marshallese landowning families and activists creatively navigated the terrain of Pacific and global anti-colonial and antinuclear protests by utilizing nonviolent direct action to leverage their power when formal, UN-sanctioned political channels failed to do so.

THE 1976 US SENATE HEARINGS: DEBATING A PATH TO DECOLONIZATION

Operation Homecoming constituted a local story of anti-colonial struggle, one of many acts playing out across the global drama of postwar decolonization during the Cold War. To understand these intersecting contexts, we need to revisit how Kwajalein came to play a central role in the Marshallese push for self-determination over the longue durée of US colonial control in the region. The historic sail-in marked a turning point that followed years of Marshallese negotiations and debates over the path of their political future. The contested status of Kwajalein was always at the forefront of these negotiations, as the island could be leveraged given its distinctive value to the military. As Marshallese expressed a range of opinions about what their future relationship with the United States should look like and what kinds of concessions and support the United States owed Marshallese in the postcolonial era (primarily compensation for nuclear radiation victims, leasing payments for Kwajalein, and greater financial support for

Ebeye), the impact of US weapons testing in the region was the focal point around which debates pivoted. These debates and eventual protests left deep cleavages between Kwajalein landowners and the emerging leaders of the Republic of the Marshall Islands government, divisions that continue to inform ongoing tension and resentment today.

While Operation Homecoming marked a historic moment when Marshallese landowning families most impactfully voiced concerns about the future status of their homelands by putting their bodies on the line, the protest built on a broader expression of Marshallese grievances about US control in the region just six years earlier in testimonies before the US Senate Subcommittee on Territorial and Insular Affairs (hereafter "Senate hearings"). Just as Operation Homecoming would do in 1982, these 1976 testimonies called attention to the imperial nature of US control in the region and advocated for Marshallese rights to self-determination on their own terms. At the same time, the testimonies pointed to the central role Kwajalein played as a site of ongoing economic dependence for Marshallese, which signaled real limitations on those terms of negotiation. Testimonies also showcased Marshallese and American observations and critiques of segregation and discrimination on Kwajalein and of US neglect of Ebeye. Some of the most damning statements centered the public health disaster plaguing Ebeye and the role segregation between Kwajalein and Ebeye played in exacerbating the deadly impact of this crisis.

While the 1976 Senate hearings foreshadowed the historic protest six years later, documenting that Marshallese grievances were nearing a tipping point, they were organized primarily to address the future political status of the region. The testimonies emerged out of a longer process of Micronesian political education sanctioned through the Trusteeship Agreement. Under UN mandate, the United States had supported political education for Micronesian elites during the first several years of the Trust Territory administration with the creation of the Congress of Micronesia (COM) in 1964 as a space for elite Micronesian political leaders, who were educated in US schools about democracy-style government, to discuss and debate the future of their islands.[5]

As revelations coming out of the Solomon Report (discussed in chapter 1) suggested, Micronesian political education historically emerged alongside US efforts to delay decolonization in the region and shape the trajectory of Micronesian sovereignty to most benefit US strategic interests. From early on, Marshallese political representatives and their Micronesian counterparts expressed skepticism about US commitments to honor the Trusteeship Agreement and support Micronesian self-determination. At a 1968 COM meeting in the Trust Territory capital, Saipan, Palauan Political Status Commission chairman Lazarus Salii warned: "'There is a danger ... that ballots for Micronesia's plebiscite will be printed in Washington."[6] Among the range of possible political paths, Micronesian leaders debated the prospect of decolonization as a unified entity. This option was encouraged by the United States because it offered an easier route toward long-term control over the region, allowing the United States to avoid multiple arrangements across the various island nations. For Marshallese leaders navigating their political future, the prospect of "Micronesian unity" contended with the distinctive local conditions that US weapons testing had brought to their islands. In these discussions, Kwajalein became a focal point. Kwajalein's strategic value to the United States informed how Marshallese political leaders discussed, debated, and imagined the possibilities of a broader *national* political future.

Opposition to Micronesian unity as a path to decolonization, one that risked erasing the distinct costs borne by Marshallese as the broader region became enfolded in the US security mission, also surfaced eight years later in Marshallese testimonies before the UN Trusteeship Council. Speaking on June 30, 1976, before the council in New York City, vice chairman of the Marshall Islands Political Status Commission Tony de Brum argued that the Marshall Islands should be allowed to negotiate their political future separately with the United States.[7] In his testimony, De Brum made a case for why unity would not benefit Marshallese, arguing:

"No one can take Marshallese, Ponapeans, Trukese, Palauans, Yapese, Kusaieans, and others, put them all together and come out with Micronesians. Micronesians unity is and has always been a myth, advanced by our so-called benefactors in order to keep us dependent, and accepted by some of our brothers in the Carolines who see it as a means of continued enjoyment of the U.S. dole system without having to give up any of their lands, without having to be displaced by the U.S. military, without having their islands blasted off the face of the earth, without being exposed to atomic radiation, without suffering discrimination or without being shot at once a week with ICBM's from Vandenberg Air Force Base in California."[8]

De Brum's statement highlighted the exceptional role that the Marshall Islands broadly, and Kwajalein specifically, had played in the US security mission. This was a role that created disproportionate costs for the Marshallese and thus necessitated a separate path toward sovereignty to ensure those costs would be specifically addressed. This position also coincided with the exceptional monetary value, the benefits connected to the military's investments in Kwajalein over time, positioning the atoll to act as a key bargaining chip in this path to self-determination. De Brum believed this value should only serve Marshallese. In his view, Marshallese had paid the highest price for their role in this broader security mission, and they alone should retain any benefits linked to those enormous costs. For De Brum, this was the cost of the Marshall Islands' unique incorporation into US empire.[9]

Prompted by the presentation of De Brum and others representing Marshallese political concerns in New York, Representative Patsy Mink (D-Hawai'i) and Delegate Antonio Borja Won Pat (D-Guam) traveled to the Marshall Islands two weeks later to head local Senate hearings to address the region's future political status. The hearings provided a forum for Marshallese to testify about the US impact on their homelands and discuss and debate their desired future relationship with the nation. One of the two representatives heading the two days of hearings in Majuro and Ebeye, Japanese American Patsy Mink was also the first Asian American woman (and first woman of color) elected to the US Congress (in 1965) and the first woman elected to Congress from the state of Hawai'i. Four years before the hearings, Mink had also become the first Asian American to seek the Democratic nomination for president of the United States.[10] Won Pat, a Chamorro politician and member of the Democratic Party of Guam, was serving as the first nonvoting delegate of Guam's at-large congressional district to the US House of Representatives at the time of the Senate hearings.[11]

Upon arriving at Ebeye, Mink explained that she and Won Pat had come to hear and record Marshallese perspectives on the matter of their political future and to bring these concerns back to the Capitol.[12] But

Senator Won Pat's opening statements at the Senate hearings on Ebeye echoed sentiments expressed in Saipan six years earlier: an awareness that Micronesians would negotiate a path toward self-determination amid the hierarchies and inequalities fostered by US empire. Speaking as a representative from Guam, noting how his people had lived under the US flag for more than half a century before becoming part of the United States, Won Pat highlighted the precarious position from which Marshallese would be negotiating their political future. As a nonvoting delegate, Won Pat compared his appearance before the Marshallese with a story about a politician addressing inmates in a prison. Won Pat said the politician first addressed the group by saying "fellow citizens," which provoked laughter among the audience because as prisoners they were no longer citizens.[13] The politician stopped to think and then addressed the group as "fellow convicts," which likewise evoked laughter because he himself was not a convict. Finally, the politician stated he had no idea what to call those before him, but he was very glad to see them. Likewise, Won Pat said he too was very happy to see his Marshallese audience.

Won Pat's remarks showcased the deeper history of US imperial control across Micronesia that began with Guam in 1898. Likening the condition of the Marshall Islands to his home of Guam, Won Pat's comments signaled the ambiguous territorial status of islanders across Micronesia who had been denied the freedom to govern their own lands following US imperial expansion into the Pacific in the late nineteenth century, as detailed in the introduction. Neglecting to specifically mark Guam's relationship to the United States through the language of colonial control, Won Pat instead pointed to the more confusing or tragically comic conundrum of an individual facing an unfree population but hesitant to name the structure confining that freedom. He alluded to this challenge in marking the freedoms and unfreedoms across the range of US territorial designations, including the many islands controlled by the United States but not part of the nation.[14]

As representatives of the US government arriving at the Marshall Islands from Guam and Hawai'i, Won Pat and Mink traversed complicated terrain in administrating a democratic discussion to determine this Pacific Island's path toward decolonization. Mink's arrival at Ebeye from Hawai'i occurred just six months after Native Hawaiian activists had sailed to reclaim one of their ancestral islands, Kahoʻolawe Island, to halt ongoing US weapons testing on the island. As noted in the introduction, the sail-in helped launch the modern Hawaiian sovereignty movement. In this respect, Marshallese testifying about a path to greater sovereignty did so in 1976 guided by representatives from two other Pacific Island territories where freedom and sovereignty remained continually constrained and contested.[15] Just as Marshallese voiced their struggles against US colonialism in their homelands, indigenous activists in Guam and Hawaiʻi were bringing global attention to shared constraints on their sovereignty under US empire during the 1970s and 1980s, as they continue to do today.[16]

While highlighting the ambiguous and constrained position from which Marshallese negotiated their political future, Won Pat opened his statements by signaling the range of options Marshallese would discuss to determine their future status. At the time of the hearings this included the option for an ongoing relationship with the United States (through the Compact of Free Association) negotiated as a broader, unified Micronesian entity or as a separate Marshallese entity. The options also included complete independence from the United States via either status. Elsewhere, I have written about Marshallese testimonies on their future political status and the centrality of Kwajalein in this path toward self-determination.[17] I briefly summarize these here to contextualize how the hearings became a dual platform for Marshallese to voice political preferences alongside grievances about Kwajalein's segregation structure.

The testimonies showcased a range of Marshallese preferences reflecting the historic and ongoing impacts of US empire and militarism in their home islands. A notable split in opinions on the question of independence hinted at the long-term implications of US imperialism in the region. Many Marshallese expressed doubts about their capacity to go it alone in a path toward decolonization by seeking full independence from the United States. This pattern suggested the level of US success in creating conditions for ongoing economic dependence in the region. To ensure continued support for its Cold War security mission, the United States had deployed colonial policies that made it difficult for Marshallese to imagine their own security in the absence of a US presence. These fears came through in the testimony of John Heine, the acting chairman for his newly formed group, Voice of the Marshallese. Arguing that Marshallese were not ready for independence, Heine said the region needed more time to learn about democratic governance and more resources and support for the training of doctors, lawyers, and political leaders and infrastructure development.[18] Heine's sentiments reflected a common concern of many decolonizing populations in the postwar era: how to navigate a postcolonial status within a context of long-term political and economic dependence fostered under the colonial administration. Given US neglect for decades of its UN obligations to support economic development across Micronesia, Marshallese found themselves debating this potential for an independent future against a backdrop of very real, material concerns. Pushing for a political path of Micronesian unity and the Compact of Free Association, Heine discounted perceived distinctions between Marshallese and other Micronesians by arguing that Marshallese had divisions from within as well based on customs of following different paramount chiefs.

While Heine's advocacy for unity proved less popular, his rejection of a path toward independence and an embrace of an ongoing political and economic relationship with the United States through the Compact of Free Association was echoed across many testimonies. Senator and member of the Congress of Micronesia and chairman of the Marshalls Political Status Commission Amata Kabua shared this vision for Marshallese sovereignty. In his testimony, he explained that the Marshallese did not need the United States managing their defense or marine resources but instead needed US financial and technical assistance in developing these resources and support to market the harvests of the sea.[19] He called on the United States to make good on the trusteeship mandate it had neglected for decades: support for economic development in the region to avoid ongoing dependence through Kwajalein. He qualified, however, that Marshallese would be "quite willing to negotiate fair and equitable agreements" with the United States to make certain their lands and waters remained available for continuing US strategic use.[20] Here Kabua alluded to the centrality of Kwajalein in determining the future political path for the nation, pointing to this bargaining chip he knew held the utmost importance to the United States.[21]

A vocal exception to broader support for ongoing free association with the United States came from Kwajalein landowner Ataji Balos. At the time of his statements, Balos had been serving for several years on the

COM Joint Committee on Future Status and participated in the Marshall Islands Political Status Commission. He couched his plea for independence alongside Marshallese separation from the rest of Micronesia while echoing Kabua's emphasis on the centrality of Kwajalein to negotiations for sovereignty. Balos pointed to the risks for Kwajalein peoples having their land leases determined by outsiders, especially given ongoing grievances associated with the 1964 Kwajalein lease. He argued: "The United States insists on the concept of Micronesian unity because it realizes no truly representative group of Marshallese leaders will ever sign an agreement embodying the 1964 Kwajalein lease."[22] For Balos, Kwajalein's leasing past, present, and future were at the center of political negotiations for broader Marshallese decolonization. Independence meant Marshallese could finally gain control over their lands and government.[23]

The history of contestation over US leasing practices, alongside disproportionate US investments in the missile base on Kwajalein and minimal investment in other sustainable economies in the region, made a vision of independence untenable to many Marshallese testifying in 1976. The prospect of redistributing any benefits or opportunities from Kwajalein's distinctive value beyond the Marshall Islands to other Micronesians who had not borne the same burdens of US weapons testing also seemed unacceptable to the majority of Marshallese who were testifying. Their testimonies showcased how US Cold War militarism had created divergent conditions across Micronesia, haunting the Marshall Islands landscape with destruction, displacement, and devastation while also marking the region as a site of new economic incentives emerging in the wake of such policies.

After listening to the testimonies of more than a dozen Marshallese speakers at the 1976 hearings, Representatives Mink and Won Pat concluded that the majority favored the Compact of Free Association with the United States, but as a separate entity from the rest of Micronesia. The representatives brought these findings back to Washington, DC, in recommendations about how the United States should proceed with negotiations.[24] But for those Marshallese who desired a different political future, the discussion did not end there. In the wake of the hearings, Ataji Balos continued his push for independence, bringing his ongoing concerns before the COM. In his statements, Balos framed the notion of any sort of democratic discussion about the Marshallese political future as a sham. He derided 1976 as the two-hundred-year celebratory anniversary of American freedom and democracy, explaining that no such luxury existed for the Marshallese. He said that as long as the Marshallese lacked an economy, no political freedom existed. Regarding enabling economic freedom, Balos highlighted Marshallese capacities in untapped areas, shifting the focus from ongoing US missile testing on Kwajalein as an economic engine and toward the Marshall Islands' marine resources. Balos explained how wealth production within an independent Marshallese nation could be built on Marshallese freedom to sell fishing rights to other nations and peoples. "Our seas are rich with tuna, and rich with minerals. Yet, we are being told we cannot support ourselves so that outsiders alone can reap the benefits from our seas," he argued.[25] Balos noted that the United States permitted nations to fish freely with no payments to Marshallese.

Balos's statements signaled the challenges for Marshallese navigating a sovereign future constrained by conditions of economic dependence upon the same colonial power whose policies had left the region's inhabitants no choice but to stay affiliated to survive. Balos questioned why Marshallese would have ever trusted the United States as a negotiating partner at the same time that Bikinians and the peoples of Enewetak and Kwajalein remained exiles due to US weapons testing on their lands. He stated, "As long as this is the case, I cannot believe that an agreement, any agreement with a nation which has so abused its sacred trust, will protect our islands and people in the future."[26] In the wake of the hearings, Balos called attention to the same predicament Won Pat had opened the hearings with: what it meant for a colonized population to discuss and debate a path to self-determination under the ongoing constraints of US empire, as subjects who were not convicts but also not free.

Marshallese testimonies, during and after the 1976 Senate hearings, foreshadowed how the transition toward decolonization would continue to be a fragile and contested path, one that stressed the tenuous nature of any solidarity across the Trust Territory region. As Micronesian political leaders negotiated divergent paths toward decolonization, these frays were marked by Marshallese critiques of their perceived focus on Kwajalein. Speaking before the COM in 1977, Amata Kabua shared his disappointment in these leaders, whom he saw as continuing to advocate for Micronesian unity with an aim to reap the material benefits of Kwajalein's value to the United States. He argued: "Leaders of this body [should] forego their obsession with leasing Kwajalein to the United States. Their attempts to do so and to coerce us into a Micronesia in the process will only make rebels out of the people of the Marshalls and jeopardize their ties of friendship to the other island groups of the Trust Territory."[27]

Kabua's statements signified the long-term impacts of US weapons testing in the region, illuminating the heterogeneity of local experiences under US colonial rule across Micronesia during the Cold War. Such distinctions contributed to how political leaders imagined different futures for their nations. The Marshallese political trajectory would differ, for example, from that of the Central Carolinean Islands in the Trust Territory (Yap, Pohnpei, Chuuk, and Kosrae), whose political leaders would opt to negotiate their political future with the United States as a newly formed entity, the Federated States of Micronesia.[28] Marshallese charted their path to decolonization along a trajectory that reflected their own distinctive experiences with US empire, one that had created divergent conditions, incentives, and perceived betrayals. This route toward Marshallese decolonization increasingly hinged on the value of Kwajalein as a key US Cold War missile installation. Over time, Kwajalein came to play *the* central role in negotiations for the nation's path toward decolonization, shaping the boundaries of how that trajectory came to be imagined.

THE SENATE HEARINGS AS A FORUM
TO PROTEST SEGREGATION ON KWAJALEIN

While the 1976 Senate hearings primarily offered a platform to discuss and debate the future political status of the Marshall Islands, it also became a forum for addressing historic and ongoing segregation between Kwajalein and Ebeye. In this respect, the hearings constituted a distinct space of protest. As detailed in previous chapters, the hearings were not the first time Marshallese or Americans had voiced concerns about differing conditions on the two islands. But the testimonies in 1976 *did* add significant evidence to the public record that comprised some of the most incriminating details about life-threatening patterns of discrimination and exclusion on Kwajalein, details that would be taken up by investigative journalists and publicized locally and globally in dozens of articles. In this way, the testimonies marked one of the most publicly documented spaces in which Marshallese traced the enormous costs they had paid as their islands historically became home to the US security mission. Numerous statements detailed how Marshallese faced increased insecurity as a consequence of this mission. The collective force of these statements, alongside the army's refusal to acknowledge any historic or ongoing responsibility to address them in the wake of the hearings, fueled the momentum that ultimately erupted six years later in Operation Homecoming.

The timing of the Senate hearings in July 1976, which coincided with the US bicentennial celebrations, made US disavowal of empire in the Marshall Islands and the structures of segregation shaping life in Kwajalein and Ebeye especially ripe for critique. In his testimony, Kwajalein landowner Ataji Balos centered the contradictions of a bicentennial honoring values of independence, freedom, and equality while the United States continued to pursue a destructive and discriminatory military colonial project in his homeland. Highlighting the extreme segregation dividing Kwajalein and Ebeye, he explained that "only a matter of hours after Trust Territory Acting High Commissioner Peter Coleman had finished telling the United Nations Trusteeship Council there was no segregation at Kwajalein (a statement he would not dare make here on Ebeye), the command of Kwajalein Missile Range celebrated the American Bicentennial by closing Kwajalein Island to any Marshallese."[29] Balos added, "So American independence was celebrated at Kwajalein Atoll by enforcement of all-out and total segregation."[30]

Balos's criticisms reflected those of several Marshallese and Americans testifying at the Senate hearings who decried discrimination in housing, educational and consumer facilities, and employment on Kwajalein. Anthropologist William J. Alexander shared his ethnographic research at the hearings, which tracked Marshallese accounts of workplace discrimination in hiring, promotion, and wages on Kwajalein. Alexander's testimony was reported on and circulated widely in an exposé published following the hearings in *Newsday* magazine, in which journalist Paul Jacobs detailed the wage gaps between Marshallese domestic servants, whose yearly earnings reached just over $2,100, and US personnel, who earned $18,000. Jacobs's article, which also detailed Marshallese perceptions that racism informed their labor conditions on Kwajalein, exemplified a series of articles that drew on the Senate testimonies to broadcast Marshallese accounts of discrimination to wider US and global audiences.[31]

The most damning statements coming out of the 1976 Senate hearings focused on the deadly repercussions of hospital exclusions and segregated medical care on Kwajalein due to US neglect of health care facilities and resources on Ebeye. As noted in previous chapters, a deeper trajectory of US disregard for Marshallese health and well-being began three decades prior to the hearings, when the navy first selected the region to become the location for nuclear testing. Since that time, Marshallese and American allies had tried and failed to call serious attention to the medical repercussions and public health crisis that accompanied US weapons testing in the region.

Testifying at the Senate hearings on the deadly impacts of US apathy about Marshallese health and well-being, Balos detailed the ongoing dire health conditions on Ebeye and exclusions from access to Kwajalein's superior facilities. Balos highlighted US negligence regarding its Trust Territory obligations, explaining that Marshallese on Ebeye suffered preventable public health crises in part because the United States had failed to develop a viable economy in the islands and excluded Marshallese from living on Kwajalein. He noted: "Since the Marshallese people are not permitted to live on islands which are rightfully ours, we are forced to live in very small apartments which may be shared by as many as 10, or even 20 people, in extreme cases."[32] Balos added that some units on Ebeye housed up to forty individuals. Positioning Ebeye's crisis within the broader context of Micronesia, Balos explained that while Ebeye had 5 percent of the Trust Territory's total population, the island accounted for 12.2 percent of the recorded cases of ameobiasis and 14.4 percent of the recorded cases of hepatitis.[33] He said that several years earlier, an official Trust Territory government report had identified Ebeye's lagoon as having a bacteria count twenty-five thousand times higher than minimum safe standards determined by US Public Health Services and the UN World Health Organization.[34]

The most extensive and damning testimony on the impact of segregation in health care in the region came from US physician Dr. Conrad P.

Kotrady. He echoed broader concerns about the public health crisis on Ebeye while adding extensive details about indifference to this crisis on Kwajalein. Kotrady had come to Ebeye in 1975 with the Brookhaven Institute to study the long-term impacts of nuclear testing in the Northern Marshall Islands among displaced and irradiated islanders resettled on Ebeye. His route to the Marshall Islands took him from examining the destructive impact of this first US weapons-testing campaign in the region (nuclear bombs) to the devastation of the second (ICBMs) as both converged on Ebeye.

Kotrady addressed the Senate committee as "a concerned physician," prefacing his statements by noting that he spoke on behalf of neither Brookhaven nor the Trust Territory.[35] He explained that during his year on Ebeye, he often volunteered seven days a week at the hospital alongside the one employed physician. He told the Senate committee, "The picture I would like to paint for Kwajalein regarding Ebeye's health care system is that Kwajalein has an attitude of indifference and apathy to what occurs at Ebeye."[36] He said this general attitude seemed pervasive among military on Kwajalein and nonmilitary personnel working at the Kwajalein hospital.[37] Kotrady recalled how the army's position was summed up to him one day when a high-level command officer "remarked that the sole purpose of the Army at Kwajalein is to test missile systems. They have no concern for the Marshallese and that it is not of any importance to their being at Kwajalein."[38] Kotrady stated that in the Kwajalein Hospital this attitude extended among personnel aware of major medical problems on Ebeye but who considered these beyond their interest or responsibility. Kotrady observed: "The Marshallese people living in Kwajalein are denied medical care in many ways, oftentimes very subtly but I contend in very accurate ways."[39] He recalled such exclusions including the case of a Marshallese boy suffering from tuberculosis meningitis. The boy's physician on Ebeye requested he be treated on Kwajalein due to better care being available on the island, but the request was denied. The boy was treated on Ebeye and recovered slowly but retained severe mental retardation.

Illuminating the ongoing challenge faced by a military dependent on both residential US workers and a segregated, colonized workforce (discussed in chapter 2), Kotrady also spoke about how the army prevented diseases on Ebeye from spreading to the homes where Marshallese labored on Kwajalein. He said Marshallese maids working in American homes were required to have yearly examinations by Kwajalein physicians. If these physicians found any problems, they referred the maids for treatment on Ebeye. Kwajalein prohibited the maids from working until they had been treated on Ebeye, often for ailments like syphilis or yaws, both common to the region. Kwajalein physicians would provide no inoculation or penicillin for any of these afflictions.[40] Marshallese domestics thus had access to be screened on Kwajalein for the purposes of protecting American families, while being denied the medical care to address any issues that were found.[41]

Kotrady's testimony seemed most consequential in motivating Representative Mink and Senator Won Pat to register their concerns about Marshallese public health on Ebeye in their report to Washington following the hearings. It is possible, if not likely, that his status as a US physician made the difference. But the broader sentiments captured by Kotrady and Marshallese testimonies marking Kwajalein's exclusionary policies came through in Mink and Won Pat's letters to US government and military officials following the hearings. Representative Mink wrote to Chairman Phillip Burton of the Subcommittee on Territorial and Insular Affairs expressing her concern about the medical care situation on Ebeye. Describing the many challenges facing Marshallese in the region, Mink asserted that "of all these problems, the most grievous, bordering on patent violation of simple basic human rights[,] is the unmet medical needs of the people of Ebeye Island, located only minutes away from the first-class modern Kwajalein hospital evidently maintained only for U.S. citizens."[42] Mink repeated the examples given at the hearings of health-care denials to Marshallese during epidemic outbreaks. She concluded that the situation violated US "commitments to the United Nations that the people of the trust territory would be protected under the laws of the United States, and beyond that it violates our simply human obligation to provide help to a fellow human being."[43]

The US representatives also voiced their criticism of the broader structure of segregation marking life on Kwajalein and Ebeye, but did so by hedging blame directed at the military. Mink and Won Pat stated they had not intended "to assign or imply Department of Army responsibility, but, rather, to provide the background of contrasting conditions of population, living, availability of professional services, etc., which prevail on Kwajalein and Ebeye."[44] While avoiding any finger-pointing, Mink and Won Pat demanded strong, corrective, and expedient action to resolve grievances surfacing in the hearings.

The 1976 Senate hearings emerged alongside and helped fuel unprecedented media attention that put pressure on the army to issue a response to the dire conditions on Ebeye and the structure of segregation between the two islands. In the wake of the hearings, the assistant secretary of defense in international security affairs issued a memorandum to the secretary of the army expressing concern about the military's reputation on Kwajalein. Calling for action, the memo stated, "The contrast in living standards is too great; in time, this will affect our ability to use Kwajalein as a base for the Ballistic Missile Defense Command."[45] Citing an attached article as exemplary of media arousing concern in the US Congress and the UN Trusteeship Council, it asserted that the situation between Kwajalein and Ebeye needed to change. Echoing Mink and Won Pat's capitulation to the military, the assistant secretary noted: "Not all of the blame belongs in the Department of the Army, but people do expect us to handle the Kwajalein-Ebeye situation with the same sort of skill and imagination that we devote to other defense problems."[46] The assistant secretary's memorandum led to the army's publication of a fact-finding report within the year.[47] The 1977 report, detailed in chapter 2, offered no concrete plans to improve conditions on Ebeye or address allegations of discrimination on Kwajalein. Instead it identified scrutiny of the two islands as part of a broader media conspiracy orchestrated to support secure, separate political status negotiations for the Marshall Islands.[48]

The army's disregard for the crisis on Ebeye fueled the flames that ultimately helped ignite Operation Homecoming in the following years. While the 1976 Senate hearings constituted the broadest attempt in a public, political forum to draw attention to the historic and ongoing crisis on Ebeye, Marshallese did not remain silent after the hearings in trying to hold the United States accountable for the demands made by Mink and Won Pat. Ebeye residents and investigative journalists continued to shine a spotlight on the ongoing deadly colonial neglect in their wake. One example, discussed in this book's introduction, was Ebeye resident Jinna Keju's letter to Juan Alcedo of the Committee on Civil Rights in San

Francisco in 1979. In it, Keju described Marshallese as caught between Trust Territory bureaucracy and the army, where nothing ever got done. Evidencing the lack of any progress made three years after the Senate hearings, Keju wrote: "It can hardly be said that the U.S. is 'protecting the health of the inhabitants' here—as the U.N. says it must—when one looks at the poor condition of the Ebeye hospital and the long list of epidemics that have claimed the lives of hundreds over the years."[49] Three years after Keju sent his letter, journalist Giff Johnson published an article in the regional periodical *Marianas Variety* revealing how Keju's desperate plea for help went unanswered. Johnson described how Ebeye residents were suffering ongoing impacts of a broken sewage system, causing many to live without "running water or toilets."[50] While Johnson's piece cataloged a range of deadly conditions detailed at the Senate hearings and in various articles since 1976, one significant difference characterized his article. By August 1982, Johnson was writing in the midst of what was becoming the most significant Marshallese protest to challenge US colonial policies in the region. His article appeared two months into Operation Homecoming.

While Operation Homecoming became the most expansively covered protest in the Marshall Islands, exacting heavy costs from the US military and concluding with the army's committing to certain concessions, the 1976 Senate hearings that preceded the protest set the stage, foreshadowing the protest's development. At the hearings, both Marshallese and American allies took advantage of the forum to have their political preferences and grievances about conditions structuring life on Kwajalein and Ebeye be heard, in hopes that such concerns would be addressed. Their concerns were met with inattention by army and Trust Territory officials, continuous infighting between the two, and ongoing negligence regarding the UN Trusteeship Agreement mandate to protect the region's inhabitants. Thus, it is not surprising that Operation Homecoming followed soon after. If the hearings showcased Marshallese participation in political channels made available to voice their concerns alongside the seeming impotence of such routes for change in a context of US empire, Operation Homecoming became a different story. It was this mass protest, and the ways it temporarily halted the gears of the US military-industrial colonial complex threatening to interfere with the army's bottom line, which ultimately shifted the ground for change. At its conclusion, Kwajalein landowning families earned higher lease payments for the island and secured funding for infrastructure improvements on Ebeye. But as the remainder of this chapter explores, along the route to winning these material concessions, all Marshallese on Ebeye would face the repercussions of the army's repressive response as the military worked to regain control over this valuable gem within its broader US base imperium.

RECLAIMING HOME ON KWAJALEIN

Before turning to the question of how a mass movement of one thousand unarmed Marshallese men, women, and children was able to gain leverage over the most powerful military in the world to win concessions, I first consider the precedent set by earlier Marshallese sail-in protests and the shifting political climate within which Operation Homecoming emerged.[51] While the earlier sail-ins were smaller and shorter in duration than the mass movement that exploded in 1982, they offered a model for how a seemingly powerless group of unarmed individuals could strategically time their protest to exert outsized influence over a powerful military. The shifting political terrain of Marshallese moving toward free association with the United States—preferences recorded as the majority opinion at the 1976 Senate hearings—also framed how a distinctive path toward decolonization hinging on the value of Kwajalein influenced the coming of Operation Homecoming.

The earlier sail-in protests that offered a model for Operation Homecoming did so by using their movements to exert pressure on the army by threatening to interrupt missile-testing operations. The first sail-in occurred in 1969, when Marshallese displaced to Ebeye from the Mid-Corridor region reclaimed their lands situated in the army's designated missile-impact zone to win higher leasing payments. A decade later, Kwajalein landowners sought (and ultimately won) a new interim lease by strategically timing their sail-in (the year before) to pose a risk to the Senate's passage of the Strategic Arms Limitations Talks (SALT) II treaty, which "in the curious logic of arms control" also hinged on development of the MX missile to gain ratification of the treaty, according to journalist Giff Johnson. He noted that "with SALT II and the MX in the balance the Kwajalein people had the leverage they needed to secure concessions from the U.S."[52]

Three years later, Marshallese protestors timed Operation Homecoming to strategically coincide with a referendum in the Marshall Islands for the Compact of Free Association with the United States. Kwajalein landowners leading the protest aimed to disrupt the referendum and influence how the newly emerging Republic of the Marshall Islands government would negotiate a long-term lease for their homelands to solidify the compact. The protest voiced concerns about the nature of that lease agreement as well as an urgent need for investments to address Ebeye's dire living conditions. For the United States, the timing of the protest was particularly inconvenient and proved a threat to broader US military policy during the Cold War. Landowners worked to gain more input in negotiations for the role Kwajalein would play in the transition toward Marshallese decolonization, as US dependence on the missile range increased to accommodate President Reagan's newest Cold War military strategy.

Framing the local political context leading to Operation Homecoming was the election of the first Marshallese president, Iroij (Chief) Amata Kabua in 1979, who led a new Marshall Islands government alongside continued Trust Territory governance through the transition to a new political status. During this interim period, Kwajalein played a central role as a bargaining chip for Marshallese leaders negotiating a new political relationship to the United States. This historic shift in political and legal authority in the Marshall Islands changed how the United States negotiated continued usage rights for Kwajalein. Whereas previously the Trust Territory administration had acted as an intermediary between the US military and Kwajalein landowners to negotiate leases through the threat of eminent domain, the emerging political transformation meant the US Army would now negotiate leases directly with the Marshall Islands government, cutting out landowner input. Complicating this new lease negotiation arrangement was the fact that Kabua was both the first president of the emerging Marshall Islands government and the most powerful Kwajalein landowning chief, one who disagreed with other Kwajalein landowners on how to negotiate with the United States.

Within this changing political landscape and informed by the precedent of earlier successful sail-ins, Kwajalein landowners strategically timed Operation Homecoming to coincide with plebiscite votes on the Compact of Free Association in 1982. By this time they had organized into a coalition called the Kwajalein Atoll Corporation (KAC), which comprised five thousand landowners. KAC supported Operation Homecoming, with one thousand of its members sailing to reclaim their home islands throughout the atoll. KAC demanded a voice in determining how the Compact of Free Association would delineate the length of the Kwajalein lease, lease compensation levels, and funding for Ebeye.[53] KAC representatives also leveraged this strategic moment to try to exact fair compensation for past use of their land.[54]

As an emerging Marshallese government worked to negotiate Marshallese decolonization as a seamless transition toward free association with the United States, it did so by leveraging its biggest bargaining chip, Kwajalein, while cutting KAC input out of the process. On May 30, 1982, the Republic of the Marshall Islands signed the Compact of Free Association with the United States. The compact ignored KAC demands for past use compensation and ignited KAC's ire by setting annual lease payments at $1.9 million (far below the $9 million won in the 1979 sail-ins). A fifty-year lease length diminished KAC capacity to leverage higher payments over time. The new lease also omitted any funding for capital improvement projects on Ebeye. According to historian David Hanlon, KAC landowners were also "bitterly disappointed that the document did not specify better, more respectful treatment of the Marshallese by the United States Army in its administration of the missile range."[55] KAC announced its opposition to the compact immediately after its signing. Operation Homecoming quickly followed in June. The protest signaled how decades of US colonial control in the region and the devastating impacts of weapons testing had created a bargaining chip to which the Marshallese path to decolonization would remain tied. That chip, the value of Kwajalein to the US military, created new divisions while exacerbating existing ones between Marshallese political leaders and landowners as negotiations for decolonization unfolded.[56]

WITH "STAR WARS" ON THE LINE, "THE EMPIRE STRIKES BACK"

If Kwajalein's value became the clay around which the shape of Marshallese decolonization was molded, a key Cold War investment helping buttress the broader US security state, Operation Homecoming claimed a stake in that new value. As the military largely ignored protests for change in the region as voiced in the Senate hearings, as well as the petitions, speeches, letters, and media coverage in the years before and after them, this mass protest spurred a moment of change. Military neglect of Marshallese concerns had persisted for decades in part because none of these other forms of protest had dramatically impacted the military's ability to continue its mission uninterrupted. Operation Homecoming changed this calculation. From its inception, the protest posed a threat to the United States by incurring financial and strategic costs through missile-testing interruptions. The United States had already felt the squeeze of earlier Marshallese sail-ins. By 1982, in addition to the material costs of delayed weapons testing, Marshallese protestors were able to leverage what historian Mary L. Dudziak has detailed in her research as the broader geopolitical pressures facing the United States during the Cold War: the battle for hearts and minds across a largely nonwhite, decolonizing world. Her work helps one think through the puzzle of how a group of unarmed Marshallese men, women, and children exerted any influence over the most powerful military in world history. Dudziak found that nonviolent resistance during the civil rights movement, which solicited violent repression, paired with globally circulating media coverage, gave protestors greater leverage in the context of Cold War geopolitical pressures.[57] As this section reveals, this distinct mixture of local and global conditions empowering civil rights activists during the Cold War also helped frame Operation Homecoming.

That this period of heightened Marshallese protests saw increased geopolitical *and* economic stakes become attached to the uninterrupted use of Kwajalein, a mission buttressing the US military-industrial colonial complex, was suggested by the market value for missile research development, production, and deployment. As noted in chapter 3, by the time Operation Homecoming erupted, military sales for missile systems and parts had reached $5.2 billion.[58] Two months into the protest, the army estimated that moving and trying to recreate similar missile facilities elsewhere would come with a price tag of more than $2 billion and take several years.[59] Between Operation Homecoming and the final Marshallese sail-in protest in 1986 (discussed in chapter 6), Kwajalein's value to the military would increase even further as the range became essential to President Reagan's Strategic Defense Initiative, his multi-billion-dollar "Star Wars" campaign.[60]

Within this context of US political and economic investment in Kwajalein, the army's response to Operation Homecoming included punitive measures directed at specific protestors *and* indiscriminately at the entire Ebeye community. I turn now to the most documented of this brutal repression through closer analysis of KAC secretary Julian Riklon's path to resistance under US colonialism. Riklon's life story further lays bare the immeasurable costs borne by Marshallese living through the multiplicity of US weapons testing campaigns in their homelands. The experiences of Riklon and his family exemplify how Marshallese insecurity under US colonial control was literally embodied through markers of trauma, disease, and death tied to nuclear testing and memories of brutal assault while reclaiming his home on Kwajalein. Riklon's was a path shaped by insecurities created in the name of US national security. But as this chapter reveals, for Riklon this also became a path toward a lifetime of activism.

As noted earlier, on the first day of Operation Homecoming Riklon was beaten unconscious by Kwajalein's guards while jailed on the island. Born on Kwajalein in 1946, the year the United States began detonating nuclear weapons in his home islands, Riklon reflected in an interview, "I was born on Kwajalein because that's where Marshallese people used to *live.*"[61] Riklon's family were landowners on both Kwajalein and Rongelap, the island contaminated by radiation in 1954 following the US hydrogen detonation. He recalled as an eight-year-old watching the Bravo Shot detonation from Kwajalein Island. While US schoolchildren were learning "duck and cover" drills as they braced for a hypothetical doomsday scenario, Riklon and other Marshallese children were witnessing the real thing taking place in their home but receiving no warnings. Instead they watched in horror as this apocalyptic story played out in their islands. At age seventy, Riklon recounted the experience while looking past me as if he were watching the detonation unfold again in the skies above Sacramento where he lived in 2016. He recalled how sound came first. A loud noise erupted, and the sky bled red. Kwajalein, more than one hundred miles away, shook. Riklon feared the world was ending. More than thirty-five years later, he said he feared *his* world was ending, as he saw stars after being beaten by US guards while reclaiming his home island of Kwajalein.

During the interim, Riklon had been living on Ebeye after being displaced from Kwajalein and temporarily resettled back onto Rongelap after the hydrogen detonation. Riklon was not living on Rongelap during the Bravo test in 1954, but was among the many Marshallese families the military resettled back onto the island three years later. Riklon was part of a control group resettled back on Rongelap so the Atomic Energy Commission could study the divergent impacts of irradiation on those directly impacted by fallout in 1954, versus those living on the contaminated island thereafter. This hybrid population would ingest food and water marked by radioactive contamination for the next twenty-five years. Riklon's brother and grandmother, both on Rongelap at the time of the detonation, had been exposed to radiation and had since passed away, his brother from cancer. His mother had also developed thyroid cancer. The Marshall Islands developed the highest rates of this form of cancer in the world following the Bravo shot. As it became clear that one of his home islands was too contaminated to live on, and the other—Kwajalein—prohibited Marshallese residency, Riklon found himself with few places to go and ended up on Ebeye in 1960.[62]

By 1982, Riklon had been working on Ebeye as a Bible translator and became the secretary for the KAC. As Riklon recalled, the protest marked the culmination of years of Marshallese struggles to survive unbearable living conditions on Ebeye under US neglect, alongside landowner grievances about ongoing, unjust lease payments. He noted that many of those protesting had been displaced throughout the atoll for missile testing and just wanted to return home. Riklon explained how so many Marshallese, especially the older people, never wanted to live on Ebeye and lost their freedom to make that choice when the United States moved them to make way for missile testing. He said the sail-ins answered a need for countless Marshallese who simply wanted to be on their own lands, to fish, gather coconuts, and collect indigenous medicines.[63] Riklon also felt that as many or more Marshallese protested because of grievances over discrimination and exclusion on Kwajalein and living conditions on Ebeye as over land leasing concerns.

For Riklon, the idea of nonviolent protest against such degrading forms of exclusion was in part inspired by what he had observed while living and studying in California and Hawai'i, where he watched in-person and

Figure 15. Marshallese participants in Operation Homecoming gathered outside the jail on Kwajalein Island, 1982. Photo from US Army.

television examples of demonstrations by civil rights activists. He recalled asking "why are they doing that?" and learning "they are doing that because they are dissatisfied with so many things."[64] Just as these demonstrations of African Americans had defied the legal and social codes of segregation in the American South, Marshallese would go on to challenge the military structure of segregation in their islands with Operation Homecoming, and Riklon would help lead this movement.

As swiftly as the military's brutal response targeted Riklon, the assault was disavowed. Within a couple of weeks of the attack, Trust Territory chief law enforcement officer Bryan J. Vila's documentation of the "Riklon incident" detailed this Marshallese "trespasser'[s]" attempt to rescue Marshallese protest leaders, which led to his jailing. According to Vila, Riklon was "physically restrained to prevent [this] illegal act." [65] Reporting the event to the Kwajalein Missile Range (KMR) commander, Vila noted: "No blows were struck nor was any physical harm done to [the officers] or RIKLON."[66] Vila's letter added that Colonel Witteried ordered

RIKLON be released after he calmed down, "as a gesture of good faith to the demonstrators."[67]

Vila's framing foreshadowed how US narratives of Operation Homecoming would unfold and hinted at military and Trust Territory officials' awareness of the need to control the spin within the broader geopolitical context of the Cold War. According to US official sources (from both Trust Territory and military representatives), those on Kwajalein responding to Marshallese protestors expressed fear but also restraint and avoided exerting unnecessary violence or excessively punitive measures. US efforts to erase evidence of violence against Marshallese protestors alluded to an awareness that their power on Kwajalein was partially checked by local and global media scrutiny. Given the barrage of investigative articles decrying US Army policies on Kwajalein during the 1970s, it is likely that such concern about ongoing scrutiny was highly sensitized to how this negative media coverage might impact the army's capacity to continue its weapons-testing mission uninterrupted.

Kwajalein's distance from population centers, a key feature of the atoll that had made it strategically ideal for US missile testing, created barriers for Marshallese protestors aiming to reach a global audience with Operation Homecoming. To gain leverage by garnering as much global attention as possible, Marshallese protestors had to make their struggles visible in a place largely invisible to the world. The army's awareness of the potential impact of this scrutiny helps explain why one of the first actions it took in response to Operation Homecoming was to impose a media blackout on the island. Controlling the spin on this event became just as important as controlling the protest itself.

That spin entailed minimizing the reality of the military's outsized security response to a movement composed of unarmed, nonviolent protestors, a demographic estimated to be 80 to 89 percent women and children.[68] Despite this presumably unthreatening demographic, Vila's report emphasized that he and Colonel Witteried were very concerned about the potential for violence. A July 28, 1982, telegram sent by the Kwajalein commanding officer requesting protective equipment alluded to this heightened level of fear: "In view of the possibility of further incidents protective riot control equipment has been obtained . . . and consisted of 30 batons, 30 helmets with face shields and 61 sets of disposable handcuffs (flexi-cuffs)."[69] Four days later the commander sent another telegram to the Huntsville ballistic missile defense commander, the secretary of state, and secretary of defense, explaining that while the present composition of demonstrators remained about 70 percent children and 30 percent older men and women, he feared future instability from "an infusion of the less responsible and more aggressive elements that are known to exist on Ebeye."[70] While this is vague, it is not hard to imagine the demographic the army feared on Ebeye as likely overlapping with the same individuals it historically worked to exclude from Kwajalein. The army's historic and ongoing structure of segregation seemed to spur ongoing paranoia about invasion from this criminalized population whose criminality was constituted of any *potential* to challenge this structure.

A concern about Marshallese protestors coming into close proximity with Kwajalein's residential community, and especially its largely white, middle-class, nuclear families, was evident in several military sources. The army's authority to secure the "comfort" of that community from any disruption was enshrined in the UN Trusteeship Agreement, which empowered Trust Territory officials and the army to respond to any protests across the territory. Until the complete dissolution of the Trusteeship Agreement, which would not occur until 1986, the United States had "the authority, by exercise of its police power, to take such action as is reasonable and proper to maintain law and order" in the region.[71] According to the Trusteeship Agreement, the freedom of Marshallese to move about freely during their protest was limited, in that

> human rights and fundamental freedoms are not unlimited, but subject to various limitations in the public interest; that the freedom of movement guaranteed by Article 7 of the Trusteeship Agreement is expressly subject to requirements of public order and security; that rights guaranteed under the United Nations Charter and Trusteeship Agreement are subject to proper exercise of police power; that the guarantee of liberty in the Trust Territory Code ... does not interfere with the proper exercise of police power; and that police power includes power to make laws to secure public peace, good order and *comfort of the community*.[72]

During Operation Homecoming, military officials worked to keep Marshallese protestors from disturbing the comfort of US families on the island *and* avert any media attention to this effort. This came through in the correspondence from Department of Defense Under Secretary for Policy Fred C. Ikle to Under Secretary Donald P. Hodel in the Department of the Interior. On July 29, 1982, Ikle wrote requesting the authority to position a small civilian law enforcement contingent to deter the risk and "threat of a physical confrontation, and the accompanying public media attention."[73] He concluded: "I am sure you will agree that the safety of 3000 Americans warrants taking every precautionary step available to this Government" and requested federal marshals be sent to KMR to secure the island.[74] Military urgency in keeping Marshallese protestors away from US families also appeared in the Kwajalein commander's telegram, sent the same day. This telegram warned the island situation could become worse "with a possibility of confrontation if demonstrators move into residential areas."[75] He added, "If this occurs additional security forces will be required to control and contain the demonstrators."[76]

While trying to keep the protest at a distance from US residents on Kwajalein, the military also worked to hasten the conclusion of Operation Homecoming through a range of punitive measures. From the get-go, the army made clear it would not bear the financial cost of any missile-testing interruption due to the protest. Those costs would be borne by the landowners who were protesting. Colonel Witteried enumerated how this would work in an open letter in the *Marshall Islands Journal* on June 22, 1982. He marked Operation Homecoming's illegality and reiterated US legal entitlement to continued "uninterrupted usage of Kwajalein."[77] Headlining his letter, "Anyone who participates will be a trespasser," Witteried warned that participants would be held responsible for the cost of any missile test delays, with costs deducted from the $2 million landowner payment due, including charges for cleanup and security and testing delays.[78] To clarify what this fee would look like, Witteried noted the daily delay cost for one upcoming test would amount to about $130,000.[79]

The costs of Operation Homecoming would not solely be borne by those participating. In an effort to put the squeeze on the island from which the protest was launched and reduce broader support for Operation Homecoming, the army enacted measures to punish *all* Ebeye residents for the "sins" of those protesting. During the four-month protest, the army banned all maids and gardeners from Kwajalein, cutting off jobs for more than two hundred Marshallese wage earners on Ebeye (or about 25 percent of the total Marshallese workforce on Kwajalein).[80] Leveraging the segregation structure it had erected over time and the precarity framing life for colonized residents on Ebeye, the army also imposed a blockade on all sales and shipments of food to merchants on Ebeye through Kwajalein. Previously available banking services on Kwajalein would now exclude Ebeye residents and businessmen.

Keeping with its historic pattern of situating Ebeye's vulnerabilities as unrelated to Kwajalein's comforts by disavowing any relational development between the two islands, the military framed its punitive policies as intended to benefit Ebeye. Principal Deputy Assistant to the Secretary of Defense for International Security Affairs Noel G. Koch explained that restricting these services would stave off what he saw as "potential overdependence upon U.S. sources," adding that both food shipment and banking privileges were always intended to be temporary.[81] He explained that Operation Homecoming had simply prompted actions long overdue by both governments. In his telegram to newly elected Marshallese president Amata Kabua in August 1982, Koch said he believed Kabua would agree "that our mutual goal of self-sufficiency for the Ebeye community can be achieved more quickly by maintaining the momentum of the efforts in self-development resulting from this demonstration."[82] Koch's ill-disguised attempt to frame a strategy to quicken the end of the protest by punishing all those struggling to survive on Ebeye as a bootstrap moment for Marshallese spurred outrage from activists and journalists following the protest.

Reporter Giff Johnson wrote a letter to US representative John F. Seiberling decrying the army's extreme measures of punishing Ebeye residents. He asserted: "Koch's pious concern for the 'potential dependency upon U.S. sources and the resultant negative effect upon independent development of Marshallese capabilities' hardly disguises the Defense Department's plan for harsh reprisals against the Marshallese people for protesting continuous violation of their basic rights by the Army—rights such as adequate hospitals, education, sanitation, and jobs—that most Americans take for granted."[83] As head of the congressional review of the Marshall Islands Compact of Free Association, Representative Seiberling responded to these allegations in support of landowner rights to protest by offering a broader condemnation of US administration in the region: "'I think the actions of the military out there are hardly becoming of a nation that is a great power. Here we have a bunch of people who are our wards. . . . We're occupying their land and we're denying them the right to peacefully assemble and petition for redress of grievances that our constitution guarantees to our own citizens. And yet we're in their country. I think it's a pretty sad spectacle.'"[84] Seiberling seemed to observe the tensions underlying US empire in the region, while unable to label them overtly as such. But his testimony added to the voices of protest expanding in support of Operation Homecoming that were rippling from the colonial Pacific back to the metropole and beyond.

Just as its decades-long structure of interisland segregation (detailed in chapter 3), enabled the army to exact swift and deadly consequences on Ebeye's insecure community in an effort to hasten the protest's conclusion, the military also drew upon its practices of intraisland segregation to control the protest on Kwajalein. In addition to cutting off life-sustaining supplies and services to Ebeye, the army also cut supplies to protestors camped out on Kwajalein. But in this instance, the cumulative impact of media scrutiny of the army seemed to inspire greater restraint. The army's awareness of how coverage of harm to Marshallese threatened its reputation, and the broader reputation of the United States, seemed to constrain its most extreme repression, especially toward the children. This was evident in an army decision to reverse course after cutting off clean water to the protest camp, when protestors alleged two Marshallese children had contracted typhoid as a result. A lawsuit quickly followed, and both Marshallese and US courts demanded the military reverse this action. The army conceded, suggesting the degree to which the 1976 Senate testimonies on Kwajalein's hospital exclusions (and accompanying media coverage) may have had ongoing influence through 1982.

The typhoid incident alluded to the ways Operation Homecoming reflected what historian Mary Dudziak found in her historic analysis of how nonviolent protest, global media coverage, and Cold War geopolitical pressures combined to give civil rights protestors leverage. Media coverage of the typhoid incident and Chief Law Enforcement Officer Vila's report evidenced such resonances. Vila's statements suggested that US officials had begun to see how restricting emergency health care for Marshallese on Kwajalein could carry potential consequences beyond the children themselves; such exclusions could be a public relations disaster for the army and by extension the US government. This was a particular risk given a changing global context that seemed increasingly attuned to the human rights of colonized peoples.[85]

Exemplifying such concerns in his report on the incident, Vila explained that as the Trust Territory's highest-ranking representative on Kwajalein, he believed the demonstrators should continue having access to clean water *and* to Kwajalein's hospital, for several reasons. First and foremost, this would be seen as a humanitarian act working favorably to show the high moral standards of the US government. Vila added that he did not believe limiting access would impact Marshallese willingness to demonstrate, since they only averaged about one hospital case every two days, and with only one exception, all had been children treated for diarrheal diseases.[86] Vila explained that diarrhea was the leading cause of children's death in Micronesia due to dehydration.[87] He emphasized: "IF A CHILD WERE TO DIE WHEN EMERGENCY MEDICAL TREATMENT AT THE KMR HOSPITAL MIGHT WELL HAVE SAVED ITS LIFE, THE DEMONSTRATORS WOULD HAVE A MARTYR AND THE USG [presumably US government] WOULD BE IN A MORALLY INDEFENSIBLE POSITION."[88] Vila stated that the long-term policy of the Kwajalein hospital had been to accept emergency medical cases from Ebeye due to the island's limited facilities. He added that a *new* policy denying access now would mean transporting a sick or injured demonstrator back to Ebeye, then back to Kwajalein, a process that could take several hours and prove fatal.[89]

Rewriting the history of the army's policy in regard to hospital access on Kwajalein, Vila's report ignored the several damning Marshallese and American testimonies in 1976 that had detailed the deadly toll of such exclusions. At the same time, his statements alluded to the impact of these testimonies and accompanying media coverage. By advising the army to take a different course in 1982, Vila seemed aware that denying Marshallese children health care would reflect poorly on a US military under increasing scrutiny. Operation Homecoming, the Senate hearings, and hundreds of articles critiquing military policy on Kwajalein leading up to it had engaged local and global audiences within the broader geopolitical context of the Cold War. Vila's report suggested how this combination of factors may have begun to show its footprint on US decision-making in the Marshall Islands.

This convergence of how local and global conditions gave Marshallese protesting greater leverage also came through in evidence of army and Trust Territory officials' attentiveness to the increasingly negative publicity about US policies in the region. Local media coverage was rippling out beyond the atoll's shores to a broader audience attuned to the context of global decolonization and the growing antinuclear movement. During the first month of Operation Homecoming, the KMR commander sent a telegram to the Huntsville ballistic missile defense commander, the secretary of defense, and secretary of state that indicated the military's close tracking of media coverage. The telegram identified quotes appearing in the *Marshall Islands Journal* and instructed recipients to pay particular attention to the "relatively inflammatory statements" made by Kwajalein landowners' attorney George Allen, in which he advised his clients of their legal right to occupy their lands.[90] This question of legality dogged the army throughout Operation Homecoming. Marshallese foreign secretary Tony de Brum discussed the issue in an interview with *Pacific Magazine* during the protest in which he described the sail-ins as "a peaceful demonstration which any democratic country must allow."[91] He added: "It was our belief that the United States would be reasonable in dealing with this, rather than cutting off banking services . . . toilet facilities, and preventing shipment of food from reaching Ebeye which punishes an entire population for the actions of a small number."[92] Emphasizing the *illegality of the US response*, De Brum noted that protestors were also denied legal counsel, violating US democratic principles.[93]

Symbolizing the various landmines exploding across the propaganda battlefield of the Cold War, the contradictions of US empire made the task of winning hearts and minds in the decolonizing world by selling values of freedom and democracy daunting. This was a sales pitch that continuously reached limits when the subjects of US empire drew upon those same values in ways that challenged US interests. With Operation Homecoming, Marshallese landowners appropriated these revered US traditions and laws to claim their right to peacefully assemble. The army's impatience with having to deal with these contradictions came through in the testimony of Ballistic Defense Systems Command commanding general Grayson D. Tate at the 1982 Military Appropriations Senate Hearings. Tate described landowners as having banded together and traveled to New York City and Washington D.C. to recruit "very clever and very smart lawyers to represent them."[94] He described these lawyers as "savvy enough to advise these people very well."[95] Tate's frustration with Marshallese capacity to seek legal support for their right to peacefully protest punctuated the ongoing tensions informing US empire, which was both empowered and restricted in seemingly arbitrary ways by the UN Trusteeship Agreement. As military and Trust Territory officials failed to reconcile these contradictions, US civilians on Kwajalein charted a variety of paths toward understanding what was unfolding around them.

CONTAINING THE PORTRAIT OF SUBURBAN FAMILY LIFE ON KWAJALEIN DURING THE PROTEST

Just as army and Trust Territory officials closely attended to media coverage of Operation Homecoming rippling beyond Kwajalein's shores to a global audience, they also showed concern about protest news reaching the island's US residents. This fear seemed less rooted in the geopolitical consequences of that reach and more about preventing any disturbance to Kwajalein's serene suburban family aura. Given the army's tremendous investments over time in creating this utopian lifestyle as a tool for recruitment and retention of its most elite workforce, this desire to maintain that mythical portrait—as something unrelated to Ebeye and any colonial context that may account for the mass protest—seemed essential to ensuring its ongoing security mission.

This was suggested by the army's decision to impose a media blackout on Kwajalein as Operation Homecoming erupted. Residents were also instructed to stay away from protest areas and refrain from any communication with Marshallese demonstrators. Keeping US residents at a distance from Marshallese protestors and any stories about their protest constituted an effort to keep daily suburban life on Kwajalein unmolested by the colonial conditions affording this privileged lifestyle. Having no access to the media coverage of Operation Homecoming that was reaching readers thousands of miles away, and restricted from visiting demonstration sites, civilians on Kwajalein relied heavily on rumor to understand what was going on.

To limit dialogue between the communities, Kwajalein security guards were put in place around the protest sites to prevent interaction. While the first three months of Operation Homecoming aligned with a lapse in Kwajalein's daily newspaper coverage from the archives, one story showed up in the final month of the protest. Appearing in early October 1982, the *Hour Glass* story notified residents that Kwajalein Atoll Corporation, the Marshall Islands government, and US negotiators were nearing an agreement and that protestors would soon evacuate Kwajalein. The article reaffirmed an earlier order by Kwajalein commander colonel John W. Banks that demonstration sites remained off limits, noting "residents must not go near the camp sites, regardless of whether demonstrators are present or not."[96] The same *Hour Glass* issue included a community notification on the final page entitled "Commander's Hot Line" that posed these questions to residents: "Are you concerned about the Marshallese protest? Have you heard *rumors* about our island community or policies affecting you? To check on the accuracy of any rumors or information about the protest and attendant problems, call the Commander's Hot Line."[97] The text reassured residents they need not divulge their names if they called.

While largely in the dark about the broader context framing Marshallese grievances and fueling the protest, some civilians did recall feeling surprised at the extreme degree of military intimidation used against the unarmed protestors. Former Kwajalein resident Robert Barclay remembered being an adolescent at the time of Operation Homecoming and seeing guards standing watch at each encampment to prevent communication between Marshallese and US residents. He said that while he had been a little foggy about what was actually going on at the time, one memory that stood out in his mind was seeing protestors march through the street and the Kwajalein commander randomly pull one of the Marshallese men from the march line and beat him. Most vivid to Barclay was how strange it seemed that the commander was wearing "a pith helmet" when confronting this group of nonviolent protestors comprising largely women and children.[98] Former Kwajalein residents and Marshallese also lamented the military's response in heightened security for all in the wake

of Operation Homecoming. The existing structure of surveillance moni-
toring the movement of people and goods on the island (detailed in chapter 3) tightened. After 1982, Kwajalein guards also started carrying guns
on the island.[99]

Commenting on what many civilians perceived as the most extreme
security measure introduced by the army during Operation Homecoming, former residents Cris Lindborg and Raymond Wolff recalled one commanding officer's effort to secure Kwajalein's borders with a concertina
fence. Characterizing the plan as "ridiculous" and "paranoid," Lindborg
and Wolff described the razor wire fence erected across the reef between
Kwajalein and Ebeye. Lindborg noted the commanding officer's "vision
was basically to block all of the Marshallese out."[100] She said he feared
Marshallese were going to "come in an invade us across the reef. So he
put this concertina wire . . . rolls of this battlefield wire, on the north end
of the island, in the water, from drop off to drop off, ocean to lagoon, and
they had these big flood lights into the reef because they thought at low
tide the Marshallese were going to come over."[101] While Lindborg and
Wolff recalled that the fence did not remain up for long, its erection as a
barrier to the perceived threat of invasion attests to the army's projection
of American exceptionalism in the Marshall Islands. In this iteration of
the national mythology, a story of imperial invasion is flipped as Kwajalein becomes an American home in need of protection from the Marshallese. Despite a context in which the US military had traveled thousands of
miles to the Central Pacific to invade Marshallese homelands in the name
of national security and then carried out the most destructive weapons-
testing campaigns in global history, the commander still perceived the
Marshallese to be the invaders.

Given the atmosphere of intimidation on Kwajalein during the protest,
US residents sympathetic to Marshallese would have felt quite limited
in their capacity to do much to help without risking being kicked off the
base. This proved the consequence for former resident Judy Rosochacki.
She recounted her efforts to skirt around the concertina fence the army
had erected to bring water to Marshallese on Ebeye. Rosochacki was a
high school student on Kwajalein during Operation Homecoming and had
befriended Marshallese workers while working at the island grocery store,
Surfway. While at work she learned the army was denying Marshallese on

Figure 16. Concertina-wire fence erected between Kwajalein and Ebeye, 1982. Photo by and courtesy of Dave Blackwell.

Ebeye fresh water in an attempt to hasten the protest's conclusion.[102] Outraged by the excessive punishment of all Marshallese on Ebeye, especially hurting the elderly and children, she recalled, "We decided one night, during low tide, to walk the reef over to Ebeye and bring as much water as we could carry."[103] Having crawled around the concertina wire, Rosochacki characterized the fence as "a joke."[104] She added: "We had no trouble getting through it unscathed."[105]

While not physically impacted by the fence, Rosochacki's deviant behavior resulted in consequences that aimed to remind all US residents on Kwajalein that their utopian suburban lifestyle existed under army surveillance. She said that she had planned to stick around Kwajalein for a couple months after she graduated high school and apply to Parsons Art Institute in Paris. Instead she found herself "unceremoniously shipped off to Colorado to live with an aunt and uncle within 2 weeks of graduation."[106] A couple years later her parents explained to her that someone had seen her crawling under the wire, and her father was informed that if she "did not depart the island immediately, [her] entire family would be thrown off."[107]

AMERICANS IN THE DARK: WORLD IN THE LIGHT

If the military was largely successful in keeping most US residents on Kwajalein in the dark about the protest and effectively sequestering those subverting the rules, it was less successful in controlling the spread of media coverage beyond the atoll to a global audience. While the army blocked media access to Kwajalein during Operation Homecoming, it was unable to contain news reported from Ebeye. The army's concern about global scrutiny was not simply paranoia but was warranted by evidence of an explosion of articles covering the protest. Many stories framed the significance of the protest within the history of US-Marshallese relations but also as connected to broader Pacific anti-colonial and antinuclear protests that had been unfolding during the 1970s and 1980s. A closer look at how Operation Homecoming was narrated and understood within this broader coalitional struggle against nuclear imperialism in Oceania helps expand our understanding of Pacific histories as both shaping and shaped by the postwar tide of global decolonization.

Local and international journalists and activists situated Operation Homecoming within a broader Pacific and global fight against nuclear armament and military colonialism. In its June/July 1982 issue, Japan's bimonthly newsletter *Han-Genpatsu News, No Nuke News Japan* ran articles about the protest, tying Operation Homecoming to the global campaign against nuclear proliferation. Vocalizing support from a nation also tragically aware of the impacts of being on the receiving end of US nuclear aggression, editor Arakawa Syungi wrote in solidarity with the Marshallese. Syunji encouraged his readers to support this "soon to be liberated colony" of the United States by signing and mailing a postcard to President Reagan.[108] Included in the newsletter, the card detailed the "continuing sit-in" at Kwajalein and stated: "I support their action and strongly protest the inhuman acts of your government. I believe the U.S. government should respect the basic human rights and the right of self-determination of the Kwajalein people."[109] It concluded with a demand that the United States close the missile installation and return the island to its owners.[110] The *Han-Genpatsu* editors also encouraged readers to send postcards to the demonstrators that included a message of support to "sisters and brothers," noting: "Your struggle is a great encouragement not only for the people of the Marshall Islands but for people all over the world who are seeking a society free from oppression and nuclear threat."[111]

Media coverage tying Operation Homecoming to a broader context of antinuclear activism also surfaced in the Philippines, another region deeply familiar with US imperialism and militarism. The September 10, 1982, issue of *Depthnews Asia*, published out of Manila, ran a Giff Johnson story that contrasted the landowners' "peaceful protest" with the army's violent response and its continuation of missile testing during the protest despite the risk to Marshallese safety.[112] Johnson reported: "The Kwajalein people say they will shut down the vital test range before they will suffer 50 more years of apartheid-like conditions in Ebeye."[113] Highlighting the significance of Operation Homecoming within a broader context of the nuclear arms race, Johnson added: "It may well be that the future of the US nuclear weapons programme rests in the hands of 5,000 Kwajalein landowners on their remote Pacific atoll."[114]

As suggested in Johnson's analysis and its circulation across the Pacific, Operation Homecoming drew local and global attention to the central role Kwajalein played in the Cold War nuclear arms race. By 1983, this awareness surfaced in the agenda and keynote address of the Nuclear Free and Independent Pacific (NFIP) conference in Port Vila, Vanuatu. The presence of Kwajalein representatives at the conference signaled the momentum that had been growing across the Pacific for nearly a decade in response to the use of this region by global imperial powers as a "nuclear playground."[115] Launched in Suva in 1975, this coalitional movement had been built by Pacific Islander leaders to halt such practices as ongoing nuclear testing in Moruroa Atoll in French Polynesia and US weapons testing on Kahoʻolawe Island in Hawaiʻi. In his keynote address at the 1983 meeting in Vanuatu, Stockholm International Peace Research Institute's Owen Wilkes highlighted Kwajalein's centrality to the larger nuclear competition, contending that "if we could shut down the Pacific Missile Range we would cut off half the momentum in the global arms

race."[116] Additional papers delivered at the conference discussed the legacy
of nuclear testing in the Marshall Islands and the historic relationship
between Kwajalein and Ebeye. Kwajalein Atoll Corporation representatives Laji Taft and Abon Jeadrik attended and presented a paper on the
events leading up to Operation Homecoming that emphasized the history
of segregation on Kwajalein.[117]

Both the participation of Operation Homecoming leaders and the
inclusion of conference resolutions addressing Kwajalein and Ebeye at
the NFIP conference illuminated the centrality of the Marshall Islands to
the US nuclear arms race. It also revealed a different path toward political
education that these Marshallese leaders were taking outside the realms
of the UN Trusteeship Agreement mandate. This trajectory constituted a
radical detour from the formal and contained forum of the Senate hearings discussed earlier in the chapter. Through participation at NFIP conferences, Marshallese activists added their voices and their stories to a
grassroots, expansive pan-Pacific coalition joining this vast Oceanic movement engaged in the postwar project of global decolonization.

Kwajalein informed the resolution agenda produced at the 1983 NFIP
conference. A key resolution identified Kwajalein as central to the arms
race, with virtually every missile in the US nuclear arsenal being tested
there.[118] This resolution condemned Kwajalein's use of first-strike weapons
and demanded the atoll's islands be returned to their rightful owners. It
noted landowners should receive just compensation for the environmental destruction caused by the base presence. Finally, addressing a very
real threat to Ebeye if the army pulled out of Kwajalein, the resolution
urged the immediate development of alternative economic strategies to
end the Kwajalein's people's dependence on the base.[119] This final point
echoed arguments made by Ataji Balos before the COM in the wake of the
US Senate hearings, that rare voice delineating what was owed to a former
colony from decades of colonial exploitation. It was not enough to simply
leave. There needed to be some accountability for the economic exploitation and economic dependences intentionally fostered over time to benefit
the United States.

Pan-Pacific collaborations fueling the NFIP movement, in which Marshallese activists participated, have gone largely understudied by scholars
who trace the trajectory of global decolonization through the lens of

European colonialisms. When US empire and the Pacific are left out, such stories of anti-colonial struggle peak in the 1960s and 1970s. This historiography erases the largest geographic feature on the planet, the Pacific Ocean, home to islands and islanders whose lack of sovereign power over their lands and sea led them to become central testing grounds for the nuclear arms race. The exclusion of such histories of anti-colonial and antinuclear protest impoverish our historic understanding of the centrality of Oceania to imperial Cold War strategies and the historic collaborations of Pacific Islander leaders and activists who shaped consequential histories of self-determination. Their stories inform the broader postwar era of global decolonization, extending that trajectory into the 1980s, 1990s, and the present.

Residing at the matrix of Pacific protests against nuclear imperialism rippling out from Kwajalein to Hawai'i, from Aotearoa/New Zealand to Palau, Operation Homecoming also inspired US activists participating in the global antinuclear movement in the continent. In January and March 1983, security officers arrested twelve hundred protestors at California's Vandenberg Air Force Base. Those arrested comprised a coalition from antinuclear organizations in Berkeley, San Luis Obispo, and San Francisco, all demonstrating against the MX missile launch to Kwajalein.[120] Highlighting the broader impact of the Marshallese sail-ins, journalist Pat Fahey characterized the coalition's nonviolent acts of civil disobedience as "greatly inspired by the Marshallese people's occupation of the Kwajalein Missile Range dubbed 'Operation Homecoming.'"[121] Fahey said the protest's aims included challenging the army's continued "apartheid policy against the Marshallese on Ebeye."[122] Subsequent protests to delay missile launches followed in 1983, 1984, and 1985.

OCEANIC WAVES OF CHANGE:
OPERATION HOMECOMING AND BEYOND

When Julian Riklon sailed to his home islands with one thousand other Kwajalein landowners in 1982, he may not have imagined the reach of his action as it rippled beyond the atoll. But such was the impact of this historic protest that brought greater attention to Marshallese struggles on Kwajalein and Ebeye to a global audience. The movement won a range of concessions (detailed in chapter 6), exerting influence over the most powerful military in world history. This leverage was brought to bear through the historic combination of nonviolent, direct action and global media coverage within the broader context of Cold War geopolitical pressures. Riklon's subsequent participation in the NFIP movement alongside other Marshallese protestors also signaled how the Marshall Islands took their place within this expansive Pacific coalition fighting against nuclear imperialism and thus within the broader postwar history of global decolonization. As this chapter has traced, when tactics of protest through Senate testimonies, speeches, and petitions to the United Nations failed to bring about change in their homelands, Marshallese activists put their bodies on the line. In doing so, they called this hegemonic military power to attention. The army's luxury of being able to ignore the destructive and deadly impacts of its colonial policies in the region while suffering no constraint on its missile-testing mission could no longer be taken for granted. Operation Homecoming changed the equation.

Julian Riklon's activism continued after Operation Homecoming, through both participation in the NFIP and the subsequent protests at Vandenberg Air Force Base. In 2016, at the age of seventy, Riklon spoke at the Lawrence Livermore Lab to share the devastating impacts of US weapons testing on his family history. Riklon has been not only an active participant in but a keen observer of the changing political landscape of his home islands during the compact era. I turn to that era now through a continuation of Riklon's observations on how Operation Homecoming influenced the shape of Marshallese sovereignty in the "postcolonial" era.

6 US Empire and the Shape of Marshallese Sovereignty in the "Postcolonial" Era

> Neo-colonialism is also the worst form of imperialism. For those who practice it, it means power without responsibility and for those who suffer from it, it means exploitation without redress.
>
> —Kwame Nkrumah, 1965

> What can you do? I mean when you grow up with your brother and he's a lot bigger than you and he slap you, what can you do? It's better to earn some money out of the situation than having nothing.
>
> —Amata Kabua, president of the Republic of the Marshall Islands, describing his relationship with the US government

REFLECTIONS ON THE "POSTCOLONIAL" ON KWAJALEIN

In an interview, Kwajalein landowner and protest leader Julian Riklon reflected on the long-term impact of Operation Homecoming in Kwajalein atoll. Acknowledging the importance of concessions won, he added that these did not alleviate ongoing grievances among landowners about lease negotiations, nor did they fully address Ebeye's perpetual crisis of density and poverty. Riklon lamented that in the wake of Operation Homecoming, Marshallese living on Ebeye continued to suffer throughout the 1980s from ongoing congestion, limited housing, unsustainable population growth, and inadequate infrastructure to address these conditions.

Riklon said one solution to the continued impacts of density would be continued encouragement for people to return to their home islands.[1] But that solution only remained an option for Ebeye residents who had not been displaced from their home islands for US weapons testing. For many living on Ebeye, the US nuclear campaign or its missile-testing extension left no "right of return" from exile.

While Riklon saw both gains and limits to Operation Homecoming's success, local journalist Giff Johnson emphasized an important and enduring win. He argued that the US Army's approach to the Marshall Islands significantly changed following Operation Homecoming. Johnson credited the mass sail-in with forcing the army to recognize "that unless they dealt more effectively with the Marshall Islands, that they would not have uninterrupted use of Kwajalein."[2]

Operation Homecoming indeed impacted the way the army would approach ongoing efforts to maintain control over Kwajalein and more broadly to retain strategic control over the entire region. What changed over time was the political arrangement for maintaining that control. Within four years of the protest, the Republic of the Marshall Islands (RMI) government became the direct line of negotiation, in the absence of any Trust Territory government intermediary. As the locus of US negotiations shifted, opportunities for internal debate, contestation, and conflict between Marshallese landowners and the newly sovereign Marshallese government became more pronounced and visible. This is not to suggest any level of pre-existing homogeneity of interests among Marshallese prior to this period, but to signal the transition away from US forms of accountability for the colonial past and its ongoing legacies—a pattern that had unfolded across the decolonizing globe. With the dissolution of the Trusteeship Agreement, the United States could wipe its hands of any responsibility to appease ongoing landowner grievances or concerns about conditions on Ebeye, opting instead to communicate and negotiate directly with the RMI government.

This chapter considers what Marshallese sovereignty looked like in the "postcolonial" era during historic waves of global decolonization, the final years of the Cold War, and the ascendance of the United States as *the* global military and economic power. It explores Marshallese politics of decolonization after 1982 and the limits of those politics. In doing this, I draw upon Ghanaian revolutionary leader and political theorist Kwame

Nkrumah's definition of neocolonialism to argue that this condition more accurately described the terrain within which the first Marshallese president, Amata Kabua, charted a course for his nation's future. Nkrumah defined neocolonialism as a condition in which "the State which is subject to it is, in theory, independent and has all the outward trappings of international sovereignty. In reality, its economic system, and thus its political policy, is directed from the outside."[3] A politics of intimidation matched by ongoing Marshallese economic dependence on its former US colonial power marked the boundaries that limited Kabua's capacity to navigate a path toward full decolonization.

As has been revealed in many histories of decolonization during the Cold War, from Latin America to Southeast Asia, from Africa to the Middle East, and beyond, the Marshall Islands would prove no exception to a common US practice of paying lip service to the value of global democracy while undercutting that vision when it threatened US interests. Despite the UN Trusteeship Agreement's mandate that the United States support free and fair elections in the region, the United States ultimately undermined Marshallese self-determination by limiting the Marshallese vote on their future political status. In the wake of the Marshallese vote for the Compact of Free Association, further boundaries on Marshallese sovereignty would be felt through the political and economic conditions within which a transition from a colonial to a postcolonial status would take place. In this respect, the 1963 Solomon Report had proven quite prescient in foreshadowing a US policy that would create conditions of enduring economic dependence. This ongoing status, created through US neglect of the UN mandate to support broad economic development in the region, alongside mass investment in Kwajalein as the primary economic engine for Marshallese, would ultimately shape the boundaries within which Marshallese sovereignty could be imagined in the postcolonial era.

OPERATION HOMECOMING AND THE THREAT OF REAL SELF-DETERMINATION

To understand how Marshallese decolonization unfolded toward a neocolonial structure that became masked under a façade of sovereign equality through the Compact of "Free" Association, I first examine why the United States reneged on its Trusteeship Agreement obligation to support the full range of political options for Micronesian self-determination. Operation Homecoming was central to this story. While the broader frame of this chapter considers how Marshallese decolonization was also dramatically bounded by the constraints of long-term economic dependence on the United States, exacted through decades of US colonial policies, this section begins with democracy, or the lack thereof, in the region. By considering US removal of a full range of voting options to support Marshallese self-determination, I show how the United States not only rejected its Trusteeship Agreement mandate but denied Marshallese access to the kind of democratic freedoms the United States boasted as its defining features to the decolonizing world during the Cold War. This pattern of Cold War US exceptionalism situated the Marshallese path toward decolonization alongside that of many other decolonizing nations in which democratic freedom was undermined by the United States when it threatened US geopolitical interests.

Before Kwajalein landowners launched Operation Homecoming in June 1982, a plebiscite had been planned for that August to allow Marshallese to vote on the future political status of their nation. One month before the mass sail-in, Foreign Secretary Tony de Brum was helping arrange the plebiscite with US ambassador Fred Zeder. In May 1982, De Brum and Zeder met and signed a memorandum of understanding calling for a plebiscite, which would give Marshallese voters a choice between free association or full independence. Both options guaranteed an end to the Trusteeship Agreement. According to De Brum, the agreement would then acquire "the necessary U.S. Congressional approval by Oct. 1, 1982. Otherwise the Marshalls would unilaterally declare the end of the 35-year U.N. trusteeship relationship and would thenceforth be independent."[4] A ten-week political education program was planned to follow the plebiscite, which would allow Marshallese to determine their future status from an informed position, leaving it up to fate with a vote on October 1.[5]

Despite De Brum and Zeder's negotiations, the United States and the RMI went ahead and signed the Compact of Free Association on May 30, 1982, ignoring Kwajalein landowners' objections. Operation Homecoming immediately followed, as did increasing pressure from personnel in the Departments of Interior, State, and Defense on Ambassador Zeder to deny any prior US commitment to the memorandum of understanding. Signaling the preeminence of US power within the United Nations, the latter "proclaim[ed] an inability—or unwillingness" to send observers to the planned August 17 plebiscite.[6] The United States ultimately imposed its Trust Territory authority to suspend the Marshallese plebiscite, postponing it indefinitely, "and announced that no wording on the ballot would be allowed that offered a clear choice for independence."[7]

For US officials negotiating the end of formal colonial control in the region, Operation Homecoming punctuated the precarity of US support for full democracy for Marshallese. In his *Pacific Islands Monthly* article "U.S. Vetoes Independence as Marshallese Landowners Occupy Kwajalein," journalist Giff Johnson highlighted potential fears informing the US decision to prevent democratic voting in the region.[8] He argued: "The U.S. Government would not have objected to the independence option *if* compact approval was a certainty."[9] But when Kwajalein landowners put compact approval in jeopardy with their protest, US officials quickly repudiated Zeder's memorandum. Johnson's article included Deputy Assistant Secretary of Defense Noel Koch's defense against allegations of bad faith negotiations in the region. Koch explained that the United States had done everything possible to expedite the process of granting Marshallese greater autonomy, but that under international law, "declaring independence simply isn't an available option to them."[10] Johnson traced how Koch's statement conflicted with UN Trusteeship provisions obligating the United States to develop Micronesia "toward self government or independence as may be appropriate."[11] As noted in chapter 3, at the time of Operation Homecoming, Pentagon officials estimated a prohibitive $2 billion cost for creating a similar missile site elsewhere. The risk of Marshallese opting for complete independence also risked ongoing US control over this valuable base.

The removal of independence from the Marshallese ballot continued a long-standing pattern in which the United States ignored any UN obligations that did not support the US government's military interests in the region. Because the United States had veto power within the UN Security Council over any decisions that could impact US national security, the United Nations proved impotent in asserting any real influence over

US practices in the region. Thus, the removal of independence not sur-
prisingly proceeded with minimal challenges, except from Marshallese
landowners and activists and journalists covering the story.

The US failure to support free and democratic voting while claiming
to be the beacon of democracy left De Brum incensed. He reflected on
his experience of spending thirteen years in political negotiations with
the United States, explaining that he had seen a side of the United States
less visible to its friends around the world. This side "violates the very
basic foundations of democracy which it boasts to the rest of the world."[12]
De Brum's experience was tragically familiar to many other political
leaders during the Cold War who were pushing forward nationalist movements for decolonization. Leaders like Jacobo Arbenz, Ho Chi Minh, and
Patrice Lumumba (among many others) also understood what it meant
to have the sovereignty of their homelands undermined by their position
as pawns in a Cold War chess match. These nationalist leaders saw their
anti-colonial struggles challenged and violently undermined when their
vision for independence was seen as a threat to US interests. While the
propaganda arm of the US Cold War arsenal deployed proclamations of
support for democracy and freedom abroad, many colonized subjects saw
their efforts to obtain a piece of this democratic pie sabotaged and felt
the deadly sting of American hypocrisy. De Brum decried the US decision
to take independence off the ballot for the Marshallese, arguing that this
choice reflected the pattern of the United States seeming to feel "they are
a little bit more equal than everyone else."[13]

Nearly three decades after the United States undermined free and
unfettered elections in the Marshall Islands, the memory remained a
bitter one for De Brum. In our 2010 interview, he contended that when
Marshallese political leaders first began working to form a new government during the 1960s, they wanted an independent one. He recalled
that these leaders saw this vision as feasible before the Solomon Report
confirmed that the United States never really planned to support such a
path.[14] De Brum said the biggest fight he encountered in his role as vice
chairman of the Status Commission for Marshall Islands was over the
wording that would appear on the Marshallese ballot. While he advocated
including independence as an option, American negotiators wanted the
wording to center on the compact. According to De Brum, US negotiators

indicated that if Marshallese voted against the compact, *then* they could begin to negotiate for independence. He said his "legal beagle" people told him the United States did not want the Marshalls "to enjoy even a scintilla moment of independence because during that scintilla moment we could say we don't want you here."[15] Pausing to reflect on whether or not Marshallese would have voted for independence if given the option, De Brum answered: "I think they would have if they had the opportunity, if only as a bargaining chip."[16]

Because independence was removed as an option in 1982, there is no way to know if Marshallese would have voted in that direction. But one thing seems certain: as an independent nation Marshallese would have had greater control over Kwajalein and thus the ability to leverage the island's importance to the United States in determining the future relationship between the two countries. The terms and conditions of the Compact of Free Association placed limitations on how much landowners could get for Kwajalein. The compact also meant landowners could not choose to do anything else with Kwajalein, either in terms of living on the island or of renting the space to other nations that might have paid more for use of this strategic space. As noted earlier, the base was valued at $2 billion in 1982. Within twelve years, its value would double.

When Marshallese cast votes on their future political status on September 7, 1983, the majority opted for free association with the United States.[17] The vote solidified the path toward decolonization after more than thirty-five years under US colonial rule. There were just two choices on the ballot: continue the ongoing Trusteeship status or transition to free association with the United States. The population was approximately thirty-four thousand, fifteen thousand of whom were eligible to vote, of which 58 percent opted for the compact.[18] Significantly, those most directly impacted by the history and ongoing legacies of US weapons testing voted against the compact: with 79 percent on Bikini/Kili, 86 percent on Rongelap, and 70 percent on Kwajalein.[19] While the compact passed by comfortable margins in most areas of the country, it was rejected by a three-to-one margin in Kwajalein Atoll.[20] Primary objections centered on the thirty-year length of the lease, which prevented Kwajalein landowners from engaging in continual renegotiations that would have given them greater leverage to demand higher compensation.[21] The compact took three more years to officially pass, awaiting US congressional approval to cement this long-term agreement between the RMI and the United States. When it was up for a vote again in 1986 in the Marshall Islands, Kwajalein landowners again broadly rejected it. In addition to noting the leasing concerns, Ebeye mayor Alvin Jacklick described the Kwajalein landowners' rejection as also tied to its wholly inadequate health and education provisions for Ebeye.[22]

The three-year interim period while the compact awaited passage in the US Congress became a crucial moment not only in Marshallese political history but also in the Reagan administration's pivot toward the strategic importance of Kwajalein. As President Reagan was going for broke on military buildup during the Cold War, the *New York Times* announced his new "Star Wars" strategic defensive initiative on March 24, 1984.[23] Kwajalein became a central site buttressing SDI research aimed at building a missile defense system to thwart potential ICBM attacks on the United States. Testing to develop army homing and intercept technology was already being carried out on Kwajalein in 1983 and 1984. The extension of this research on ICBM missile interception carried a projected price tag of at least $25 billion between 1984 and 1989.[24]

President Reagan's increasing dependence on Kwajalein for missile defense placed heightened pressure on a stable transition toward free association. On January 14, 1986, President Reagan signed the bill passed by Congress that December to create the Compact of Free Association between the two nations. This bill authorized "a 30 year contract, with 15 year renewal timeframe, negotiated for control of Kwajalein Missile Range in support of missile testing and Reagan's SDI. The U.S. recognized the sovereignty of the Republic of the Marshall Islands (RMI) but retained the right of 'strategic denial' to other foreign nations and American military protection."[25] Other concessions included health-care and food support for islands that suffered most from the atomic testing, economic aid of $2.6 billion, and trade and tax concessions. "The agreement also gave the RMI the authority to conduct its own foreign affairs in areas not related to defense and security, including consular, cultural and economic relations. As well the compact permitted the free movement of citizens from the Marshalls to the United States without the usual immigration requirements such as passports and visas."[26]

The 1986 compact solidified the long-term free association relationship between the United States and the newly sovereign RMI, disregarding overwhelming opposition from Kwajalein landowners. The vote signaled the climax of decades of political negotiations, leasing deals, testimony, and protests, and cemented Amata Kabua's role as president of the newly decolonized nation. At a United Nations University conference in 1986, historian Stewart Firth offered his analysis of the compact vote and the limits on decolonization in the region.[27] In a paper entitled "Staying While Leaving: The Americans in Micronesia," Firth argued: "The future for the Marshallese at Kwajalein will be defined by the needs of the military. Once the Compact goes into effect their bargaining power will be weak."[28] While for the new RMI, the Compact of Free Association marked the end of nearly forty years of US rule through UN-sanctioned colonialism, the suggestion of sovereign equality through "free association" proved misleading.

As the remainder of this chapter explores, what ensued instead was an era of political inequality marked by President Amata Kabua's efforts to navigate a path for his new nation in an atmosphere of ongoing US political intimidation. The legacy of economic dependence fostered under decades of US colonial control gave this tone of intimidation a mark of coercion on Kabua's presidential policies that proved a lasting legacy in the "postcolonial era." This period more accurately reflected the defining features of neocolonialism commonly experienced by other decolonizing nations in the postwar era. I next examine the tumultuous years of this political transition leading up to and in the immediate wake of the 1986 compact signing. Analysis of President Kabua's public statements during this period and his consequential responses to a final landowner protest will provide a better understanding of the limits on Marshallese sovereignty in this neocolonial era.

THE POLITICS OF INTIMIDATION
AND THE NEOCOLONIAL SHIFT

Kwajalein's strategic value as an ongoing missile-testing facility influenced US decisions to limit the Marshallese vote on their future political status.

The assessment of Kwajalein's value over time—to the United States, to landowners, and to the newly sovereign Marshallese government—not only determined the path of Marshallese decolonization by impacting the vote, but also played a central role in how Marshallese politics unfolded following formal decolonization. As I explore the ways that first Marshallese president Kabua navigated this transition for his new nation, I show how his was a path traversed under conditions of neocolonialism. The obstacles facing Kabua reflected those that Kwame Nkrumah delineated in his globally influential 1965 book analyzing neocolonialism, a structure that bounded many nations newly forming in the ashes of imperialism. This structure replaced direct political control with a range of other levers of coercion that limited nominally sovereign countries from exercising any full capacity to dictate the terms of their own collective future.[29] While Nkrumah's analysis of neocolonialism centered ongoing economic dependencies determining the shape of decolonization across Africa and Southeast Asia, his political theory resonated with the conditions in the Marshall Islands. For Marshallese, these historic and ongoing economic dependencies were linked both to Kwajalein's development as a key US missile installation and to US neglect of its Trusteeship Agreement mandate to support any other viable forms of economy within the region.

As Marshallese emerged from nearly four decades of US colonial control and US neglect of its UN mandate to support economic development in the region, the political economy of the new nation remained tied to the fate of Kwajalein. By the 1980s, the Solomon Report's recommendations (made two decades earlier) had borne fruit. The United States no longer needed any formal structure of colonial control to ensure an ongoing and indefinite strategic presence in the region. As President Kabua made clear in several public statements, the sustainability of the Marshallese economy depended on remaining connected to the US military.

As Kabua emerged in 1979 as president to lead the decolonizing Marshall Islands government, Kwajalein landowners expressed ongoing concerns about their marginalization from a political process that hinged on the value of their lands. For the United States, decolonization brought relief after years of direct conflict with Kwajalein landowners over land control. In the postcolonial era, that responsibility would shift onto the RMI government. The United States could wipe its hands of any responsibility

to deal with the political turmoil that accompanied its historic and ongoing legacy of colonial control and economic neglect within the region.
Under the Compact of Free Association, the primary battles over Kwajalein would be internally fought between Marshallese. As historian David
Hanlon observed, US and Marshallese government negotiations worked
to divide or exacerbate existing divisions among Marshallese. This "would
be one of the legacies of American colonialism in a postcolonial order that
was really not postcolonial at all."[30]

In our 2010 interview, when Kwajalein senator Tony de Brum bitterly quipped about Kwajalein having been "given away" by the Marshallese government, his words reflected these lasting divisions. De Brum's
impressions of Kabua as having betrayed Kwajalein landowners by showing greater loyalty to the United States echoed the experience of others
during this political transition. Kabua's position as a high chief and landowner complicated these issues and perhaps exacerbated the sense of
betrayal among other landowners, whose historic influence and power
became marginalized with the imposition of a foreign government system.

Kabua was tasked with navigating a new dynamic of free association
with the United States, a former colonial overseer and increasingly hegemonic global imperial power.[31] His path to the presidency was long in the
making, informed by his inherited chiefly (*iroij*) status as son of principal
Kwajalein landowner *iroij* Lejolan Kabua.[32] He obtained a US political
education under the Trust Territory government and became a founding
member of the Congress of Micronesia in 1964, serving as president of its
Senate for two terms.[33] During this period, Kabua played an active role
in trying to shape the conditions of governance under which Marshallese
lived. This included his scathing critique of US control over the region,
labeling conditions under US governance as exemplary of a "neo-colonial
situation." As discussed in previous chapters, this allegation was made in
Kabua's coauthored Nitijela resolution, sent to the UN Trusteeship Council in 1968, calling for an end to the Trusteeship Agreement and delineating these neocolonial conditions.[34] As Kabua neared election to the
most powerful position of governance over his decolonizing nation, such
radical criticisms became tempered. Appointed by the Nitijela as the first
Marshallese president in 1979, Kabua began navigating a strategic path
of cooperation with the United States that informed the development

of the Compact of Free Association and the legacy of that relationship thereafter.[35]

During Kabua's tenure as president he received mixed reviews from Marshallese; many praised his leadership during the historic transition, while others criticized what they viewed as support for US interests over Marshallese. In contrast, US political leaders continually applauded Kabua's support for the ongoing US presence in the region, support solicited through US coercion and intimidation. As head of state, President Kabua often acknowledged that the limits of his power in the newly sovereign nation extended to the limits of US interests on Kwajalein. A politics of intimidation framed the boundaries of his decision-making and came through in his commentary on this historic transition. These statements illuminate that while Kabua may have left the *label* of neocolonialism behind him with the 1968 Nitijela resolution, he was never fully able to escape the *conditions* of neocolonialism to chart a course of sovereignty for his people unimpaired by their impacts.

Kabua's public statements on how he navigated this path toward Marshallese sovereignty over time suggest his leadership was informed by a level of pragmatic realism. During the 1970s and 1980s Kabua publicly chronicled his efforts to secure the best deal he could for his people within a context of US global imperial dominance. This pragmatism signaled a shift from a more radical vision he had voiced during the 1960s. Four years after penning the 1968 defamation of US neocolonialism in his home islands, Kabua's public tune shifted toward one more reconciled to an ongoing future relationship with the imperial power. In a 1972 interview published in the *Micronesian Reporter*, Kabua no longer advocated for complete removal of the United States from the region. He said he did not believe in the kind of independence expressed by some Marshallese youth in which one had nothing to do with those around him: "Independence is just a degree of a person's or a nation's being able to control his or its own fate and not always in an unfriendly way."[36] Kabua argued that he knew no nation in the world to be purely independent and cited coexistence as much more important than isolation from the world community.[37]

By the late 1970s, Kabua was traversing a complex terrain in negotiating a path toward national sovereignty *and* interdependence with the United States as the new president of the Marshall Islands. Kabua highlighted that interdependence in his inaugural address, which began with his acknowledging the historic nature of the day. He said that from "this day forward, let no one doubt our full and complete sovereignty over the Marshall Islands," but went on to assert his continued commitment to the United States following the Trust Territory administration's disintegration.[38] He also highlighted the central role Kwajalein would continue to play in this ongoing partnership.[39] Kabua emphasized that after the government, Kwajalein Missile Range remained the second largest employer in the Marshalls. He said the base employed directly or indirectly more than eight hundred Marshallese people. The speech reaffirmed his commitment to supporting Kwajalein families to reach fair and equitable agreements alongside his support for US national security requirements. He likewise acknowledged that the cost of meeting such requirements had been, and remained, high for the Marshallese people.[40]

Less than a year after his inauguration, Kabua spoke to the *New Pacific Magazine* on what free association meant to him: "Free Association is a contract between our two sovereign countries wherein we have delegated the U.S. certain responsibilities, and in this case it is defense and security. In return for providing them with what they consider to be a legitimate defense need, we receive a certain amount of economic assistance."[41] Pointing to US neglect of its Trust Territory obligations, Kabua explained how compact economic assistance built on the fact that for the prior thirty years the United States had done little to help build any economic base for the Marshalls. Thus, the United States had a continuing responsibility to deal with the economic situation it caused.[42] Kabua said that since World War II, the United States had viewed the Marshalls as an important strategic space: "So we said, fine. If you want to stay here, you want to control defense and security, fine; that's your responsibility, fine; that's what it is. It is not a continuation of a colonial relationship."[43] Kabua asserted that his nation retained full control over foreign affairs unless they were defense related, and this new relationship recognized Marshallese sovereignty.[44]

While many of Kabua's public statements framed the path forward with the United States as one marked by partnership, rooted in mutual *inter*dependence, mutual respect, and mutual interest, some of his public comments also hinted at the unequal nature of this historic and ongoing relationship. The absence of any true reciprocity marking Marshallese negotiations for greater sovereignty with the United States came through in one of Kabua's interviews in 1983. Associate Press journalist Todd Carrol captured the limitations on Marshallese sovereignty in his article's title, "Self-Government But Missiles Too." Speaking with Carrol, Kabua reflected on his limited influence even as the most powerful politician of his decolonizing nation. When asked his impressions of President Reagan's latest "peacekeeper" MX missile landing near Kwajalein that June, Kabua subverted the euphemistic title of the missile, describing the tests as "'killer' weapons" and as the "business of the United States."[45] He said he was "'too small' to understand U.S.-Soviet Missile politics" and preferred to associate with the kind of guy without a gun.[46] When asked how Kabua could allow the United States to continue missile testing at Kwajalein if he was so opposed to such weapons, Kabua replied: "'If I didn't let them use it, they would have taken it anyway.'"[47]

Political cartoonist John Bauman satirized this power imbalance under which Kabua was tasked with leading his nation toward a new political status in a 1985 issue of the *Guardian*. Bauman's editorial cartoon highlighted the limited degree of influence Kabua brought to these negotiations. Illustrating the extent to which US military interests eclipsed Marshallese sovereignty when it came to the compact vote, the cartoon centered the atmosphere of intimidation informing the compact signing. It shows a man (presumed to be Kabua) sitting in a chair atop the Marshall Islands looking fearfully at an incoming missile as he is being pressured to sign the "New Compact" by Uncle Sam and a US military commander. Suggesting an atmosphere of intimidation, the cartoon's caption reads: "Hurry up and sign."[48] Of the three men in the image, only the two Americans are bestowed the honor of wearing hats, and they both sit taller than Kabua. Alluding to the Cold War context informing this political transition, the cartoonist included a Soviet bear spying on the men off in the distance.[49]

Portrayed by Bauman as a hatless dupe and decried by some Kwajalein landowners as "betrayer in chief," Kabua seemed a leader highly aware of the global political reality that his new republic was entering in the 1980s. Kabua defended his pragmatic stance during the final landowner protest in 1986, summing up his alliance with the United States. In an interview he allowed to be filmed, which would ultimately appear in Adam

Horowitz's 1991 documentary film *Home on the Range*, Kabua alluded to the tensions underlying the ongoing hierarchical relationship between the United States and the Marshall Islands: "What can you do? I mean when you grow up with your brother and he's a lot bigger than you and he slap you, what can you do? It's better to earn some money out of the situation than having nothing.'"[50] Kabua's defeatist sentiments accented the realist thread operating under the surface of previous statements on Marshallese sovereignty and partnership with the United States. That some Marshallese were critical of this persistent power dynamic informing the neo-colonial structure of the compact era was evident in Kwajalein landowner and activist Julian Riklon's comments. Also in an interview filmed during the 1986 protest, Riklon explained: "The Marshall Islands government says they are independent and that they possess power and authority, but I feel our government is not really independent because in fact, almost all the money that the Marshall Islands government has come from the American government." Riklon concluded that given this reality, the RMI government had to do whatever the US government demanded.[51] Riklon's comments hinted at the continual divide that would remain for those with the most to lose, given their landowner status and residency on Ebeye.

Another critical response came from John Heine, a former Marshallese representative to the Congress of Micronesia. His reflections appeared in anthropologist Geoffrey M. White's 1991 edited volume, *Remembering the Pacific War*, in which Heine highlighted both the economic and political constraints on Marshallese politics during this period. In his analysis, Heine traced the three successive administrations in the region (Germany, Japan, and the United States) leading up to the contemporary Marshallese republic. He raised questions about Marshallese capacity for true sovereignty within that context, asking: "When you examine that republic, and you think about how that republic was led into being what it is through the training of three different administrations, is that a republic, a product of our own desires, of our own making?"[52] Heine considered how economic conditions complicated Marshallese independence. Without directly criticizing US economic neglect in the region during the colonial era, he noted the lack of any material base in the region other than coconut sales, which yielded minimal returns. "So, in the absence of an economic base," he argued, "we see that because of the Kwajalein testing ground, we cannot really say no to the United States. While the taking is good, we are using it."[53] Heine's comments echoed the pragmatic, realistic approach of Kabua, who spoke candidly at different moments of his presidency about these constraints on Marshallese sovereignty following decolonization.

Hailed as the Father of the Nation, Kabua had served eighteen years as president (five consecutive terms) by the time of his passing in 1996. In the obituaries that followed, he was credited for having led the new nation's transition into the compact era and securing increasing financial gains for the republic during that time.[54] Among the many tributes to Kabua, longtime friend and former chief secretary Oscar de Brum lauded him for having restored Marshallese sovereignty, bringing the small country "'into the modern world to take its place within the family of nations.'"[55]

De Brum's familial commemoration echoed a familiar trope also used by US political leaders over time to mark Kabua's historic navigation of the nation toward free association. A family metaphor infused President Reagan's framing of the transition to free association and the cessation of the Trusteeship Agreement. Drawing on this sentimentalized framework, Reagan disavowed the historic and ongoing hierarchical nature of negotiations by euphemizing decades of colonial control as a "family affair." In his January 31, 1983, "Message on Micronesian Plebiscite," Reagan acknowledged the historic nature of the occasion and reflected on what he called "a very special relationship" existing between the United States and the Trust Territory peoples for many years.[56] He explained that "under the trusteeship we've come to know and respect you as members of our American family. And now, as happens to all families, members grow up and leave home."[57] Evoking an image of parents sending adolescents out into the adult world, Reagan said Americans wished the Marshallese the best as they assumed full responsibility for their domestic affairs and foreign relations. He wished them luck as they charted their own course for economic development and entered the world as a sovereign nation. Reagan concluded: "We look forward to continuing our close relationship with you in your new status, but you'll always be family to us."[58] Reagan's paternalistic tone obscured the deeper history of destruction, violence, and injustice characterizing US policies in the region. Likewise, by positioning the Marshall Islands as residing within the American family, Reagan's remarks

furthered—on a global scale—a narrative that Kwajalein's physical transformation into small-town suburbia had accomplished on a local level.
As the Marshall Islands transitioned from the formal confines of colonial
control, this domestic nostalgia—the notion that this had always been a
family affair—obscured an ongoing reality of violence more akin to domestic abuse than familial bliss.

As Reagan wished the Marshallese well on their journey, he did so in
a context of ongoing landowner efforts to secure greater compensation
for Kwajalein, continuing struggles facing Marshallese trying to survive
Ebeye's ongoing crisis of poverty, and continued pressures for the United
States to acknowledge the true extent of destruction and devastation
brought about by its nuclear-testing campaign in the region. Just two
years after Reagan's speech was penned, reminding Marshallese "family
members" of their special relationship, the Greenpeace vessel *Rainbow
Warrior* sailed to Rongelap to rescue and resettle Marshallese individuals
who had been living on the irradiated island for decades. Like Julian Riklon and his family members (discussed in chapter 5), other Rongelapese
had been "fearful about the implications of their continued exposure to
radiation" after being resettled onto their island after the Bravo detonation
and studied by researchers from Brookhaven National Laboratory and the
Department of Energy for decades.[59] As historian Martha Smith-Norris
has traced, after their request to the Department of Energy to remove them
from the contaminated atoll was declined, Rongelapese "took matters into
their own hands" and solicited help from Greenpeace. In 1985, Greenpeace
activists used their ship to transport 350 Rongelapese to safety on a small
uninhabited island within Kwajalein Atoll called Mejatto.[60]

During the 1980s, Reagan mythologized a US relationship to the Marshall Islands as defined through familial support and rooted in the sacrosanct values of democracy. He concluded his 1983 address by reflecting
on all the positive projects the United States and Marshall Islands built
together over the years. He applauded the construction of roads, airports,
schools, and hospitals. He emphasized that the most important project
built together was the "understanding of the meaning of democracy and
freedom and the dignity of self-determination."[61] Reagan concluded the
Marshallese had built "a strong foundation for [their] future. Together
in free association, [the United States and Marshalls] can and will build

a better life for all."[62] By emphasizing a relationship built around mutual efforts toward Marshallese democracy, freedom, and self-determination, Reagan erased the history and continuity of domination, military destruction, and political coercion and intimidation that more accurately characterized the US impact in the region. This emphasis on democratic values and support for self-determination also obscured the US decision to undermine Marshallese voting rights when Operation Homecoming raised the possibility that Marshallese might opt for independence if given a real choice.

In an interview, Tony de Brum reflected on how a politics of intimidation historically infected Marshallese and US political negotiations and continued to characterize the culture between the nations into the twenty-first century. Having spent the majority of his career negotiating a Marshallese political future with the United States, De Brum described what he saw as the "anomaly" of many Marshallese viewing their relationship with the United States as one of friendship. He said these Marshallese did not see the military's "spear line" as the true relationship they dealt with, even though the United States continued to operate from a place of hierarchy and intimidation.[63] Exemplifying this continuity of intimidation in the region, De Brum recounted a recent incident on Kwajalein in which the wife of the highest-ranking Marshallese political representative living on the island was barred for thirty days. The Marshallese woman had given a cola to someone on Ebeye, and the Kwajalein commander charged her with attempting to smuggle soda onto the black market. De Brum said the woman intended to remain on a smaller island for her thirty-day ban, until he got word and remedied the situation. He concluded: "The *intimidation* of 50 to 60 years is so real that . . . that is normal. The Army tells you to move off, even if your husband is a representative of our government on Kwajalein, they pack up and move."[64]

De Brum's story illustrating the continuity of a politics of intimidation over time further demystified any illusion of equivalent political sovereignty between the United States and the RMI inferred by a formal, legal contract: the Compact of Free Association. It raises questions about the "free" nature of such an association voted on under conditions limiting Marshallese democratic options and bounded by a material reality of economic dependence fostered over nearly four decades of US colonial rule.

As the imperative of US colonial administrators was always the pursuit of national security mandated by the UN Trusteeship Agreement alongside neglect of the dual obligation to foster sustainable economic development within the region, the Marshall Islands had been left in a state of economic precarity and thus political vulnerability. Having considered these neocolonial legacies on the national level that shaped the Marshallese path toward decolonization, I now look at how this history played out locally on the ground, or the coral, at Kwajalein Atoll.

PROTEST IN THE NEOCOLONIAL ERA AND THE RETURN OF EMINENT DOMAIN

The extent to which Marshallese sovereignty remained bounded by a politics of intimidation came through poignantly in President Kabua's response to a final landowner protest in 1986. During the protest, Kabua supported US interests by endorsing punitive and violent responses to nonviolent Marshallese protesters. He also declared eminent domain on Kwajalein, arguing that a US missile base constituted a public good. Both of Kabua's responses elicited an array of criticism from Marshallese and investigative journalists covering the protest. This final landowner movement emerged just before the final Marshallese vote on the Compact of Free Association. While the length of the 1986 sail-ins slightly exceeded that of Operation Homecoming, the participation level significantly declined, from the 1,000 Marshallese involved in 1982 to about 150 by 1986.[65] By analyzing the political climate of this final protest, I further examine the limits of Marshallese sovereignty, bound by an ongoing neocolonial structure in an era of US global imperial ascendance.

The conditions that preempted the 1986 Marshallese protest against the army grew out of landowner objections to a lease negotiated in September 1985 to cover the period until the compact went into effect in 1986. In October, Kwajalein landowners requested concessions from the United States, including the rehiring of the approximately 200 Marshallese domestics fired as a punitive action during Operation Homecoming four years earlier. The landowners also demanded a $6 million lump sum payment in addition to funds promised under the compact.[66] The military rejected the monetary request in February but agreed in part to some of the other requests. Unsatisfied with the US response, approximately 150 Kwajalein Atoll Corporation landowners sailed to Kwajalein in early February. Characterizing the 1986 sail-in as "low key" compared to the sail-in by 1,000 Marshallese four years earlier, journalist Giff Johnson wrote: "Nevertheless, the army flew in additional security personnel, stating that the occupation was disrupting normal KMR operations."[67] Various factors seemed to influence the reduced number of protestors participating by 1986. Julian Riklon was absent in the 1986 protest because he was in Australia acting as a Marshallese representative at the Nuclear Free and Independent Pacific meeting. But he said he believed fewer participated in this sail-in because of the earlier concessions won, including some funding for Ebeye improvement projects. He also felt the lease was unlikely to change by 1986.[68]

Marshallese landowner Sato Maie voiced another reason fewer landowners protested in this final sail-in: fear of the army's punitive response. Signaling new divisions that had taken place among Kwajalein landowners since Operation Homecoming, Maie represented the interests of a new landowner group, the Kwajalein Association of Landowners (KAL). Maie wrote a letter to President Kabua on behalf of his landowner group suggesting the degree to which economic fears may have influenced many to abstain. He said KAL believed the demonstrators did not represent the majority of landowners and in fact only comprised those holding about 27 percent of acreage used by the missile range.[69] He asserted that his organization's members would not take part in the demonstration and they wanted the record to clearly reflect their position so that when the United States deducted the protest costs under the new compact, as they had done during Operation Homecoming, KAL's members would not suffer. He stated, "It must be clearly understood by all concerned that we will not stand idly by as we did in early 1983, allowing our people to suffer for the misdeeds of others."[70] Maie requested Kabua's government take a clear public position regarding who would pay the protest costs so everyone would know the penalty for their conduct. He also asked that Kabua make his position clear to the US government and act in whatever way possible to protect the interests of those committed to peaceful negotiations.[71]

Maie's letter exemplified how the army's punitive measures during Operation Homecoming may have been successful in deterring broader protest participation four years later. The letter revealed how, in its wake, Operation Homecoming had sown the seeds for new divisions among landowners. Like other decolonizing nations in the postwar era, new incentives and punishments created by the former imperial power also exacerbated existing divisions among the Marshallese. The sail-ins made those divisions between Kwajalein landowners and the emerging RMI government more visible.[72]

Diverging slightly from Operation Homecoming's tactics, landowners protesting in 1986 attempted to put additional pressure on the army by blockading the Ebeye pier. The protest involved a labor strike, preventing most Marshallese employed on Kwajalein from getting to work. The RMI government declared a state of emergency in response to the blockade, while commander Colonel William Spin tried to hasten an end to the protest by firing and working to permanently replace all Marshallese workers stranded on Ebeye. Spin's recruitment efforts motivated a large number of Marshallese from Ebeye to risk their lives walking across the reef at low tide to reach work before losing their jobs. Neibanjan Lavin was among the several hundred Marshallese workers who made the journey.[73] In an interview, Lavin recalled having to work during the protest because she had just given birth and needed to feed her daughter.[74] She described how she set out with a group of men to walk the reef but quickly fell into a hole in the ocean. She said the experience was scary but noted that luckily others knew how to swim; presumably she did not. They assisted her in getting back to Ebeye. Lavin managed to keep her job, as the dock blockade lasted only a short time. Her reflections complicated a narrative running through articles written at the time, which alleged that protesting landowners threatened to destroy the homes of the so-called strike breakers. Lavin said nobody had ever threatened her. In fact, she recalled that most people on Ebeye supported the protest, including the workers, despite the increased difficulty in getting to work. She said all on Ebeye stuck together as one.[75]

That the historic and ongoing wounds of segregation continued to fester just below the surface during the sail-ins in 1986 came through in media coverage of the protest. During the protest, the army's efforts to replace Marshallese workers caught the critical attention of the media and Marshallese political leaders. Responding to the pier blockade,

Marshall Islands government attorney general Greg Danz said that while forty dependents at Kwajalein were hired to replace Marshallese workers, the army planned to bring in expatriates to fill essential positions. Danz explained in a *Marshall Islands Journal* article that Colonel Spin said: "'KMR could not house or feed the 420 Marshallese who [walked the reef] to Kwajalein.'"[76] Kwajalein landowner and protest leader Ataji Balos questioned the colonel's plan to recruit and accommodate additional workers on Kwajalein by highlighting the island's continued structure of segregation. In another *Marshall Islands Journal* article Balos argued: "'The Colonel says he can't house and feed all 420 workers, that they must return to Ebeye. Why then did he say he's going to hire hundreds of outsiders to come and work at Kwajalein. How will he house and feed them?'"[77] Balos concluded, "The Americans just don't want Marshallese to live on Kwajalein.'"[78] Four years after Operation Homecoming, Balos saw little change in the demoralizing structure of segregation.

Another distinction marking Operation Homecoming and the 1986 protest was collaboration between the United States and the newly formed RMI government in supporting an armed response to protestors. Julian Riklon had been one of several Marshallese protestors beaten by Kwajalein guards after arriving unarmed to peacefully demonstrate on his homeland in 1982; four years later the official army response included the threat of lethal force.[79] Kwajalein army authorities issued a "shoot to wound" order if any occupying landowners crossed over a type of "'line-of-death'" boundary painted yellow on the island.[80] The RMI government supported the army's approach. "Missile Range Commander Colonel William Spin ordered his guards to 'use deadly force only in extreme necessity' noting the caveat that if the guards pull out their weapons, they should 'shoot to wound and not to kill.'"[81]

Lasting four months, the protest concluded in the first week of May, after President Kabua met with landowners and promised to seek better lease compensation and developmental assistance for Ebeye. But the manner in which the Marshallese government had collaborated with the army to remove protestors from Kwajalein and the legal means through which the army enacted the removal left a bitter taste throughout the newly decolonized nation. In addition to Kabua supporting the army's punitive approach to workers on Ebeye and armed force to quell the protest, he took another, drastic measure that distinguished the 1986 sail-in from the earlier protest: he declared eminent domain on Kwajalein Island. Attorney General Greg Danz explained that the government made this declaration to help remove Kwajalein protestors because the protest had gone on "long enough."[82] Journalist Giff Johnson reported on the unprecedented nature of this move, explaining how by authorizing the government to take possession of land belonging to the protesting landowners, the Marshall Islands Cabinet had identified the US and RMI activities conducted at the Kwajalein Missile Range as constituting "public use."[83] The government's position on eminent domain relied on an argument that US use of Kwajalein offered defense protection and other services to the RMI government. This in turn allowed the RMI government to provide services to the Marshallese people.[84]

President Kabua's eminent domain order raised questions about the RMI government's responsibility to the United States versus its own people. While the Trust Territory government had historically declared eminent domain on Ebeye to take land in support of the army's missile-testing purposes, it was a meaningfully unprecedented move for the newly decolonized government to be issuing the same directive in this presumed-to-be "postcolonial" moment. As noted in chapter 2, twenty years earlier Kabua had spoken before the Congress of Micronesia, on behalf of Ebeye landowners, decrying the use of eminent domain by the Trust Territory government. Then he had warned about the precedent being set on Ebeye that could ripple out to the rest of Micronesia.[85] By 1986, his tune had changed.

Seen by protesting landowners as a betrayal, Kabua's eminent domain order also garnered broader condemnation by Marshallese onlookers not involved in the protests who expressed concern about the implications for the newly decolonized nation. Kabua's decision highlighted how ongoing economic dependence centered on Kwajalein's value to the United States shaped the nature of Marshallese sovereignty following formal decolonization. This seemed especially apparent to Marshallese who warned of the frightening precedent set by the eminent domain order. The Marshallese Opposition Coalition Party published a statement in the *Marshall Islands Journal* critical of the Marshall Islands High Court for issuing the order. Speaking on behalf of the coalition, Senator Carl Heine stated: "We strongly believe that the M.I. government with all the enormous powers at its command has done to the weak and helpless people of Kwajalein what many a dictator the world over has done to gain and usurp unnecessary power and authority."[86] He added that his party viewed the use of eminent domain as both dangerous and unnecessary. He stated: "Occupation by an alien military power of privately owned lands does not constitute 'public use.'"[87] Heine added that his party felt the government had betrayed the Kwajalein people in order to support the powerful US government and military.

Editorials appearing in the *Marshall Islands Journal* further voiced concern about the use of eminent domain on Kwajalein. One editorial questioned the idea that military activities conducted in Kwajalein's segregated setting constituted a public use, noting that "Marshallese don't have free access to KMR and public use of facilities there."[88] The piece acknowledged the RMI government's concern about a minority of landowners jeopardizing "the government's access to benefits, security and services which the U.S. provides as a result of the Compact and control of KMR for weapons development."[89] And yet, the author concluded, the eminent domain order represented an unsettling precedent given the singular importance of land in the region.[90]

Contrasting with Marshallese criticism of Kabua's eminent domain order, the US secretary of defense showered the president with praise. In his May 13, 1986, correspondence, the defense secretary explained that President Kabua's order strengthened the alliance between the United States and the RMI governments. The secretary of defense expressed "deep personal appreciation" to the president, adding that Kabua's "strong and effective personal leadership in ending the demonstrations" and his "courage and wisdom deserve the admiration of [his] countrymen, and have earned [him] a place of honor in the history of the Republic of the Marshall Islands."[91] He thanked President Kabua, saying that despite the challenges confronting the Marshall Islands, the emerging nation appeared to be in very good hands.[92]

For the US military and the RMI government, 1986 marked a watershed moment in containing Marshallese unrest on Kwajalein. After that point, no more protests would interfere with the US mission on Kwajalein. The consequential shift away from landowner influence over the process of negotiating compensation for their islands was reflected in the statements of US State Department representative Mike Senko, who noted: "The Kwajalein Atoll is part of the Marshall Islands. And the United States policy is very clearly to deal with other governments on a government to government basis when it involves a military lease agreement."[93] Senko added that the United States dealt with the governments of Japan, Germany and Spain. He concluded: "We don't go direct to the local people and this is just a continuation of that precedent."[94] Senko's words obscured the prior two decades' protocol, established under the colonial confines of the Trusteeship Agreement. They marked the military's final departure from recognizing Kwajalein landowners' legitimacy in negotiating any compensation or conditions for use of their lands. As the Marshall Islands officially decolonized, the creation of the new nation-state relocated all power and political negotiations in the hands of each successive Marshallese president under a mixed parliamentary-presidential system. After 1986, the army no longer had to contend with Marshallese protests, and since then it has been able to operate Kwajalein's missile testing uninterrupted.

The Compact of Free Association had structured a continuing relationship between the United States and the RMI that included US financial support, access to certain US domestic programs, residency, and jobs in exchange for continued exclusive US military access in the region. US policies of economic neglect, which had helped foster greater dependence during the colonial period, necessitated ongoing US financial support to avoid an economic crisis in the region. Decades of broader economic neglect in the region, alongside mass investment in the base at Kwajalein, meant the Marshallese economy would suffer greatly in the absence of US support. Such has been the legacy of Cold War weapons testing in the Marshall Islands in shaping the economic and political trajectory of the nation's path toward sovereignty.

The impact of nuclear testing was also written into the 1986 Compact of Free Association, as Marshallese continued to suffer ongoing displacement from their homelands and irradiation of their bodies at the time of its signing. The compact included the section 177 agreement to address such legacies. The section stated that the "government of the United States accepts the responsibility for compensation owing citizens of the Marshall Islands for loss or damage to property and person resulting from the nuclear testing program."[95] The two governments agreed that the United States would provide compensation "for the just and adequate settlement of all such claims which have arisen in regard to the Marshall Islands and its citizens and which have not yet been compensated or which in the future may arise."[96] Alongside the compact, the Nuclear Claims Tribunal was created to adjudicate personal injury and land damage claims, with $45.75 million provided to address all claims. This initial funding proved wholly inadequate. In the more than three decades since the compact was signed, there have been ongoing legal battles for greater compensation and for recognition of the wider impact of irradiation beyond the four atolls initially identified as affected (Bikini, Rongelap, Enewetak, and Utirik).[97]

As the history of both weapons-testing campaigns—nuclear and missile—shaped the contours of the Compact of Free Association, the legacies of the colonial past morphed with the neocolonial present, threatening a sovereign Marshallese future. At Kwajalein, those legacies resonated with those living segregated lives on Ebeye, comprising nuclear refugees and their families alongside Marshallese displaced from within the atoll to make way for missile testing. Both remained in exile from their home islands. As the US quest for security historically and continually created new insecurities for Marshallese residing within Kwajalein Atoll, US civilians on Kwajalein continued to enjoy a life of leisure under the veil of suburban innocence.

"STRESSES" OF LIFE FOR AMERICANS ON KWAJALEIN AND BACK TO SCHOOL FOR EBEYE "GUESTS"

In 1986, as the United States and the RMI government signed the Compact of Free Association against the backdrop of a "shoot to wound" order against protestors, and as Neibanjan Lavin nearly drowned walking the reef to keep her job, US civilians on Kwajalein faced their own "stresses." These were delineated in great detail in a March 27 article that ran in the island newspaper in the middle of this final Marshallese protest. In her *Kwajalein Hourglass* piece, "Even Paradise Can Be Stressful . . . ," Ruth Horne delved into a range of anxieties that American civilians faced living on Kwajalein, as recounted by Kwajalein's physicians. Horne's piece illustrated the gulf separating life on Kwajalein and life on Ebeye. As Horne lamented the variety of cabin-fever-style stresses facing US residents on their isolated suburban island home, the article stood as a testament to the army's success in creating not simply a physical barrier between Kwajalein and Ebeye through segregation, but also a psychological one.

Shortly after the article was published, the army introduced a quasi-school integration program on Kwajalein, resembling one-way busing, or in this case ferrying, to remedy the ongoing chasm of abundance and scarcity, privilege and poverty marking life between the two islands. The remainder of this chapter looks more closely at these features of civilian life on Kwajalein that played out during this historic transition toward Marshallese decolonization. As this final protest was erupting around them, marking the contestations embedded in this transition, Kwajalein's residents carried on with the humdrum of everyday suburban life. Over time, they also hailed the island's tokenized school integration program as a sign of laudable US benevolence in the region. In doing so, these civilian residents contributed to the ongoing disavowal of the deadly and destructive impacts of a colonial past as it transitioned into a neocolonial present by buttressing the enduring myth of middle-class, suburban innocence on Kwajalein.

Horne began her 1986 *Hourglass* article with two words: "Almost heaven." The phrase had become a popular slogan that Americans used to describe Kwajalein over the years and today adorns paraphernalia created for and consumed by former residents nostalgic about their time on the island. In this story, Horne employed the phrase as a question, asking readers whether when they saw these two words they wondered if they had missed the boat.[98] Horne explained that while expectations on a small Pacific island often conjured up visions of stress-free living, Kwajalein physicians Eric Lindborg and Paula Barclay had identified various stresses and anxieties afflicting Kwajalein residents. The physicians discussed the island's remoteness as one potential reason some felt out of control, trapped, or even guilty for neglecting family or friends far away. Both physicians also discussed the fishbowl effect created by the smallness of the community alongside the difficulty of living in a controlled military environment. Barclay described "the limited living space in bachelor

quarters, trailers and houses [affecting] almost all KMR residents," adding that additional stress was attributed to a "limited variety of activities,"
especially for those who didn't enjoy water sports, jogging, or other physical fitness activities.[99] Horne said some missed mall shopping and could
feel stressed about being confined to the island's few stores.

These laments evidenced how for many of those residing on Kwajalein,
the reference point for situating the deprivations of daily life remained
thousands of miles away in the suburban United States. In some ways, this
again affirmed the army's success in creating a landscape that for many US
residents abstracted Kwajalein from any Marshallese context and instead
simply extended American suburbia into the Pacific. Barclay described
some patients who seemed stressed due to their busy lives, filled with too
many leisure opportunities. She explained that patients came in with tension headaches due to a full day's work followed by tennis, meetings, and
sometimes a movie. She cautioned: "The drive to take advantage of the
leisure opportunities on Kwajalein—even if they are enjoyable—can put
more stress on a person's life."[100]

The timing of Horne's lengthy analysis of such "stresses" facing Kwajalein residents, appearing in the middle of the 1986 protests, poignantly
captured the divergence in realities existing between Kwajalein and Ebeye.
Just as it had during Operation Homecoming, the army continued to limit
civilian access to protest sites and news in 1986, and US residents would
have continued to be aware of severe punishments awaiting anyone who
challenged army protocol. The distance in perceptions of daily life highlighted in Horne's piece seemed to illustrate something beyond ignorance
or fear. Her article illuminated the deeper pattern of *unseeing* that infused
the lives of US residents on Kwajalein over time. From miniature golf and
beauty pageants on Kwajalein accompanying the first nuclear detonations in 1946, through four decades of leisure and recreation to follow, this
American capacity to engage with everyday suburban life in the midst of
Marshallese trauma proved a consistent feature informing the work of US
empire in the region.

As noted in chapter 5, this continuity of perceived apathy toward the
daily struggles of Marshallese living segregated lives three miles across
the reef should come as no surprise, according to former resident Robert
Barclay. He saw this as predictable, even as Marshallese protests unfolded

within eyeshot of American homes and recreational spaces. Barclay identified the typical civilian on Kwajalein as well-meaning and decent, with good intentions, but also intent on getting along and not making waves.[101]

Echoing a common refrain from several former and current Kwajalein residents, Barclay explained that those on Kwajalein were there for one purpose: to make money. He said even if Americans saw injustices toward the Marshallese, they would back off as soon as they caught wind of them because that reality would be problematic and would complicate their purpose for being there. Barclay said injustices against Marshallese are not something Americans want to think about, and they have an easier picture to put in place.[102] The physical landscape constructed for civilians on Kwajalein helped enable that "easier picture." The readily available spatial and cultural narrative of small-town, suburban USA seemed to help many Americans avoid any confrontation (externally or internally) with the broader military-colonial context framing their lives on Kwajalein. Even as Marshallese protests most overtly challenged the simplicity of that portrait, presumably forcing US residents on Kwajalein to confront or at least complicate that mythology, the façade remained in place for many.

These spatial and cultural signifiers had traveled thousands of miles into the Central Pacific, having already successfully informed the peace of mind and sense of security of many suburban residents back at home in the continental United States. Kwajalein's residents were no different than those in the United States who during urban uprisings in the 1960s, which aimed to challenge structures of segregation and disinvestment, racial discrimination, and police abuse, could retreat to the psychic and physical refuge of their suburban homes and employ this "easier picture." In both contexts, from the United States to Kwajalein, Americans could draw on what historian Matthew Lassiter has identified as "the dominant ethos of American suburbia [that] has always idealized the present and celebrated the future at the expense of any critical reflection on the past."[103] In the postwar era, segregation of these landscapes helped maintain a storied and physical barrier distancing racialized urban poverty and discrimination from any relational link to suburban privilege, and in the case of Kwajalein and Ebeye, the military-colonial context that created that local replica.[104] Here, in the local context of US empire in the Pacific, Kwajalein residents could indulge the idealized present of their utopian lifestyle without probing into the colonial context enabling that privilege, even as Marshallese protests erupted around them pointing to the contested nature of that history.

Another way an "easier picture" was created on Kwajalein in the compact era—a picture that allowed some US civilians to reconcile ongoing disparities between Kwajalein and Ebeye (if and when they *did* confront these realities)—was through the creation of educational opportunities for Marshallese children on Kwajalein. Just as urban uprisings within the United States threatened to unsettle a *national* narrative of postwar security embodied through the tranquil segregated suburban image, so too did the acts of Marshallese protestors sailing from Ebeye's urban landscape to reclaim their "home" on Kwajalein. Americans living on Kwajalein, like their suburban counterparts in the United States, were tasked with making "concessions" through limited educational opportunities to acknowledge the historic and ongoing impact of segregation and structural inequalities. These concessions never aimed to dismantle the broader structures of racial and economic inequality and oppression in either place. Rather, they were token gestures. On Kwajalein, in addition to exporting the model of postwar suburban segregation, the US military also exported a tokenized remedy to address the grievances that this structure of segregation created: school integration.

Identified as a compact-era concession aimed at "improving diplomatic relations" between the United States and the RMI government, the army decided in 1987 to create a program that would allow five Marshallese children to bus, or "ferry," daily to attend school on Kwajalein. Demands by Marshallese for adequate educational resources on Ebeye had persisted alongside the range of grievances expressed about US neglect of its UN mandate for decades. Schooling was always a concern, included in requests for greater attention to public health resources, housing, and other infrastructure on Ebeye. A *Marshall Islands Journal* editorial appearing the year before Operation Homecoming drew upon the historic language of Jim Crow segregation within the US context to highlight grievances about Ebeye residents' second-class status. Discussing divergences in schooling between Kwajalein and Ebeye, the editorialist described facilities on each island as "at best 'separate but equal.'"[105] Highlighting how Marshallese had paid a high price for the US security mission, he concluded that the dynamic between Kwajalein and Ebeye exemplified how the army "has not been forced to pay the social cost of the activity it performs in the interest of national security."[106]

In the wake of Marshallese protests interrupting missile-testing operations, army leaders began to consider how education could potentially ease tensions in the compact era. Kwajalein commanding Lt. General John F. Wall remarked on the possibility of educational integration on Kwajalein in a letter to President Kabua in January 1986 just prior to the compact signing. The letter addressed several "non-monetary requests" made during the 1986 sail-in protest, which included snack bar access for those visiting Kwajalein on official business and approving visitation rights for Marshallese peoples to home islands blocked off for missile tests.[107] On the subject of education, Wall stated he could not permit open access to Kwajalein's school system. He explained, "Even if we were to recover all costs associated with education at KMR [Kwajalein Missile Range], I fear the costs to RMI [Republic of Marshall Islands] parents would be prohibitive."[108] Wall added he was seriously investigating the possibility of implementing a scholarship program for several deserving candidates to be selected for their academic quality by governmental authorities for school attendance. Within the year, a select group of Marshallese children would be entering Kwajalein's classrooms. In 1957, Little Rock had its nine; in 1987, the army decided Kwajalein would have its five.

In the early years, this concession was called the "Ebeye Guest Program," a title that reinforced the narrative of Kwajalein as an American home where Marshallese remained visitors. The 2001 *Ekatak* yearbook on Kwajalein emphasized the program's early aims to improve "diplomatic relations" while highlighting the "guest" status of its Marshallese beneficiaries. The yearbook explained: "Each day the Ebeye Guest students are "welcomed" onto Kwajalein" with "selected Marshallese students [given] an opportunity to experience American education."[109] Following challenges from older Marshallese students over time, the title would be switched to its contemporary iteration, "Rikatak," a Marshallese word meaning people who study or learn (hereafter, Rikatak is used).

The Rikatak program highlighted the persistence of segregation between Kwajalein and Ebeye, while simultaneously diverting attention from the roots of historic and ongoing structural inequality between the two islands. By inviting a handful of Marshallese children to study on Kwajalein annually, the army could avoid ongoing scrutiny about the continuity of segregation policies characterizing the two islands. This change on Kwajalein in some ways mirrored how racial segregation in the United States was addressed through busing programs during the 1970s. This approach focused on schooling to address historic housing segregation and neglect of equitable community investments and accountable taxation across urban and suburban divides. But in contrast to busing, and more reminiscent of Little Rock, Kwajalein's quasi-integration program was a one-way exchange. Marshallese children were ferried to Kwajalein each day to learn; US kids were not ferried to attend school on Ebeye. Such tokenized concessions could be made without the kind of backlash from Kwajalein parents that had marked the previous decade of busing, most infamously in Boston.[110]

Signaling the colonial distinctions of this program emerging in the Marshall Islands, school integration on Kwajalein lacked the kind of national framework of racial entitlements marked by constitutional change undergirding its US model. Whereas in the United States efforts toward school integration followed the *Brown vs. Board of Education* ruling in 1954 marking "separate but equal" as unconstitutional, on Kwajalein school integration emerged at the matrix of colonialism and its legacies alongside the simultaneous disavowal of both. In that context, allowing Marshallese students to attend school on Kwajalein was framed within a narrative of American charity and goodwill toward an impoverished foreign population: a "good-neighbor" policy.[111] Another distinction marking the Rikatak program was the particular shape Kwajalein's history of military colonialism took when it came to disciplining segregation between the two islands. The military's historic and ongoing policies of army surveillance, strict curfews for workers, and shopping bans also applied to Marshallese students coming from Ebeye. Unless they obtained special permission, these students (K–12) had to and still have to vacate the island after school each day by a certain hour. Just like their Marshallese worker counterparts, the students were and continue to be prohibited from patronizing most of the island's stores and eateries.

Like many racialized US children enrolled in busing and integration programs, Rikatak students carried the weight of an entire community on their shoulders as they entered this segregated suburban school to pursue an "equal opportunity." Echoing US school integration discourse, the Rikatak program enabled a focus on individual educational achievement while deflecting attention from the history and continuity of structural inequalities. With five Marshallese children selected each year, the Rikatak program reinforced US celebratory narratives emphasizing the limitless possibilities for the individual child lucky enough to be selected in the educational lottery and move on to their successful future.

And this lottery was highly competitive. As former Rikatak student Shem Livai explained, typically one hundred students applied each year. To determine eligibility, program administrators tested the children's English literacy and social skills.[112] When Livai enrolled in 1990, he was chosen alongside six other children and was among the few selected who had not come from an elite family.[113] While status did not appear in public documentation of selection rules, rumors surfaced over the years among Americans and Marshallese, who discussed the unfair nature of the lottery, noting the disadvantages faced by most children on Ebeye trying to get into the program (as most lacked chiefly family status or connections).[114]

Livai's path through Rikatak is illustrative of convergences and distinctions from other histories of student integration in the United States. The program employed the American exceptionalist myth of individual opportunity to frame Marshallese student successes on Kwajalein, further normalizing Kwajalein as an American space. Because Marshallese remained foreign to this narrative, their educational opportunities were framed as charity rather than entitlements for those included in national citizenry. The Ebeye student receiving this charitable gift now became responsible for the success of their family and community, which continued to struggle under the structure of poverty and segregation created by a history of military colonialism on Kwajalein. Livai suggested that this expectation often carried too much pressure, noting that since the program's implementation in 1987, an average of about two of the five children enrolled each year actually made it through to Kwajalein's high school graduation.[115] He said he was the only student who graduated in his cohort. Livai's experiences of alienation within the Rikatak program echoed those of other students who have been bused across U.S. segregated landscapes. He recalled how traveling between seemingly separate worlds on Kwajalein and Ebeye marginalized him in both spaces. Livai remembered being called "ribelle" (meaning "American") by Marshallese on Ebeye.[116] Excluded from living on Kwajalein, Livai also felt out of place among Americans. He said he learned how to switch hats as needed. Another Rikatak graduate, Jefferson Bobo, described the experience as "like being caught in-between two worlds."[117]

As a senior, Livai participated in a program that highlighted the distances in educational opportunities between Kwajalein and Ebeye and the seemingly insidious ways he was co-opted into championing these. As president of the Marshall Islands Club, which began at Kwajalein High School during the 1990s, Livai helped organize a day for hosting Ebeye's seniors on Kwajalein. The seniors came over on the ferry in the morning and attended one of Kwajalein High School's classes. After class they went bowling and ate with the Rikatak students. When asked his impression of what this experience was like for Ebeye's seniors, Livai responded: "It was kind of good and bad. When they came they were really amazed and they kind of felt like they missed out on a lot, and they kind of felt like embarrassed, like how the school was so good and they were just . . . there for a day."[118]

Livai's reflection on the Ebeye seniors signaled the complicated experience framing his individual access. He seemed aware of tensions undergirding his opportunities, burdens carried by individual students historically traversing segregated spaces marking US national and imperial landscapes. These journeys have been historically applauded through American meritocratic discourse hailing individual success that simultaneously has worked to obscure historic policies structuring inequality. On Kwajalein, successes of students like Livai are spotlighted by program supporters in ways that have diverted attention from the thousands of students on Ebeye lacking educational opportunities and the colonial history and legacy that has structured that divergent relationship.

Livai's path upon graduation mirrored that of other Rikatak graduates who made a beeline to college in the United States, a route perceived by many as a marker of success. The Kwajalein Army Command and RMI government have showcased the Rikatak program as enabling such success stories. In so doing, each could wipe their hands of any broader responsibility to address the educational needs of the rest of Ebeye's children. By focusing on and celebrating the few annual Marshallese "success" stories at Kwajalein's school, military and government administrators could avoid planning and investing in equitable educational opportunities for all of Ebeye's children through teacher training, resources for books and other school materials, and safe school buildings. This pattern has mirrored how school segregation has historically been addressed in the United States, where urban districts facing drained resources following white flight to suburbs have had to rely on policies that emphasized temporary busing solutions over more equitable regional tax sharing or mixed-income housing.

Kwajalein civilian and military residents continue to champion the Rikatak program today. For the army, this ongoing celebration of the program as a symbol of progress between the two nations was exemplified by a 2013 article headlining the US Army's official home page. "From Ri'Katak Student to RMI Ambassador: Charles Paul Returns to His Stomping Grounds" applauded Rikatak graduate Charles Paul, who became the RMI ambassador to the United States. The article chronicled Paul's meeting with current Rikatak students, in which he encouraged them to work hard so they could succeed as he had. He shared how his schooling on "Kwaj" had given him a leg up, recalling how when he was young he wanted to be the president of the United States. "'Now I know I can't because I'm not a U.S. citizen,'" he said. "'But, you have to dream and you have to think you can do big things.'"[119] Paul's reflections signaled the confusion a child might experience when educated in an American school that might imply a promise of inclusion within that nation, only to later understand the limitations of that promise.

The army's veneration of Paul's success further reflected what political and urban historians have identified as a growing political discourse focused on meritocratic, individual achievement in postwar US history. Like narratives about educational opportunity in the United States, the military and American civilians on Kwajalein have spotlighted individual success stories while avoiding direct confrontation with the deeper history of colonialism and segregation that perpetuates the continued structural inequalities between the two islands. Many stories have revealed how those Marshallese who first made the ferry trip to enter school in this "American space" on Kwajalein continued on to enter additional American spaces of education and employment. As US workers have historically and continually pursued professional and family goals of amassing wealth by living subsidized lives on this Marshallese homeland—claiming it as *their* home—Marshallese like Shem Livai could pursue opportunities only by moving thousands of miles away from home and joining the diaspora. But as Paul's story suggests, not all. Some eventually come home.

SUBURBAN INNOCENCE IN THE NEOCOLONIAL ERA

Just as a politics of intimidation worked to frame US negotiations with the newly decolonized RMI government as mutual and reciprocal, diverting attention from persistent hierarchies and the neocolonial structure bounding these negotiations, the Rikatak program contributed to an erasure of the historic and ongoing power dynamics in the region. In recent years, Marshallese leaders and workers and local and US journalists have attributed Ebeye's ongoing struggles to policies of the RMI government and Marshallese cultural values of extended family support. The army has increasingly escaped scrutiny for historic and continuous policies of displacement and segregation. Military leaders can now point to the RMI and local governments as accountable for the socioeconomic problems plaguing their people. With Rikatak, the army can also now hail this flagship program as an example of US benevolence toward the Marshallese and wipe its hands of any further accountability for decades of colonial exploitation in the region. This suburban school program has reinforced the myth of US innocence in the region, helping to disavow a colonial past and a neocolonial present.

Through the 1986 compact's signing and dissolution of the Trust Territory administration, suddenly the history of structural inequalities and failing infrastructure on Ebeye shifted to Marshallese political responsibility. Blame for Ebeye's persistent problems fell on a government whose economic decisions still depended on US approval and which now was expected to take on the task of undoing the persistent legacies of US colonial policies of economic neglect in the region.[120] A shift in focus onto Marshallese governmental policies obscured the continued impact of US colonial history on Kwajalein and Ebeye, which has included the army's ongoing enforcement of segregation alongside dehumanizing search and seizure policies and preventing displaced Marshallese from returning to their home atolls. While Americans on Kwajalein continue to reap the benefits of this history, as do military and civilian contractors profiting from the army's multi-billion-dollar missile-testing program, accountability for all related consequences has shifted to the Marshallese. Americans continue to take comfort in knowing that they annually allow five Marshallese children the privilege of sitting in classrooms with theirs. That privilege continues today and likely will into future years, as long as those Marshallese kids remember to leave the island on time each day.

Conclusion

> I don't think the choice is any longer between violence and
> nonviolence in a day when guided ballistic missiles are
> carving highways of death through the stratosphere. I think
> now it is a choice between nonviolence and nonexistence.
>
> —Dr. Martin Luther King Jr., 1961

> I am just sad . . . that the Americans brought the word of
> God for us to love one another, and then used my islands
> for testing weapons to kill other people.
>
> —Julian Riklon, May 2010

"THE MARSHALLESE DON'T EVEN HAVE A WORD FOR ENEMY"

Three years before the RMI transitioned from US colonial rule with the signing of the Compact of Free Association, Marshallese activist, graduate student, and nuclear fallout survivor Darlene Keju-Johnson spoke before the World Assembly of Churches in Vancouver to share the plight of her people.[1] In 1983, she came before this global constituency of faith leaders to ask for their support in the Marshallese fight for independence from the United States. Keju-Johnson detailed the history of the US presence in her homelands, one rooted in the destructive nuclear-testing campaign in the Northern Marshall Islands between 1946 and 1958 and ongoing missile testing at Kwajalein Atoll. She said the United States had explained that it was in the region to protect the Marshallese. Taking this Cold War

269

military imperative to task, she said, "It's very funny, when the United States tells us it's there to protect us, we turn around and ask them: 'protect us from who? We have no enemies. In fact, you might be interested to know that us Marshallese do not have a word for enemy.'"[2]

Keju-Johnson told the Vancouver audience that Marshallese people needed help to gain their independence, lamenting the devastating legacy of US nuclear testing and her own personal struggles with its effects. She said, "'The Marshallese are dying out now,'" admitting she too had three tumors growing in her. She expressed fear about getting pregnant because she did not know if her child might be born with defects, "'a jelly fish baby,'" like so many others had been under the effects of radiation.[3] Keju-Johnson ended her speech with a call to action: "'We must travel throughout the world and share this kind of experience from the bombs so that we must stop it before it gets to you. Remember we are the victims of the nuclear age; don't become a victim.'"[4] Eight years after she spoke in Vancouver, Darlene succumbed to the cancer that plagued her body. She never had children and was forty-five years old when she passed.

Keju-Johnson's Vancouver speech helped to open the eyes of church leaders around the world to the devastating impact of US nuclear testing in the Marshall Islands.[5] It was one among hundreds of speeches she had given throughout the United States and the world to raise global consciousness about these impacts and the ongoing struggle of her peoples to gain sovereignty. Her poignant words in Vancouver powerfully unsettled the narrative set in place during the 1940s that married US national security to global security, a story that included Marshallese as presumed beneficiaries of such global protection. Instead she painted a portrait of ongoing *insecurity* that had plagued Marshallese ever since the US military entered their homelands, and she cried out for global support for independence from this colonial power.

Just as Keju-Johnson had begun to question the dynamics of segregation between Kwajalein and Ebeye as a toddler in the early 1950s, she continued to probe this structure in 1983. During the Vancouver speech, she attributed the ongoing struggles and insecurity of her peoples to the conditions on Ebeye created by historic and ongoing US weapons testing. She noted: "They use our islands for missiles. They relocated the people into a very tiny island called Ebeye. . . . [T]he U.S. has taken two thirds of our islands. It

Figure 17. Darlene Keju-Johnson playing a song with brother Deo Keju (behind), cousin Tadashi Lometo (left), and cousin Rejine Capitol (right) during her oral presentation for her master's degree in public health at the University of Hawai'i, 1983. Photo by and courtesy of Giff Johnson.

means we cannot go fishing. We cannot go visit our islands and get more food for the more than eight thousand people. It means we are stuck into what we call a jail. Can you imagine? The United States is only leasing our islands. And we have to have passes to go onto our own islands?"[6]

Keju-Johnson never relented in calling attention to the injustice of segregation in her homelands. Here she continued marking that which had increasingly become unremarkable to onlookers within an expanding US base imperium throughout the Cold War. In her speech, she described the inadequate health-care facilities on Ebeye and the challenges in accessing Kwajalein's superior hospital three miles away, a situation to which she attributed the tragic death of her sister Alison, who had passed away after a complicated labor that began on Ebeye four years earlier. As her widower, Giff Johnson, explained in his memoir of her life, Darlene's grief over this devastating loss provided insight into "why she developed into a fierce advocate for justice and change in the Marshall Islands."[7]

Many of the insecurities governing life on Ebeye that Darlene tirelessly protested throughout the 1980s remain in place today. While the island saw some significant improvements following the Compact of Free Association, given a $6 million funding allotment to address Ebeye infrastructure, the comparison with Kwajalein three miles away remains just as stark. Since the transition to the Republic of Marshall Islands governance throughout the 1980s, 1990s, and into the twenty-first century, Ebeye residents have continued to face challenges in the wake of the US colonial era and ongoing neocolonial dependency on the Kwajalein missile range. Today, the island remains a repository for those displaced by US weapons testing and Kwajalein's segregated labor sector and their families. As the missile installation at Kwajalein continues to be hailed as an essential site for US and global security, the insecurities facing Marshallese on Ebeye persist, just as they have for decades. Media coverage of the island's density peaked in the 1970s, exposing the deadly conditions facing eight thousand people living on eighty acres, yet in recent years that number has nearly doubled. By 2017, the population had reached approximately fifteen thousand. In 2010, the density crisis had already found residents running out of space to bury their dead. A *Marianas Variety* article explained that this predicament left some on Ebeye with little choice but to dig up existing graves and place new caskets on top of the remains of those previously buried.[8] Pacific scholar and former Kwajalein resident Greg Dvorak commented on the ongoing gulf between Ebeye's density and Kwajalein's spatial abundance. As Kwajalein's residential workforce decreased to approximately twelve to seventeen hundred people on nine hundred acres, Dvorak observed that "one cannot help noticing how much vast open space is now available, land where Marshallese people could live if they were allowed to do so."[9] He noted that while Marshallese continue to be segregated to Ebeye, open space on Kwajalein has been converted into a dog park. "That even dogs can run free on land that is off-limits to ordinary Marshall Islanders is yet another cruel joke," he wrote. It is a joke punctuating decades of US Army segregation policies in the region.[10]

Today, Kwajalein and Ebeye continue to resemble the apartheid conditions decried during the 1970s and 1980s. Token concessions made through the Rikatak program (detailed in chapter 6) only highlight the stark contrasts. In addition to schooling, another exception that illuminates the rule of segregation in the region is the story of the Kemems' migration from Ebeye to Kwajalein. This Marshallese family's unprecedented path to residency on Kwajalein began with Yoshi Kemem's employment in the island's security and law enforcement as a constable, translating for the police department in 1985.[11] As he moved up to the position of investigator, Kwajalein Command permitted Yoshi to move his family from Ebeye to Kwajalein in 1998. Aside from RMI government representative Noda Lojkar, Yoshi's family became the first Marshallese family to live on Kwajalein.[12]

In a 2010 interview, Yoshi and his wife Fumiko Kemem shared how their lives had changed when they moved to Kwajalein. Yoshi talked about the convenience of living somewhere with consistent power and electricity, explaining how in 1998, Ebeye's power still only came on half the time.[13] While the Kemems lived and worked on Kwajalein, Yoshi said he and his wife's social world remained on Ebeye. He said they went to Ebeye every day to see family and to socialize, and went to attend church on Sundays. Exemplifying Kwajalein's continued structure of segregation that made socializing with friends and family from Ebeye difficult, Yoshi said he and his wife constantly sponsored Marshallese to come onto the island. While Yoshi and Fumiko could move freely to visit their community on Ebeye, any visitors coming from Ebeye continued to require sponsorship approval and remained under strict time limits. When asked if he felt his family was treated differently on Ebeye because they lived on Kwajalein, Yoshi said yes, and especially when they first moved. He described how people assumed that living on Kwajalein came with "good things" happening and meant they were "up here" (raising his hand high). "People think because I live here, I am somebody. But we don't think that way; we were the same person that we were over there."[14]

ROUTES TO AND AWAY FROM HOME

The Kemems' path to Kwajalein represented an exceptional migration away from Ebeye, from one Marshallese island to another that remained under the control of the United States. Such migrations from one Pacific home to others within the sphere of US imperial control are common. Many Marshallese living in the diaspora have settled in Hawai'i. The Compact of Free Association expanded opportunities for Marshallese to travel to and live, study, and work in the United States without a visa. In its wake, many Marshallese took advantage of the chance to pursue higher income, education, and importantly, health-care services to address illnesses linked to historic and ongoing impacts of US military colonialism in their homelands. Aside from Kwajalein's hospital facilities, from which Marshallese continue to be excluded, the Marshall Islands have lacked adequate medical resources to address the range of health issues facing thousands of Marshallese. These have included radiation-related cancers (Marshallese have the highest rate of thyroid cancer in the world) and diabetes linked to dietary patterns that emerged during the US colonial period.

While arriving from island homes that share histories of destruction, devastation, and exploitation under US colonialism, militarism, and weapons-testing campaigns that helped fuel sovereignty movements in both the Marshall Islands and Hawai'i, Marshallese have largely faced hostility in Hawai'i, marked by virulent racism. Marshallese have struggled with these obstacles alongside other Micronesians living in the diaspora in Hawai'i, all of whom have been afforded the rights to live and work in Hawai'i and the United States under their respective Compacts of Free Association. Given a broad lack of awareness in Hawai'i about these colonial histories and "postcolonial" agreements, Micronesian migrants are viewed with open disdain for not speaking English, for their poverty, and for undeservedly using public resources, particularly health-care services. The latter issue has become a significant area of debate in Hawai'i, especially given the extensive health-care needs of those coming from the Marshall Islands.[15]

In addition to moving to Hawai'i, large numbers of Marshallese living in the diaspora have made new homes in California, Washington, and Oregon. But the largest population of Marshallese living outside of the Marshall Islands resides in Arkansas. During the 1980s, the Tyson chicken factory began recruiting Marshallese workers to go to Springdale, Arkansas. Northwest Arkansas is home to an estimated ten to fifteen thousand Marshallese residents. In our 2010 interview, Kwajalein landowner Tony de Brum reflected on the specific history of diasporic movements of Kwajalein's landowning families who continued to receive lease payments through the compact. He explained: "When you remove people from their land, you chop off half of their soul. This is where people from Kwajalein are today."[16] De Brum lamented how when Kwajalein people received money, they left.[17] He said most second-generation Kwajalein people lived outside the Marshall Islands, but emphasized they were not living well. He said they lived on food stamps and subsidized housing. They opted to "cut chicken for $7 an hour" rather than "clean toilets on Kwajalein for $2 an hour."[18] In 2020, these chicken-cutting workers in Springdale were deemed "essential" and thus faced disproportionate rates of COVID-19 infection. Accounting for only 3 percent of northwest Arkansas's population, Marshallese comprised half of all COVID-19 deaths in the region by June 2020.[19]

UNSEEING EMPIRE IN THE MARSHALL ISLANDS

As Marshallese have migrated outward from their islands to create new homes in the diaspora, US workers have continued to migrate inward to Kwajalein to find their new home in the Marshall Islands. They do so in support of the ongoing missile-testing mission, which has averaged six ICBM tests per year since 2018.[20] As detailed in chapter 4, the ongoing lure of Kwajalein's subsidized storybook setting continues to afford financial savings for many US workers and their families. This "Mayberry" in the middle of the ocean, as Colonel Rod Stuckey called it, is a site few ever want to leave.[21] Stuckey highlighted how the return home for many former "Kwajers" continues to be an ongoing challenge. And as also noted in chapter 4, the nostalgia industry is going strong today.[22] This persistence of seeing Kwajalein as an *American* home over time has continually required the *unseeing* of it as a Marshallese one.

This unseeing, which historically incorporated Kwajalein into a postwar imaginary of Andy Griffith's small-town suburban innocence, has expanded to situate the island within another realm of historic American identity. This one harkens back to Boston and the origins of the nation at the moment of revolution. In 2002, Kwajalein's civilian workers expressed outrage at a base income tax increase imposed by the Republic of Marshall Islands government. As detailed in the Kwajalein *Hour Glass*, Kwajalein residents quickly responded with claims of "no taxation without representation."[23] US worker Chris A. Danals detailed the protest in his letter to the newspaper and encouraged his fellow workers to remember they indeed had a representative, Michael Senko, the US ambassador to the RMI embassy. Danals urged everyone outraged by the tax increase to contact Senko, adding that he "would like to think that, as a community, we can show the same resolve and unity that our forefathers did."[24]

That American workers living on a US base in the Marshall Islands could imagine their plight of taxation on base income as somehow connected to deeper roots of an anti-imperial struggle against the British monarchy hinted at the persistent, unreconciled tensions of American exceptionalism. It is impossible to gauge the seriousness of Danals's plea to fellow workers on Kwajalein in joining their protest of "no taxation without representation" (nor the seriousness of that chant). But nothing in the article seemed to suggest a satirical or ironic take on the issue. Thus, one can consider the meanings of some US workers' capacities to conjure up an image of the Marshall Islands government as replicating the historic oppression of American colonial subjects by the British imperial power. This capacity would seem to be in line with the more enduring ability of many Americans to imagine Kwajalein as an American home, a feat dependent on the historic and ongoing erasure of the island as a Marshallese home. The moment further offers a profound illustration of Americans' incapacity to *see* where they are in the world. This propensity to unsee, birthed at the moment American identity was forged in the erasure of indigenous histories in the continental landscape, persists temporally and geographically in the twenty-first-century US global base imperium.

"The wheels of militarization," Cynthia Enloe has argued, "are greased by ... popular inattention."[25] She was referring to Iraq, Afghanistan, South Korea, the Philippines, and Japan, but this is no less true of Kwajalein. But at work is more than only inattention. No less important has been the way in which engagements within and across the US empire have been premised on these compartmentalizations. On Kwajalein, civilians dwell in a level of privilege many may have never experienced in the United States. That privilege was built on Marshallese dispossession and segregation and a tremendous amount of spatial and cultural work that went into obscuring that relational truth. Noted in this book's introduction, but worth revisiting here, historian Philip J. Deloria has written of

American culture: "From the beginning, national identity and the nation itself have relied upon such separations. The plotting out and expanding of the United States have for a long time meant celebrating the nation's growing power and its occasionally wise, often tragic, sometimes well-intentioned deployment of that power on the continent and around the world. The celebration of national character, on the other hand, has frequently involved the erasure of such exercises of power."[26] On Kwajalein, most Americans have seemed content to inherit the power and privilege that came with their engagement in this historic moment of imperial expansion. They seemed to struggle more with the fact that their colonial privilege came in relation to the oppression of others, and thus worked to disavow that history in various ways, even to the extent of potentially seeing themselves as oppressed by a *Marshallese* imperial attack.

These contradictions have long been observed by other historians of empire and have little purchase in US national histories. But they lie at the heart of US imperial histories and were encapsulated in the 1947 Trusteeship Agreement. The UN agreement sanctioned US administration of Micronesia under contradictory directives, deploying the US military to use the territory to ensure national security while imploring a new Trust Territory government to support Micronesians toward self-determination. As traced in this book, these two entities remained arms of the same imperial body, just as the military continues to remain a powerful arm, if not the most powerful arm, of US empire today. American inattention has few consequences for Americans; they suffer few repercussions of this imperial expansion, but continue to benefit from it enormously, even, to inattentive eyes, invisibly. As US citizens ignore this history, they also ignore the localized and global repercussions of the impact of their expanding empire. Few, if any, places in the world have felt the repercussions of US military expansion to the same degree as the Marshall Islands. The region has historically borne the brunt of that expansion through US weapons testing in its home islands. The Marshall Islands continue to feel the impact of US empire today as Marshallese continue to suffer the consequences of displacement, radiation-related illnesses, and broader national economic dependence on the United States. All the while Kwajalein remains an indispensable location, the laboratory of strategic defense, and now also a port in a new private space industry.

I have argued throughout this book that alongside the geopolitical structures framing this historic trajectory, equally important in erasing empire have been the local physical, cultural, and spatial transformations that have marked this distinct US imperial formation during the Cold War. The postwar convergence of US military power expanding alongside the global context of decolonization made this imperial project in the Pacific one for which its devastating impacts of dispossession, displacement, and destruction necessitated simultaneous disavowal. This book has situated Kwajalein's history within the longue durée of American exceptionalism, illustrating the continuity of this pattern of disavowal across time and space. But what I have also tried to reveal is the distinct iteration of this pattern in a moment of political, military, and cultural investment in selling a postwar image of the nation to the world. While the United Nations became a geopolitical partner in helping to buttress that myth through a global framing of imperial innocence, the export of suburbia to Kwajalein further supported that project. This restaging of the postwar American dream in the Marshall Islands helped to physically and culturally erase some of the most destructive features of a growing base imperium taking root on the ground by burying these histories under the sheen of miniature golf, beauty pageants, and ballparks; Macy's fare; and annual "karnivals." The mapping of a growing number of installations in this base imperium with such features of small-town Americana has infused these spaces tied to the expansion of increasingly destructive US military power with the everyday innocence of Cold War suburban family life. That was, and continues to be, the mark of "suburban empire."

RISING SEAS, RAISING CONSCIOUSNESS . . .

As Marshallese continue to live with the destructive and deadly costs of wars they did not contribute to waging, today they also live with the imminent, existential threat posed by a rapidly changing planet they did not contribute to warming. As legal scholar Michael Gerrard recently argued: "More than any other place, the Marshall Islands is a victim of the two greatest threats facing humanity—nuclear weapons and climate change. . . . The United States is entirely responsible for the nuclear testing there, and its emissions have contributed more to climate change than those from any other country."[27] Alongside other low-lying atoll nations, the Marshall Islands face a distinctive threat posed by climate change and the impacts of rising sea levels. In 2017, the US Department of Defense Environmental Research Program conducted a study at Roi Namur, one of the islands within Kwajalein Atoll, with an aim to assess the precarity of its military installations in the Pacific. While the DoD report's findings have implications beyond Kwajalein Atoll (identifying patterns relevant to other low-lying atolls), the military's significant investments in the base at Kwajalein over time directed the report's concerns toward the US Army's aim of long-term use of this key missile installation. The findings suggest that goal may be unrealistic. The report noted that low-lying islets within Kwajalein Atoll will be threatened when sea level rise reaches 0.4 meter higher than in 2017, "at which point, without active management measures, the annual amount of seawater flooding onto the islands would be sufficient to make ground water nonpotable year-round."[28] This tipping point for flooding was projected to arrive as early as 2030–2040, if the Atlantic ice sheet were to melt, as is predicted.[29]

Flooding caused by what are called "king tides" poses a risk to many low-lying atolls, where inundation with seawater flooding threatens to contaminate crops and freshwater sources and necessitates increased support for desalination infrastructure. As just one of the twenty-nine atolls and five islands comprising the RMI, Kwajalein Atoll faces a shared precarity posed by climate change through the impacts of king tide flooding, alongside climate-related drought. The military's preoccupation with the sustainability of its installation has produced research that reveals the challenges of ongoing habitation in the atoll by 2055–2065. These catastrophic effects of rising seas traced in the report are already being disproportionately felt among Ebeye residents. Given the deep colonial histories and neocolonial legacies of divergent investments and support for infrastructure on Kwajalein and Ebeye over time (which this book has extensively traced), it should come as no surprise that the crisis of climate change is differentially impacting Ebeye and Kwajalein.

A *PBS NewsHour* report in 2017 illustrated the ongoing influence of these historic inequalities in infrastructure mapping the two islands' landscapes as they have been brought into sharp relief in a new era of climate crisis. Journalist Mike Taibi reported on how extreme drought and rising seas have converged to threaten the freshwater supply on Ebeye.[30] Taibi spoke to several Marshallese residents on the island, including seventy-four-year-old Belma Marok, who described his biggest worry as access to enough fresh water. His family had been relying on rainwater catchment tanks, but those had nearly dried up due to relentless drought.[31] Likewise, the freshwater wells and underground aquifers were at risk of contamination by salt water due to frequent flooding connected to high tides. Ebeye's main freshwater source—a fourteen-year-old desalination plant—was undergoing a nearly $5 million upgrade at the time, leaving residents limited to accessing water for their households to just two days a week. This water required boiling for safety, as waterborne illnesses ranked among the three most common conditions treated at Ebeye's hospital. Signaling the ongoing divergence between Kwajalein's and Ebeye's infrastructures, which has also included desalination plants, Ebeye resident Jim Sheema noted: "I don't drink the water here, I drink the water from Kwaj."[32] Sheema was referring to the daily routine of Marshallese lugging water in five-gallon jugs (weighing forty pounds each) from Kwajalein to Ebeye on the ferry. Given the army's investment in a state-of-the-art desalination plant for its residents on Kwajalein, there was an ample supply of clean water to share with Ebeye.[33]

As Marshallese living on Ebeye and throughout the rest of the Marshall Islands share the existential threat of rising seas with other low-lying atoll nations around the world, they also face a uniquely layered risk located at the intersection of the historic nuclear and contemporary climate catastrophes. These threats converge today at Runit Dome. Referred to by locals as "the tomb," the dome was constructed by the United States at Runit Island in Enewetak Atoll to cover up contaminated soil from nuclear testing. The dome "holds more than 3.1 million cubic feet—or 35 Olympic-sized swimming pools—of U.S.-produced radioactive soil and debris, including lethal amounts of plutonium."[34] As Los Angeles Times journalist Susanne Rust chronicled, the Runit Dome contains not only this deadly mix from nuclear testing done at Enewetak, but also toxic waste transported thousands of miles across the Pacific from the irradiated Nevada testing site.[35] Rust explained that "this concrete coffin" is now at risk of collapse due to rising sea levels.

While the US government continues to pour billions of dollars into missile and space surveillance research at the Kwajalein installation, it remains unclear what level of investment will be made to prevent the imminent catastrophe at Runit Dome, the (literal) by-product of its nuclear campaign.[36] Outraged at an ongoing lack of accountability for the fallout (again literally) of this campaign in his homeland, seventy-two-year-old Rongelapese Nerje Joseph asked: ""If the U.S. can land a man on the moon, why can't they clean up my island?"[37] From the technological feats and mass expenditures involved in US military and space programs enabled by a history of US colonialism in the Marshall Islands, one wonders if the costs Marshallese have paid for their unchosen participation in the US military mission will ever be fully acknowledged with truth and accounted for with any meaningful reconciliation.

In 2016, activist Julian Riklon reflected on the historic and ongoing costs of US weapons testing in his Marshallese homelands from his new home in Sacramento, California. The year marked both his seventieth birthday and the seventieth anniversary of the US launch of its nuclear campaign in his islands. During our interview, Riklon reflected on the passing of his brother and grandmother from cancer; both were on Rongelap during the US hydrogen detonation. He said, "I have lesions on me too, but they haven't caused me problems . . . *yet.*"[38] He pondered why the United States exposed his family to radiation, echoing other Marshallese suspicions of intentionality. In our earlier interview on Ebeye, Riklon had also discussed the centrality of faith in his life, and how this made his relationship to the United States complicated. He said that while he felt grateful that US missionaries had brought religion and provided him with educational opportunities, he also felt anguish that other Americans had such a destructive impact on his homelands: "I am just sad . . . that the Americans brought the word of God for us to love one another and then used my islands for testing weapons to kill other people."[39] Riklon said he assumed the US public knew nothing about the acts of their government. He added that he wished the American people would realize the importance of these islands to the Marshallese people. Riklon had reflected on the long-term implications of this history over many years and had commented on them twenty-five years earlier. In a 1991 interview, he had lamented: "For my children, and their children, and their children's children, the life they will face is something I cannot [bear] to think about."[40]

Such concerns continue to fuel Riklon's ongoing work in educating US citizens about the legacies of nuclear testing in his islands. His decades-long leadership and activism has been a path shared by the late Marshallese senator Tony de Brum, who up until his passing in 2017 remained a prominent voice on the global stage fighting for nuclear and climate justice. One year after leading the 2014 Nuclear Zero campaign, which brought before the Hague a lawsuit against the United States and the eight other nuclear-armed countries to meet their obligations of disarmament, De Brum spoke at the Paris Climate Conference (COP21).[41] As he worked in Paris to form the "High Ambition Coalition," cobbling together a collective of "100 rich and poor nations" to secure a committed global effort toward limiting warming to 1.5 degrees Celsius, De Brum was joined by Marshallese climate activist Selina Neirok Leem.[42] As the summit's youngest delegate, eighteen-year old Leem spoke in Paris and represented a new generation of Marshallese leaders. Addressing a global audience, Leem asserted that the Paris Agreement "is for those of us whose identity, whose culture, whose ancestors, whose whole being is bound to their lands."[43] She cautioned attendees against seeing these crises as detached from their own fates. "I have only spoken about myself and my islands but the same story will play out everywhere in the world. If this is a story about our islands, it is a story for the whole world."[44]

Building on the path paved by her elders, Leem is just one among a rising generation of Marshallese women who have been stepping into the global spotlight, speaking out on nuclear and climate justice at some of the most significant international forums.[45] Four years after Paris, Tony de Brum's daughter, Doreen de Brum, took up the baton passed by her late father to push for change in her role as ambassador and Marshall Islands permanent representative to the United Nations Office. After the Marshall Islands had secured a seat on the UN Human Rights Council, Doreen spoke in Madrid about nuclear and climate justice.[46] At the December 2019 meeting, she delineated Marshallese commitments to reach net zero carbon emissions by 2050, arguing that "more countries needed to follow in Marshallese footsteps." She stated: "We must do more than simply offer our thoughts and prayers."[47] Common to all of these statements by

Marshallese global leaders, young and old, has been a call for accountability to the past, present, and future. This is not simply a demand to support Marshallese, but rather a capacious and coalitional vision asserting the lessons the world must learn from the devastating histories Marshallese have been forced to endure.

Moving in lockstep with this younger cohort speaking truth to power is Julian Riklon, who continues to resist weapons testing in his homelands in the twenty-first century. Just as he refused to sit idly by during the 1980s, this church pastor remained busy at age seventy, raising awareness about militarism in the Marshall Islands. Our June 2016 interview followed upon a presentation Riklon had given at the Lawrence Livermore Lab, where he spoke about the devastating impacts of US weapons testing on his family. During our discussion, I asked Riklon how he faced the fear and risks involved with standing up to the most powerful military in the world during the 1980s. He said: "You know it's funny because although I knew the U.S. was the most powerful country in the world, I was not afraid of telling them what I believe they were doing wrong to our people. I was not afraid of dying for what I believe the U.S. was doing wrong to the people, to the small people. . . . [T]hat was my thinking then, and still. If you think that something is right you should not be afraid of losing your life, dying for what you believe is right."[48]

Alongside a rising generation of Marshallese activists carving their path in the twenty-first century, Riklon's words echo the spirit and courage of Darlene Keju-Johnson, which she carried throughout a lifetime of activism. As her widower, journalist, and co-conspirator in activism Giff Johnson noted in his biography of her life, Darlene was driven to ask questions that could transform societies on local and global levels. Darlene's legacy leaves us with the challenge, in her own words: "Why settle for being a spectator when you might be able to change the world? Or at least one small piece of it?"[49]

Acknowledgments

For a book project that has taken so many years to complete, it seems impossible to thank everyone who has helped along the way to bring this to fruition, so I start out of the gate with apologies for anyone I have missed here. Digging into this research in 2008 as a graduate student at the University of Michigan means I have incurred innumerable intellectual and personal debts over the years.

Because the idea for this book grew out of the stimulating, interdisciplinary, and collaborative approach that signifies the University of Michigan's history doctoral program, I start with the inspiring mentors I had the privilege to train with. Gratitude to Penny Von Eschen, a deeply caring mentor who always reminded me of my potential as a scholar long before I ever saw it, and Damon Salesa, whom I still fondly recall knocking me over on the soccer field several times during my tenure at Ann Arbor. It turns out Damon was far gentler off the field; as co-chair of my dissertation, he was a genuinely kind and thoughtful mentor who pushed me intellectually with questions that lingered with me years later. I also was gifted the mentorship and support of Matt Lassiter during my journey in Ann Arbor, learning from his example as a scholar and teacher. Matt's kindness and confidence in me from day one still humble me. Deep gratitude as well to Phil Deloria, who has been so generous with his time and support over the years, and whose scholarship greatly inspired my thinking with this book. I am also grateful for the opportunity I had to work with Vince Diaz at Michigan and the chance to learn from so many other incredible scholars, including Geoff Eley, Gina Morantz-Sanchez, and Mary Kelley. The friendship and support of

Lily Geismer, Laura Ferguson, Suzi Linsley, and Elspeth Martini were among the many Michigan gifts.

I have also been terribly fortunate to have a vast collective of mentors take an interest in me and my work beyond Michigan, offering invitations for conferences, writing workshops, and publication opportunities. Some of my biggest champions have been Paul Spickard (whom I will always be grateful to for welcoming me into the hui), Cynthia Enloe, Jana Lipman, Julie Greene, and Paul Kramer. I am also thankful for the encouragement of my research over the years from other tremendous scholars, including the late Teresia Teaiwa, Jessica Wang, Dan Bender, David Vine, Andy Urban, Andrew Friedman, and Vernadette Gonzalez.

In addition, I have been fortunate to be welcomed into a network of Pacific scholars during my time researching and thereafter at the University of Hawai'i, Mānoa. I received support and feedback from faculty in the History Department and the Center for Pacific Islands Studies, and I especially want to thank Juli- anne Walsh and David Hanlon for that support. David's reading of my political history analysis while in progress greatly helped my thinking. He also generously made time to speak with me over the years and connected me with other students and colleagues.

If the University of Hawai'i became a second academic home while I was conducting my research after Michigan, UCLA was definitely a third. I enjoyed tremendous support, both financially for my research and through the mentorship of incredible scholars via the ACLS New Faculty Fellows Award in the UCLA History Department. Among the many who supported my work while at UCLA, I would like to thank Valerie Matsumoto, Joan Waugh, Teo Ruiz, David Myers, Ellen Dubois, Robin D. G. Kelley, Kelly Lytle Hernández, and Eric Avila. Also a shout-out to my Pacific writing group organized by UCLA mentors and incredible scholars of the Pacific: Liz Deloughrey and Keith Camacho. UCLA also expanded my network of rising Pacific scholars and new friends, whose work has enriched my own, including Christen Sasaki and Alfred Flores. Big shout out to Sophia Cole, my phenomenal UCLA undergraduate student, who helped support my research during my tenure there. A generous postdoctoral fellowship in the Thinking Matters program at Stanford University further provided me financial support for my research, in a rich intellectual and professionally supportive environment that made this book possible. I would like to express gratitude to Stanford mentors and friends Parna Sengupta, Ellen Woods, Gordan Chang, Zenia Kish, Katie Lennard, Risa Cromer, Dave Blome, and Tiffany Liew. Special thank you to Stanford comrade Anna Corwin for her friendship and intellectual support in reading several chapters in progress. It was at Stanford that I also had the opportunity to audit Michele Elam's class on James Baldwin, which deeply influenced my book revisions. Deep gratitude as well for the care of Meredith Singer Garcia, whom I connected with during my tenure in Palo Alto, and without whose support this book would not be possible.

I would also like to thank the early institutions that funded my research, including the University of Michigan's History Department and the Rackham School of Graduate Studies, the Andrew W. Mellon Foundation and the American Council of Learned Societies, the Society for Historians of American Foreign Relations, the American Historical Association, and the George C. Marshall Foundation. The collective generosity of these various institutions enabled me to complete the vast bulk of my research trips for archival collecting and oral history interviews in the Marshall Islands, Hawai'i, Maryland, Washington, DC, and the Bay Area.

In each of my archival endeavors I was guided by fantastic librarians and archivists. I heavily relied on the Pacific Collection and the Trust Territory of the Pacific Islands archives at the University of Hawai'i at Mānoa and was fortunate to have been supported in that work early on by the Karen Peacock. Karen's commitment and dedication to her work was exemplary, and her bright spirit lit up Hamilton Library's fifth floor. I want to thank all of the staff on the fifth floor, especially Stu Dawrs for his tremendous support over the years. During several trips to the Pacific branch of the National Archives in San Bruno, the kind and knowledgeable archivist Robert Glass also provided tremendous help in assisting with my research on the US naval period on Kwajalein. Gratitude as well to my "research library yoda," Melissa DeWitt, at Regis University, for support with eleventh-hour book revision questions.

In addition to help in the archives, I worked with a number of amazing individuals to guide my oral history work. As the Pacific scholar Epeli Hau'ofa revealed, the Pacific is a space defined by vast networks of connections between islands and individuals. This project has greatly depended on those networks, with new friends and colleagues emerging along the way in Hawai'i and the Marshall Islands. I would like to specifically acknowledge those who shared their hospitality and kindness in my travels through Hawai'i and the Marshalls and others who connected me to friends and colleagues to interview and learn from. These included Ingrid Ahlgren, Terry and Andrea Hazzard, and Deo Keju. Huge thanks to Monica LaBriola for connecting me with Deo, who was instrumental in planning my stay on Ebeye and arranging all of my oral histories on the island. This project would not have been possible without Deo's help; *kommol tata Deo*! I also want to thank Greg Dvorak, who has generously shared insights and encouragement over the years and also connected me with Jimmy Matsunaga. A special thanks to Jimmy for his warm hospitality to me while I was on Kwajalein. Jimmy shared stories with me, he and his wife Doreen fed me, he lent me his bike to get around the island, and he always kept an eye out for me.

My oral histories on Ebeye with non-English-speaking Marshallese individuals were made possible by the support and linguistic skills of my dear friend and interpreter Rachel Miller. Rachel's experiences in the Marshalls, and her time on Namdrik as a teacher, also afforded me the opportunity, alongside the generous hospitality of Liton and Clara Beasa, to spend time on Namdrik. That experience was not only memorable, but also greatly impacted my thinking on space, culture, and history in the region. I would also like to mention those individuals who took a significant amount of time to speak with me in the Marshalls, Hawai'i, and California, including Tony de Brum, Iroij Michael Kabua, Bob Butz, Neibanjan Lavin, Julian Riklon, Yoshi and Fumiko Kemem, Cris Lindborg, Nate Jackson Jr., Raymond Wolff, Shem Livai, Sue Rosoff, QB Keju, and CJ Johnson. Gratitude to those who shared insights through correspondence, including Chi Chi Kemem and Judy Rosachacki. And to all of those who trusted me with their stories and reflections: the perspectives you offered in our conversations, which were less evident in the archives, deeply enriched my work. I hope I have represented those stories and experiences that infuse this larger history sensitively and thoughtfully in this book.

I would like to give a special shout-out to Giff Johnson for his ongoing support of this book through its final iteration, and to Robert Barclay, who was tremendously helpful in assisting me with my countless questions along the way. Special thanks as well to Bill Remick and Sue Rosoff for their support with image selections, as well as Phil Bradley White for the wonderful maps he created for this book. Deep gratitude to my incredible Regis student Fatima Ibrahiem for her tremendous research support on the nuclear testing era. I could not be more proud of Fatima as she's begun law school to further her path toward environmental and racial justice work. A very special thanks as well to my bestie Jaja Chan for her design expertise and support with my image selections all the way from dissertation to book stage. Jaj has been a tremendous support alongside other "chosen family members" for decades, including Amna Khan, Ellen Keith Shaw, my "aunty" Janie Keith, and the late, beautiful Don Keith.

Several friends and fellow writers were also kind enough to look over versions of chapters in the final editing stage. Big thank you to Clay Howard and Ethan Sanders for that support, as well as to Michigan comrade Colleen Woods, for helping me tie up those analytic lose ends. Huge thank you to another Michigan fellow traveler and dear friend, Tiana Kahakauwila, whose literary genius and insights on narrative style undoubtedly strengthened this book's introduction. Our many "board meetings" on the waves in O'ahu likewise enriched this work along the way. I would also like to thank University of California Press's Niels Hooper for his tremendous patience and support for this project over time, and Naja Pulliam Collins for her help in bringing it all together at the final production stage.

Finally there is family to thank for their patience and ongoing support, as I (and thus they) have lived with this project for over a decade. Thank you to my sister Jodi Foster and brother-in-law Clay Foster for their loving support along the way. I'm also grateful to have supportive in-laws Craig Zuckerman, Syd Zuckerman, Bree Zuckerman, Arto Artinian, and B. Artinian Zuckerman. A special note of gratitude to Liz Gibson (and Soozie), whose warm and loving home and endless support provided an oasis during the year of plague in which this book was finally completed.

And to my parents Joan and Fred Hirshberg (also known as "Joanie the Brave" and Freddie, "a well-known, folk-singing personality"), my forever cheerleaders. They have always encouraged me to reach for the stars and made it so much easier to do so because I knew they were there to catch me if and when I slipped along the way. This book would not exist without their love and support. Finally, to Ian Zuckerman, the love of my life, who read every single page of this book and helped me transform it from a jumbled mess into something readable, while also keeping me well fed every step of the way with his exquisite cooking. Of course more important than his support of my work has been the daily joy he has brought into my life, the unbelievable gift of his partnership, for which I am eternally grateful.

Notes

A NOTE ON LANGUAGE

1. A main reference I have employed in this effort is the most recent 2018 scholarship on the Marshall Islands, Greg Dvorak's *Coral and Concrete: Remembering Kwajalein Atoll between Japan, America, and the Marshall Islands* (Honolulu: University of Hawai'i Press, 2018), which includes a rich glossary on Marshallese language and orthography (as well as Japanese and English). One Marshallese source and friend from Ebeye, who graciously helped me double check on language/spelling and translation questions, has been Deo Keju (brother of Darlene Keju-Johnson).

2. The challenge of selecting the most accurate descriptive terms meant moving mostly between "US residents," "US workers and family members," "US civilians," and "Kwajalein residents" to try to indicate the range of people residing on Kwajalein during the US colonial and neocolonial eras. While the vast majority of Kwajalein residents during these periods have been US citizens, not all were, nor have they all been workers on the island; many have been resident dependents. I have tried in each instance to capture the most accurate phrasing for what that book section is referencing. That said, there are still many instances in which I use "American" or "Americans" because the other options felt too ambiguous or unclear, and/or in rare instances to retain stylistic flow.

INTRODUCTION

1. Ian Zuckerman, "The Politics of Emergencies: War, Security and the Boundaries of the Exception in Modern Emergency Powers" (PhD diss., Columbia University, 2012).

2. Giff Johnson, *Don't Ever Whisper: Darlene Keju, Pacific Health Pioneer, Champion for Nuclear Survivors* (Majuro: self-published, 2013), 16.

3. Johnson, *Don't Ever Whisper*, 16.

4. See Patricia Nelson Limerick, "Empire of Innocence," in *The Legacy of Conquest: The Unbroken Past of the American West* (New York: W. W. Norton, 1987).

5. James Baldwin, *The Fire Next Time* (New York: Dial Press, 1963), 19–20.

6. Greg Dvorak, *Coral and Concrete: Remembering Kwajalein Atoll between Japan, America and the Marshall Islands* (Honolulu: University of Hawai'i Press, 2018), 2–3. Dvorak's work has been essential to this book. His scholarly research has constituted key secondary support for contextualization, while his writings on experience as a former Kwajalein resident have also informed my primary source analysis, particularly in chapter 4's focus on memory and commemoration. Also, while this geology description uses the term "islet" to describe Kwajalein and Ebeye, throughout the book I use the term "island," which much more commonly appears throughout all primary and secondary sources to describe the two.

7. Dvorak, *Coral and Concrete*, 4.

8. Dvorak, *Coral and Concrete*, 4.

9. Dvorak, *Coral and Concrete*, 4.

10. Dvorak, *Coral and Concrete*, 4.

11. Epeli Hau'ofa, "Our Sea of Islands," *Contemporary Pacific* 6, no. 1 (Spring 1994): 148–161.

12. Hau'ofa, "Our Sea of Islands."

13. Martha Smith-Norris, *Domination and Resistance: The United States and the Marshall Islands during the Cold War* (Honolulu: University of Hawai'i Press, 2016), 44.

14. See Nuclear Claims Tribunal, Republic of the Marshall Islands, accessed December 12, 2020, www.nuclearclaimstribunal.com/testing.htm. As detailed in Stewart Firth's *Nuclear Playground* (Honolulu: University of Hawai'i Press, 1987), the United States was not alone in using the Pacific as a Cold War testing ground. Firth's book examines US nuclear testing in the Marshall Islands within a comparative context alongside British nuclear testing in Australia and on Christmas Island and French nuclear testing in French Polynesia. For global comparative histories outside the Pacific, see Gabrielle Hecht, *Being Nuclear: Africans and the Global Uranium Trade* (Cambridge, MA: MIT Press, 2012).

15. In 2017, the population had reached approximately fifteen thousand. See Wyatt Olson, "Under the Radar: Life Is Low-Tech at Army Missile Defense

Base in the Pacific," *Stars and Stripes*, March 12, 2017, accessed November 18, 2020, www.stripes.com/news/pacific/under-the-radar-life-is-low-tech-at-army -missile-defense-base-in-the-pacific-1.458322.

16. Republic of the Marshall Islands 2011 Census, Economic Policy, Planning, and Statistics Office, Office of the President, accessed December 15, 2020, www .rmieppso.org/social/census-report.

17. Jinna A. Keju to Mr. Juan Alcedo, Committee on Civil Rights, September 15, 1979, Giff Johnson Marshall Islands Resource Materials, Pacific Manuscripts Bureau 1172, University of Hawai'i, Mānoa.

18. Keju to Alcedo, September 15, 1979.

19. Keju to Alcedo, September 15, 1979.

20. Keju to Alcedo, September 15, 1979.

21. Keju to Alcedo, September 15, 1979. Kwajalein's hospital exclusions continue today as Ebeye residents struggle to maintain adequate medical staff and resources to meet the island population's needs. Those living on Ebeye not employed by Kwajalein who require emergency care are first directed to Majuro (approximately $300 for a one-hour flight) or to Honolulu (approximately $1,800 for a five-hour flight). Most Ebeye residents cannot afford these options. After those expensive emergency care options are exhausted, only then will Kwajalein make the rare exception to allow an Ebeye resident to enter the island's hospital, even though the two islands are only three miles apart.

22. For more on the history of the overthrow see Noenoe K. Silva, *Aloha Betrayed: Native Hawaiian Resistance to American Colonialism* (Durham, NC: Duke University Press, 2004). I use this term here in place of "Native Hawaiian" as a gesture to self-identification in the historical and contemporary sovereignty movement, discussed in this paragraph. For more on the use of this term, see Noelani Goodyear-Ka'ōpua, introduction to *A Nation Rising: Hawaiian Movements for Life, Land, and Sovereignty*, ed. Noelani Goodyear-Ka'ōpua, Ikaika Hussey, and Erin Kahunawaika'ala (Durham, NC: Duke University Press, 2014).

23. Kyle Kajihiro, "The Militarizing of Hawai'i: Occupation, Accommodation and Resistance," in *Asian Settler Colonialism: From Local Governance to the Habits of Everyday Life in Hawai'i*, ed. Candace Fujikane and Jonathan Y. Okamura (Honolulu: University of Hawai'i Press, 2008), 174.

24. I was unable to get sponsorship to stay overnight on base for my first research trip, so I stayed on Ebeye and organized sponsorship for afternoon visits to Kwajalein, which I made under the close supervision of my daytime sponsor.

25. I have chosen to keep this individual anonymous because his refusal to speak with me on Kwajalein clearly signaled his lack of consent to be included by name in this project. But this correspondence took place in October/November 2010.

26. Anonymous correspondent, October/November 2010.

27. Firth, *Nuclear Playground.*

28. Dvorak, *Coral and Concrete,* 5.

29. Holly M. Barker, *Bravo for the Marshallese: Regaining Control in a Post-Nuclear, Post-Colonial World* (Belmont, CA: Wadsworth/Thomson Learning, 2004), 17.

30. Julianne M. Walsh, "Imagining the Marshalls: Chiefs, Tradition, and the State on the Fringes of U.S. Empire" (PhD diss., University of Hawai'i at Mānoa, 2003), 125.

31. Dvorak, *Coral and Concrete,* 6.

32. Guam was not part of the Trust Territory region, as it had already come under US colonial control in 1898 and was administrated by the US Navy thereafter (except during the brief period of Japanese control during World War II). Within three years of the Trust Territory of the Pacific Islands (TTPI) Agreement's signing, Guam transitioned to an unincorporated territory of the United States through the 1950 Guam Organic Act. The map uses the historic spelling "Truk" (as it was spelled during the Trusteeship era) and the contemporary spelling "Chuuk."

33. David Vine, *Base Nation: How U.S. Military Bases Abroad Harm America and the World* (New York: Metropolitan Books, 2015), 19.

34. Vine, *Base Nation.*

35. David Vine, *Island of Shame: The Secret History of the U.S. Military Base on Diego Garcia* (Princeton, NJ: Princeton University Press, 2009), 48.

36. Vine, *Base Nation,* 24.

37. Vine, *Base Nation,* 27.

38. Vine, *Base Nation,* 30.

39. Vine, *Base Nation,* 3.

40. Bruce Cumings, "Archipelago of Empire: An American Grid for the Global Garden," in *Dominion from Sea to Sea: Pacific Ascendancy and American Power* (New Haven, CT: Yale University Press, 2009).

41. Vine, *Island of Shame,* 54. In addition to *Island of Shame* and Vine's more recent *Base Nation,* a number of scholars have contributed to our historic understanding of this vast base network over time. Growing out of Cynthia Enloe's field-inspiring *Bananas, Beaches and Bases: Making Feminist Sense of International Politics* (Berkeley: University of California Press, 1989), these works include Mark L. Gillem, *America Town: Building the Outposts of Empire* (Minneapolis: University of Minnesota Press, 2007); Jana K. Lipman, *Guantánamo: A Working Class History between Empire and Revolution* (Berkeley: University of California Press, 2009); and Catherine Lutz, ed., *The Bases of Empire: The Global Struggle against U.S. Military Posts* (New York: New York University Press, 2009).

42. I am grateful to Colleen Woods for her feedback on my analysis of the military industrial colonial complex in February 2021.

43. Sandra Crismon, "Negotiating the Borders of Empire: An Ethnography of Access on Kwajalein Atoll, Marshall Islands" (PhD Diss., University of Georgia, 2005), 215.

44. Crismon, "Negotiating the Borders of Empire," 215.

45. "United States Army Kwajalein Atoll," published by US Army Space and Strategic Defense Command, 1994, Government Documents, Hamilton Library, University of Hawai'i, Mānoa.

46. "Kwajalein Missile Range: Analysis of Existing Facilities, Ballistic Missile Defense System Command, U.S. Army," prepared by Production Engineering Control Department, Global Associates, 1982, reel no. 2197, 6, Trust Territory of the Pacific Islands Archives, University of Hawai'i, Mānoa (hereafter TTA).

47. "Kwajalein Missile Range."

48. Eugene C. Sims, *Kwajalein Remembered*, 3rd printing (Eugene, OR: Eugene Print, 1996), 27–28. Note that Macy's was named after but not part of the US department store franchise.

49. Barker, *Bravo for the Marshallese*, xiii.

50. Vine, *Base Nation*, 212.

51. Vine, *Base Nation*.

52. Philip J. Deloria, *Playing Indian* (New Haven, CT: Yale University Press, 1998), 36.

53. Deloria, *Playing Indian*, 190 (emphasis added).

54. With "formation" I am invoking the work of sociologists Michael Omi and Howard Winant and their concept of "racial formation" as rooted in the historic specificity of that production. See Michael Omi and Howard Winant, *Racial Formations in the United States: From the 1960s to the 1980s*, 3rd ed. (New York: Routledge, 2014).

55. Vine, *Island of Shame*, 54.

56. Vine, *Island of Shame*.

57. Lipman, *Guantánamo*; Vine, *Island of Shame*; Katherine T. McCaffrey, *Military Power and Popular Protest: The U.S. Navy in Vieques, Puerto Rico* (New Brunswick, NJ: Rutgers University Press, 2002); Wesley Iwao Uenten, "Rising Up from a Sea of Discontent: The 1970 Koza Uprising in U.S.-Occupied Okinawa," in *Militarized Currents: Toward a Decolonized Future in Asia and the Pacific*, ed. Setsu Shigematsu and Keith L. Camacho (Minneapolis: University of Minnesota Press, 2010); and Gillem, *America Town*.

58. An array of base studies grew out of Cynthia Enloe's feminist analysis of US military base histories and US military colonialism more broadly, centering gender and sexuality in their analysis. These include Teresia K. Teaiwa, "bikinis and other s/pacific n/oceans," *Contemporary Pacific* (Spring 1994): 87–109; Kathy E. Ferguson and Phyllis Turnbull, *Oh Say Can You See? The Semiotics of the Military in Hawai'i* (Minneapolis: University of Minnesota Press, 1999);

Greg Dvorak, "'The Martial Islands': Making Marshallese Masculinities between American and Japanese Militarism," *Contemporary Pacific* 20, no. 1 (Spring 2008): 55–86; and Setsu Shigematsu and Keith L. Camacho, eds., *Militarized Currents: Toward a Decolonized Future in Asia and the Pacific* (Minneapolis: University of Minnesota Press, 2010). Themes of displacement, discrimination, and segregation have also infused other studies examining the local impact of US bases around the world, including Wesley Iwao Ueunten's consideration of segregation at the US Kadena Airforce Base in Okinawa. See Uenten, "Rising Up from a Sea of Discontent."

59. Uenten, "Rising Up from a Sea of Discontent"; and Lipman, *Guantánamo*.

60. Gillem, *America Town*, 77.

61. Matthew D. Lassiter, "The Suburban Origins of 'Color-Blind' Conservatism: Middle-Class Consciousness in the Charlotte Busing Crisis," *Journal of Urban History* 30, no. 4 (May 2004): 552 (emphasis added).

62. Lassiter, "The Suburban Origins of 'Color-Blind' Conservatism," 557.

63. Dvorak, *Coral and Concrete*, 12.

64. Scholars of metropolitan and Sunbelt studies have traced such patterns of post–World War II suburban transformations within the United States as tied to postwar defense spending and the rise of the military industrial complex. These works include collections such as Richard M. Bernard and Bradley R. Rice, eds., *Sunbelt Cities: Politics and Growth since World War II* (Austin: University of Texas Press, 1983) and comparative histories such as Margaret Pugh O'Mara, *Cities of Knowledge: Cold War Science and the Search for the Next Silicon Valley* (Princeton, NJ: Princeton University Press, 2005).

65. Sims, *Kwajalein Remembered*, 121.

66. Dvorak, *Coral and Concrete*, 12.

67. Sims, *Kwajalein Remembered*, 1–2. Estimates of the size of the population have ranged across primary and secondary sources documenting these numbers throughout the 1960s and 1970s. In her ethnography of Kwajalein, Crismon, in "Negotiating the Borders of Empire," traced the base population peaking at over five thousand residents in the early 1970s, drawing upon numbers in *The Kwajalein Hourglass* (July 2000). Dvorak, in *Coral and Concrete*, has written of the island's population peaking at four thousand in the 1960s.

68. Dvorak, *Coral and Concrete*, 7.

69. This divergence in civilian/military tenure on the island created a complicated and often fraught social setting in which a civilian population far more familiar with life on the island perceived itself as vulnerable to the whims of changing governance rules and policies as different military colonels cycled in and out every two years.

70. Gillem, *America Town*, 118.

71. Here I am referring to the history of all-White suburban landscapes emerging from private and public policies, including restrictive racial covenants

most infamously deployed to segregate William J. Levitt's postwar Levittown housing developments.

72. The racial landscape of the island changed over time, with a larger percentage of White workers in recent decades. The 1960s and 1970s saw a greater number of workers of color arriving to support construction labor, with a sizable number of Native Hawaiian workers arriving from Hawai'i.

73. Dr. Martin Luther King Jr., interview, *Meet the Press*, April 17, 1960. It also important to keep in mind that the military remained a thoroughly segregated institution across all bases until 1948, when President Truman issued Executive Order 9981 abolishing discrimination on the basis of race, color, religion, or national origin in the US Armed Forces.

74. Chapter 3 explores these army regulations imposed in 1968, which banned Marshallese shopping privileges on the island.

75. See, for example, Kenneth T. Jackson, *Crabgrass Frontier: The Suburbanization of the United States* (New York: Oxford University Press, 1987).

76. These works include Thomas J. Sugrue, *The Origins of the Urban Crisis: Race and Inequality in Postwar Detroit* (Princeton, NJ: Princeton University Press, 1996); Robert O. Self, *American Babylon: Race and the Struggle for Postwar Oakland* (Princeton, NJ: Princeton University Press, 2003); Eric Avila, *Popular Culture in the Age of White Flight: Fear and Fantasy in Suburban Los Angeles* (Berkeley: University of California Press, 2004); and Matthew D. Lassiter, *Silent Majority: Suburban Politics in the Sunbelt South* (Princeton, NJ: Princeton University Press, 2007).

77. For more on this topic, see Elaine Tyler May, *Homeward Bound: American Families in the Cold War Era* (New York: Basic Books, 1988), and Sugrue, *Origins of the Urban Crisis.*

78. Elaine Tyler May, "Security against Democracy: The Legacy of the Cold War at Home," *Journal of American History* 97 (March 2011): 939–957.

79. See, for example, Penny M. Von Eschen, *Satchmo Blows Up the World: Jazz Ambassadors Play the Cold War* (Cambridge, MA: Harvard University Press, 2004).

80. In addition to Von Eschen's *Satchmo Blows Up the World*, these works include Christian G. Appy, ed., *Cold War Constructions: The Political Culture of United States Imperialism, 1945–1966* (Amherst: University of Massachusetts Press, 2000); Mahmood Mamdani, *Good Muslim, Bad Muslim: America, the Cold War, and the Roots of Terror* (New York: Pantheon Books, 2004); and Greg Grandin, *Empire's Workshop: Latin America, the United States, and the Rise of the New Imperialism* (New York: Henry Holt, 2006).

81. Mary L. Dudziak, *Cold War Civil Rights: Race and the Image of American Democracy* (Princeton, NJ: Princeton University Press, 2000).

82. For additional comparative analysis on U.S. disavowal of empire, see Amy Kaplan and Donald E. Pease, eds., *Cultures of United States Imperialism* (Durham, NC: Duke University Press, 1994).

83. Keith H. Basso, *Wisdom Sits in Places: Landscape and Language among the Western Apache* (Albuquerque: University of New Mexico Press, 1996), 7.

84. Basso, *Wisdom Sits in Places*.

85. See, for example, Edward W. Soja, *Postmodern Geographies: The Reassertion of Space in Critical Social Theory* (London: Verso, 1989); and David Harvey, *Spaces of Capital: Towards a Critical Geography* (New York: Routledge, 2001).

86. There are recent, notable exceptions to this trend most exemplary in Pacific history and Pacific cultural studies, history of science and technology, and anthropology. See Dvorak, *Coral and Concrete*; Smith-Norris, *Domination and Resistance*; David Hanlon, *Remaking Micronesia: Discourse over Development in a Pacific Territory, 1944–1982* (Honolulu: University of Hawai'i Press, 1998); Barker, *Bravo for the Marshallese*; Giff Johnson, *Nuclear Past: Unclear Future* (Majuro: Micronitor, 2009); Barbara Rose Johnston, *The Consequential Damages of Nuclear War: The Rongelap Report* (Walnut Creek, CA: Left Coast Press, 2008); and Firth, *Nuclear Playground*.

87. Hau'ofa, "Our Sea of Islands," 148–161.

88. Mary L. Dudziak, *War Time: An Idea, Its History, Its Consequences* (New York: Oxford University Press, 2012), 5.

89. In this forever war era, these targets have been the "enemies" of North Korea and China.

90. Vine, *Base Nation*.

91. A phenomenon that both Greg Dvorak's and Sandra Crismon's historic and ethnographic research has illuminated.

92. One notable exception to this absence is Monica C. LaBriola, "Iien Ippan Doon (This Time Together): Celebrating Survival in an 'Atypical Marshallese Community'" (MA thesis, University of Hawai'i, Mānoa, 2006), which centered the voices of Marshallese women on Ebeye and offered the first significant documentation of those experiences and narratives.

93. There was also one individual I interviewed through correspondence, who was employed on Kwajalein at the time of the interview, who also requested anonymity (as noted in chapter 4).

94. My research was likewise enriched by the work of scholars such as David Hanlon, Greg Dvorak, Monica C. LaBriola, and Sandra Crismon, who lived in the region (Hanlon in Pohnpei, the other three in Kwajalein Atoll) and brought invaluable linguistic and cultural knowledge to their work.

CHAPTER 1. FROM WARTIME VICTORY TO COLD WAR CONTAINMENT IN THE PACIFIC

The first epigraph is from Lt. John Useem, USNR, "Social Reconstruction in Micronesia," February 7, 1946, Stanford University, School of Naval

Administration, docs. NA1–NA14, Hoover Institution Archives, Stanford University (hereafter HIA).

The second epigraph is from *Half Life: A Parable for the Nuclear Age* (Dennis O'Rourke, dir., 1985).

1. Geoffrey M. White, "Remembering the Pacific War" (Occasional Paper 36, Center for Pacific Islands Studies, School of Hawaiian, Asian and Pacific Studies, University of Hawai'i, Honolulu, 1991), 116.

2. White, "Remembering the Pacific War," 113.

3. Heine noted that he arrived at Kwajalein around 1946 or 1947, in Lin Poyer, Suzanne Falgout, and Laurence Marshall Carucci, *The Typhoon of War: Micronesian Experiences of the Pacific War* (Honolulu: University of Hawai'i Press, 2001), 214.

4. Poyer, Falgout, and Carucci, *Typhoon of War*, 121.

5. David Hanlon, *Remaking Micronesia: Discourse over Development in a Pacific Territory, 1944–1982* (Honolulu: University of Hawai'i Press, 1998), 23.

6. "The Battles of Kwajalein and Roi-Namur," published by Bell Laboratories in 1974 as special edition to the company newsletter *The Interceptor*. Republished by the Kwajalein Veterans of Foreign Wars Post 10268, 11, Pacific Collection in Hamilton Library, University of Hawai'i, Mānoa (hereafter PCH).

7. "The Battles of Kwajalein and Roi-Namur," PCH.

8. Poyer, Falgout, and Carucci, *Typhoon of War*, 121.

9. White, "Remembering the Pacific War," 116.

10. White, "Remembering the Pacific War," 116.

11. Catherine Lutz, ed., *The Bases of Empire: The Global Struggle against U.S. Military Posts* (New York: New York University Press, 2009), 15.

12. Suzanne Falgout, Lin Poyer, and Laurence Marshall Carucci, *Memories of War: Micronesians in the Pacific War* (Honolulu: University of Hawai'i Press, 2008), 82.

13. Handel Dribo, interview in *Home on the Range* (Adam Horowitz, dir., 1991). The date range in various published sources on this film's release has spanned 1989, 1990, and 1991. I have used the citation included in Hanlon, *Remaking Micronesia*.

14. Dribo interview, 1991.

15. Dribo interview, 1991.

16. Dribo interview, 1991.

17. See Vicente M. Diaz, "Deliberating Liberation Day: Memory, Culture and History in Guam," in *Perilous Memories: The Asia-Pacific War(s)*, ed. T. Fujitani, Geoffrey M. White, and Lisa Yoneyama (Durham, NC: Duke University Press, 2001); and Keith L. Camacho, *Cultures of Commemoration: The Politics of War, Memory and History in the Mariana Islands* (Honolulu: University of Hawai'i Press, 2011).

18. See Greg Dvorak, "Capturing Liberation," in *Coral and Concrete: Remembering Kwajalein Atoll between Japan, America and the Marshall Islands*

(Honolulu: University of Hawai'i Press, 2018). Dvorak offers what he calls a "deep-time" history of Marshallese, Japanese, and American experiences, and thus his analysis aims to challenge the erasures of the images and their captions.

19. Dvorak, *Coral and Concrete*, 97.

20. Franklin D. Roosevelt, "State of the Union Address," January 6, 1945, and Harry S. Truman, "Special Message to the Congress on Winning the War with Japan," June 1, 1945, The American Presidency Project, John T. Woolley & Gerhard Peters, University of California at Santa Barbara, accessed October 10, 2010, www.presidency.ucsb.edu/ws/.

21. An exception to this pattern came through in US soldiers' *visual* documentation of Marshallese in the Kwajalein battle story through photography; see Dvorak, "Capturing Liberation."

22. *Hour Glass* 2, no. 5 (February 5, 1948), souvenir issue; and E. H. Bryan Jr., "Life in Micronesia: *Hour Glass* Special, The Marshalls and the Pacific," nos. 1–23 (June 4, 1965–January 21, 1966), PCH.

23. "Life in Micronesia," PCH.

24. "Battles of Kwajalein and Roi-Namur," 1, PCH.

25. "Battles of Kwajalein and Roi-Namur," 29, PCH.

26. In *Coral and Concrete* (121–122), Dvorak traces how in Japanese commemorations of the war, the same "lone palm tree" represented how the battle was an example of *gyokusai*, in which all were lost (even though there were close to three hundred Japanese and Korean survivors).

27. "Battles of Kwajalein and Roi-Namur," 30, PCH.

28. "Battles of Kwajalein and Roi-Namur," 30, PCH.

29. "Battles of Kwajalein and Roi-Namur," 30, PCH (emphasis added).

30. "Battles of Kwajalein and Roi-Namur," 65, PCH.

31. "Battles of Kwajalein and Roi-Namur," 65, PCH.

32. Jim Bennett, "The Battle for Kwajalein," *Soldiers* 55, no. 11 (November 2000): 21.

33. Bennett, "Battle for Kwajalein," 21.

34. Bennett, "Battle for Kwajalein," 21.

35. Bennett, "Battle for Kwajalein," 21.

36. David Vine, *Island of Shame: The Secret History of the U.S. Military Base on Diego Garcia.* (Princeton, NJ: Princeton University Press, 2009), 16.

37. Of the eleven original trusts, nine were no longer trusts by 1975, either having gained independence or integrated with a neighboring territory. New Guinea, the tenth, under Australian administration, gained independence in union with Papua in 1975, leaving the United States the only remaining administrator of a UN Trust Territory by 1975. Donald F. McHenry, *Micronesia, Trust Betrayed: Altruism vs. Self Interest in American Foreign Policy* (New York: Carnegie Endowment for International Peace, 1975), 34.

38. McHenry, *Micronesia, Trust Betrayed*, 33–34.

39. See, for example, Emily S. Rosenberg, "World War I, Wilsonianism, and Challenges to U.S. Empire," *Diplomatic History* 38, no. 4 (September 2014): 852–863.

40. McHenry, *Micronesia, Trust Betrayed*, 66–67.

41. K. R. Howe, Robert C. Kiste, and Brij V. Lal, eds., *Tides of History: The Pacific Islands in the Twentieth Century* (Honolulu: University of Hawai'i Press, 1994), 229, as cited in Sandra Crismon, "Negotiating the Borders of Empire: An Ethnography of Access on Kwajalein Atoll, Marshall Islands" (PhD diss., University of Georgia, 2005), 157.

42. "Trusteeship Agreement for the Former Japanese Mandated Islands," signed by Harry S. Truman, July 18, 1947, reel no. 106, 4, TTA.

43. "Trusteeship Agreement for the Former Japanese Mandated Islands."

44. "Trusteeship Agreement for the Former Japanese Mandated Islands."

45. Jon A. Anderson, "Trusteeship in Turmoil—The Agreement," *Micronesian Reporter* 19, no. 2 (1971): 26, PCH.

46. Anderson, "Trusteeship in Turmoil," PCH.

47. Anderson, "Trusteeship in Turmoil," PCH.

48. McHenry, *Micronesia, Trust Betrayed*, 33–34.

49. Anderson, "Trusteeship in Turmoil," 26, PCH.

50. McHenry, *Micronesia, Trust Betrayed*, 66–67.

51. McHenry, *Micronesia, Trust Betrayed*, 67–68.

52. Lt. John Useem, USNR, "Social Reconstruction in Micronesia," HIA (emphasis added).

53. Useem, "Social Reconstruction in Micronesia," HIA.

54. "Comparative Colonial Administration Syllabus," Stanford University, School of Naval Administration, Documents, NA1-NA14, Prepared at the School of Naval Administration, 1946, HIA.

55. "The United States Indian Service Evolution of the Policy of the United States Government toward Indians" by Dr. Whitaker, Stanford University, School of Naval Administration, Documents, NA1-NA14, Prepared at the School of Naval Administration, 1946, HIA.

56. Useem, "Social Reconstruction in Micronesia," HIA.

57. Useem, "Social Reconstruction in Micronesia," HIA.

58. Martha Smith-Norris, *Domination and Resistance: The United States and the Marshall Islands during the Cold War* (Honolulu: University of Hawai'i Press, 2016), 44.

59. Smith-Norris, *Domination and Resistance*, 44.

60. Smith-Norris, *Domination and Resistance*, 44.

61. See Nuclear Claims Tribunal, Republic of the Marshall Islands, accessed December 12, 2020, www.nuclearclaimstribunal.com/testing.htm.

62. Smith-Norris, *Domination and Resistance*, 46.

63 *The Atomic Blast*, June 15, 1946, Beth Flippen Scheel Papers, box 1, 85070-9.17, HIA.

64. *Atomic Blast*, June 15, 1946, HIA.

65. *Atomic Blast*, June 15, 1946, HIA.

66. *Atomic Blast*, June 15, 1946, HIA.

67. *The Atomic Blast*, June 22, 1946, Beth Flippen Scheel Papers, box 1, 85070-9.17, HIA.

68. *The Atomic Blast*, June 29, 1946, Beth Flippen Scheel Papers, box 1, 85070-9.17, HIA.

69. *Atomic Blast*, June 29, 1946, HIA.

70. Teresia K. Teaiwa, "bikinis and other s/pacific n/oceans," *Contemporary Pacific* 6, no. 1 (Spring 1994): 87–109. Reard said he "hoped that the raunchy two-piece would elicit the same shock and horror that the atomic bomb did," as reported by Rose Eveleth in "The Bikini's Inventor Guessed How Much It Would Horrify the Public," *Smithsonian Magazine*, July 5, 2013, accessed November 20, 2017, www.smithsonianmag.com/smart-news/the-bikinis-inventor-guessed-how -much-it-would-horrify-the-public-6914887/.

71. Teaiwa, "bikinis and other s/pacific n/oceans."

72. Micronesia Support Committee, *Marshall Islands, a Chronology: 1944–1981* (Honolulu: Makaʻainana Media, 1981), 9, PCH.

73. "Monthly Report on Military Government Administration from the Island Commander Kwajalein," August 19, 1946, RG 313, folder "Military Affairs," Pacific Branch of the National Archives (hereafter PBNA).

74. "Monthly Report on Military Government Administration," PBNA.

75. Micronesia Support Committee, *Marshall Islands, a Chronology*, 7, PCH.

76. Micronesia Support Committee, *Marshall Islands, a Chronology*, 9, PCH.

77. Smith-Norris, *Domination and Resistance*, 50.

78. Jack Niedenthal, *For the Good of Mankind: A History of the People of Bikini and Their Islands* (Majuro: Bravo Publishing, 2001), 68. For more on Bikinian displacement history see Robert C. Kiste, *The Bikinians: A Study in Forced Migration* (Menlo Park, CA: Benjamin-Cummings, 1974).

79. Correspondence on Civil Administration Unit, Kwajalein Quarterly Report for the months of January, February, and March, 1948, report no. 9 from Governor of the Marshalls, May 12, 1948, RG 313 Records of Naval Operating Forces, Trust Territory of the Pacific Islands, Office of the Deputy High Commissioner, General Administrative Files, 1, US National Archives and Records Administration (hereafter NARA).

80. Correspondence on Civil Administration Unit, NARA.

81. "Navy Can cope with Atomic War: Ramsey," from *Honolulu Advertiser*, in *Marshall Post Inquirer*, March–September 1948, PCH.

82. "Navy Can Cope with Atomic War," PCH.

83. "Navy Can Cope with Atomic War," PCH.

84. "Navy Can Cope with Atomic War," PCH.

85. Micronesia Support Committee, *Marshall Islands, a Chronology*, 11–13.

86. By the categories established through the United Nations Convention Relating to the Status of Refugees in 1951, Bikinians were never identified as falling within this classification of "refugees," nor were they afforded the international rights and protections that are presumed to accompany such status recognition.

87. Giff Johnson, *Nuclear Past, Unclear Future* (Majuro: Micronitor, 2009), 3.

88. Johnson, *Nuclear Past, Unclear Future*; and Stewart Firth, *Nuclear Playground* (Honolulu: University of Hawai'i Press, 1987), 15.

89. Micronesia Support Committee, *Marshall Islands, a Chronology*, 10.

90. Firth, *Nuclear Playground*, 18.

91. Firth, *Nuclear Playground*, 18.

92. Firth, *Nuclear Playground*, 18.

93. Firth, *Nuclear Playground*, 18.

94. See Smith-Norris, *Domination and Resistance*; Holly M. Barker, *Bravo for the Marshallese: Regaining Control in a Post-Nuclear, Post-Colonial World* (Belmont, CA: Wadsworth/Thomson Learning, 2004); Johnson, *Nuclear Past: Unclear Future*; Barbara Rose Johnston, *The Consequential Damages of Nuclear War: The Rongelap Report* (Walnut Creek, CA: Left Coast Press, 2008); Firth, *Nuclear Playground*.

95. For more on this history, see Smith-Norris, "U.S. Nuclear Tests, the Environment, and Medical Research: Case Studies of the Rongelapese and Utirikese," in *Domination and Resistance*.

96. Smith-Norris, *Domination and Resistance*, 77.

97. Arakawa Syunji, "Report from the Marshall Islands: The Number of 'Hibakusha' Is Growing (an Interview with Mr. Nelson Anjain)," *Han-Genpatsu News, No Nuke News Japan* (June/July 1982), Pacific Manuscripts Bureau 1172, Giff Johnson Marshall Islands Resource Materials, University of Hawai'i, Mānoa.

98. Joseph P. Masco, "'Survival Is Your Business': Engineering Ruins and Affect in Nuclear America," *Cultural Anthropology* 23, no. 2 (2008): 374.

99. Masco, "'Survival Is Your Business,'" 373.

100. Masco, "'Survival Is Your Business,'" 372–373.

101. Masco, "'Survival Is Your Business,'" 373. Masco also notes that more than 150 industrial associations participated to ensure a wide range of consumer items would be included in the test. See also "Cue for Survival," Operation Cue A.E.C. Nevada Test Site, May 5, 1955, a report by the Federal Civil Defense Administration, and "Operation Teapot: Report of the Test Manager Joint Test Organization" (extracted version), Nevada Test Site, Spring 1955, prepared for Director,

Defense Nuclear Agency, Washington ,DC, November 1, 1981, 145, Defense Technical Information Center as a Department of Defense Field Activity, accessed November 1, 2019, https://discover.dtic.mil/.

102. Masco, "'Survival Is Your Business,'" 376.

103. Smith-Norris, *Domination and Resistance*, 39.

104. Johnson, *Nuclear Past, Unclear Future*, 21–22. Bikinians were to receive $5 million annually; Enewetakese, $3.25 million annually; and Utirikese, $1.5 million annually. Compensation was paid into trust funds established by each local government and invested to generate further revenue. Each atoll was allowed to use a percentage for compensation payments and operations, while retaining a portion for investment. According to Johnson, in 2000, 2,126 people on the Bikini compensation list had received about $275 in quarterly compensation payments. But from 2017 onward the Bikinian leadership obtained complete control of the trust fund and was spending more, including more frequent distributions of money to Bikinians, bringing the per capita amount down to $102 in the last couple of years. These most recent numbers were obtained through correspondence with Johnson on March 7, 2021.

105. Johnson, *Nuclear Past, Unclear Future*, 6–16.

106. Smith-Norris, *Domination and Resistance*, 84.

107. Neither the film *Half Life* nor follow-up research into the National Archives Records and Administration in College Park and correspondence with Martha Smith-Norris unearthed the original source of this footage to reveal the targeted audience of this clip. But we can speculate that this may have either been broadcast to a broader public audience to teach about laboratory research or used as an instructional video circulated internally to scientists working within the laboratory.

108. *Half Life* (emphasis added).

109. *Half Life*.

110. *Half Life*.

111. *Half Life* (emphasis added).

112. Johnson, *Nuclear Past, Unclear Future*, 17.

113. *Half Life*.

114. Useem, "Social Reconstruction in Micronesia," HIA.

115. "Relationship of the United Nations to the Trust Territory of the Pacific Islands," speech by Rear Admiral Leon. S. Fiske, US Navy, Deputy High Commissioner Trust Territory of the Pacific Islands, United Nations, October 23, 1950, reel no. 166, file Correspondence, Dispatches, and other information regarding the Trust Territory of the Pacific Islands (General Info), UN, Trusteeship Documents, 1952–1978, 2, TTA.

116. "Relationship of the United Nations to the Trust Territory of the Pacific Islands," 14.

117. Hanlon, *Remaking Micronesia*, 34.

118. See Noenoe K. Silva, *Aloha Betrayed: Native Hawaiian Resistance to American Colonialism* (Durham, NC: Duke University Press, 2004); Jonathan Kay Kamakawiwoʻole Osorio, *Disemembering Lahui: A History of the Hawaiian Nation to 1887* (Honolulu: University of Hawaiʻi Press, 2002); and Paul A. Kramer, *The Blood of Government: Race, Empire, the United States, and the Philippines* (Chapel Hill: University of North Carolina Press, 2006).

119. Historians Penny M. Von Eschen, Kevin K. Gaines, and Greg Grandin, among others, have traced US executive-level discourse marking colonized and racialized peoples incapable of self-governance across Africa, Southeast Asia, and Latin America during the Cold War, and the ways such narratives were used to justify the undermining of democratic elections for fear of decolonizing nations falling to communism. See Von Eschen, *Satchmo Blows Up the World: Jazz Ambassadors Play the Cold War* (Cambridge, MA: Harvard University Press, 2004); Kevin K. Gaines, *American Africans in Ghana: Black Expatriates and the Civil Rights Era* (Chapel Hill: University of North Carolina Press, 2006); and Grandin, *Empire's Workshop: Latin America, the United States, and the Rise of the New Imperialism* (New York: Henry Holt, 2006).

120. "Russia Critical of T.T. Administration," *Micronesian Monthly*, November 1952–January 1954, PCH. (Mr. Zonov's first name was not listed in the UN report).

121. "Russia Critical of T.T. Administration," PCH.

122. "High Commissioner Midkiff Answered Questions, Criticism before UN Trusteeship Council," *Micronesian Monthly*, November 1952–January 1954, PCH.

123. "High Commissioner Midkiff Answered Questions," PCH.

124. "High Commissioner Midkiff Answered Questions," PCH (emphasis added).

125. Howe, Kiste, and Lal, *Tides of History*, cited in Crismon, "Negotiating the Borders of Empire," 142–143.

126. Hanlon, *Remaking Micronesia*, 51.

127. McHenry, *Micronesia, Trust Betrayed*, 14.

128. McHenry, *Micronesia, Trust Betrayed*, 14.

129. McHenry, *Micronesia, Trust Betrayed*, 16.

130. McHenry, *Micronesia, Trust Betrayed*, 16.

131. McHenry, *Micronesia, Trust Betrayed*, 16–17 (emphasis added).

132. McHenry, *Micronesia, Trust Betrayed*, 17; and Hanlon, *Remaking Micronesia*, 93.

133. McHenry, *Micronesia, Trust Betrayed*, 17.

134. McHenry, *Micronesia, Trust Betrayed*, 19.

135. McHenry, *Micronesia, Trust Betrayed*, 20.

136. McHenry, *Micronesia, Trust Betrayed*, 16.

137. "The Trusteeship System: How the United Nations Works for People of Trust Territories," circa late 1960s-mid-1970s, reel no. 166, file Correspondence, Dispatches and other information regarding the Trust Territory of the Pacific Islands (General Information), UN, Trusteeship Documents, TTA.

138. During the Trust Territory era, the Nitijela could propose bills and write petitions, but nothing was binding without US approval. Nonetheless, the legislative body clearly understood the geopolitical pressures on the United States and played a very active role during this era in pushing forth Marshallese demands for self-determination.

139. Resolution no. 71 and accompanying correspondence submitted to the Fifteenth Regular Session, United Nations requesting reconsideration of legal and political status of the Trust Territory of the Pacific Islands, signatures Amata Kabua (Speaker) and Atlan Anien (Legislative Secretary), October 21, 1968, Newspaper Room, UN collection, Library of Congress (hereafter LOC).

140. Resolution no. 71 and accompanying correspondence, LOC.

141. Resolution no. 71 and accompanying correspondence, LOC.

142. Resolution no. 71 and accompanying correspondence, LOC.

143. Resolution no. 71 and accompanying correspondence, LOC.

144. *The Marshall Islands Journal* was published out of the capital, Majuro.

145. Editorial on Resolution 71, *Marshall Islands Journal*, November 6, 1968, *The Marshall Islands Journal* (1967, 1968, 1969), reel no, 105, TTA.

146. Editorial on Resolution 71, TTA.

147. "Military Activities and Arrangements by Colonial Powers in Territories under Their Administration Which Might Be Competing in the Implementation of the Declaration on the Granting of Independence to Colonial Countries and Its Peoples," 1969, presented at the UN General Assembly, reel no. 166, file Correspondence, Dispatches and other information regarding the Trust Territory of the Pacific Islands (General Information), UN, Trusteeship Documents, TTA.

148. "Military Activities and Arrangements by Colonial Powers in Territories," TTA.

149. US representative to the United Nations Charles Yost sent a letter to the UN General Assembly stating that despite prior US membership on the committee since its creation in 1962, the United States would no longer be participating, remarking that committee membership had changed several times before. Permanent Representative of the United States of America, Charles Yost, to the United Nations, Secretary-General, regarding the Implementation of the Declaration on the Granting of Independence to Colonial Countries and Peoples, January 11, 1971, reel no. 166, file Publication, correspondence and other info., regarding territories (UN Committee on Territories), Decolonization, TTA.

150. Resolution no. 71 and accompanying correspondence, LOC.

151. Resolution no. 71 and accompanying correspondence, LOC.

152. Bill Remick, *Just Another Day in Paradise: A History of Kwajalein, Marshall Islands* (Sun City: Bill Remick Publishing, 2005), 159.

CHAPTER 2. NEW HOMES FOR NEW WORKERS

The epigraph is from Statement of Hon. Ataji Balos, a Representative in the Micronesian Congress from the Seventh District, Hearings before the Subcommittee on Territorial and Insular Affairs on the Current Problems in the Marshall Islands held on Ebeye, July 13, 1976, and Majuro, July 14, 1976, PCH.

1. Handel Dribo to High Commissioner Goding, April 18, 1966, reel, no. 3849, TTA.

2. Dribo to Goding, April 18, 1966, TTA.

3. Dribo to Goding, April 18, 1966, TTA.

4. Dribo to Goding, April 18, 1966, TTA.

5. Statement of Handel Dribo, Landowner, in Marshallese and Translated by the Interpreter, Hearings before the Subcommittee on Territorial and Insular Affairs on the Current Problems in the Marshall Islands held on Ebeye, July 13, 1976, and Majuro, July 14, 1976, PCH (emphasis added).

6. See Eric Avila, *Popular Culture in the Age of White Flight: Fear and Fantasy in Suburban Los Angeles* (Berkeley: University of California Press, 2004).

7. For more on this history see Roxanne Dunbar-Ortiz, *An Indigenous Peoples' History of the United States* (Boston: Beacon Press, 2014); and Nick Estes, *Our History Is the Future* (London: Verso, 2019).

8. Shibusawa introduced this framing through feedback offered to my writing at the Organization for American Historians conference (Houston, 2011), where she distinguished this from other modes of colonialism in which resource extraction tended to be geared toward life-sustaining materials like food or cotton. Shibusawa argued that in cases of expansive US military settler colonialism across the globe, the extraction of wealth accompanies the creation of death-producing resources.

9. Greg Dvorak, *Coral and Concrete: Remembering Kwajalein Atoll between Japan, America and the Marshall Islands* (Honolulu: University of Hawai'i Press, 2018), 57.

10. Holly M. Barker, *Bravo for the Marshallese: Regaining Control in a Post-Nuclear, Post-Colonial World* (Belmont, CA: Wadsworth/Thomson Learning, 2004), 9.

11. Barker, *Bravo for the Marshallese*, 10.

12. Barker, *Bravo for the* Marshallese, 10.

13. Mark R. Peattie, *Nan'yo: The Rise and Fall of the Japanese in Micronesia, 1885–1945,* Pacific Islands Monograph Series, no. 4 (Honolulu: University of Hawai'i Press, 1988), 96-100.

14. Ruth Douglas Currie, *Kwajalein Atoll, the Marshall Islands and American Policy in the Pacific* (Jefferson: McFarland, 2016), 70.

15. I draw here on historian Amy Dru Stanley's analysis of "freedom of contract" as she traced the concept of "free" labor following emancipation in the United States to deconstruct how the presumed legal legitimacy and mutual agreement embedded in the notion of contract obscured ongoing forms of unfreedom. While her analysis focuses on labor, I argue that US colonial history at Kwajalein fell into a similar pattern, in which a fetishization of "contract" through land leases helped obscure the coercive colonial nature of US land control in the region over time. See Amy Dru Stanley, *From Bondage to Contract: Wage Labor, Marriage, and the Market in the Age of Slave Emancipation* (New York: Cambridge University Press, 1998).

16. "Land Agreement Trust Territory of the Pacific Islands," signed by Assistant Secretary of the Navy, R. H. Fogler and Assistant Secretary of the Interior, Wesley A. D' Ewart, September 15, 1955, reel no. 3849, TTA. This three-page land agreement is part of a larger file labeled "Attorney General File—Kwajalein and Ebeye Miscellany, Quarry Site, Snack Bar Sit-in, Power Plant, Interim Use Agreement, Bucholz Airfield Agreement, Post-Office, Housing Rehab, '64 Land Settlement, Agreement, more." "Using Agencies" comprised the departments of the US Army, Navy, Air Force, and Coast Guard and the Atomic Energy Commission.

17. "Land Agreement Trust Territory of the Pacific Islands," TTA.

18. Martha Smith-Norris, *Domination and Resistance: The United States and the Marshall Islands during the Cold War* (Honolulu: University of Hawai'i Press, 2016), 105–106.

19. Francis X. Hezel, S.J., *Strangers in Their Own Land: A Century of Colonial Rule in the Caroline and Marshall Islands*, Pacific Islands Monograph Series, no. 13 (Honolulu: University of Hawai'i Press, 1995), 325.

20. Hezel, *Strangers in Their Own Land*

21. Amata Kabua, "Petition from Amata Kabua concerning the Pacific Islands," presented to the United Nations Trusteeship Council," August 25, 1959, T/PET.10/30/Add.1, LOC.

22. Kabua, "Petition from Amata Kabua concerning the Pacific Islands," LOC.

23. Kabua, "Petition from Amata Kabua concerning the Pacific Islands," LOC.

24. Kabua, "Petition from Amata Kabua concerning the Pacific Islands," LOC.

25. Kabua, "Petition from Amata Kabua concerning the Pacific Islands," LOC.

26. Executive Order no. 79, Subject: Addition of Chapter 20 to the Code of the Trust Territory of the Pacific Islands, August 28, 1959, Trust Territory of the Pacific Islands, Office of High Commissioner, Agana, Guam, Record Group 126, Office of Territories: Land, Kwajalein, NARA.

27. Executive Order no. 79, NARA.

28. David Hanlon, *Remaking Micronesia: Discourse over Development in a Pacific Territory, 1944–1982* (Honolulu: University of Hawai'i Press, 1998), 192. The lease also contained no "past use" compensation for the twenty years the US military had already been using Kwajalein, a point of contention fueling future protests. See Dvorak, *Coral and Concrete*, 209, in which he also traces Lejolan's lease signing, an act representing fifty other landowners.

29. Amata Kabua, "Petition from Marshall Islands Nitijela Concerning the Trust Territory of the Pacific Islands," presented to the United Nations Trusteeship Council, October 22, 1968, T/Pet.10/46, LOC.

30. High Commissioner Edward E. Johnston to Secretary of Interior Walter J. Hickel, July 24, 1969, reel no. 3849, TTA. This three-page letter is part of a larger file labeled "Attorney General File—Kwajalein and Ebeye Miscellany, Quarry Site, Snack Bar Sit-in, Power Plant, Interim Use Agreement, Bucholz Airfield Agreement, Post-Office, Housing Rehab, '64 Land Settlement, Agreement, more."

31. Johnston to Hickel, July 24, 1969, TTA.

32. In naval documents the labor camp is identified as home to "Micronesian" workers, but scholars have identified this as a combined population of at least 559 Marshallese workers and their dependents (of Ri-Kuwajleen, meaning specifically people of Kwajalein). See Dvorak, *Coral and Concrete*, 172; and Smith-Norris, *Domination and Resistance*, 103.

33. Hanlon, *Remaking Micronesia*, 194.

34. September Monthly Activities Report, submitted by W. C. White, Dist. Land Titles Officer to District Administrator Mr. Maynard Neas, September 1, 1954, reel, no. 106, TTA.

35. September Monthly Activities Report, TTA.

36. Jack Tobin (District Anthropologist Marshall Islands), *Ebeye Village: An Atypical Marshallese Community* (Majuro, 1954), 30–31, PCH.

37. Tobin, *Ebeye Village*, PCH.

38. Dvorak, *Coral and Concrete*, 209.

39. Hanlon, *Remaking Micronesia*, 193.

40. Hanlon, *Remaking Micronesia*, 193.

41. Hanlon, *Remaking Micronesia*, 195.

42. Hanlon, *Remaking Micronesia*, 195.

43. Hanlon, *Remaking Micronesia*, 195.

44. Congressman Amata Kabua to the Attorney General and Landowners of Ebeye, April 4, 1966, reel, no. 3849, TTA.

45. Kabua to the Attorney General and Landowners, April 4, 1966, TTA.

46. Hermios Kibin, letter to the editor, *Ebeye Voice*, September 2, 1968, reel, no. 991, TTA.

47. Kibin, letter to the editor, September 2, 1968, TTA.

48. The overlap in landownership across multiple islands throughout Kwajalein Atoll should be noted here. Some landowners retained land parcels on the islands of Kwajalein and Ebeye as well as other islands throughout the atoll. The "mid-corridor" islands (labeled as such by the US military) reside within the midsection of Kwajalein Atoll that the military used for its missile impact zone. Those Marshallese residing within these islands were displaced to Ebeye to make way for US missile testing during the 1960s.

49. For examples in urban landscapes across the United States, see Avila, *Popular Culture in the Age of White Flight*; Richard Rothstein, *Color of Law: A Forgotten History of How Our Government Segregated America* (New York: Liveright, 2017); and Keeanga-Yamahtta Taylor, *Race for Profit: How Banks and the Real Estate Industry Undermined Black Homeownership* (Chapel Hill: University of North Carolina Press, 2019).

50. Senator Tony de Brum, May 3, 2010, interview with author, Majuro Atoll, Republic of the Marshall Islands.

51. Anonymous, interview with author, May 2010, Kwajalein Island, Republic of the Marshall Islands.

52. Tony de Brum, oral history interview with author, November 22, 2010, Honolulu, Hawaiʻi.

53. Tobin, *Ebeye Village*, 3, PCH.

54. Dorothy E. Richard, *United States Naval Administration of the Trust Territory of the Pacific Islands* (Washington, DC: Office of the Chief of Naval Operations, 1957), 3:558.

55. Richard, *United States Naval Administration of the Trust Territory of the Pacific Islands*, 3:558.

56. Richard, *United States Naval Administration of the Trust Territory of the Pacific Islands*, 3:557.

57. Richard, *United States Naval Administration of the Trust Territory of the Pacific Islands*, 3:559.

58. While many scholars have traced this dynamic across time and space, Philip J. Deloria, *Indians in Unexpected Places* (Lawrence: University Press of Kansas, 2004), offers an especially instructive analysis of this ideology.

59. Richard, *United States Naval Administration of the Trust Territory of the Pacific Islands*, 3:559.

60. Correspondence from Chief Administrator, Field Headquarters, Trust Territory of the Pacific Islands, Subject: Proposed Move of Kwajalein Marshallese Village to Ebeye Island: Comments and Recommendations, September 12, 1950, 2, RG 313, box Records of Naval Operating Forces, Naval Air Base, Roi-Namur, Kwajalein, Marshall Islands, General Correspondence (Formerly Classified), 1946[-], PBNA.

61. Correspondence from Chief Administrator, September 12, 1950, 4, PBNA.

62. Correspondence from Chief Administrator, September 12, 1950, 6–7, PBNA.

63. Tobin, *Ebeye Village*, 9–10, PCH.

64. Tobin, *Ebeye Village*, 19, PCH.

65. See Daniel E. Bender and Jana K. Lipman, eds., *Making the Empire Work: Labor and United States Imperialism*, Culture, Labor, History Series (New York: New York University Press, 2015). Included in this volume is Lauren Hirshberg, "Home Land (In) Security: The Labor of U.S. Cold War Military Empire in the Marshall Islands." For more comparative analysis on the historic range of labor supporting US global military expansion and war during and beyond World War II, see Alfred Flores, "'No Walk in the Park': U.S. Empire and the Racialization of Civilian Military Labor in Guam, 1944–1962," *American Quarterly* 67, no. 3 (2015): 813–835; Andrew Friedman, "U.S. Empire, World War 2 and the Racialising of Labour," *Race & Class* 58, no. 4 (April–June 2017): 23–38; and Adam Moore, *Empire's Labor: The Global Army That Supports U.S. Wars* (Ithaca, NY: Cornell University Press, 2019).

66. Richard, *United States Naval Administration of the Trust Territory of the Pacific Islands*, 3:558.

67. *The New Yorker* staff writer Sarah Stillman found that by May 2011 there were more than seventy thousand third-country nationals working for the US military in military war zones alone, not including bases not located within these zones. See Stillman, "The Invisible Army," *New Yorker*, May 30, 2011. Stillman and historian Jana K. Lipman have each found that third-country nationals faced increasing vulnerability, abuse, and human trafficking. See also Jana K. Lipman, *Guantánamo: A Working Class History between Empire and Revolution* (Berkeley: University of California Press, 2008), 223–226.

68. Lipman, *Guantánamo*, 191–194.

69. Tobin, *Ebeye Village*, 30–31, PCH.

70. Hanlon, *Remaking Micronesia*, 39–41.

71. Hanlon, *Remaking Micronesia*, 38–39.

72. Eve Grey, *Three Children*, illus. Tambi Larsen, (published by the High Commissioner, Trust Territory of the Pacific Islands, Department of Education, 1951), 8–25, HIA (emphasis added).

73. For more information on how Chuukese themselves have defined their own historic and ongoing sense of responsibility for guardianship over their environment and their communities, see Myjolynne Marie Kim, "Nesor Annim, Niteikapar (Good Morning, Cardinal Honeyeater): Indigenous Reflections on Micronesian Women and the Environment," *Contemporary Pacific* 32, no. 1 (2020): 147–163. In this section I use the contemporary spelling of "Chuuk" or "Chuukese" to acknowledge the historic shift away from the colonial spelling "Truk" or "Trukese" that was used in the Trusteeship era. I defer to this contemporary spelling throughout the

book except when the former spelling of "Truk" or "Trukese" is in quoted historic documents.

74. Correspondence on Military Government-Native Employee Directive, Marshall Islands, from Commander Marshalls Gilberts Area, June 1, 1945, RG 313, box Naval Air Base Ebeye, 1944–1947, PBNA.

75. Correspondence on Military Government-Native Employee Directive, PBNA.

76. Memorandum No. 23-52 by Commanding Officer E. M. Arnold of US Naval Station, Navy 824, Subject: Employment of Marshallese as Domestic Servants, June 21, 1952, RG 313, box Naval Station Kwajalein, 1–3, PBNA.

77. Memorandum No. 23-52, PBNA.

78. Memorandum No. 23-52, PBNA.

79. Memorandum No. 23-52, PBNA.

80. Hirshberg, "Home Land (In) Security: The Labor of U.S. Cold War Military Empire," in Bender and Lipman, *Making the Empire Work.*

81. Hanlon, *Remaking Micronesia,* 193–194.

82. Report including excerpts from meeting minutes sent in correspondence from Attorney General R. K. Shoecraft to High Commissioner re: Conference at Honolulu Re Ebeye, May 4, 1964, reel, no. 486, TTA.

83. Report including excerpts from meeting minutes, May 4, 1964, TTA.

84. Giff Johnson, "Collision Course at Kwajalein," *Bulletin of Concerned Asian Scholars* 18, no. 2 (April–June 1986): 29.

85. Report of Joint Study Group on the Impact of Nike-Zeus and Nike-X Planning on Marshallese Population on Kwajalein Atoll, December 6, 1963, reel no. 512, TTA.

86. Meeting of December 9, 1965, on Ebeye Improvement Program, included in file with Report on Ebeye Improvement Program, master construction plan 1963–1966, reel, no. 512, TTA.

87. Meeting of December 9, 1965, on Ebeye Improvement Program, TTA.

88. Meeting of December 9, 1965, on Ebeye Improvement Program, TTA.

89. Dever, Greg, MD, "Ebeye, Marshall Islands: A Public Health Hazard," Micronesian Support Committee Report, 1978, 9–10, PCH. While the polio vaccine had become available eight years earlier, the military and Trust Territory government failed to immunize those on Ebeye.

90. Assistant Commissioner, Community Services and Acting Assistant Commissioner, Administration, to the High Commissioner, re: Ebeye planning, March 28, 1968, reel, no. 987, TTA.

91. Hanlon, *Remaking Micronesia,* 193–194.

92. Hanlon, *Remaking Micronesia,* 196–197.

93. Final Report of Kwajalein-Ebeye Fact Finding Team, Department of the Army, January 28, 1977, PCH.

94. K. R. Howe, Robert C. Kiste, and Brij V. Lal, eds., *Tides of History: The Pacific Islands in the Twentieth Century* (Honolulu: University of Hawai'i Press, 1994), 231–232.

95. Hanlon, *Remaking Micronesia*, 170. Thereafter, the Trust Territory government received about $120 million in welfare assistance funds between fiscal years 1974 and 1979, approximately $20 million a year for that period for the entire region. A 1978 report by the Department of the Interior found the Trust Territory was participating in only 166 of the 482 programs for which it was eligible.

96. See Thomas J. Sugrue, *Origins of the Urban Crisis: Race and Inequality in Postwar Detroit* (Princeton, NJ: Princeton University Press, 1996); Robert O. Self, *American Babylon: Race and the Struggle for Postwar Oakland* (Princeton, NJ: Princeton University Press, 2003); and Avila, *Popular Culture in the Age of White Flight*.

97. Final Report of Kwajalein-Ebeye Fact Finding Team, Department of the Army, January 28, 1977, PCH.

98. Final Report of Kwajalein-Ebeye Fact Finding Team, PCH.

99. Final Report of Kwajalein-Ebeye Fact Finding Team, PCH.

100. Colonel Donald B. Millar to Mr. R. Earle II, Principal Deputy Assistant Secretary of International Security Affairs, October 30, 1968, RG 126, Records of the Office of Territories: Land, Kwajalein, NARA.

101. Millar to Earle, October 30, 1968, NARA.

102. Millar to Earle, October 30, 1968, NARA.

103. Millar to Earle, October 30, 1968, NARA.

104. Lipman, *Guantánamo*, 104.

105. Catherine Lutz, ed., *The Bases of Empire: The Global Struggle against U.S. Military Posts* (New York: New York University Press, 2009), 24–26.

106. Lutz, *The Bases of Empire*, 24–26.

107. Final Report of Kwajalein-Ebeye Fact Finding Team, PCH.

108. Final Report of Kwajalein-Ebeye Fact Finding Team, PCH..

109. Final Report of Kwajalein-Ebeye Fact Finding Team, PCH (emphasis added).

CHAPTER 3. DOMESTIC CONTAINMENT IN THE PACIFIC

The first epigraph is from Petition Concerning the Trust Territory of the Pacific Islands to the President of the Trusteeship Council, signed "A True Micronesian," March 19, 1968, reel, no. 166, TTA.

The second epigraph is from Matthew D. Lassiter, "The Suburban Origins of 'Color-Blind' Conservatism: Middle-Class Consciousness in the Charlotte Busing Crisis," *Journal of Urban History* 30, no. 4 (May 2004): 557.

1. Giff Johnson (editor of *Marshall Islands Journal*), interview with author, May 13, 2010, Majuro Atoll, Republic of the Marshall Islands.

2. Johnson interview, May 13, 2010 (emphasis added, reflecting Johnson's tone of voice during the interview).

3. Tony de Brum (Marshall Islands senator), interview with author, May 3, 2010, Majuro, Republic of the Marshall Islands. Cris Lindborg and Raymond Wolff, interview with author, October 16, 2010, Kailua-Kona, Hawai'i.

4. Lindborg and Wolff interview, October 16, 2010.

5. Mark L. Gillem, *America Town: Building the Outposts of Empire* (Minneapolis: University of Minnesota Press, 2007). Unlike the bases Gillem chronicles, Kwajalein's borders were bounded by the Trusteeship Agreement, which delineated regulations for entry to Kwajalein privileging access to military personnel and civilian workers supporting the mission. Those employed by the US Armed Forces stationed in the territory and their dependents could bypass lengthy application procedures for entry. While in the 1950s the Navy located its authority to enforce security clearance through the region's status as a "'strategic trusteeship,' by 1967 the secretary of the interior explained to the secretary of the navy that entry guidelines comprised a combination of naval security considerations and existing US *immigration* policies. These new border policies included separate security checks for US and foreign nationals. See "Travel in the Pacific and Adjacent Areas; Clearance For," directive from Commander in Chief US Pacific Fleet, November 10, 1952, reel no. 563, TTA; Secretary of Interior to Secretary of Navy, correspondence ca. April 10, 1967, reel no. 554, TTA; "Entry Authorization Procedure, Kwajalein Test Site," produced by US Army Material Command, Nike-X Project Office, March 15, 1965, reel no. 540, TTA; and "Entry Authorization Procedure for Kwajalein Missile Range," produced by Kwajalein Range Directorate, US Army Safeguard System Command, June 15, 1970. This manual is located in record group 126, Office of Territories: Land, Kwajalein, NARA.

6. Restricted access policies did not target only Marshallese but also Americans who were not employees of the base, or even the dependents of employees once they reached a certain age. Nonresidents of the base might be given access to visit, but that would usually be confined to a certain period of time and require sponsorship.

7. Report/narrative on the experience at Kwajalein for Bell Laboratories employees between 1960 and 1975, ca. 1975, folder "Kwajalein Island Battlefield," 28, Archive Repository National Register, National Historic Landmarks, Washington, DC.

8. Lauren Hirshberg, "Nuclear Families: (Re)producing Suburban America in the Marshall Islands," *OAH Magazine of History* 26, no. 4 (October 2012): 39–43.

9. These various island amenities are listed throughout the following sources: "A Guide to Kwajalein Pacific Missile Range Facility," Bell Telephone Laboratories

Incorporated, January 1961, and "Welcome to Kwajalein," Transport Company of Texas, published circa 1963–1964, PCH; report/narrative on the experience at Kwajalein, ca. 1975. This report is prefaced by C.A. Warren, Executive Director of SAFEGUARD Division of Bell Laboratories; "United States Army Kwajalein Atoll," published by US Army Space and Strategic Defense Command, 1994, Government Documents, Hamilton Library, University of Hawai'i, Mānoa.

10. This 1950s iteration of the Karnival was covered in the *Kwajalein Post*, June 15, 1953, US Naval Station, Kwajalein, Marshall Islands.

11. Greg Dvorak, *Coral and Concrete: Remembering Kwajalein Atoll between Japan, America and the Marshall Islands* (Honolulu: University of Hawai'i Press, 2018), 95.

12. Directive from Army Colonel Peter F. Witteried to Visiting Personnel, Subject: Welcome to Kwajalein Missile Range, June 1, 1980, reel no. 637, file "A Visitor's Guide to Kwajalein Missile Range," TTA (emphasis added).

13. "Kwajalein Missile Range: Analysis of Existing Facilities, Ballistic Missile Defense System Command, US Army," prepared by Production Engineering Control Department, Global Associates, 1982, reel no. 2197, 5, TTA.

14. "A Small Pamphlet on the Nike-X Project on Kwajalein Island, Marshalls," October 10, 1964, reel no. 993, 13, TTA.

15. Estimates on the size of the population have ranged across secondary and primary sources, including Sandra Crismon's ethnography of Kwajalein, which found the base population peaking at over five thousand residents in the early 1970s ("Negotiating the Borders of Empire: An Ethnography of Access on Kwajalein Atoll, Marshall Islands" [PhD diss., University of Georgia, 2005]); Pacific scholar Greg Dvorak's estimation of the population peaking at four thousand in the 1960s (*Coral and Concrete*, 8); and former resident and self-published memoirist Eugene C. Sims's location of the 1960s peak at four to five thousand (*Kwajalein Remembered* [Eugene, OR: Eugene Print, 1996], 1–2).

16. Bill Patton, financial column, *Pacific Echo*, Kwajalein Missile Range, Kentron Hawai'i Ltd. employee newsletter, October 1975, reel no. 095, 4, TTA.

17. Cris Lindborg and Raymond Wolff, oral history interview with author, October 16, 2010, Kailua-Kona, Hawai'i; Nathaniel Jackson Jr., oral history interview with author, October 17, 2010, Kailua-Kona, Hawai'i; and Jimmy Matsunaga, oral history interview with author, November 11, 2010, Kwajalein Island, Republic of the Marshall Islands.

18. Examples of primary construction contracts in the early 1960s include the Honolulu Engineering District of the US Army Corps of Engineers for $55 million and Pacific Martin Zachry for $15 million. See "Kwajalein Missile Range: Analysis of Existing Facilities," reel no. 2197, 6, TTA.

19. Sims, *Kwajalein Remembered*, 27–28. As noted in this book's introduction, the Kwajalein Macy's was not connected to the US department store franchise.

20. Sims, *Kwajalein Remembered*, 27–28.

21. Owen Wilkes, Megan van Frank, and Peter Hayes, "Chasing Gravity's Rainbow: Kwajalein and US Ballistic Missile Testing" (Strategic and Defence Studies Centre, Research School of Pacific Studies, Australian National University, 1991), 11.

22. Wilkes, van Frank, and Hayes, "Chasing Gravity's Rainbow," 15.

23. "United States Army Kwajalein Atoll," Hamilton Library, University of Hawai'i, Mānoa.

24. Kate Brown, *Plutopia: Nuclear Families, Atomic Cities, and the Great Soviet and American Plutonium Disasters* (New York: Oxford University Press, 2013). Brown offered a comparative analysis of two atomic cities, tracing continuities and divergences across Richland and Ozersk, in the Southern Russia Urals.

25. Elaine Tyler May, *Homeward Bound: American Families in the Cold War Era* (New York: Basic Books, 1988), 8.

26. "A Small Pamphlet on the Nike-X Project on Kwajalein Island, Marshalls," October 10, 1964, reel no. 993, TTA.

27. "Small Pamphlet on the Nike-X Project on Kwajalein Island, Marshalls," 7, TTA.

28. Harry Hargett, "New Heights Attained over Kwajalein," *The American Pacific* (1977), PCH.

29. "Small Pamphlet on the Nike-X Project on Kwajalein Island, Marshalls," 13, TTA.

30. Open House Nike Zeus Facilities, Army Rocket and Guided Missile Agency, US Army Corps of Engineers, November 20, 1960, PCH.

31. Open House Nike Zeus Facilities, PCH.

32. Open House Nike Zeus Facilities, PCH.

33. Open House Nike Zeus Facilities, PCH.

34. Report/narrative on the experience at Kwajalein, ca. 1975, 1.

35. Report/narrative on the experience at Kwajalein, ca. 1975, 1.

36. "A Guide to Kwajalein," prepared by the Kwajalein Office of the Defense Information Office, Bell Telephone Laboratories, September 1, 1966, reel no. 993, file "A Publication on the Nike-X Kwajalein Test Site," TTA.

37. "A Guide to Kwajalein," TTA.

38. "A Guide to Kwajalein," TTA.

39. Statements from Que Keju in *Home on the Range* (Adam Horowitz, dir., 1991).

40. Statements from Harold Keju in *Home on the Range* (Adam Horowitz, dir., 1991).

41. "A Small Pamphlet on the Nike-X Project on Kwajalein Island, Marshalls," TTA.

42. Sims, *Kwajalein Remembered*, 40; and Dvorak, *Coral and Concrete*, 173.

43. David Vine, *Base Nation: How U.S. Military Bases Abroad Harm America and the World* (New York: Metropolitan Books, 2015), 212 (emphasis added).

44. Petition Concerning the Trust Territory of the Pacific Islands to the President of the Trusteeship Council, signed "A True Micronesian," March 19, 1968, reel, no. 166, TTA.

45. Petition Concerning the Trust Territory of the Pacific Islands, TTA.

46. Petition Concerning the Trust Territory of the Pacific Islands, TTA.

47. Neilat Zackhrias, oral history interview with author, May 2010, Ebeye Island, Republic of the Marshall Islands, interpreted by Rachel Miller.

48. Gertruth Clarence, oral history interview with author, May 2010, Ebeye Island, Republic of the Marshall Islands, interpreted by Rachel Miller.

49. Kenye Kobar, oral history interview with author, May 2010, Ebeye Island, Republic of the Marshall Islands, interpreted by Rachel Miller.

50. Jana K. Lipman, *Guantánamo: A Working Class History between Empire and Revolution* (Berkeley: University of California Press, 2008), 128.

51. Lauren Hirshberg, "Home Land (In)Security: The Labor of U.S. Cold War Military Empire," in *Making the Empire Work: Labor and United States Imperialism*, ed. Daniel E. Bender and Jana K. Lipman (New York: New York University Press, 2015), 343.

52. Hirshberg, "Nuclear Families," 4.

53. Hirshberg, "Nuclear Families," 4 (emphasis added).

54. Hirshberg, "Nuclear Families," 4.

55. Hirshberg, "Nuclear Families," 4.

56. Hirshberg, "Nuclear Families," 4.

57. Hirshberg, "Nuclear Families," 4.

58. Hirshberg, "Nuclear Families," 4.

59. Hirshberg, "Nuclear Families," 4. For more on the subject of disciplining intimacy in colonial spaces see Ann Laura Stoler, *Carnal Knowledge and Imperial Power: Race and the Intimate in Colonial Rule* (Berkeley: University of California Press, 2002); and Ann Laura Stoler, ed., *Haunted by Empire: Geographies of Intimacy in North American History* (Durham, NC: Duke University Press, 2006). For recent scholarship exploring US colonial concerns about contagion and disease in Micronesia, see Anne Perez Hattori, *Colonial Dis-ease: U.S. Navy Health Policies and the Chamorros of Guam, 1898–1941* (Honolulu: University of Hawai'i Press, 2004).

60. Military policies segregating the Marshallese colonial service sector on Kwajalein resided within a broader context of labor segregation on US bases globally. In her research on the pre- and postrevolutionary history of Guantánamo, historian Jana K. Lipman traced structures of social segregation between Cuban workers and US military personnel at Guantánamo Bay Naval Base (GTMO). Unlike Kwajalein, Cuban domestic workers and other Cuban personnel were allowed to live on base (the domestics in American family homes), but they

faced segregation in certain social spaces, like movie theaters and dance halls. See "Good Neighbors and Good Revolutionaries" in Lipman, *Guantánamo*.

61. For more on how mass consumption framed Cold War nuclear family life see Lizabeth Cohen, *A Consumers' Republic: The Politics of Mass Consumption in Postwar America* (New York: Vintage Books, 2003).

62. Lassiter, "Suburban Origins of 'Color-Blind' Conservatism," 552.

63. Lassiter, "Suburban Origins of 'Color-Blind' Conservatism," 552.

64. "Purchase and Removal of Goods—KTS," Global Associates Procedure 4520-1, December 1967 and January 1968, reel no. 987, TTA.

65. "Purchase and Removal of Goods—KTS," TTA.

66. "Purchase and Removal of Goods—KTS," TTA.

67. P.F. Kluge, "Micronesia's Unloved Islands: Ebeye," *Micronesian Reporter* 16, no. 3 (1968), PCH.

68. Robert Barclay, *Melal: A Novel of the Pacific* (Honolulu: University of Hawai'i Press, 2002), 7–8.

69. Resolution no. 71 and accompanying correspondence submitted to the Fifteenth Regular Session, United Nations requesting reconsideration of legal and political status of the Trust Territory of the Pacific Islands, signatures Amata Kabua (Speaker) and Atlan Anien (Legislative Secretary), October 21, 1968, Newspaper Room, UN collection, LOC.

70. Lomes McKay, letter to the editor, *Ebeye Voice*, November 12, 1968, PCH.

71. McKay, letter to the editor, November 12, 1968, PCH.

72. Mary. E. Russell to the Director of Marshallese Affairs, United Nations Building, October 21, 1970, RG 126, Records of the Office of Territories: Land, Ebeye, NARA.

73. John D. Beall to Senator Murphy, April 24, 1970, RG 126, Records of the Office of Territories: Land, Ebeye, NARA.

74. Beall to Murphy, April 24, 1970, NARA

75. Chris Christensen (publication adviser), letter to the editor, *Ebeye View*, April 27, 1971, PCH.

76. Christensen (publication adviser), letter to the editor, April 27, 1971, PCH.

77. Kluge, "Micronesia's Unloved Islands: Ebeye," PCH.

78. High Commissioner W. R. Norwood to Colonel Frank C. Healy, Commanding Officer, Kwajalein Test Site, February 3, 1968, RG 126, Records of the Office of Territories: Land, Ebeye, NARA.

79. "Purchase and Removal of Goods—KTS," TTA.

80. "Purchase and Removal of Goods—KTS," TTA.

81. Representatives of the Kwajalein workforce, Kwajalein Atoll Congress, Council Members, Medical Officers and Distad Representatives to Colonel Healy, January 19, 1968, reel, no. 987, TTA.

82. Representatives of the Kwajalein workforce et al. to Healy, January 19, 1968, TTA.

83. Representatives of the Kwajalein workforce et al. to Healy, January 19, 1968, TTA.

84. Representatives of the Kwajalein workforce et al. to Healy, January 19, 1968, TTA.

85. Colonel Frank C. Healy to Mr. Ataji Balos, Acting Assistant DISTAD Representative, January 25, 1968, reel, no. 987, TTA.

86. Healy to Balos, January 25, 1968, TTA.

87. Neilat Zackhrias, oral history interview with author, May 14, 2010; Getruth Clarence, oral history interview with author, May 18, 2010; Cinderella Silk, oral history interview with author, May 15, 2010; Kenye Kobar, oral history interview with author, May 2010; Madeline Balos, oral history interview with author, May 20, 2010. All interviews took place on Ebeye Island, Republic of the Marshall Islands, and were interpreted by Rachel Miller.

88. For more on the politics of laundry within spaces of US empire, see Cynthia Enloe, "The Laundress, the Soldier and the State," in *Maneuvers: The International Politics of Militarizing Women's Lives* (Berkeley: University of California Press, 2000).

89. Barclay, *Melal*, 110.

90. Barclay, *Melal*, 111.

91. Barclay, *Melal*, 111 (emphasis added).

92. Robert Barclay, follow-up correspondence with author, February 1, 2011, to answer questions that followed oral history interview, December 23, 2010, Kaneohe, Oʻahu.

93. Barclay, follow-up correspondence with author, February 1, 2011.

94. "A Guide to Kwajalein," TTA.

95. Crismon, "Negotiating the Borders of Empire," 291.

96. Crismon, "Negotiating the Borders of Empire," 291.

97. Prostitution on Ebeye was discussed in Crismon, "Negotiating the Borders of Empire," and in William J. Alexander, "The Destruction of Paradise: America's Legacy in Micronesia," *The Progressive*, February 19, 1979, in which Alexander wrote that on Ebeye "Marshallese women from pre-teens up sell their bodies to men from the Missile Range." For more on US military bases and prostitution see Cynthia Enloe, *Bananas, Beaches and Bases: Making Feminist Sense of International Politics* (Berkeley: University of California Press, 1989); Catherine Lutz, ed. *The Bases of Empire: The Global Struggle against U.S. Military Posts* (New York: New York University Press, 2009); and Setsu Shigematsu and Keith L. Camacho, eds. *Militarized Currents: Toward a Decolonized Future in Asia and the Pacific* (Minneapolis: University of Minnesota Press, 2010).

98. Kwajalein Atoll Inter-Island Community Relations Committee meeting minutes, June 8, 1978; June 9, 1979; March 7, 1980; and June 24, 1980, PCH. The minutes did not identify the ages of Marshallese "girls," and it is not clear if the use of the term referenced age or common colonial discourse that has

paternalistically positioned indigenous peoples as childlike. In this case, however, it is likely that the age of Marshallese working on Kwajalein could have ranged between adolescent and adult, so it is possible the use of the term "girls" referenced Marshallese adolescent workers.

99. Kwajalein Atoll Inter-Island Community Relations Committee meeting minutes, PCH.

100. Kwajalein Atoll Inter-Island Community Relations Committee meeting minutes, PCH.

101. Kwajalein Atoll Inter-Island Community Relations Committee meeting minutes, PCH.

102. Kwajalein Atoll Inter-Island Community Relations Committee meeting minutes, PCH.

103. Kwajalein Atoll Inter-Island Community Relations Committee meeting minutes, PCH.

104. Yoshi Kemem was working as a constable on Kwajalein when he moved his family from Ebeye in 1995.

105. Lynn A. Jacobson, *Kwajalein: An Island Like No Other* (self-published, 2013), xvii.

106. *The Kwajalein Hourglass*, August 5, 2006.

107. Gillem, *America Town*, 113.

108. Directive to all visitors to Kwajalein Test Site, prepared by US Army Material Command, circa 1966, reel no. 993, file "A Publication on the Nike-X Kwajalein Test Site," TTA.

109. Directive to all visitors to Kwajalein Test Site, TTA.

110. Directive to all visitors to Kwajalein Test Site, TTA.

111. As Gillem notes, this overlaps with segregation in recent years on bases where "officers usually have their own clubs. Senior enlisted soldiers have their own clubs. And junior enlisted soldiers have their own clubs and dining halls. The justification for all of this is to avoid fraternization, which could undermine the military's chain of command." See *America Town*, 113.

112. "A Guide to Kwajalein," TTA.

113. "Welcome to Kwajalein," PCH; and "A Guide to Kwajalein," TTA.

114. "Welcome to Kwajalein," PCH.

115. "Welcome to Kwajalein," PCH.

116. "Welcome to Kwajalein," PCH.

117. Robert Barclay, oral history interview with author, December 23, 2010, Kaneohe, O'ahu; and Bill Remick (former resident), email correspondence with author, July 2015. Barclay recalled the sign being taken down sometime during the mid-1970s.

118. My analysis of Kwajalein's heteronormative mapping drew upon insights from Greg Dvorak, "Remapping Home: Touring the Betweenness of Kwajalein" (MA thesis, University of Hawai'i, Mānoa, 2004).

119. I chose not to list the defendants' names here to protect their privacy. See Court Martial Orders No. 4-45, 12-7-44, 12-20-44 (for charges on November 8, 1944, November 11, 1944, November 21, 1944, November 22, 1944, March 15, 1945), United States Pacific Fleet and Pacific Ocean Areas, Commander Task Force Ninety-Six, RG 313, Records of Naval Operating Forces, Naval Air Base Kwajalein, General Correspondence 1943–1947, box S900, PBNA.

120. See Allan Bérubé, *Coming Out under Fire: The History of Gay Men and Women in World War II* (New York: Free Press, 1990); and Margot Canaday, *The Straight State: Sexuality and Citizenship in Twentieth-Century America* (Princeton, NJ: Princeton University Press, 2009).

121. Executive Officers Notice: Visiting Hours, Nurses' Quarters, US Naval Base, Navy 824, August 13, 1945, RG 313, Records of Naval Operating Forces, Naval Air Base Kwajalein, General Correspondence 1943–1947, box S899, PBNA.

122. Executive Officers Notice: Visiting Hours, Nurses' Quarters, PBNA.

123. Executive Officers Notice: Visiting Hours, Nurses' Quarters, PBNA.

124. Executive Officer's Memorandum no. 94-45: Building and Areas Occupied by Women-Out of bounds of, US Naval Base, Navy 824, August 30, 1945, RG 313, Records of Naval Operating Forces, Naval Air Base Kwajalein, General Correspondence 1943–1947, box S899, PBNA.

125. Executive Officer's Memorandum no. 94-45, PBNA.

126. Anonymous interview with author, May 2010, Kwajalein Island, Republic of the Marshall Islands.

127. *Pacific Echo*, Kwajalein Missile Range, Kentron Hawai'i Ltd. employee newsletter, October 1975, reel no. 095, 2, TTA. Offering scientific and technical services, Kentron was a subsidiary of LTV Aerospace Corporation.

128. *Pacific Echo*, , 5, TTA.

129. See Pat Cramer, "The Shop That Serves," *Guam and Micronesia Glimpses*, 3rd quarter 1990, and Congress of Micronesia House Resolution no. 6-2, H.D.1, H.D.2, Expressing Sincere Appreciation to the Yokwe Yuk Women's Club of Kwajalein, Marshall Islands District, Sixth Congress of Micronesia, First Regular Session, 1975, PCH. As Enloe traced in her chapter "Diplomatic Wives" in *Bananas, Beaches and Bases*, the "imperial diplomacy" that governs spaces of US colonialism (including military bases) involves the assertion of control and authority that has long relied on the work of both husbands and their wives, the latter often doing "diplomatic housework." The Yokwe Yuk Women's Club exemplifies this kind of "diplomatic housework," which Enloe argues was essential to mediating and perhaps softening the power relations and operations of empire.

130. Anonymous source, interview with author, May 2010.

131. This is not to suggest a complete demise of gender inequity within the continental United States, but rather to highlight *degree*, to signal that Kwajalein's gendered landscape reflects the more extreme binaries and rigidities of an earlier period in US history.

132. Crismon, "Negotiating the Borders of Empire," 246.

133. Anonymous source, interview with author, May 2010.

134. Jacobson, *Kwajalein*, 102–103.

135. Jacobson, *Kwajalein*, 102–103.

136. Jacobson, *Kwajalein*, 102–103.

137. Jacobson, *Kwajalein*, 102–103.

CHAPTER 4. "MAYBERRY BY THE SEA"

The epigraph is from an anonymous source, sentiments shared via correspondence in November 2016.

1. A. J. B. Lane, "Meet the 'Kwaj' Alumni," *Boston Globe*, July 28, 2019.

2. Lane, "Meet the 'Kwaj' Alumni."

3. Lane, "Meet the 'Kwaj' Alumni."

4. David Vine, *Base Nation: How U.S. Military Bases Abroad Harm America and the World* (New York: Metropolitan Books, 2015), 151.

5. Anonymous, November 2016.

6. Keith H. Basso, *Wisdom Sits in Places: Landscape and Language among the Western Apache* (Albuquerque: University of New Mexico Press, 1996), 7.

7. This includes the waged and unwaged labor on Kwajalein, the latter largely performed by wives through family care work.

8. "General Information for Visitor and TDY Personnel Arriving Kwajalein Missile Range," prepared by EC Services Company, 1988, PCH (emphasis added).

9. Eugene C. Sims, *Kwajalein Remembered* (Eugene, OR: Eugene Print, 1996), I.

10. Sims, *Kwajalein Remembered*.

11. Sims, *Kwajalein Remembered*, 2, and echoed across various oral history interviews with former residents and social media reunion sites.

12. Jana K. Lipman, *Guantánamo: A Working Class History between Empire and Revolution* (Berkeley: University of California Press, 2008), 179.

13. Lipman, *Guantánamo*.

14. Greg Dvorak, *Coral and Concrete: Remembering Kwajalein Atoll between Japan, America and the Marshall Islands* (Honolulu: University of Hawai'i Press, 2018), 235–236.

15. Dvorak, *Coral and Concrete* (emphasis added).

16. Report/narrative on the experience at Kwajalein for Bell Laboratories employees between 1960 and 1975, ca. 1975, preface by C. A. Warren, Executive Director of SAFEGUARD Division of Bell Laboratories, Archive Repository National Register, National Historic Landmarks, Washington, DC folder "Kwajalein Island Battlefield," p. 44.

17. While metaphoric in the allusion to ICBMs constituting a traffic jam one might imagine clogging up a Los Angeles freeway, the act of displacement to clear the space of a trafficked area mirrors histories of displacement connected to *real* freeway construction in metropolitan spaces like LA. Among other urban historians, Eric Avila has traced these historic patterns in *Popular Culture in the Age of White Flight: Fear and Fantasy in Suburban Los Angeles* (Minneapolis: University of Minnesota Press, 2004) and *The Folklore of the Freeway: Race and Revolt in the Modernist City* (Minneapolis: University of Minnesota Press, 2014).

18. Kwajalein Test Site, US Army Material Command, Kwajalein, Marshall Islands, 1968, PCH.

19. Kwajalein Test Site, 1968, PCH.

20. "A Guide to the Marshall Islands," Bell Laboratories, 1972, 53, PCH.

21. "A Guide to the Marshall Islands," 1972, 53, PCH.

22. "A Guide to Kwajalein Pacific Missile Range Facility," Bell Telephone Laboratories Incorporated, January 1961, 51, PCH (emphasis added).

23. "Guide to Kwajalein Pacific Missile Range Facility," January 1961, 51, PCH.

24. "Guide to Kwajalein Pacific Missile Range Facility," January 1961, 52, PCH.

25. "Guide to Kwajalein Pacific Missile Range Facility," January 1961, 52, PCH.

26. "Handbook on the Trust Territory of the Pacific Islands: A Handbook for Use in Training and Administration," prepared at the School of Naval Administration, Hoover Institute, Stanford University, by the Navy Department, Office of the Chief of Naval Operations, Washington, DC, 1948, 38, HIA.

27. See Nicolas Thomas, *Colonialism's Culture: Anthropology, Travel and Government* (Princeton, NJ: Princeton University Press, 1994), in which the author traces how the field of anthropology was a "modern discourse that has subsumed humanity to the grand narratives and analogies of natural history," becoming deeply implicated "in the practical work of colonialism." (6–7).

28. Here I am referring to a vast literature that analyzes colonial cultural productions framing the Pacific, including Haunani-Kay Trask, *From a Native Daughter: Colonialism and Sovereignty in Hawai'i* (Honolulu: University of Hawai'i Press, 1993); Catherine A. Lutz and Jane L. Collins, *Reading National Geographic* (Chicago: University of Chicago Press, 1993); Amy Kaplan, *The Anarchy of Empire in the Making of U.S. Culture* (Cambridge, MA: Harvard University Press, 2002); Teresia K. Teaiwa, "bikinis and other s/pacific n/oceans," *Contemporary Pacific* 6, no. 1 (Spring 1994): 87–109; and Thomas, *Colonialism's Culture*.

29. Michael Omi and Howard Winant, *Racial Formation in the United States: From the 1960s to the 1980s*, 3rd ed. (New York: Routledge, 2014), in which they trace the "establishment and reproduction of different regimes of domination, inequality, and difference in the United States . . . drawing upon concepts of difference, hierarchy, and marginalization based on race" (106–107). See also

the more recent analysis of social and cultural constructions of racial ideology by Karen E. Fields and Barbara J. Fields in *Racecraft: The Soul of Inequality in American Life* (London: Verso, 2012).

30. Julian Riklon, oral history interview with author, May 17, 2010, Ebeye Island, Republic of the Marshall Islands.

31. Riklon interview, May 17, 2010.

32. Anonymous, oral history interview with author, Kwajalein Island, Republic of the Marshall Islands, May 2010.

33. Robert Barclay, oral history interview with author, December 23, 2010, Kaneohe, Oʻahu.

34. Barclay interview, December 23, 2010.

35. Cris Lindborg and Raymond Wolff, oral history interview with author, October 16, 2010, Kailua-Kona, Hawaiʻi.

36. Lindborg and Wolff interview, October 16, 2010.

37. Jimmy Matsunaga, oral history interview with author, November 11, 2010, Kwajalein Island, Republic of the Marshall Islands.

38. Lindborg and Wolff interview, October 16, 2010.

39. Bob Butz, oral history interview with author, November 14, 2010, Kwajalein Island, Republic of the Marshall Islands.

40. Dvorak, *Coral and Concrete*, 12.

41. Dvorak, *Coral and Concrete*, 235.

42 "Yokwe" is another common spelling.

43. *Ekatak* Kwajalein High School Yearbook, 1967, and *Pacific Echo* (1975), Kwajalein Missile Range, Kentron Hawaiʻi Ltd. employee newsletter, reel no. 095, TTA.

44. Dvorak found an earlier example of this following the 1944 battle on Kwajalein Atoll in his analysis of photographs of Marshallese girls and women displaying and selling grass skirts to US soldiers, which did not align with any Marshallese traditions of dress but may have been an effort to play along with "American Hawaiiana stereotypes." See Dvorak, *Coral and Concrete*, 148–149.

45. J. J. Klein, "40 and Counting: Matsunaga Turns Two-Year Tour to Forty Years of Living on Kwaj," *The Kwajalein Hourglass*, August 5, 2006.

46. Klein, "40 and Counting.".

47. Matsunaga interview, November 11, 2010.

48. Matsunaga interview, November 11, 2010.

49. See Chad Blair, "Health Care: Migration Is Often a Matter of Survival," *Civil Beat*, October 21, 2015. Fellow journalist Anita Hofshneider also illuminated the tensions increasing in Hawaiʻi following federal budget cuts to Medicaid for COFA citizens (from the 1996 Welfare Reform Act), which left Hawaiʻi's state-funded Medicaid to foot the bill; in 2018 it reached more than $38.5

million. See Hofshneider, "Micronesians in Hawaii Still Struggle to Get Health Care," *Civil Beat*, April 3, 2019.

50. Barclay interview, December 23, 2010.

51. Trask, *From a Native Daughter*, 144. Political scientist Trask traces how US appropriation of Hawaiian culture historically mirrored similar appropriations of Native American culture. Trask and historian Philip J. Deloria have each respectively explored how American performances of perceived Native Hawaiian and Native American rituals helped ease American settlement by culturally appropriating and displacing a presumed "vanishing native." For more on the historic circulation of a touristic vision of "aloha" culture through hula, see Adria L. Imada, *Aloha America: Hula Circuits through the U.S. Empire* (Durham, NC: Duke University Press, 2012).

52. Deloria, *Playing Indian* (New Haven, CT: Yale University Press, 1998), 191.

53. For analysis of the contested history of the statehood vote, see Dean Itsuji Saranillo, "Colliding Histories: Hawai'i Statehood at the Intersection of Asians 'Ineligible to Citizenship' and Hawaiians 'Unfit for Self-Government,'" *Journal of Asian American Studies* 13, no. 3 (October 2010): 283–309.

54. For more on the contradictions in the foundations of this mythology, see John Chock Rosa, "'The Coming of the Neo-Hawaiian American Race': Nationalism and Metaphors of the Melting Pot in Popular Accounts of Mixed Race Individuals," in *The Sum of Our Parts: Mixed Heritage Asian Americans*, ed. Teresa Kay Williams-León and Cynthia Nakashima (Philadelphia: Temple University Press, 2001); Camilla Fojas, Rudy P. Guevarra Jr., and Nitasha Tamar Sharma, eds., *Beyond Ethnicity: New Politics of Race in Hawai'i* (Honolulu: University of Hawai'i Press, 2018); and most recently Sarah Davenport, *Gateway State: Hawai'i and the Cultural Transformation of American Empire* (Princeton, NJ: Princeton University Press, 2019). For an example of the ongoing persistence of this myth, see Moises Velasquez-Manoff, "Want to Be Less Racist? Move to Hawai'i: The "Aloha Spirit" May Hold a Deep Lesson for All of Us," *New York Times*, June 28, 2019, op-ed.

55. Sue Ellen Moss, "Culture Shock," *Winston-Salem Journal*, n.d., op-ed, posted to Friends of Kwajalein, 1960s–70s, May 29, 2016. This solicited fifty-seven comments (all agreeing with this unique dynamic on the island) and seven shares. I retain the anonymity of the individual posting and those commenting.

56. Moss, "Culture Shock."

57. Giff Johnson, "Ebeye: Apartheid, U.S. Style," *The Nation*, December 25, 1976.

58. In addition to Robert Barclay, these sentiments were expressed in the following: Lindborg and Wolff interview, October 16, 2010; Nathaniel Jackson Jr., oral history interview with author, October 17, 2010, Kailua-Kona, Hawai'i;

Matsunaga interview, November 11, 2010; and Butz interview, November 14, 2010.

59. Sandra Crismon, "Negotiating the Borders of Empire: An Ethnography of Access on Kwajalein Atoll, Marshall Islands" (PhD diss., University of Georgia, 2005), 263–264.

60. Crismon, "Negotiating the Borders of Empire," 262.

61. C. J. Johnson, oral history interview with author, 2015, Los Angeles, California.

62. While this Marshallese phrase was used as the title of the Kwajalein yearbook for more than five decades, giving the Marshallese *language* a presence at the school on Kwajalein, Marshallese *students* remained absent. They were excluded from any opportunity "to study" on Kwajalein until 1987, when five were selected annually from Ebeye through the quasi-integration program (discussed in chapter 6).

63. Johnson interview, 2015.

64. Johnson interview, 2015.

65. Johnson interview, 2015.

66. Johnson interview, 2015.

67. *Ekatak*, 1967. US civilians on Kwajalein have historically used "the rock" and Kwajalein interchangeably.

68. *Ekatak*, 1967.

69. *Ekatak*, 1967.

70. *Ekatak*, 1967 (underscore in original).

71. While in current times this presumption of degradation and humiliation associated with drag would be identified as transphobic, this pattern showed up in several yearbook issues, including the 1989 *Ekatak*. The relationship between gender play and high school hazing over several decades is ripe for further analysis to consider this dynamic within Kwajalein's distinctive setting of traditional gender norms over time, discussed in chapter 3.

72. *Ekatak*, 1982. The one non-White student may have been Marshallese.

73. *Ekatak*, 1982.

74. Robert Barclay, follow-up correspondence with author, November 29, 2019.

75. Rhae Lynn Barnes, "The Troubling History behind Ralph Northam's Blackface Klan Photo: How Blackface Shaped Virginia Politics and Culture for More Than a Century," *Washington Post*, February 2, 2019.

76. Mark L. Gillem, *America Town: Building the Outposts of Empire* (Minneapolis: University of Minnesota Press, 2007), 106 (emphasis added).

77. Abel Meeropol, comp., "Strange Fruit," 1937, performed by Billy Holiday, 1939.

78. For additional context to situate these questions in deeper histories of the US circulation of White supremacy throughout the Pacific over time, see Gerald

Horne, *The White Pacific: U.S. Imperialism and Black Slavery in the South Seas after the Civil War* (Honolulu: University of Hawai'i Press, 2007).

79. See sociologist and Assistant Secretary of Labor Daniel Patrick Moynihan, "The Negro Family: The Case for National Action" (Office of Policy Planning and Research, United States Department of Labor, 1965; also known as "The Moynihan Report"). Moynihan framed racial segregation and apartheid landscapes of US ghettos and suburbs through a "culture of poverty" analysis.

80. Dvorak, *Coral and Concrete*, 188.

81. Dvorak, *Coral and Concrete*, 188.

82. Dvorak, *Coral and Concrete*, 188.

83. Anonymous, oral history interview with author, November 2010, Kwajalein Island, Republic of the Marshall Islands.

84. Anonymous interview, November 2010.

85. Anonymous interview, November 2010.

86. Here I am referring to other *noncontinental* spaces of US colonial settlement as well, such as Hawai'i.

87. Douglas S. Massey and Nancy A. Denton, *American Apartheid: Segregation and the Making of the Underclass* (Cambridge, MA: Harvard University Press, 1993).

88. Dvorak, *Coral and Concrete*, 156.

89. James Baldwin, *The Fire Next Time* (New York: The Dial Press, 1963), 19–20 (emphasis added).

90. Renato Rosaldo, "Imperialist Nostalgia," in "Memory and Counter-Memory," special issue of *Representations*, no. 26 (Spring 1989): 108.

91. Rosaldo, "Imperialist Nostalgia," 108.

92. Sims, *Kwajalein Remembered*, 185.

93. Steve Johnson, "Why Kwajalein Atoll in the Pacific Ocean Is Almost Part of Redstone Arsenal," *WHNT* [Alabama] *News*, January 5, 2017. The second quote in this passage expresses Stuckey's sentiments paraphrased by Johnson.

94. Johnson, "Ebeye," 677.

95. While Sims referenced the "1983–1984 sail-in," I am assuming here that he may have meant Operation Homecoming in 1982, which was the largest sail-in and whose impacts for the army would have rippled into 1983 and 1984 as well.

CHAPTER 5. RECLAIMING HOME

The first epigraph is from Julian Riklon, oral history interview with author, May 17, 2010, Ebeye Island, Republic of the Marshall Islands (emphasis added).

The second epigraph is from Giff Johnson, "US Evicts Pacific Islanders to Build Secret Missile Base," *Depthnews ASIA*, September 10, 1982.

1. See Martha Smith-Norris, *Domination and Resistance: The United States and the Marshall Islands during the Cold War* (Honolulu: University of Hawai'i Press, 2016), in which she traces how Senator Imada Kabua was the first recipient of US violence against nonviolent protest in the atoll when he was clubbed by a security guard on Roi Namur during the 1979 sail-in after "'he and the first contingent of 25 men, women, and children climbed out of their boats and onto their beaches.'" (119).

2. Giff Johnson, "Atoll Protestors 'Occupy' Missile Sites," *National Catholic Reporter*, August 27, 1982.

3. Riklon interview, May 17, 2010. While the Kwajalein police chief was from the United States, it was initially unclear if the other Kwajalein policemen who knocked Julian unconscious were US or Marshallese workers. Riklon noted they could not understand Marshallese, so it seems safe to speculate they were also from the United States.

4. Riklon interview, May 17, 2010.

5. As noted in chapter 1, the COM retained limited governing authority under US colonial administration. Micronesian representatives of the Congress could write bills and resolutions that remained subject to the Trust Territory government's veto.

6. Marjorie Smith, "The Summer of Dissent," *Micronesian Reporter*, (4th quarter 1968), 26.

7. *Current Problems in the Marshall Islands: Hearings before the Subcommittee on Territorial and Insular Affairs of the Committee on Interior and Insular Affairs House of Representatives, Oversight Hearings on the Marshall Islands District Trust Territory of the Pacific Islands*, 94th Cong., 2nd sess., July 13, 1976 (Ebeye) and July 14, 1976 (Majuro), 1, PCH (hereafter *Current Problems in the Marshall Islands*).

8. *Current Problems in the Marshall Islands*.

9. *Current Problems in the Marshall Islands*.

10. For more on Mink's historical political trajectory, see Judy Tsu-Chun Wu, "The Dead, the Living, and the Sacred: Patsy Mink, Antimilitarism, and Reimagining the Pacific World," *Meridians* 18, no. 2 (October 1, 2019).

11. Won Pat was the first Chamorro to hold this nonvoting delegate position in the US House of Representatives, beginning in January 1973, a position that remains nonvoting today.

12. *Current Problems in the Marshall Islands*, 2.

13. *Current Problems in the Marshall Islands*, 42.

14. In addition to Guam, a range of island colonies spanning the Pacific and Caribbean were identified through the 1901 Supreme Court case *Downes v. Bidwell* as "foreign in a domestic sense," spaces where the Constitution does not follow the flag. For more on this history see Christina Duffy Burnett and Burke Marshall, eds., *Foreign in a Domestic Sense: Puerto Rico, American Expansion*

and the Constitution (Durham, NC: Duke University Press, 2001); and Sam Erman, *Almost Citizens: Puerto Rico, the U.S. Constitution, and Empire* (Cambridge: Cambridge University Press, 2019).

15. For more on Japanese American politics in Hawai'i, which was one local context situating Mink's political path, see Candace Fujikane and Jonathan Y. Okamura, *Asian Settler Colonialism: From Local Governance to the Habits of Everyday Life in Hawai'i* (Honolulu: University of Hawai'i Press, 2008).

16. For more on these ongoing movements in Hawai'i, see Noelani Goodyear-Ka'ōpua, Ikaika Hussey, and Erin Kahunawaika'ala, eds., *A Nation Rising: Hawaiian Movements for Life, Land, and Sovereignty* (Durham, NC: Duke University Press, 2014); and in Guam, see Julian Aguon, *Just Left of the Setting Sun* (Tokyo: Blue Ocean Press, 2006).

17. Lauren Hirshberg, "Navigating Sovereignty under a Cold War Military Industrial Colonial Complex: U.S. Military Empire and Marshallese Decolonization," *History and Technology: An International Journal* (December 30, 2015): 259–274.

18. *Current Problems in the Marshall Islands*, 20.

19. *Current Problems in the Marshall Islands*, 57.

20. *Current Problems in the Marshall Islands*.

21. *Current Problems in the Marshall Islands*.

22. *Current Problems in the Marshall Islands*, 6.

23. *Current Problems in the Marshall Islands*, 7.

24. *Current Problems in the Marshall Islands*, Appendix.

25. Statement by Rep. Ataji Balos of Marshall Islands to the House of Representatives of the Sixth Congress of Micronesia, 2nd spec. sess., July 24, 1976, PCH.

26. Statement by Rep. Ataji Balos of Marshall Islands.

27. Remarks of Amata Kabua to the Senate of the Congress of Micronesia Regarding Separation of the Marshall Islands from the Trust Territory of the Pacific Islands, February 8, 1977, reel no. 323, TTA.

28. In this respect the Marshall Islands mirrored the paths taken by Palau and the Northern Mariana Islands, as each charted its own course toward self-determination with the dissolution of the Trust Territory government; the Northern Mariana Islands toward a commonwealth status with the United States in 1986; and Palau toward independence in 1994. Here again, I am using the contemporary spelling of Chuuk to acknowledge the historic shift away from the colonial spelling "Truk" that was used in the Trusteeship era.

29. *Current Problems in the Marshall Islands*, appendix.

30. *Current Problems in the Marshall Islands*.

31. Paul Jacobs, "The Natives Are Forbidden to Shop on a U.S.-Administered Pacific Isle," *Newsday*, February 13, 1977.

32. *Current Problems in the Marshall Islands*, 4.

33. *Current Problems in the Marshall Islands*.

34. *Current Problems in the Marshall Islands*.

35. *Current Problems in the Marshall Islands*, 28.

36. *Current Problems in the Marshall Islands*, 33.

37. *Current Problems in the Marshall Islands*.

38. *Current Problems in the Marshall Islands*.

39. *Current Problems in the Marshall Islands*.

40. *Current Problems in the Marshall Islands*, 35.

41. This would determine if a domestic worker would be disqualified for employment due to bad health and thus need to be replaced by a healthier worker, to protect US families.

42. *Current Problems in the Marshall Islands*, appendix.

43. *Current Problems in the Marshall Islands*, appendix.

44. *Current Problems in the Marshall Islands*, appendix.

45. Final Report of Kwajalein-Ebeye Fact Finding Team, Department of the Army, January 28, 1977, with correspondence from Assistant Secretary of Defense, International Security Affairs, September 1976, attached, PCH.

46. Final Report of Kwajalein-Ebeye Fact Finding Team.

47. Final Report of Kwajalein-Ebeye Fact Finding Team.

48. David Hanlon, *Remaking Micronesia: Discourse over Development in a Pacific Territory, 1944–1982* (Honolulu: University of Hawai'i Press, 1998), 204.

49. Jinna A. Keju to Mr. Juan Alcedo, Committee on Civil Rights, September 15, 1979, Giff Johnson Marshall Islands Resource Materials, Pacific Manuscripts Bureau 1172.

50. Giff Johnson, "Marshallese Treated as Second Class Citizens," *Marianas Variety*, August 20, 1982.

51. In my oral history interview with movement leader Julian Riklon in June 2016, Riklon also confirmed the civil rights movement was an inspiration from the 1960s and included references to Martin Luther King Jr., a claim that Greg Dvorak confirmed in *Coral and Concrete*, when describing the protest as in part modeled on the civil rights movement. See *Coral and Concrete: Remembering Kwajalein Atoll between Japan, America and the Marshall Islands* (Honolulu: University of Hawai'i Press, 2018), 211.

52. Giff Johnson, *Collision Course at Kwajalein: Marshall Islanders in the Shadow of the Bomb* (Honolulu: Pacific Concerns Resource Center, 1984).

53. Hanlon, *Remaking Micronesia*, 210.

54. This included both the period from 1944 to 1964, in which the United States failed to pay any compensation for Kwajalein, and also the period between 1964 and 1979, when before sail-in protests pushed the army to increase leasing payments to $9 million per year, landowners only received $10 per acre per month. This fifteen-year period of lower payments followed the 1964 lease negotiations discussed in chapter 2.

55. Hanlon, *Remaking Micronesia*, 211.

56. Hanlon, *Remaking Micronesia*, 211.

57. See Dudziak, *Cold War Civil Rights: Race and the Image of American Democracy* (Princeton, NJ.: Princeton University Press, 2000); and Penny M. Von Eschen, *Satchmo Blows Up the World: Jazz Ambassadors Play the Cold War* (Cambridge, MA: Harvard University Press, 2004) for more on these transnational histories.

58. Owen Wilkes, Megan van Frank, and Peter Hayes, "Chasing Gravity's Rainbow: Kwajalein and US Ballistic Missile Testing" (Strategic and Defence Studies Centre, Research School of Pacific Studies, Australian National University, 1991), 11.

59. Johnson, *Collision Course at Kwajalein*, 46.

60. Journalist John M. Broder traced the Reagan administration's estimates of the program investment costs for Phase 1 of SDI as ranging between $75–$150 billion. See Broder, "'Star Wars' First Phase Cost Put at $170 Billion: System Would Intercept Only 16% of Soviet Missiles, Report of 3 Senate Democrats Says,'" *Los Angeles Times*, June 12, 1988.

61. Riklon interview, May 17, 2010 (emphasis added).

62. Riklon interview, May 17, 2010.

63. Riklon interview, May 17, 2010.

64. Julian Riklon, oral history interview with author, June 6, 2016, Sacramento, California.

65. Correspondence Reports from Chief Law Enforcement Officer, Trust Territory of the Pacific Islands, Bryan J. Vila, "18 June Incident at KMR Police Station," July 21, 1982, Micronesian Bureau of Investigation File, reel no. 3810, TTA. Vila's trajectory to chief law enforcement officer on Kwajalein followed a career path he described as transitioning after nine years as a "street cop in the ghettos and barrios of Los Angeles." See Brian Vila and Cynthia Morris, *Micronesian Blues: A True Story* (self-published, 2017), preface. Vila's policing work in the Trust Territory overlapped with a broader Cold War labor history of global "police professionalizers" chronicled by Stuart Schrader in *Badges without Borders: How Global Counterinsurgency Transformed American Policing* (Berkeley: University of California Press, 2019).

66. Correspondence Reports from Chief Law Enforcement Officer, July 21, 1982, TTA (all caps in original).

67. Correspondence Reports from Chief Law Enforcement Officer, July 21, 1982, TTA.

68. Correspondence Reports from Chief Law Enforcement Officer, July 21, 1982, TTA. Vila estimated that those protesting Riklon's arrest comprised about forty Marshallese men above age fifteen, seventy-five Marshallese women above age fifteen, ninety Marshallese children under age fifteen, and twenty infants. An affidavit produced by Principal Deputy Assistant to the Secretary of Defense

for International Security Affairs Noel Koch and Marshall Islands president Amata Kabua estimated the Marshallese protestors on Kwajalein as 21 men, 39 women, and 138 children, meaning 89 percent were women and children.

69. Telegram from Commander KMR Kwajalein to Commander Ballistic Missile Defense at Huntsville, AL, Commander Westcom Ft. Shafter, Secretary of State, Washington, DC, July 28, 1982, Micronesian Bureau of Investigation File, reel no. 3810, TTA.

70. Commander KMR Kwajalein to Commander Ballistic Missile Defense, July 28, 1982, TTA.

71. Memorandum from Associate Solicitor, Division of General Law, to Director, Office of Territorial Affairs, on the Subject "Law Enforcement in Kwajalein," September 25, 1979, Attorney General File—Kwajalein and Ebeye Miscellany, reel no. 3849, TTA.

72. Memorandum from Associate Solicitor, Division of General Law, to Director, Office of Territorial Affairs, TTA (emphasis added).

73. Fred C. Ikle, Under Secretary for Policy, Department of Defense, to Donald P. Hodel, Under Secretary, Department of the Interior, July 29, 1982, file on correspondence, memos and other information related to protestors, landowners, entry to Kwajalein Atoll, reel no. 886, TTA.

74. Ikle to Hodel, July 29, 1982, TTA.

75. Commander KMR Kwajalein to Commander Ballistic Missile Defense, July 28, 1982, TTA.

76. Commander KMR Kwajalein to Commander Ballistic Missile Defense, July 28, 1982, TTA.

77. Peter F. Witteried, Commanding Colonel, "Colonel Witteried: Anyone Who Participates Will Be a Trespasser: Open Letter to the Landowners of Kwajalein Atoll," *Marshall Islands Journal*,. June 22, 1982 (underscore in original).

78. Witteried, Commanding Colonel, "Colonel Witteried: Anyone Who Participates Will Be a Trespasser."

79. Witteried, Commanding Colonel, "Colonel Witteried: Anyone Who Participates Will Be a Trespasser."

80. Giff Johnson and Darlene Keju-Johnson, "Kwajalein: Home on the 'Range,'" *Pacific Magazine*, November/December 1982, 27 (underscore in original).

81. Johnson and Keju-Johnson, "Kwajalein."

82. Johnson and Keju-Johnson, "Kwajalein."

83. Giff Johnson to Representative John F. Seiberling, United States House of Representatives, August 31, 1982, Giff Johnson Marshall Islands Resource Materials, Pacific Manuscripts Bureau 1172.

84. Johnson to Seiberling, August 31, 1982, 38.

85. While the UN Declaration of the Granting of Independence to Colonial Countries and Peoples came two decades earlier (in December 1960) and

included language on the 1948 Universal Declaration of Human Rights, the creation by July 1982 of a UN Working Group on Indigenous Populations suggested increasing global attention to these issues over time.

86. Fact Sheet, Subject: "Emergency Access to KMR Hospital for Demonstrators," submitted by Bryan J. Vila, Chief Law Enforcement Officer, Trust Territory of the Pacific Islands, July 2, 1982, Micronesian Bureau of Investigation File, reel no. 3810, TTA.

87. Fact Sheet, "Emergency Access to KMR Hospital for Demonstrators," TTA.

88. Fact Sheet, "Emergency Access to KMR Hospital for Demonstrators," TTA (all caps in original).

89. Fact Sheet, "Emergency Access to KMR Hospital for Demonstrators," TTA (emphasis added).

90. Telegram from Commander KMR Kwajalein to Commander Ballistic Missile Defense at Huntsville, AL, Commander Westcom Ft. Shafter, Secretary of State and Secretary of Defense, on "Marshall Islands Journal Articles," circa late June 1982, Washington, DC, Micronesian Bureau of Investigation File, reel no. 3810, TTA.

91. Greg Knudsen, "The Marshalls Besieged: Foreign Secretary Tony de Brum on Washington, the U.N., Kwajalein, the Northern Atolls, . . . and Independence," *Pacific Magazine*, September/October 1982.

92. Knudsen, "Marshalls Besieged."

93. Knudsen, "Marshalls Besieged."

94. Giff Johnson, "Collision Course at Kwajalein: Marshall Islands," *Bulletin of Concerned Asian Scholars* 18, no. 2 (April–June 1986): 37.

95. Johnson, "Collision Course at Kwajalein," 37.

96. "U.S.-Marshalls Talks 'Progress Favorably,'" *Kwajalein Hourglass*, October 6, 1982.

97. "U.S.-Marshalls Talks 'Progress Favorably'" (emphasis added).

98. Robert Barclay, oral history interview with author, December 22, 2010, Kaneohe, O'ahu.

99. Neilat Zackhrias, oral history interview with author, May 14, 2010;, Cinderella Silk, oral history interview with author, May 15, 2010;, Getruth Clarence, oral history interview with author, May 18, 2010; Telki Amon, oral history interview with author, May 20, 2010; and Neibanjan Lavin, oral history interview with author, November 15, 2010. All interviews were interpreted by Rachel Miller and conducted on Ebeye Island, Republic of the Marshall Islands. Also noted in Cris Lindborg and Raymond Wolff, oral history interviews with author, October 16, 2010, Kailua-Kona, Hawai'i. Information about increased security, including gun carrying, noted in Sandra Crismon, "Negotiating the Borders of Empire: An Ethnography of Access on Kwajalein Atoll, Marshall Islands" (PhD diss., University of Georgia, 2005), 386 and 391.

100. Lindborg and Wolff interviews, October 16, 2010.

101. Lindborg and Wolff interviews, October 16, 2010.

102. Judy Rosochacki, interview correspondence with author, March 4–7, 2011.

103. Rosochacki interview, March 4–7, 2011.

104. Rosochacki interview, March 4–7, 2011.

105. Rosochacki interview, March 4–7, 2011.

106. Rosochacki interview, March 4–7, 2011.

107. Rosochacki interview, March 4–7, 2011.

108. Arakawa Syunji, "Report from the Marshall Islands: The Number of 'Hibakusha' Is Growing (an Interview with Mr. Nelson Anjain)," *Han-Genpatsu News, No Nuke News Japan*, June/July 1982, Giff Johnson Marshall Islands Resource Materials, Pacific Manuscripts Bureau 1172.

109. Syunji, "Report from the Marshall Islands."

110. Syunji, "Report from the Marshall Islands."

111. Syunji, "Report from the Marshall Islands."

112. Giff Johnson, "US Evicts Pacific Islanders to Build Secret Missile Base," *Depthnews ASIA*, September 10, 1982.

113. Johnson, "US Evicts Pacific Islanders."

114. Johnson, "US Evicts Pacific Islanders."

115. Stewart Firth, *Nuclear Playground* (Honolulu: University of Hawai'i Press, 1987).

116. Firth, *Nuclear Playground*.

117. Laji Taft and Abon Jeadrik (Kwajalein Atoll Corporation), "Kwajalein Atoll: The Impact of Foreign Military Presence" (paper presented at the Nuclear Free and Independent Pacific Conference, July 10–20, 1983, Port Vila, Vanuatu), PCH.

118. "Resolutions Adopted by NFIPC/83" (paper presented at the Nuclear Free and Independent Pacific Conference, July 10–20, 1983, Port Vila, Vanuatu), PCH.

119. "Resolutions Adopted by NFIPC/83."

120. Pat Fahey, "MX Delay Temporary," *Micronesian Support Committee Bulletin*, 1st quarter 1983, Micronesian Support Committee Bulletin file, Pacific Manuscripts Bureau 447.

121. Fahey, "MX Delay Temporary."

122. Fahey, "MX Delay Temporary" (underscore in original).

CHAPTER 6. US EMPIRE AND THE SHAPE OF MARSHALLESE SOVEREIGNTY IN THE "POSTCOLONIAL" ERA

The first epigraph is from Kwame Nkrumah, *Neo-colonialism: The Last Stage of Imperialism* (New York: International Publishers, 1966), xi.

The second epigraph is from statements by President Amata Kabua in the 1991 documentary film *Home on the Range* (Adam Horowitz, dir., 1991).

1. Julian Riklon, oral history interview with author, May 17, 2010, Ebeye Islands, Republic of the Marshall Islands.

2. Giff Johnson, oral history interview with author, May 13, 2010, Majuro Atoll, Republic of the Marshall Islands.

3. Kwame Nkrumah, *Neo-colonialism: The Last Stage of Imperialism* (New York: International Publishers, 1966), ix.

4. Greg Knudsen, "The Marshalls Besieged: Foreign Secretary Tony de Brum on Washington, the U.N., Kwajalein, the Northern Atolls, . . . Independence," *Pacific Magazine.* September/October 1982, 17.

5. Knudsen, "Marshalls Besieged."

6. Knudsen, "Marshalls Besieged."

7. Knudsen, "Marshalls Besieged." See also Ruth Douglas Currie, *Kwajalein Atoll, the Marshall Islands and American Policy in the Pacific* (Jefferson, NC: McFarland, 2016), 142.

8. Giff Johnson, "U.S. Vetoes Independence as Marshallese Landowners Occupy Kwajalein," *Pacific Islands Monthly,* September 1982, 31.

9. Johnson, "U.S. Vetoes Independence" (emphasis added).

10. Johnson, "U.S. Vetoes Independence."

11. Johnson, "U.S. Vetoes Independence."

12. Knudsen, "Marshalls Besieged," 17.

13. Knudsen, "Marshalls Besieged," 17.

14. Tony de Brum, oral history interview with author, November 22, 2010, Honolulu, Hawai'i.

15. De Brum interview, November 22, 2010.

16. De Brum interview, November 22, 2010.

17. Underlying publicly documented discourse on the future political negotiations for the country remained several other influences, including conflicts and loyalties based on personality, kinship relations, and backroom economic negotiations. Information about these factors surfaced during my research via hearsay and thus remains outside the bounds of this project. Just like other contested political histories, what can be analyzed about the path toward Marshallese decolonization in documented statements remains only the tip of an iceberg for understanding the complexities and varied relationships informing political negotiations from both US and Marshallese sides.

18. Martha Smith-Norris, *Domination and Resistance: The United States and the Marshall Islands during the Cold War* (Honolulu: University of Hawai'i Press, 2016), 144.

19. Smith-Norris, *Domination and Resistance*, 144.

20. David Hanlon, *Remaking Micronesia: Discourse over Development in a Pacific Territory, 1944–1982* (Honolulu: University of Hawai'i Press, 1998), 212.

21. Hanlon, *Remaking Micronesia.*

22. "Mayor Jacklick's Statement to U.S. Senate Subcommittee" (press release, January 19, 1984), *Marshall Islands Journal*, January 31, 1984.

23. Currie, *Kwajalein Atoll*, 151.

24. Giff Johnson, *Collision Course at Kwajalein: Marshall Islanders in the Shadow of the Bomb* (Honolulu: Pacific Concerns Resource Center, 1984), 46.

25. Currie, *Kwajalein Atoll*, 152.

26. Smith-Norris, *Domination and Resistance*, 142.

27. Stewart Firth, "Staying While Leaving: The Americans in Micronesia" (paper presented at the United Nations University Conference, Auckland, April 3-6, 1986), 20.

28. Firth, "Staying While Leaving," 21.

29. Nkrumah, *Neo-colonialism.*

30. Hanlon, *Remaking Micronesia*, 211.

31. In considering the challenges Kabua faced in leading the Marshallese toward a path of greater sovereignty, one comparative example is Puerto Rico's historic trajectory toward Commonwealth status and some of the dilemmas faced by Governor Luis Muñoz Marín in political status debates during this political transition. For more on this history, see José A. Cabranes, "Some Common Ground," in *Foreign in a Domestic Sense: Puerto Rico, American Expansion and the Constitution*, ed. Christina Duffy Burnett and Burke Marshall (Durham, NC: Duke University Press, 2001), 39–47.

32. Smith-Norris, *Domination and Resistance*, 107.

33. Giff Johnson, "Amata Kabua—1928–1996: The Father of a Nation," *Pacific Magazine*, March/April 1997, 14.

34. Amata Kabua, "Petition from Marshall Islands Nitijela Concerning the Trust Territory of the Pacific Islands," presented to the United Nations Trusteeship Council, October 22, 1968, T/Pet.10/46, LOC.

35. The Republic of the Marshall Islands created a mixed parliamentary-presidential system with a bicameral legislature comprising the upper house Council of Iroij (twelve Iroij) and lower house of thirty-three senators, the Nitijela. As noted in chapter 1, the Nitijela coexisted with the Trust Territory government as a political entity empowered to make proclamations and statements before the United Nations but with limited authority and power over decision-making.

36. "Interview: Amata Kabua," *Micronesian Reporter*, 4th quarter 1972, 4.

37. "Interview: Amata Kabua."

38. Amata Kabua, President of the Marshall Islands, inaugural address, "Marshall Islands Constitutional Government Inaugurated," *Micronesian Reporter*, 2nd quarter 1979, 10.

39. Kabua, inaugural speech.

40. Kabua, inaugural speech.

41. "Interview: President Amata Kabua," *New Pacific Magazine*, March/April 1980, 59.

42. "Interview: President Amata Kabua."

43. "Interview: President Amata Kabua."

44. "Interview: President Amata Kabua."

45. Todd Carrol, "Self-Government But Missiles Too," Associated Press, news cable on the Marshall Islands and Amata Kabua, 1983, reel no. 613, TTA.

46. Carrol, "Self-Government But Missiles Too," TTA.

47. Carrol, "Self-Government But Missiles Too," TTA.

48. John Bauman, "Hurry Up and Sign," *Guardian*, August 9, 1985, 1.

49. Bauman, "Hurry Up and Sign."

50. President Amata Kabua, statements in *Home on the Range* (Adam Horowitz, dir., 1991).

51. Julian Riklon, statements in *Home on the Range* (Adam Horowitz, dir., 1991).

52. Geoffrey M. White, "Remembering the Pacific War" (Occasional Paper 36, Center for Pacific Islands Studies, School of Hawaiian, Asian and Pacific Studies, University of Hawai'i, Mānoa, 1991), 116.

53. White, "Remembering the Pacific War," 121.

54. Johnson, "Amata Kabua—1928–1996," 14.

55. Johnson, "Amata Kabua—1928–1996," 14.

56. White House Office of Speechwriting, Speech Drafts, folder "Taping: Micronesian Plebiscite, Jan. 31, 1983," box 72, Ronald Reagan Presidential Library and Archives. This speech appeared as a televised address to the people of the Marshall Islands in *Half Life: A Parable for the Nuclear Age* (Dennis O'Rourke, dir., 1985).

57. White House Office of Speechwriting, Speech Drafts.

58. White House Office of Speechwriting, Speech Drafts.

59. Smith-Norris, *Domination and Resistance*, 99.

60. Smith-Norris, *Domination and Resistance*, 99.

61. White House Office of Speechwriting, Speech Drafts.

62. White House Office of Speechwriting, Speech Drafts.

63. De Brum interview, November 22, 2010. In addition to economic, military, and political factors potentially influencing what De Brum identified as a spirit of friendship with which Marshallese approached Americans, another factor likely has been the significant role of religion. Both Kwajalein and Ebeye have historically been and remain today heavily Christian spaces. The importance of religion as another layer in a history of US colonial relations in the region may help explain in part the spirit of friendship guiding some Marshallese approaches to Americans. It is a subject this book does not address, but one

worthy of further scrutiny and no doubt relevant to how the longer history of US missionary influence in the region impacted these more recent Cold War events.

64. De Brum interview, November 22, 2010 (emphasis added).

65. Ed Rampell, "Islanders Sit in Against 'Apartheid,'" *Pacific Islands Monthly*, June 1986, 13.

66. Giff Johnson, "Protests at the Missile Range," *Islands Business*, June 1986, 27–28.

67. Johnson, "Protests at the Missile Range."

68. Riklon interview, May 17, 2010.

69. Sato Maie (representing Kwajalein Association of Landowners) to President Amata Kabua, Republic of the Marshall Islands, February 27, 1986, Attorney General File-Kwajalein Missile Range, reel no. 3849, TTA.

70. Maie to Kabua, February 27, 1986, TTA.

71. Maie to Kabua, February 27, 1986, TTA.

72. As Greg Dvorak has traced, these divisions had a long history in the Marshalls, going back for centuries of landowners' battles with each other over land and power. See *Coral and Concrete: Remembering Kwajalein Atoll between Japan, America and the Marshall Islands* (Honolulu: University of Hawai'i Press, 2018), 200–232.

73. Niebanjan Lavin, oral history interview with author, November 15, 2010, Ebeye Island, Republic of the Marshall Islands. Lavin was the younger sister of Darlene Keju-Johnson.

74. Lavin interview, November 15, 2010.

75. Lavin interview, November 15, 2010.

76. "KMR Workers Walk Ebeye Reef to Get to Jobs on Kwaj.," *Marshall Islands Journal*, May 2, 1986, 10.

77. "KAC Blockade Will Continue," *Marshall Islands Journal*, May 2, 1986, 4.

78. "KAC Blockade Will Continue."

79. For coverage of additional allegations of brutality against Riklon and other landowners protesting in 1986, see "KMR Slaps KAC with 'Assault,'" *Marshall Islands Journal*, February 21, 1986.

80. "KAC Victorious in Court," *Marshall Islands Journal*, April 18, 1986, 1 and 5.

81. *Home on the Range* (Adam Horowitz, dir., 1991).

82. Giff Johnson, "Protests at the Missile Range," *Islands Business*, June 1986, 28.

83. Johnson, "Protests at the Missile Range."

84. Johnson, "Protests at the Missile Range."

85. Congressman Amata Kabua to the Attorney General and Landowners of Ebeye, April 4, 1966, reel no. 3849, TTA.

86. "Heine: RepMar Cause of Kwajalein Unrest," *Marshall Islands Journal*, May 9, 1986, 1 and 4.

87. "Heine: RepMar Cause of Kwajalein Unrest," 1 and 4.

88. "Eminent Domain a Sticky Issue for RepMar," *Marshall Islands Journal*, May 2, 1986, 2.

89. "Eminent Domain a Sticky Issue for RepMar," 2.

90. "Eminent Domain a Sticky Issue for RepMar," 2.

91. Secretary of Defense to Republic of the Marshall Islands President Amata Kabua, May 13, 1986, file Situation Reports on the Kwajalein "Sit-in" of Early 1986, reel no. 3748 F093, TTA.

92. Secretary of Defense to Kabua, May 13, 1986, TTA.

93. US State Department Representative Mike Senko, interview in *Home on the Range* (Adam Horowitz, dir., 1991).

94. Senko interview in *Home on the Range*.

95. Giff Johnson, *Nuclear Past: Unclear Future* (Majuro: Micronitor, 2009), 20.

96. Johnson, *Nuclear Past*.

97. Johnson, *Nuclear Past*. It has taken the United States nearly four decades to begin acknowledging the impact of radioactive fallout in the region. Tracing ongoing Marshallese struggles for just compensation, historian Martha Smith-Norris has written about the huge gap in US funding provisions for the Nuclear Claims Tribunal, which limited the NCT to paying only $3.9 million of the more than $2 billion of compensation awarded for environmental damage in the Marshall Islands. For more information on these gaps, as well as those in health compensation payments and other claims, see Smith-Norris, *Domination and Resistance*, 156–159.

98. Ruth Horne, "Even Paradise Can Be Stressful . . .," Hourglass, March 27, 1986, reprinted in *Marshall Islands Journal*, April 4, 1986, 14.

99. Horne, "Even Paradise Can Be Stressful . . . ."

100. Horne, "Even Paradise Can Be Stressful . . . ."

101. Robert Barclay, oral history interview with author, December 22, 2010, Kaneohe, Oʻahu.

102. Barclay interview, December 22, 2010.

103. Matthew D. Lassiter, "The Suburban Origins of 'Color-Blind Conservatism': Middle-Class Consciousness in the Charlotte Busing Crisis," *Journal of Urban History* 30, no. 4 (May 2004): 549–582.

104. As noted earlier, in addition to Lassiter's scholarship, examples of these urban/suburban histories in the United States have been traced in Thomas J. Sugrue, *Origins of the Urban Crisis: Race and Inequality in Postwar Detroit* (Princeton, NJ: Princeton University Press, 1996); Kenneth J. Jackson, *Crabgrass Frontier: The Suburbanization of the United States* (New York: Oxford University Press, 1987); Elaine Tyler May, *Homeward Bound: American Families in the Cold War Era* (New York: Basic Books, 1988); Eric Avila, *Popular Culture in the Age of White Flight: Fear and Fantasy in Suburban Los Angeles* (Berkeley:

University of California Press, 2004); and Robert O. Self, *American Babylon: Race and the Struggle for Postwar Oakland* (Princeton, NJ: Princeton University Press, 2003), among others.

105. "Kwajalein" [editorial], *Marshall Islands Journal*, March 13, 1981. It is unclear if this was written by editor Daniel C. Smith or another contributor to the editorial section.

106. "Kwajalein."

107. Army Commanding Lieutenant General John F. Wall to President Amata Kabua, Republic of the Marshall Islands, January 31, 1986, file Kwajalein sit-in and use rights negotiations, reel no. 4122, TTA.

108. Wall to Kabua, January 31, 1986, TTA.

109. "Ebeye Guest Students," *Ekatak* yearbook, Kwajalein High School, 2001.

110. For more on this history see J. Anthony Lukas, *Common Ground: A Turbulent Decade in the Lives of Three American* Families (New York: Random House, 1985); Ronald P. Formisano, *Boston against Bussing: Race, Class, and Ethnicity in the 1960s and 1970s* (Chapel Hill: University of North Carolina Press, 1991); and Lily Geismer, *Don't Blame Us: Suburban Liberals and the Transformation of the Democratic Party* (Princeton, NJ: Princeton University Press, 2014).

111. See Jana K. Lipman, "Good Neighbors, Good Revolutionaries, 1940–1958," in *Guantánamo: A Working Class History between Empire and Revolution* (Berkeley: University of California Press, 2008).

112. Shem Livai, oral history interview with author, December 12, 2010, Honolulu, Hawai'i. Livai also recalled being placed in a room with American children on Kwajalein to see how they got along to measure these social skills.

113. While typically just five students were admitted annually, Livai recalled seven being admitted the year he enrolled.

114. The veracity of such rumors can be difficult to disentangle because *iroij* connections and the resources that would have helped support academic skills and English fluency for children on Ebeye were often correlated. Across several years of Kwajalein yearbook photographs, many of the Rikatak students carried common *iroij* family names.

115. Livai interview, December 12, 2010.

116. Livai also wrote extensively about this experience for the 2005 *Ekatak* yearbook in a piece he titled "Got Culture?"

117. Amber Morse, "A Handshake across the Water: An Exploration of the Rikatak Program, Kwajalein Atoll, Republic of the Marshall Islands (presented for Dartmouth College MALS Independent Study, spring 2008).

118. Morse, "Handshake across the Water."

119. Mrs. Sheila C. Gideon (SMDCARSTRAT), "From Ri'katak Student to RMI Ambassador: Charles Paul Returns to His Stomping Grounds," US Army, February 8, 2013, accessed November 12, 2019, www.army.mil/article/96178

/from_rikatak_student_to_rmi_ambassador_charles_paul_returns_to_his
_stomping_grounds.

120. I do not intend to ignore a common challenge in histories of decolonization: how former colonial powers have navigated forms of accountability for colonial histories of extraction and exploitation in ways that avoid ongoing colonial influence. Rather, this chapter aims to highlight that this pattern is shared by Marshallese in their historic path toward, and obstacles preventing, full decolonization.

CONCLUSION

The first epigraph is from Dr. Martin Luther King Jr., interview with BBC, 1961.

The second epigraph is from Julian Riklon, oral history interview with author, May 17, 2010, Ebeye Island, Republic of the Marshall Islands.

1. "Keju-Johnson" was her married name by this date.

2. "Darlene Keju Speech to World Council of Churches, Vancouver 1983," posted April 29, 2013, accessed October 16, 2016, www.youtube.com/watch?v=1hxCGlA50JQ.

3. "Darlene Keju Speech."

4. "Darlene Keju Speech." See also Johnson, *Don't Ever Whisper*, 142-143.

5. Giff Johnson, *Don't Ever Whisper: Darlene Keju, Pacific Health Pioneer, Champion for Nuclear Survivors* (Majuro: Self-published, 2013), back cover.

6. Johnson, *Don't Ever Whisper*, 142-143.

7. Johnson, *Don't Ever Whisper*, 46.

8. Giff Johnson, "Marshall's Ebeye Out of Room for Dead: Cemeteries Are Full on the Tiny Atoll," *Marianas Variety*, July 16, 2010.

9. Greg Dvorak, *Coral and Concrete: Remembering Kwajalein Atoll between Japan, America and the Marshall Islands* (Honolulu: University of Hawai'i Press, 2018), 229; population numbers, 7. The estimates in residential decline have varied across sources, including a 2016 report that tracked Kwajalein's residential population from 2004 to 2016 and found that by 2016 the population had fallen from about twelve to nine hundred (Republic of the Marshall Islands, Fiscal 2016 Statistical Appendices, Graduate School USA, Pacific Islands Teaching Initiative, economic report). Correspondence with *Marshall Islands Journal* editor Giff Johnson on March 7, 2021, indicated Kwajalein's residential population had hovered around three thousand for decades, but since the late 2000s it had dwindled to around seventeen hundred. Johnson also reported on the decline in the Marshallese workforce, from around fourteen hundred in the early 2000s to between nine hundred and one thousand in recent years. For more on Johnson's coverage of why these numbers have decreased, including US budget

cuts, see Johnson, "Job Cuts to Hit Kwaj Workers," *Marshall Islands Journal*, July 15, 2011.

10. Dvorak, *Coral and Concrete*, 229.

11. Yoshi Kemem and Fumiko Kemem, oral history interview with author, November 14, 2010, Kwajalein Island, Republic of the Marshall Islands.

12. Kemem and Kemem interview, November 14, 2010. As of 2010, the Kemem family remained one among only a few Marshallese families and bachelors living and working on Kwajalein. Yoshi and Fumiko told me that two years after they moved to Kwajalein the second Marshallese family came, which consisted of a Department of Energy employee moving from Majuro (not Ebeye) to help care for those Marshallese living on Ebeye impacted by radioactive fallout. Yoshi and Fumiko noted the few other Marshallese living on Ebeye lived in the bachelors' quarters, one working in finance and three pilots who used to work for Air Marshall Islands in Majuro.

13. Kemem and Kemem interview, November 14, 2010.

14. Kemem and Kemem interview, November 14, 2010.

15. Tensions surrounding health care costs may ease in the future, as the US Congress voted in December 2020 to restore Medicaid access to COFA citizens (this includes citizens from the Marshall Islands, Palau, and the Federated States of Micronesia living in the United States). See Anita Hofshneider, "How Decades of Advocacy Helped Restore Medicaid Access to Micronesian Migrants," *Civil Beat*, December 23, 2020.

16. Tony de Brum, oral history interview with author, November 22, 2010, Honolulu, Hawai'i.

17. De Brum interview, November 22, 2010.

18. De Brum interview, November 22, 2010.

19. Alex Golden and Doug Thompson, "Marshallese Contracting, Dying from Covid-19 at Disproportionate Rate," *Arkansas Democrat Gazette*, June 14, 2020, accessed July 16, 2020, www.arkansasonline.com/news/2020/jun/14/marshallese-contracting-dying-from-covid-19-at/?news-arkansas.

20. Giff Johnson (editor, *Marshall Islands Journal*), correspondence with author, March 7, 2021. Johnson cited Ministry of Foreign Affairs and Trade notices provided by the US Army Garrison, Kwajalein Atoll, that are issued to him in advance of tests, citing annual totals as seven in 2018, six in 2019, and five in 2021 (one by March 2021).

21. Steve Johnson, "Why Kwajalein Atoll in the Pacific Ocean Is Almost Part of Redstone Arsenal," *WHNT* [Alabama] *News*, January 5, 2017.

22. See The Kwajalein Community Website, 'www.shermiewiehe.com/kwaj.html, updated September 28, 2021, accessed September 20, 2021; Kwaj-Net: Kwajalein News from Around the Web, www.kwaj-net.blogspot.com, accessed September 20, 2021; and Virtual Simmons, www.kwajkat.com, accessed

September 20, 2021. While various blogs and social networking sites primarily house photographs, stories, and news updates on Kwajalein with a nostalgic tone focused on US residential experiences, some sites also showcase stories and images that devote attention to Marshallese history, culture, and news. One such site is Friends of Kwajalein, 1960s–1970s on Facebook.

23. Sandra Crismon, "Negotiating the Borders of Empire: An Ethnography of Access on Kwajalein Atoll, Marshall Islands" (PhD diss., University of Georgia, 2005), 285. She offers analysis of this story appearing in the Kwajalein *Hour Glass*, October 1, 2002.

24. Crismon, "Negotiating the Borders of Empire," 285.

25. Setsu Shigematsu and Keith L. Camacho, eds., *Militarized Currents: Toward a Decolonized Future in Asia and the Pacific* (Minneapolis: University of Minnesota Press, 2010), vii.

26. Philip J. Deloria, *Playing Indian* (New Haven, CT: Yale University Press, 1998), 190.

27. Susanne Rust, "How the U.S. Betrayed the Marshall Islands, Kindling the Next Nuclear Disaster," *Los Angeles Times*, November 10, 2019.

28. "The Impact of Sea-Level Rise and Climate Change on Department of Defense Installations on Atolls in the Pacific Ocean RC-2334," report to the US Department of Defense Strategic Environmental Research and Development Program, 2017, 1–2.

29. "Impact of Sea-Level Rise and Climate Change on Department of Defense Installations," 1–2.

30. Mori Rothman and Melanie Saltzman, "Fighting for Fresh Water amid Climate Change," *PBS News Hour*, June 25, 2017, accessed April 10, 2021, www .wnyc.org/story/fighting-for-freshwater-amid-climate-change/.

31. Rothman and Saltzman, "Fighting for Fresh Water amid Climate Change."

32. Rothman and Saltzman, "Fighting for Fresh Water amid Climate Change."

33. Rothman and Saltzman, "Fighting for Fresh Water amid Climate Change."

34. Rust, "How the U.S. Betrayed the Marshall Islands."

35. Rust, "How the U.S. Betrayed the Marshall Islands."

36. The installation received a massive investment in 2014, with Lockheed Martin winning a $915 million contract to construct a "space fence" on Kwajalein to detect space debris. See Doug Cameron, "Lockheed Martin Wins $915 Million Space Fence Deal," *Wall Street Journal*, June 2, 2014.

37. Susanne Rust, "Huge Waves and Disease Turn Marshall Islands into 'a War Zone,' Health Official Says," *Los Angeles Times*, December 5, 2019.

38. Julian Riklon, oral history interview with author, June 6, 2016, Sacramento, California.

39. Julian Riklon, oral history interview with author, May 17, 2010, Ebeye Island, Republic of the Marshall Islands.

40. Julian Riklon, interview in *Home on the Range* (Adam Horowitz, dir., 1991).

41. See Julian Borger, "Marshall Islands Sues Nine Nuclear Powers over Failure to Disarm," *Guardian*, April 24, 2014, accessed September 15, 2015, www .theguardian.com/world/2014/apr/24/marshall-islands-sues-nine-nuclear -powers-failure-disarm. Citing the 1968 nuclear nonproliferation treaty while signaling the distinct historical experiences of Marshallese, de Brum asked "'if not us, who? and 'if not now when?'" Although the lawsuit was dismissed, de Brum's movement garnered tremendous support, with a coalition of fifty-five international peace and activist groups backing the initiative.

42. Associated Press, "Tony de Brum, Champion of Paris Climate Agreement, Dies Aged 72, *Guardian*, August 23, 2017, accessed April 10, 2021, www .theguardian.com/world/2017/aug/23/tony-de-brum-champion-of-paris-climate -agreement-dies-aged-72.

43. "Marshall Islands 18-Year-Old Thanks UN for Climate Pact," *Climate Home News*, accessed March 12, 2021, www.climatechangenews.com/2015/12/14 /marshall-islands-18-year-old-thanks-un-for-climate-pact/.

44. "Marshall Islands 18-Year-Old Thanks UN for Climate Pact."

45. Also at the forefront of this movement has been Marshallese activist and poet Kathy Jetñil-Kijiner, who gained international attention after sharing her poem, "Dear Matafele Peinem," with a global delegation at the opening ceremony of the UN Secretary General's Climate Change Summit in New York in 2014. See Katie Zavadski, "A Young Mother's Poem at the U.N. Climate Summit Was Completely Heartbreaking," *New York*, September 24, 2014, accessed July 21, 2020, https://nymag.com/intelligencer/2014/09/mother-reads-heartbreaking-climate -poem-at-un.html.

46. Nanettew, "We Must Do More Than Simply Offer Our Thoughts and Prayers—Marshall Islands on the World Stage at COP25," Secretariat of the Pacific Regional Environmental Program, December 13, 2019, accessed December 10, 2020, www.sprep.org/news/we-must-do-more-than-simply-offer-our -thoughts-and-prayers-marshall-islands-on-the-world-stage-at-cop25.

47. Nanettew, "We Must Do More Than Simply Offer Our Thoughts and Prayers."

48. Riklon interview, June 6, 2016.

49. Johnson, *Don't Ever Whisper*, 5.

Works Cited

ABBREVIATIONS FOR ARCHIVES

HIA: Hoover Institution Archives, Stanford University
LOC: Library of Congress, Washington, DC
NARA: US National Archives and Records Administration, College Park, Maryland
PBNA: Pacific Branch of the National Archives, San Bruno, California
PCH: Pacific Collection in Hamilton Library, University of Hawai'i, Mānoa
TTA: Trust Territory of the Pacific Islands Archives, University of Hawai'i, Mānoa

SELECTED BIBLIOGRAPHY

Aguon, Julian. *Just Left of the Setting Sun*. Tokyo: Blue Ocean Press, 2006.
Appy, Christian G., ed. *Cold War Constructions: The Political Culture of United States Imperialism, 1945–1966*. Amherst: University of Massachusetts Press, 2000.
Avila, Eric. *The Folklore of the Freeway: Race and Revolt in the Modernist City*. Minneapolis: University of Minnesota Press, 2014.
———. *Popular Culture in the Age of White Flight: Fear and Fantasy in Suburban Los Angeles*. Berkeley: University of California Press, 2004.

Baldwin, James. *The Fire Next Time*. New York: Dial Press, 1963.

Barclay, Robert. *Melal: A Novel of the Pacific*. Honolulu: University of Hawai'i Press, 2002.

Barker, Holly M. *Bravo for the Marshallese: Regaining Control in a Post-Nuclear, Post-Colonial World*. Belmont, CA: Wadsworth/Thomson Learning, 2004.

Basso, Keith H. *Wisdom Sits in Places: Landscape and Language among the Western Apache*. Albuquerque: University of New Mexico Press, 1996.

Bender, Daniel E., and Jana K. Lipman, eds. *Making the Empire Work: Labor and United States Imperialism*. Culture, Labor, History Series. New York: New York University Press, 2015.

Bernard, Richard M., and Bradley R. Rice, eds. *Sunbelt Cities: Politics and Growth since World War II*. Austin: University of Texas Press, 1983.

Bérubé, Allan. *Coming out Under Fire: The History of Gay Men and Women in World War II*. New York: Free Press, 1990.

Brown, Kate. *Plutopia: Nuclear Families, Atomic Cities, and the Great Soviet and American Plutonium Disasters*. New York: Oxford University Press, 2013.

Burnett, Christina Duffy, and Burke Marshall, eds. *Foreign in a Domestic Sense: Puerto Rico, American Expansion and the Constitution*. Durham, NC: Duke University Press, 2001.

Camacho, Keith L. *Cultures of Commemoration: The Politics of War, Memory and History in the Mariana Islands*. Honolulu: University of Hawai'i Press, 2011.

Canaday, Margot. "Building a Straight State: Sexuality and Social Citizenship under the 1944 G.I. Bill." *Journal of American History* 90, no. 3 (December 2003): 935–957.

———. *The Straight State: Sexuality and Citizenship in Twentieth Century America*. Princeton, NJ: Princeton University Press, 2009.

Carucci, Laurence Marshall. "The Source of the Force in Marshallese Cosmology." In *The Pacific Theater: Island Representations of World War II*, edited by Geoffrey M. White and Lamont Lindstrom, 73–96. Honolulu: University of Hawai'i Press, 1989.

Cohen, Lizabeth. *A Consumers' Republic: The Politics of Mass Consumption in Postwar America*. New York: Vintage Books, 2003.

Crismon, Sandra. "Negotiating the Borders of Empire: An Ethnography of Access on Kwajalein Atoll, Marshall Islands." PhD diss., University of Georgia, 2005.

Crocombe, Ron, and Ahmed Ali. *Politics in Micronesia*. Suva: Institute of Pacific Studies of the University of the South Pacific, 1983.

Cumings, Bruce. *Dominion from Sea to Sea: Pacific Ascendancy and American Power*. New Haven, CT: Yale University Press, 2009.

Currie, Ruth Douglas. *Kwajalein Atoll, the Marshall Islands and American Policy in the Pacific.* Jefferson, NC: McFarland, 2016.

Davenport, Sarah. *Gateway State: Hawai'i and the Cultural Transformation of American Empire.* Princeton, NJ: Princeton University Press, 2019.

Deloria, Philip J. *Indians in Unexpected Places.* Lawrence: University of Kansas Press, 2006.

——. *Playing Indian.* New Haven, CT: Yale University Press, 1998.

Diaz, Vicente M. "Deliberating Liberation Day: Memory, Culture and History in Guam." In *Perilous Memories: The Asia-Pacific War(s),* edited by T. Fujitani, Geoffrey M. White, and Lisa Yoneyama, 155–180. Durham, NC: Duke University Press, 2001.

——. *Repositioning the Missionary: Rewriting the Histories of Colonialism, Native Catholicism, and Indigeneity in Guam.* Honolulu: University of Hawai'i Press, 2010.

Dudziak, Mary L. *Cold War Civil Rights: Race and the Image of American Democracy.* Princeton, NJ.: Princeton University Press, 2000.

——. *War Time: An Idea, Its History, Its Consequences.* New York: Oxford University Press, 2012.

Dunbar-Ortiz, Roxanne. *An Indigenous Peoples' History of the United States.* Boston: Beacon Press, 2014.

Dvorak, Greg. *Coral and Concrete: Remembering Kwajalein Atoll between Japan, America and the Marshall Islands.* Honolulu: University of Hawai'i Press, 2018.

——. "The 'Martial Islands': Making Marshallese Masculinities between American and Japanese Militarism." *Contemporary Pacific* 20, no. 1 (Spring 2008): 55–86.

——. "Remapping Home: Touring the Betweenness of Kwajalein." MA thesis, University of Hawai'i, Mānoa, 2004.

Enloe, Cynthia. *Bananas, Beaches and Bases: Making Feminist Sense of International Politics.* Berkeley: University of California Press, 1989.

——. *Maneuvers: The International Politics of Militarizing Women's Lives.* Berkeley: University of California Press, 2000.

Erman, Sam. *Almost Citizens: Puerto Rico, the U.S. Constitution, and Empire.* Cambridge: Cambridge University Press, 2019.

Estes, Nick. *Our History Is the Future.* London: Verso, 2019.

Ferguson, Kathy E., and Phyllis Turnbull. *Oh Say Can You See? The Semiotics of the Military in Hawai'i.* Minneapolis: University of Minnesota Press, 1999.

Fields, Karen E., and Barbara J. Fields. *Racecraft: The Soul of Inequality in American Life.* London: Verso, 2012.

Firth, Stewart. *Nuclear Playground.* Honolulu: University of Hawai'i Press, 1987.

Flores, Alfred. "'No Walk in the Park': U.S. Empire and the Racialization of Civilian Military Labor in Guam, 1944–1962." *American Quarterly* 67, no. 3 (2015): 813–835.

Fojas, Camilla, Rudy P. Guevarra Jr., and Nitasha Tamar Sharma, eds. *Beyond Ethnicity: New Politics of Race in Hawai'i.* Honolulu: University of Hawai'i Press, 2018.

Formisano, Ronald P. *Boston against Bussing: Race, Class, and Ethnicity in the 1960s and 1970s.* Chapel Hill: University of North Carolina Press, 1991.

Friedan, Betty. *The Feminine Mystique.* New York: W. W. Norton, 1963.

Friedman, Andrew. *Covert Capital: Landscapes of Denial and the Making of U.S. Empire in the Suburbs of Northern Virginia.* Berkeley: University of California Press, 2013.

———. "U.S. Empire, World War 2 and the Racialising of Labour." *Race & Class* 58, no. 4 (April–June 2017): 23–38.

Fujikane, Candace, and Jonathan Y. Okamura, eds. *Asian Settler Colonialism: From Local Governance to the Habits of Everyday Life in Hawai'i.* Honolulu: University of Hawai'i Press, 2008.

Gaines, Kevin. *American Africans in Ghana: Black Expatriates and the Civil Rights Era.* Chapel Hill: University of North Carolina Press, 2006.

Geismer, Lily. *Don't Blame Us: Suburban Liberals and the Transformation of the Democratic Party.* Princeton, NJ: Princeton University Press, 2014.

Gillem, Mark L. *America Town: Building the Outposts of Empire.* Minneapolis: University of Minnesota Press, 2007.

Goodyear-Ka'ōpua, Noelani, Ikaika Hussey, and Erin Kahunawaika'ala, eds. *A Nation Rising: Hawaiian Movements for Life, Land, and Sovereignty.* Durham, NC: Duke University Press, 2014.

Grandin, Greg. *Empire's Workshop: Latin America, the United States, and the Rise of the New Imperialism.* New York: Henry Holt, 2006.

Grey, Eve. "Three Children." High Commissioner, Trust Territory of the Pacific Islands, Department of Education, 1951.

Half Life: A Parable for the Nuclear Age. Directed by Dennis O'Rourke. 1985.

Hanlon, David. *Remaking Micronesia: Discourse over Development in a Pacific Territory, 1944–1982.* Honolulu: University of Hawai'i Press, 1998.

Harvey, David. *Spaces of Capital: Towards a Critical Geography.* New York: Routledge, 2001.

Hattori, Anne Perez. *Colonial Dis-Ease: U.S. Navy Health Policies and the Chamorros of Guam, 1898–1941.* Honolulu: University of Hawai'i Press, 2004.

Hau'ofa, Epeli. "Our Sea of Islands." *Contemporary Pacific*, 6, no. 1 (Spring 1994): 147–161.

Hecht, Gabrielle. *Being Nuclear: Africans and the Global Uranium Trade.* Cambridge, MA: MIT Press, 2012.

Heine, Carl. *Micronesia at the Crossroads: A Reappraisal of the Micronesian Political Dilemma*. Honolulu: University of Hawai'i Press, 1974.

Hezel, Francis X., S.J. *Strangers in Their Own Land: A Century of Colonial Rule in the Caroline and Marshall Islands*. Pacific Islands Monograph Series, no. 13. Honolulu: University of Hawai'i Press, 1995.

Hirshberg, Lauren. "Domestic Containment in the Marshall Islands: Mapping American Family Life onto Cold War Military Empire in the Pacific." *LABOR* 13, nos. 3–4 (2016): 177–196.

———. "Home Land (In) Security: The Labor of U.S. Cold War Military Empire." In *Making the Empire Work: Labor and United States Imperialism*, edited by Daniel E. Bender and Jana K. Lipman, 335–356. New York: New York University Press, 2015.

———. "Navigating Sovereignty under a Cold War Military Industrial Colonial Complex: US Military Empire and Marshallese Decolonization." *History and Technology: An International Journal* (December 30, 2015): 259–274.

———. "Nuclear Families: (Re)producing Suburban America in the Marshall Islands." *OAH Magazine of History* 26, no. 4 (October 2012): 39–43.

Howe, K. R., Robert C. Kiste, and Brij V. Lal, eds. *Tides of History: The Pacific Islands in the Twentieth Century*. Honolulu: University of Hawai'i Press, 1994.

Imada, Adria L. *Aloha America: Hula Circuits through the U.S. Empire*. Durham, NC: Duke University Press, 2012.

Jackson, Kenneth T. *Crabgrass Frontier: The Suburbanization of the United States*. New York: Oxford University Press, 1987.

Jacobson, Lynn A. *Kwajalein: An Island Like No Other*. N.p.: Self-published, 2013.

Johnson, Giff. *Collision Course at Kwajalein: Marshall Islanders in the Shadow of the Bomb*. Honolulu: Pacific Concerns Resource Center, 1984.

———. "Collision Course at Kwajalein." *Bulletin of Concerned Asian Scholars* 18, no. 2 (April–June 1986): 29.

———. *Don't Ever Whisper: Darlene Keju, Pacific Health Pioneer, Champion for Nuclear Survivors*. Majuro: Self-published, 2013.

———. *Nuclear Past: Unclear Future*. Majuro: Micronitor, 2009.

Johnston, Barbara Rose. *The Consequential Damages of Nuclear War: The Rongelap Report*. Walnut Creek, CA: Left Coast Press, 2008.

Kajihiro, Kyle. "The Militarizing of Hawai'i: Occupation, Accommodation and Resistance." In *Asian Settler Colonialism: From Local Governance to the Habits of Everyday Life in Hawai'i*, edited by Candace Fujikane and Jonathan Y. Okamura, 170–194. Honolulu: University of Hawai'i Press, 2008.

Kaplan, Amy. *The Anarchy of Empire in the Making of U.S. Culture*. Cambridge, MA: Harvard University Press, 2002.

Kaplan, Amy, and Donald E. Pease, eds. *Cultures of United States Imperialism*. Durham, NC: Duke University Press, 1994.

Kiste, Robert C. *The Bikinians: A Study in Forced Migration*. Menlo Park, CA: Benjamin-Cummings, 1974.

Kramer, Paul A. *The Blood of Government: Race, Empire, the United States and the Philippines*. Chapel Hill: University of North Carolina Press; 2006.

Kupferman, D. W. "On location at a non-entity: Reading Hollywood's 'Micronesia.'" *Contemporary Pacific* 23, no. 1 (2011): 141–168.

LaBriola, Monica C. "Iien Ippan Doon (This Time Together): Celebrating Survival in an 'Atypical Marshallese Community.'" MA thesis, University of Hawai'i, Mānoa, 2006.

Lassiter, Matthew D. *Silent Majority: Suburban Politics in the Sunbelt South*. Princeton, NJ: Princeton University Press, 2007.

———. "The Suburban Origins of 'Color-Blind' Conservatism: Middle-Class Consciousness in the Charlotte Busing Crisis." *Journal of Urban History* 30, no. 4 (May 2004): 549–582.

Leibowitz, Arnold H. *Embattled Island: Palau's Struggle for Independence*. Westport, CT: Praeger, 1996.

Limerick, Patricia Nelson. *The Legacy of Conquest: The Unbroken Past of the American West*. New York: W. W. Norton, 1987.

Lipman, Jana K. *Guantánamo: A Working Class History between Empire and Revolution*. Berkeley: University of California Press, 2008.

Lukas, J. Anthony. *Common Ground: A Turbulent Decade in the Lives of Three American Families*. New York: Random House, 1985.

Lutz, Catherine, ed. *The Bases of Empire: The Global Struggle against U.S. Military Posts*. New York: New York University Press, 2009.

Lutz, Catherine A., and Jane L. Collins. *Reading National Geographic*. Chicago: University of Chicago Press, 1993.

Mamdani, Mahmood. *Good Muslim, Bad Muslim: America, the Cold War, and the Roots of Terror*. New York: Pantheon Books, 2004.

Marshall, S. L. A. *Island Victory: The Battle of Kwajalein Atoll*. Lincoln: University of Nebraska Press, 1944.

Masco, Joseph P. *The Nuclear Borderlands: The Manhattan Project in Post-Cold War New Mexico*. Princeton, NJ: Princeton University Press, 2006.

———. "'Survival Is your Business': Engineering Ruins and Affect in Nuclear America." *Cultural Anthropology* 23, no. 2 (2008): 361–398.

Massey, Douglas S., and Nancy A. Denton. *American Apartheid: Segregation and the Making of the Underclass*. Cambridge, MA: Harvard University Press, 1993.

May, Elaine Tyler. *Homeward Bound: American Families in the Cold War Era*. New York: Basic Books, 1988.

———. "Security against Democracy: The Legacy of the Cold War at Home." *Journal of American History* 97, no. 4 (March 2011): 939–957.

McCaffrey, Katherine T. *Military Power and Popular Protest: The U.S. Navy in Vieques, Puerto Rico*. New Brunswick, NJ: Rutgers University Press, 2002.

McHenry, Donald F. *Micronesia, Trust Betrayed: Altruism vs. Self Interest in American Foreign Policy*. New York: Carnegie Endowment for International Peace, 1975.

Micronesian Support Committee. *Marshall Islands, A Chronology: 1944–1981*. Honolulu: Maka'ainana Media, 1981.

Moore, Adam. *Empire's Labor: The Global Army That Supports U.S. Wars*. Ithaca, NY: Cornell University Press, 2019.

Morse, Amber. "A Handshake across the Water: An Exploration of the Rikatak Program, Kwajalein Atoll, Republic of the Marshall Islands. Presented for Dartmouth College MALS Independent Study, spring 2008.

Ngai, Mai. *Impossible Subjects: Illegal Aliens and the Making of Modern America*. Princeton, NJ: Princeton University Press, 2004.

Niedenthal, Jack. *For the Good of Mankind: A History of the People of Bikini and Their Islands*. Majuro: Bravo Publishers, 2001.

Nkrumah, Kwame. *Neo-colonialism: The Last Stage of Imperialism*. New York: International Publishers, 1966.

O'Mara, Margaret Pugh. *Cities of Knowledge: Cold War Science and the Search for the Next Silicon Valley*. Princeton, NJ: Princeton University Press, 2005.

Omi, Michael, and Howard Winant. *Racial Formation in the United States: From the 1960s to the 1980s*. New York: Routledge, 2014.

Osorio, Jonathan Kay Kamakawiwo'ole. *Dismembering Lahui: A History of the Hawaiian Nation to 1887*. Honolulu: University of Hawai'i Press, 2002.

Peattie, Mark R. *Nan'yo: The Rise and Fall of the Japanese in Micronesia, 1885–1945*. Pacific Islands Monograph Series. Honolulu: University of Hawai'i Press, 1988.

Poyer, Lin, Suzanne Falgout, and Laurence Marshall Carucci. *Memories of War: Micronesians in the Pacific War*. Honolulu: University of Hawai'i Press, 2008.

———. *The Typhoon of War: Micronesian Experiences of the Pacific War*. Honolulu: University of Hawai'i Press, 2001.

Remick, Bill. *Just Another Day in Paradise: A History of Kwajalein, Marshall Islands*. Sun City, AZ: Bill Remick Publishing, 2005.

Richard, Dorothy E. *United States Naval Administration of the Trust Territory of the Pacific Islands*. Vol. 3. Washington, DC: Office of the Chief of Naval Operations, 1957.

Rosa, John Chock. "'The Coming of the Neo-Hawaiian American Race': Nationalism and Metaphors of the Melting Pot in Popular Accounts of Mixed

Race Individuals." In *The Sum of Our Parts: Mixed Heritage Asian Americans*, edited by Teresa Kay Williams-León and Cynthia Nakashima, 49–56. Philadelphia: Temple University Press, 2001.

Rosaldo, Renato. "Imperialist Nostalgia." *Representations*, no. 26 (Spring 1989): 107–122.

Rosenberg, Emily S. "World War I, Wilsonianism, and Challenges to U.S. Empire." *Diplomatic History* 38, no. 4 (September 2014): 852–863.

Rothstein, Richard. *Color of Law: A Forgotten History of How Our Government Segregated America*. New York: Liveright Publishing, 2017.

Saranillo, Dean Itsuji. "Colliding Histories: Hawai'i Statehood at the Intersection of Asians 'Ineligible to Citizenship' and Hawaiians 'Unfit for Self-Government.'" *Journal of Asian American Studies* 13, no. 3 (October 2010): 283–309.

Schrader, Stuart. *Badges without Borders: How Global Counterinsurgency Transformed American Policing*. Berkeley: University of California Press, 2019.

Self, Robert O. *American Babylon: Race and the Struggle for Postwar Oakland*. Princeton, NJ: Princeton University Press, 2003.

Shigematsu, Setsu, and Keith L. Camacho, eds. *Militarized Currents: Toward a Decolonized Future in Asia and the Pacific*. Minneapolis: University of Minnesota Press, 2010.

Silva, Noenoe K. *Aloha Betrayed: Native Hawaiian Resistance to American Colonialism*. Durham, NC: Duke University Press, 2004.

Sims, Eugene C. *Kwajalein Remembered*. Eugene, OR: Eugene Print, 1996.

Smith-Norris, Martha. *Domination and Resistance: The United States and the Marshall Islands during the Cold War*. Honolulu: University of Hawai'i Press, 2016.

Soja, Edward W. *Postmodern Geographies: The Reassertion of Space in Critical Social Theory*. London: Verso, 1989.

Stanley, Amy Dru. *From Bondage to Contract: Wage Labor, Marriage, and the Market in the Age of Slave Emancipation*. New York: Cambridge University Press, 1998.

Stoler, Anne Laura. *Carnal Knowledge and Imperial Power: Race and the Intimate in Colonial Rule*. Berkeley: University of California Press, 2002.

———, ed. *Haunted by Empire: Geographies of Intimacy in North American History*. Durham, NC: Duke University Press, 2006.

Sugrue, Thomas J. *The Origins of the Urban Crisis: Race and Inequality in Postwar Detroit*. Princeton, NJ: Princeton University Press, 1996.

Taylor, Keeanga-Yamahtta. *Race for Profit: How Banks and the Real Estate Industry Undermined Black Homeownership*. Chapel Hill: University of North Carolina Press, 2019.

Teaiwa, Teresia K. "bikinis and other s/pacific n/oceans." *Contemporary Pacific* 6, no. 1 (Spring 1994): 87–109.

Thomas, Nicolas. *Colonialism's Culture: Anthropology, Travel and Government.* Princeton, NJ: Princeton University Press, 1994.

Trask, Haunani-Kay. *From a Native Daughter: Colonialism and Sovereignty in Hawai'i.* Honolulu: University of Hawai'i Press, 1993.

Trouillot, Michel-Rolph. *Silencing the Past: Power and the Production of History.* Boston: Beacon Press, 1995.

Ueunten, Wesley Iwao. "Rising Up from a Sea of Discontent: The 1970 Koza Uprising in U.S.-Occupied Okinawa." In *Militarized Currents: Toward a Decolonized Future in Asia and the Pacific,* edited by Setsu Shigematsu and Keith L. Camacho, 91–124. Minneapolis: University of Minnesota Press, 2010.

Vila, Brian, and Cynthia Morris. *Micronesian Blues: A True Story.* Self-published, 2017.

Vine, David. *Base Nation: How U.S. Military Bases Abroad Harm America and the World.* New York: Metropolitan Books, 2015.

———. *Island of Shame: The Secret History of the U.S. Military Base on Diego Garcia.* Princeton, NJ: Princeton University Press, 2009.

Von Eschen, Penny M. *Satchmo Blows Up the World: Jazz Ambassadors Play the Cold War.* Cambridge, MA: Harvard University Press, 2004.

Walsh, Julianne M. "Imagining the Marshalls: Chiefs, Tradition, and the State on the Fringes of U.S. Empire." PhD diss., University of Hawai'i, Mānoa, 2003.

Weisgall, Jonathan M. *Operation Crossroads: The Atomic Tests at Bikini Atoll.* Annapolis, MD: Naval Institute Press, 1994.

White, Geoffrey M. "Remembering the Pacific War." Occasional Paper 36, Center for Pacific Islands Studies, School of Hawaiian, Asian and Pacific Studies, University of Hawai'i, Mānoa, 1991.

Wilkes, Owen, Megan van Frank, and Peter Hayes. "Chasing Gravity's Rainbow: Kwajalein and US Ballistic Missile Testing." Strategic and Defence Studies Centre, Research School of Pacific Studies, Australian National University, 1991.

Williams, William Appleman. *Empire as a Way of Life: An Essay on the Causes and Character of America's Present Predicament, along with a Few Thoughts about an Alternative.* New York: Oxford University Press, 1980.

Wu, Judy Tsu-Chun. "The Dead, the Living, and the Sacred: Patsy Mink, Antimilitarism, and Reimagining the Pacific World." *Meridians* 18, no. 2 (October 1, 2019): 304–331.

Zuckerman, Ian. "The Politics of Emergencies: War, Security and the Boundaries of the Exception in Modern Emergency Powers." PhD diss., Columbia University, 2012.

Index

AMERICAN CROSSROADS

Edited by Earl Lewis, George Lipsitz, George Sánchez, Dana Takagi, Laura Briggs, and Nikhil Pal Singh

Founded in 1893,
UNIVERSITY OF CALIFORNIA PRESS
publishes bold, progressive books and journals
on topics in the arts, humanities, social sciences,
and natural sciences—with a focus on social
justice issues—that inspire thought and action
among readers worldwide.

The UC PRESS FOUNDATION
raises funds to uphold the press's vital role
as an independent, nonprofit publisher, and
receives philanthropic support from a wide
range of individuals and institutions—and from
committed readers like you. To learn more, visit
ucpress.edu/supportus.